Jack!
No. 4-92 #

UNDERSTANDING
THE ARTS

▶UNDER

Henry Holt and Company

STANDING

THE ARTS

Bernard S. Myers

THE CITY COLLEGE, NEW YORK

New York

FOR LUCY ELLEN

Preface

FOR SOME TIME interested readers no less than art departments throughout the country have felt the need for a book dealing with general ideas concerning art, a book that would be in every sense introductory, defining the various approaches, outlining the different technical problems—and relating these two types of material to the creative side of art as well as to its uses in everyday life.

Understanding the Arts is neither a history of art nor a book of esthetics—although historical and esthetic materials are included within its scope. It is rather, as the title implies, a simple approach to the understanding of the plastic arts (drawing, architecture, sculpture, painting, graphics, minor arts, industrial art) on a conceptual basis. Paralleling the approach of some introductory music books, it is more or less a kind of "what to look for in art."

Briefly, the aims of the book are as follows: to outline a number of approaches to art (physical, intellectual, religious, symbolic, historical, etc.) ; to describe and characterize the different techniques or media in art with their respective limitations and advantages; to convey an idea of the planning (or designing) of the art object; to evaluate the meaning of the art of the past and its value for us today (that is, the various kinds of information it gives us, including that on taste and style). It surveys earlier art forms or styles from Ancient through Renaissance forms, then observes the importance of the individual's contributions to these styles. It examines, thereafter, the role played by such factors as proportion, space, and composition in the evolution of style. After presenting in some detail the work of a major traditional artist it brings our stylistic evolution down to the present day, noting how special problems arise in the modern world and examining the evolution of a major modern artist in contrast to that of a major traditional artist.

Throughout the book it is shown that the traditional artist and the modern artist must be judged in terms of their respective backgrounds, that the modern artist cannot be judged in terms that are necessarily valid for the Renaissance artist or vice versa. Is it possible, then, to arrive at some standard of judgment, however rudimentary? It is proposed here that objects can only be compared with objects of the same general type and period, where similar, if not identical, demands are made on the spectator's perceptions. From this it can follow, for example, that we encounter a poor Cubist painting or an outstanding Baroque painting once we have established some sort of norm for each of these phases or styles of art.

This qualitative aim, like the other purposes of the book, is accomplished through an extensive series of direct comparisons of works of art reproduced in the text, comparisons which bring out the particular point involved. Although the history of art is necessarily subordinated to the general concepts we try to establish here, there are two extensive chapters devoted to the development of historical styles from ancient man to the present day. The objects reproduced in this section may be amplified by others of the various periods which have been previously shown in other connections.

The treatment of certain technical factors is also historical. Here it is shown not only that each period has its own style (and each artist within that period) but that specific artistic factors such as space, proportion, and composition change from one epoch to another. Thus under each of these brief but very specific technical discussions we find a miniature history of art with concrete examples tracing the development of space, proportion, and composition through the ages.

Many colleges have been giving such a course, either as a preliminary to the usual art history survey or as something that would satisfy the student's need for general orientation in this particular fashion. For many years the present writer has taught courses of this type, first at New York University (where the basic outline of the present book took its first form), then at the University of Southern California, and more recently at The City College in New York.

For the teacher as well as the student *Understanding the Arts* offers a relatively new way of looking at art. Presenting a number of avenues through which one may approach the subject, it opens the way to the establishment of other paths as well. Its principles of design, discussed within the framework of many specific works, may be elaborated to include other principles. Most important, however, it comes to grips with the problem of value judgments, projecting one way in which both teacher and student can attempt to solve one of the thorniest problems in the understanding of art. The practical exercises offered in substantiation of this method, exercises wherein pairs of objects are compared in very concrete terms (the regular method of this book), may be extended and varied in any manner found desirable. What is significant about this comparative method, whether used for investigating our problem of value judgments or for any other purpose in approaching our material, is that it forces the reader to look at a good many different kinds of art objects for very specific purposes. In the experience of the writer over a long period of time this method has proved very valuable.

However the teacher chooses to use the material presented here, whether in its actual printed form or with his own elaborations and emendations, it is hoped that *Understanding the Arts* will be a useful tool in bringing the student to art and in helping him look at it more intelligently and sympathetically than before.

Although the author has tried to credit all the photographs, he would like to extend special thanks to those who have been particularly generous with their material. The Photographic Division of the Metropolitan Museum of Art, the Library of The Museum of Modern Art, and the information services of many European countries have been very helpful. These countries include Eire, the Federal Republic of Germany, France, Italy, and the Netherlands. Belgium and France have also been helpful through their official photographic archives.

If the author cannot find new and fresh words to thank his wife for her unfailing editorial help and patience with this newest book, he can still marvel (and be grateful) that one person can so successfully combine the roles of wife, mother, and editor.

B. S. M.

New York City
February 10, 1958

Contents

Illustrations

I. *St. John on Patmos* (Byzantine Gospel page). London, British Museum.

II (above). SANDRO BOTTICELLI: *Birth of Venus*. Florence, Italy, Uffizi Gallery. III (below). KU K'AI-CHIH: *Admonitions of the Imperial Preceptress* (detail). London, British Museum.

IV. TITIAN: *Pope Paul III*. Naples, Italy, Picture Gallery.

▶PART I

Introduction to the Arts

▶❙

The Approach

WE ARE CONCERNED in this book with the three-dimensional (or plastic) arts of painting, sculpture, architecture, graphics, the minor and industrial arts. Approaching these plastic arts, we are drawn into an exciting world of tangible sensation where our senses of sight, touch, and balance are strongly engaged. Colors, forms, textures, movements, emotions, and ideas are spread before us with kaleidoscopic variety and stimulation. The signposts along this road to the arts point to certain special aspects of meaning, function, and creation.

In this initial *Approach*, therefore, we shall be concerned with such special problems as the kinds of pleasure the contemplation of art can give us, what we learn of the past from looking at art, the difference between the original meaning and purpose of the work of art and its present meaning, the technical language of the artist, the meaning of style, the question of taste or preference in the arts, and the all-important question of artistic standards of quality and our personal judgment of art.

From time to time in later chapters, many of these problems will be recalled and discussed in greater detail. We shall thereby find them falling into place as part of a broader viewpoint or approach. We shall find that we live surrounded by the work of the creative artist—painter, sculptor, architect—and by the products of the industrial and commercial designer. This has, of course, been true of peoples all through the ages. Their everyday usages, like ours, were influenced by all kinds of artistic expression; and their lives also were enriched even when they, like many of us, were unaware of the relationship and the effect. It is one of the functions of art in human society to help provide and condition the background against which we exist.

Our Personal Enjoyment of Art

Art may provide certain personal satisfactions, comparable to those we feel in reading books, witnessing plays or ballets, or listening to music. These satisfactions come from physical, intellectual, and emotional responses to what the artist has experienced and what he is trying to communicate to us. Our sheer physical appreciation of a powerful and monumental work of sculpture, the exaltation inspired by an imposing building, the visual and intellectual gratification of grasping a painting's compositional arrangement, the emotional surge of awe, pity, rage, or joy aroused by many different types of works—all these leave us with the same feeling of fulfillment as does a great symphony or fugue or a well-performed drama.

But the function of art goes beyond this. It may project in symbolic (that is, indirect) form certain universal truths. These may ultimately have the greatest potential meaning for us. We shall try here to identify as many as possible of the tangible personal satisfactions that enter into enjoyment and understanding of art. Nevertheless there will be certain elements on the intuitive (nonrational) level, the existence of which we can point out but certainly not explain. As in the nonplastic arts of music and playwriting, this very circumstance gives an elasticity, indeed an endlessness, to the possible reactions and degrees of pleasure to be derived, depending on our own sensitivity. These added intangible factors, these satisfactions of the soul, make the reaction to art potentially one of the great experiences man can undergo.

Our Acquaintance with Other Peoples and Other Times

Art is also a part of our evidence of how people in past ages lived and died. It survives as a record of their physical and psychological experiences, of their thoughts and aspirations. We shall see presently the many ways in which our ancestors reveal themselves to us through their arts.

As for understanding, we must bear in mind that art—however unusual and strange it may appear at first—is produced by human beings for other human beings. In some cases our approach to the art object may be blocked by our ignorance of the language of art—that is, of its technical aspects. This can be overcome more readily in traditional art, with which many of us are familiar, than in contemporary forms. Where the problem is to absorb and understand nonrepresentational and other modern viewpoints, perhaps less familiar to us, it is somewhat more complex but far from hopeless.

In this same category may fall certain non-Western forms, the art of primitive man, and ancient Mediterranean art. Here the contemporary spectator may have certain difficulties since expressions of unfamiliar cultures do not always correspond to our preconceived notions. These notions may have been derived from an often lagging educational system as well as from a generation-long impact of magazines with exclusively naturalistic and sentimental illustrations. The attitude of those who still reject modern art is also affected by a long tradition of prejudice expressed in the clichés and stereotypes of the antimodern cartoon, magazine story, motion picture, or television program.

Some of us may, therefore, be inclined to reject these strange expressions as unworthy or even insincere. As we become more and more familiar with art, however, we find that one of the strongest motivations in artistic or esthetic reaction is the element of recognition. This refers not only to the obvious fact that continuous exposure to a given mode of painting or sculpture will tend to make that mode more acceptable; it even extends to such naïve reactions as attributing excellence to a work of art or music merely because we recognize its type or style, its subject matter, or its very title.

Even a brief consideration of the reasons for rejecting certain art forms (lack of familiarity with them and, contrariwise, constant exposure to traditional Western naturalistic art) may help us realize that most legitimate formulations, even those we may at first consider in bad taste, in bad perspective, or badly drawn (that is, different from the familiar and the expected—see Chapter 14), represent thoughtful and planned efforts on the part of often long-lived cultures and are not simply aberrations or ignorant maunderings.

The study of different kinds of art objects will give us additional benefits. We will gain a notion of how different races and cultures operated, how they thought and felt; and even more important, we will profit by our increased receptivity to other men's ideas. The moment we realize that the differences are genuine, that they are due not to ignorance but rather to varying backgrounds, religions, or social systems, we have made an important step toward understanding our fellow man.

This may seem at first a rather academic problem, inasmuch as the average person will seldom concede that he is intolerant of other people and their ideas. A little thought, however, will reveal large areas of intolerance, especially in the intellectual field. Although many people will admit the validity of, let us say, Oriental or medieval ideas and even make some attempt to understand them (after all, they *are* old and respectable), the same people may not be ready to accept contemporary ideas that are at variance with theirs. The study of art will do something—perhaps a great deal—to dispel some of these prejudices, through the very attempt to understand what an artist is saying, as well as through the process of examining into the motivations of artists in the past, in far-off countries, or of those today who for various reasons are removed from reality.

Discovering the Original Meaning of a Work of Art

Obviously, then, the "snap" judgment on a work of art is out of place; more examination is called for. With further study we discover, for example, that the original purpose and the present function of many works of art may be entirely different. This means that a sculpture like Michelangelo's *Moses* (Fig. 1, p. 7), a building like the *Louvre,* and a painting like Géricault's *Raft of the Medusa* (Fig. 2, p. 8) were made for one reason—generally practical in a religious, political, or other sense—and now serve a changed purpose altogether, that of purely esthetic enjoyment.

The *Moses* was conceived as part of a large tomb for Pope Julius II, which was never executed; this figure is one of the few elements to be completed. It was to have been one of four corner figures on a gigantic structure designed for the specially enlarged and altered interior of St. Peter's in Rome. In its present state it is centered in a reconstructed composition set up after the sculptor's death in a different church. Thus the purpose, meaning, and location of this work have been significantly changed.

Fig. 1. Tomb of Pope Julius II. (*Moses*, center figure, bottom row.) Rome, San Pietro in Vincoli.

The Louvre, originally a palace for the kings of France, now serves as one of the greatest public museums in the world. The Géricault painting was created specifically to protest the abandonment of a group of sailors by their officers after the wreck of the *Medusa*, a French naval vessel, off the coast of Africa. After weeks of horrible suffering, the sailors were rescued. This painting was so controversial that the government would not permit it to be shown. Today in the Louvre, like other objects of its kind, the picture is looked upon exclusively as a work of art.

With so many works of art from the past in museums, we must often remind ourselves that a particular piece of sculpture or painting was originally part of a temple or church, set in an altogether different kind of light or high up on a different eye level or tinted with color which it has since lost. These and other changes show how far we may have come from the original function, locale, and intrinsic meaning of the work of art.

Along these same lines, we find that many works of art refer to a world or sphere of activity not immediately concerned with the tech-

Fig. 2. THÉODORE GÉRICAULT: *Raft of the Medusa*. Paris, Louvre.

nique of the object, that is, with painting or sculpture. There are many that evoke the world of the theater, such as Watteau's *Gilles* (Fig. 3, p. 9), social life, sports, such as Myron's *Discobolus* (or *Discus Thrower,* Fig. 86, p. 132), political events, such as Géricault's *Raft of the Medusa* (Fig. 2, p. 8), or the realm of religion. These special meanings indicate a wide scope of reference within the figurative arts, and they often add greatly to the interest and significance of the objects themselves.

The Technical Language of the Artist

The arts have an important technical aspect which must be considered for greater understanding and enjoyment. This technical side, as we shall see, has direct bearing on what the artist can accomplish physically (in other words, the limitations or advantages of the various media) and on what this may mean in ultimate spiritual terms, such as the rich translucency of stained glass, the clarity and smoothness of marble, the tight precision of the engraved line.

In the technical area we shall become aware of the major role played by drawing, particularly in the traditional arts. The artist is first and foremost a sensitive organism receiving visual and emotional stimuli from the outside world. These stimuli are absorbed and translated into the language of art through various technical media as well as through the artistic idiom of the time, rendered in the artist's personal manner. Many, if not most, of the arts do this with the aid of drawing, which here acts in the capacity of a planning device.

We must not discount the independent function of the drawing as an art form by itself, especially since the Renaissance, but its chief traditional use has been as a basis, a preliminary sketch for buildings, paintings, sculpture, and the industrial arts. Although many sculptors prefer a three-dimensional preliminary model, an equal number are addicted to the use of the drawn sketch of an idea on paper or the drawing made directly on the block itself before they begin carving.

What Determines Style?

Not only are we to investigate the various techniques of the arts but also their history, which we should understand at least in general terms.

Fig. 3. JEAN ANTOINE WATTEAU: *Gilles*. Paris, Louvre.

This will bring in its turn a realization of the different standards of taste that prevail in each period, and something of the relationship between the social and historical forces of each epoch and the cultural expression of that time as revealed in its arts. We must think of these epochs as differing from each other and yet linked together in the sense that one period is often a reaction in many ways to the period preceding. Moreover, certain artistic traditions are handed on from one generation to another, as revealed in techniques such as bronze casting, lithography, etching, and oil painting. Sometimes techniques are revived after many generations, such as the revival of Renaissance fresco painting in modern Mexican art.

Furthermore, the general cultural forces of an age may necessitate a kind of style or manner of execution that can only be found in some previous period. Thus the early nineteenth-century Romantics, with their need for violent expression and sometimes pathos, will show a conscious imitation of the emotive art of the seventeenth-century Baroque (*cf.* Delacroix and Rubens). We may say then that similar psychological needs will possibly produce similar, or parallel, emotional and esthetic expressions in the arts. And yet, since the historical circumstances of one period are never the exact counterpart of those of any previous period, there are bound to be serious differences.

We should note that the history of art is related to the history of each separate epoch and to history as a whole, and that the individual arts (painting, sculpture, etc.) are related to each other as well as to the period. This means that the arts influence each other; in given periods one art may perhaps be dominant, as in the Gothic age when the architectural concept (that is, the idea of the cathedral) was the most important. No one art exists entirely apart from any other in a particular era; they are all connected with the general cultural spirit of the time. This may not always be easy to demonstrate, but it is a useful idea to keep in mind. Its value for us lies in the fact that if we know, for example, that a certain period is dominated by the sculptural, pictorial, or architectonic concept, we have an important clue to the artistic standards and tastes of the time.

Just as art in general is part of a continuous development, each artist will be found to have a history of his own which, although part of the cultural expression of his age, is still an individual and personal thing. After his work with one master or another for a period of apprenticeship, he may become an imitative personality with little to contribute. Or he may take what the teacher has to offer and add to it in a new and creative fashion, to emerge with something meaningful and important, something individualistic.

The actual steps in this process constitute the events in the history of the particular artist. Generally there is a hesitant, even fumbling, adjustment to what is being learned as well as to the process of growing up mentally. Then the young personality begins to add elements of his own. Finally, the old and the new combine in what ultimately stands as the artist's own contribution to history. In this personal story it is difficult for us, the outsiders, to weigh the relative contributions of the period itself as a force and of the unique personality. Both are significant, and we must consider them as forces balancing and complementing each other.

We may also speak of esthetic or artistic problems as having their own history. By this we mean that the actual elements which go into the creation of a work of art: space, light, proportion, etc., proceed in a parallel fashion to that of art as a whole. Space, for example, is treated differently from one culture to another, and yet it remains part of a total development process. In the change from the Romanesque to the Gothic kind of space, for instance, we find a continuity and yet a significant difference as well (see Chapter 4) .

We have seen that each period has its own specific artistic character and dominant trends—sculpturesque, architectonic, or pictorial. This character or trend is the result in part of the socio-historical forces of that particular time, their relationship to the immediate or distant past, and finally the many expressions of thousands of creative individualities. The three elements are mutually interdependent and interactive, stimulating and restraining each other, and, taken together, ultimately constitute the creative attitude of the time.

The Question of Taste

This creative attitude expresses itself in a kind of artistic taste which differs from period to period. Just as the attitude toward physical beauty changed from the Victorian age to our own, from the preference for the hourglass figure in women to the svelte figure of the 1950's, so our attitude toward artistic beauty also changes from era to era. In one age the preference is for a flamboyant emotional or physical quality —as in certain aspects of seventeenth-century art—and in others it is for a more controlled expression or physical quality—as in the early sixteenth century.

Two things must be noted here: first, that those separate periods had their own taste in art (just as we have ours today); second, that our attitude toward their art is conditioned to a great extent by the prevailing taste of our own time. A simple illustration will help make the latter point clear. Rembrandt, who died in 1669, outlived his own era, so that by the time of his death, Dutch painting had already entered into a somewhat formal and even aristocratic type of expression best represented by Vermeer, who was born a quarter of a century after him. Further, during the eighteenth century, in the face of the dominantly elegant and decorative Rococo art of France, the serious and soulful heritage left by Rembrandt would necessarily be less popular than ever. On the other hand, during the Romanticism of the early nineteenth century (see Delacroix) Rembrandt's emotional quality, his dramatic lighting effects, and his specific concern with the human being made him very popular.

An equally striking change in taste from one era to another is seen in the varying attitudes toward use of the same material. Classical (that is, Greek and Roman) ornaments in architecture and sculpture have been applied differently in different periods, each era handling this vocabulary or language of form in a manner consistent with the taste of the time. There is a certain spareness in the fifteenth-century treatment, a richness in the seventeenth, a lightness in the eighteenth. In literature we may recall the different productions of Shakespeare's plays from one century to another. Not only costumes and scenery, but even the actual manner of delivery, have varied, and the text itself has been altered, added to, or cut to conform to the taste of the time.

We also find that translations of Homer and other classics vary in character from one era to another.

Thus we have two separate problems: how a given period looks on its own art, and how it looks on the art of another period or culture removed in time or space. Furthermore, the way we view the art of others is conditioned to a great extent by the way we perceive our own, that is, what we consider good or worth while.

A question that naturally emerges is whether or not we have the right to criticize and condemn any type of artistic, literary, or musical taste because it does not conform to our own. Can we take the position that Rubens' women are too heavy, or Egyptian painting too flat, or Chinese music too discordant? Or should we, rather, try to realize that since each of these art forms is a legitimate and serious expression of its own time and place, designed (usually unconsciously) to meet certain spiritual needs, we must give it the same careful consideration that we feel our own taste is entitled to receive?

We can readily realize that standards of physical beauty as well as standards of artistic beauty were different in Rubens' time, because we ourselves have experienced such changes. In our times the standards of physical beauty are to a large extent controlled and dictated by fashion magazines, movies, television, and other media of mass communication. These same organs of information have also helped disseminate certain artistic ideas, especially in the realm of industrial art—furniture and fabric design, home appliances, and the like—that represent a serious shift from the prevailing taste of only a generation ago. When we encounter an old-fashioned automobile of the 1920's or 1930's, we may smile, but this car was appropriate to its period, and we were just as proud of our cars then as we are now.

Since the industrial arts are more obviously a part of our everyday lives than the so-called fine arts, painting and sculpture, the evolution of industrial forms is familiar, acceptable, and understandable. Because of this familiarity we are perhaps more interested in changes in the applied arts—but there is a certain evidence of everyday concern with the fine arts. For example, styles in interior decoration (home furnishing and home design) have changed, much like the design of appliances, vehicles, or packages. This necessarily includes our notion of color ensembles as well as the pictures appropriate to the kind of interior that may be popular at a given moment. Not too long ago, Old Master reproductions were the prevailing taste for home decoration. Later, for a period of about ten to fifteen years there was great use of Impressionist and post-Impressionist material (Monet, Renoir, van Gogh, and others) —originals when the buyer could afford them, but usually color reproductions. More recently taste has shifted to the use of Fauve and Cubist material as exemplified by Matisse, Vlaminck, and Derain and by Picasso and Braque. All this means that we have been and are still concerned with matters of taste even on the fine arts level.

As for the industrial arts, the modern shift in taste, as between the old-fashioned automobile and the streamlined vehicle, has actually been influenced by a new kind of painting, sculpture, and architecture. This has created new attitudes whose effects have recently appeared in the industrial arts. It may be illustrated by the relationship between the Mondrian *Composition* (see Fig. 33, p. 50) and the kind of layout or design found in such objects as the Kleenex package, the compact linear organization of the modern kitchen, and such examples of modern architecture as the *Tugendhat House* at Brno (see Fig. 64, p. 101), and the many later examples derived from it.

Artistic Standards and Our Judgment

Although there is no statute that compels everyone to like the same things, and many of us may have a distaste for some style of the past or for some contemporary phenomenon in the arts, these forms have a right to exist as much as our own preferred styles. One may even speak of a moral obligation to let these nonfavored types of expression be heard, however much we dislike them. In this process also, the critic and the historian have a valuable function to fulfill, giving us the benefit of their knowledge and experience.

There is a school of thought that maintains it is impossible to set up objective standards by which works of art may be judged. This reflects an honest belief that the virtues possessed by the object of art reside within the eye of the observer, that since there are so many possible reactions, these may be as readily caused by the viewer himself as by the object viewed. With this belief there necessarily goes a refusal to state or even hazard any value or quality judgments.

In opposition, we maintain that since works of art are products of a given period with its attendant historical and other circumstances, our knowledge of these historical, cultural, and artistic circumstances helps us to judge a work in terms of its own environment and execution. Balancing the aims of the period as a whole and the aims of the individual artist within this framework, we begin to arrive—not always completely or successfully, it is true—at a standard of value, a fairly rough rule of thumb.

This enables us to say, for example, that within the artistic complex of the fifteenth century in Italy, there exist certain types of pictorial, sculptural, and other artistic performance. These constitute the cultural climate of that period. Varying groups of artists will adhere to each of these forms of expression, some driven by affinity, others by the fact that they are pupils or followers of the initiators of the separate movements or schools. After we examine enough of the material in a particular type of creation, it appears almost inevitable that certain individuals in that group are better able to transmit to the spectator the particular things for which the group stands: its striving for monumentality or color richness, its two-dimensional decorativeness, or other qualities.

Most people will agree that there is such a thing as a skillfully drawn line, a sensitively applied texture, a dynamically balanced composition, or a rich and moving combination of colors. They agree because they themselves are stirred by such demonstrations of skill and sensitivity in certain artists; and they remain unaffected by works of others of the same school. Here we are speaking of our own reaction rather than that of the period itself. It will be evident that there can be conflicts between the standards of an age like ours, increasingly dominated by the idea of nonrepresentational art, and a period primarily devoted to narrative and representational art. What is important is that although we may or may not like the art of a given period, our reaction by no means disqualifies it from serious consideration.

When we have made some investigation of the elements of art, that is, of the vocabulary of the artist's language, we shall try to compare the work of one artist in a given era with that of another—or, equally important, one work by a certain artist with another by the same man. From this we shall see that we can approach a judgment, though it is all but impossible to achieve absolute standards where there are so many unmeasurable or intuitive qualities.

Admittedly, two artists of the same period are different people with different mental and physical equipment; and however much they may share the qualities of a school of thought, they will differ ultimately in their interpretations, in their artistic language. For this reason it will be possible for us to see that one seventeenth-century Dutch painter is more serious in outlook and more subtle as a colorist than his contemporary, that one eighteenth-century French painter is comparable to another on these and other grounds.

With different works by the same artist, it will be somewhat easier to arrive at a judgment, since within a limited period his aims and standards are not likely to change very much. Once we can isolate these factors, it will become possible for us to speak of a more or less "successful" work by this master. All the works of Shakespeare, Beethoven, or Rembrandt are not equally great, and we shall attempt to discover just what it is that determines such a circumstance.

Leaving our general view, we may now go a little closer to the men and their works, by exploring in more leisurely fashion the various avenues of our approach to art.

▶2

What to Look for in Art

FOR THE AVERAGE uninitiated person, enjoyment and appreciation of the fine arts are often limited by an approach which measures
the importance of a work of art by the degree of excitement and
drama in the life of the artist.

Even without biographical fireworks, however, the initial approach
to a work of art need not be mysterious or complicated. Many people
without any artistic knowledge whatsoever derive pleasure from the
simplest contact with a painting, sculpture, building, or other work.
This primarily physical response is enjoyed by many persons who may
have color prints of paintings in their homes or reproductions of
sculpture or pottery. Understanding may come later to enhance their
original pleasure, as intellectual, symbolic, and other values are added.

Physical Appeal

This first sensation of physical enjoyment is the kind of pleasure we
might feel in looking at a handsome man or beautiful woman or a
pleasant scene in nature. No profound understanding of art is required, for example, to appreciate the sheer physical good looks and
well-being of the young men and women in Renoir's paintings (Fig. 4,
p. 18) . Their rich glossy hair, glowing complexions, their air of health
and enjoyment of life can all be grasped without knowing anything
about art as such. Without understanding the specific technical means
by which Renoir has conveyed these qualities, one is somehow in ac-

Fig. 4. PIERRE AUGUSTE RENOIR: *Luncheon of the Boating Party*. Washington, D. C., Phillips Memorial Gallery.

cord with him. Yet it is also true, here as elsewhere in the arts, that when the element of understanding is added, when we realize what the artist was trying to do and how he accomplished his purpose, the potential enjoyment becomes much greater.

The elementary physical approach—for example, to the beauty of human beings—may be applied to innumerable works of art from all periods and cultures. We may choose at random the artificial elegance of the goddess *Diana* in Goujon's work (Fig. 5, p. 19), the poetic glorification of the flesh in the dreamy *Aphrodite* by Praxiteles (Fig. 6, p. 20), or the virile appeal of the *Artemision Zeus* (Fig. 7, p. 20).

But this physical attraction, at least for the faces and forms of human beings, is not necessarily always in force. In van Eyck's *Arnolfini Marriage* (Fig. 8, p. 21) we find certain immediate objections to both figures on such grounds. This may mean that the conception of physical beauty was different in fifteenth-century Flanders, or that what the artist wished to achieve had little to do with obvious physical beauty but instead with such elements as texture, compositional strength, light, and emotional quality.

We may therefore realize that a work of art need not have the physical appeal of a Renoir painting to be beautiful. Beauty in art is, rather, a consequence of the successful bringing together of lines, forms, textures, and colors in order to convey a form idea or an emotional idea. The important factor in the *Arnolfini Marriage* is its spiritual mood (resulting from certain technical devices and less tangible elements), rather than any beauty of the lady or gentleman. In another example, Daumier's *Washerwoman* (Fig. 9, p. 22), we see that the feeling of quiet strength and dignity, the simple motherly protectiveness of the monumental woman, outweigh any other consideration.

These understandings come only after experience, after we have learned to look. At this stage the physical reaction is still the simplest; and just as we approached some works for the obvious beauty of their human participants, we come to others which deal primarily with nature. Whereas in the human form and face we may be hampered in our appreciation by differing standards of physical beauty, this is less likely to happen in representations of nature. If we take two considerably different treatments of landscape—the early nineteenth-century English *Childe Harold's Pilgrimage* (Fig. 10, p. 23) by Turner

Fig. 5. JEAN GOUJON: *Diana*. Paris, Louvre.

Fig. 6 (*left*). PRAXITELES: *Aphrodite*. Rome, Vatican Museum. Fig. 7 (*right*). *Artemision Zeus*. Athens, National Museum.

and the nineteenth-century French *Peasants Resting* (Fig. 11, p. 24) by Pissarro—it would appear that nature is interesting and attractive to us in many forms.

Although the philosophy behind these two works is as different as the respective artistic techniques (and these we may still leave aside at this point), both have immediate interest and appeal to the degree that they convey some of the pleasure we always feel in the presence of nature. At the same time it is true that as we look, even for a relatively short while, other factors begin to operate in addition to the obvious physical ones—emotion, memory (that is, recognition), sentiment, poetry. We must therefore admit that although we are trying here to present the primary reactions as separate entities, it is very seldom, if ever, that one of them is present without some admixture of other and increasingly complex stimuli.

The physical beauty of paintings, sculptures, or prints is not merely a matter of the subject itself, its rich curves or muscular strength; we may also be attracted by lovely color or texture (surface quality). The paintings of Renoir or of such Venetians as Giorgione or Titian possess an added coloristic allure, the effect of which is just as immediate as that of the lush forms themselves. This color quality, varying in meaning and character with each school of art, can be of interest for its own sake and without reference to esthetic, that is, artistic, factors.

The appeal of color extends from paintings through sculpture, architecture, and lesser forms such as textiles, jewelry, and pottery. A great deal of ancient sculpture and architecture enjoyed the benefits of color —a fact not always apparent from architectural ruins and museum fragments. In our own time colored sculpture and architecture have been revived, and we can readily enjoy the color of certain kinds of woods or exotic stones in sculpture as well as the color of particular types of residences, like the California redwood houses (see Fig. 56, p. 89), or industrial buildings, like Frank Lloyd Wright's *Johnson Wax Company Laboratory Tower* (see Figs. 75 and 75a, p. 116) at Racine, Wisconsin, with its red brick and glass tubing.

In the same elementary way that we enjoy form and color, we may also react to the nature of the surface—what is called the texture of a given art object. Perhaps the simplest example would be the skin

Fig. 8. JAN VAN EYCK: *Arnolfini Marriage.*
London. National Galley.

Fig. 9. HONORÉ DAUMIER: *Washerwoman*. New York, Metropolitan Museum of Art.

quality in a work of sculpture like Praxiteles' *Aphrodite* (Fig. 6, p. 20) or Bernini's *Apollo and Daphne* (see Fig. 177, p. 311). In works of this type the translucence or light-absorptive quality of the marble creates a soft glow about the body, especially in such smaller areas as the nose, ears, and lips that protrude sufficiently to catch and absorb the light more directly. Here, as with many other sculptures, we have an urge to touch the surface, to come into direct contact with a skin texture, the quality of which the artist has managed to convey so effectively in this hard material.

Sculpture in general offers a wide variety of textural or surface possibilities to interest us, each material, such as stone, wood, bronze, or clay, offering its own surface interest and excitement. This may be illustrated by the simple experience of touching a piece of sculpture and sensing in a direct physical manner the nature of the particular surface. A bronze sculpture (see *Zeus*, p. 20) will not only look different from a wooden figure, it will actually feel different. Each of the sculptural media gives a unique reception to the light falling on it or to the touch of a hand; each gives us a separate sensation in the fingertips as we learn how it feels to touch its surface. In fact, the sculptor himself works as much by the sense of touch as by the sense of sight.

Textural quality is also present to a high degree in architecture, where materials are deliberately chosen, as in sculpture, both for their different surface qualities and their technical advantages. The smooth white marble of the Greek *Parthenon* is different in this respect from the rougher grayish stone of the Gothic *Chartres Cathedral* and the grained California redwood house of today. Here again, without being more than generally aware of the need for a different type of material in each case, we can appreciate the stately effect of the marble, the rugged simplicity of the stone, or the natural beauty of the redwood surface as it blends into its environment.

Texture in painting is not quite so obvious as in sculpture and architecture, but it is there nevertheless, and often so important that it can immediately concern our beginning view. There are many different possibilities of direct and effective appreciation of paint texture—a few instances will suggest the range. Frans Hals' *Malle Bobbe* (Fig. 12, p. 24) shows a casual application of strokes of paint that allows us to trace the path of the artist's brush, lends a sense of spontaneity and movement, and adds to the surface interest of the picture. In the Im-

Fig. 10. J. M. W. TURNER: *Childe Harold's Pilgrimage—Italy*. London, Tate Gallery.

Fig. 11 (*left*). CAMILLE PISSARRO: *Peasants Resting*. Toledo, Ohio, Toledo Museum of Art. Fig. 12 (*right*). FRANS HALS: *Malle Bobbe*. New York, Metropolitan Museum of Art.

pressionist school, painters like Renoir (see Fig. 4, p. 18), Monet, and Pissarro (Fig. 11, p. 24) emphasize the application of small dots of color that are fused by the eye into an effect of constant twinkling light and brilliant coloristic quality. This rough application of paint—in other words, its shaggy texture—is attractive in itself, adds enormously to the sense of movement on the canvas, and instantly affects us even when we are not quite aware of what is happening. Paintings like *Peasants Resting* illustrate this textural quality and also point up the important effect of color as such.

Another and more subtle textural experience in painting (which may, however, be felt even on an elementary level) can be illustrated in such pictures as Terborch's *Curiosity* (Fig. 13, p. 25). Here, in contrast to the Hals or the Monet, we are no longer dealing with surface roughness. Terborch's canvas shows no single point of paint raised above the surface; and yet it conveys in the glossy, highly polished finish a sense of the touch quality of the various objects shown: the chandelier, furniture, picture frame, cloth. The painter has created an *illusion* of the surface qualities of various materials instead of trying to reproduce in paint the actual roughness or movement in nature.

Architecture and sculpture may also be apprehended physically by walking about and into the former and around the latter. It is a genuine physical experience to ride in a high-speed elevator in the *R.C.A. Building* or to walk down the lofty nave of a Gothic cathedral (Fig. 14, p. 26). It is also a physical experience to take in the overwhelming bulk of an Egyptian statue like the *Sphinx* or to move visually through a modern figure by Pevsner (see Fig. 84, p. 129) or Henry Moore. But from the physical to the emotional is only a short distance, for every one of these examples leaves us with an emotional reaction as well.

We may sense physically the balance of such buildings as the serene Parthenon, the impressive *Palace of Versailles,* the dignified *Palazzo Farnese,* the delicate *Pazzi Chapel* (see Fig. 30, p. 45); but this balance invariably results in an emotional reaction of peacefulness, quiet, respect. In painting, works like Giorgione's *Castelfranco Madonna* (Fig. 15, p. 27) may have the same effect.

Fig. 13. GERARD TERBORCH: *Curiosity.* New York, Metropolitan Museum of Art.

Fig. 14. Amiens Cathedral. View of interior, showing nave and choir. Amiens, France.

Conversely, we may be disturbed by an unbalanced or diagonal composition, as in the *Ecstasy of St. Theresa* by Bernini (see Fig. 98, p. 153) or in the Hellenistic sculpture group known as the *Laokoön* (see Fig. 187, p. 325). Or we may be exalted by the sweeping grandeur of a Gothic interior or by its soaring towers. In reactions of this sort, too, it seems that after a brief interval the physical may become the emotional.

Emotional Approach

The same person who enjoys a work of art for its obvious physical qualities of form, color, texture, and balance can often derive from it an equally elementary and pleasurable emotional reaction. Just as the physical implications become more complex as we go along, the emotional meanings of art become more and more profound, adding to themselves elements of the narrative, associational, intellectual, symbolic, or religious.

A mixture of physical and emotional can be illustrated in the *Aphrodite* of Praxiteles which appeals to us for its beauty of form and also for a certain dreamy mood. Similarly, the *Concert Champêtre* (or *Pastoral Concert*) by Giorgione (see Fig. 175, p. 308) gives us beautiful forms and colors as well as hauntingly poetic suggestions, however vague.

There are works whose quality is either primarily physical or primarily emotional. We have seen the *Artemision Zeus* (Fig. 7, p. 20), an idealized human form that is attractive for its virility and the nobility of its proportions rather than for any emotional reasons. In contrast we have a Raphael Madonna and Child, *The Alba Madonna* (Fig. 16, p. 28), a basically sentimental expression, whatever other qualities

Fig. 15. IL GIORGIONE: *Castelfranco Madonna*. Castelfranco Veneto, Italy, Cathedral.

Fig. 16. RAPHAEL: *The Alba Madonna*. Washington, D. C., The National Gallery of Art (Mellon Collection).

it may possess. Although this picture is presumably a religious work, the motherliness of the Madonna and the simple affection of the Child are immediately important impressions. For a fuller understanding of the painting, however, we must go beyond this initial naïve reaction. We need to consider intellectual, religious, and other aspects in order to grasp the painting's real meaning as a work of art.

On a more powerful emotive level are such works as the *Ecstasy of St. Theresa* by Bernini, noted above. Although we, as modern spectators, may have little idea of what is happening, we cannot help being disturbed by the clearly expressed anguish of the saint at the right. It is also possible that some of us might be repelled by what seem to be exaggerations of feeling and might therefore not like this work particularly; but it is scarcely likely that we will remain completely unmoved. If later we discover the narrative and religious implications of the scene and the historical milieu of which it is a part—in other words, if we learn why such works were produced—we will understand its expression better and perhaps be readier to accept it, at least intellectually. Right now we are concerned simply with the fact that it is possible for us to be moved, positively or negatively, by a work of art even when our understanding of it is limited.

We may, then, be moved by sentimentality, as in *The Alba Madonna,* by anguish, as in the *Ecstasy of St. Theresa,* or by pain, as in the *Laokoön* (see Fig. 187, 325). In these latter two works, even without any narrative knowledge, we are affected by the obvious facts that in the first someone is undergoing a great emotional experience and that in the second human beings are suffering terrific anguish.

The Narrative Factor

The narrative factor, the story content of a given work, has many possible uses in our initial approach; first and foremost, it helps us understand what the artist had in mind for his picture or sculpture. We should, therefore, always look for the narrative content (where there is any) as a beginning. Sometimes the narrative approach is the only contact with which we can start. Rubens' *Descent from the Cross* and Chardin's *Child with a Top* (Figs. 17 and 18, pp. 29, 30), whatever

Fig. 17. PETER PAUL RUBENS: *Descent from the Cross* (altar triptych). Antwerp, Belgium, Cathedral.

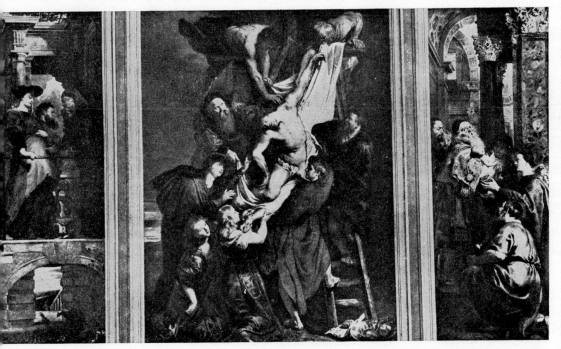

Fig. 18. J. B. S. CHARDIN: *Child with a Top*. Paris, Louvre.

their other virtues, tell simple and clear-cut stories. The melodramatic
feeling of the first picture, its strong lighting and violent movement—
the components of its mood—become more understandable as we scan
the picture for story. In the Chardin painting we become interested
in examining the child with his picturesque costume of the past and his
quiet, pleasant, self-absorbed game. Both pictures show a balancing of
story and emotional quality, one adding to the other and the two combined giving added meaning to the paintings.

After looking at a number of pictures of these two diverse emotional
types, we realize that works with an exciting narrative content or story
are arranged accordingly, that is, in such a way that we, the spectators,
are disturbed or agitated so as to receive the full emotional impact.
This may be illustrated by the difference between the strong light of
the Rubens and the gentle lighting of the Chardin work, as well as by
the diagonal thrust of the first versus the balanced arrangement of the
shapes in the second. Indeed we can always expect to find a close re-

lationship between the form of a work and its content or story.

Some paintings and sculptures lead us to scrutinize them quite carefully for the story interest they contain. Sometimes our motivation is simple curiosity—the thing is there to be examined. At times our motives are more complex, as when the work suggests an experience we have had or something we have seen.

The idea of ordinary curiosity needs no great elaboration. We may be thumbing through an illustrated book on the eighteenth century and encounter one of Hogarth's *Marriage à la Mode* prints (Fig. 19, p. 31) or the paintings from which they were made. The sight of a slovenly man seated on one chair, a rather disagreeable woman on another, and an older man going out of the picture with a pen behind his ear and accounts of various kinds in his hands arouses our curiosity, especially in view of the picture title. Though we lack additional information, the title of the series, *Marriage à la Mode* (or *Fashionable Marriage*), and the subtitle, *Shortly after Marriage,* convey the fact

Fig. 19. WILLIAM HOGARTH: *Marriage à la Mode—Scene 2 (Shortly after Marriage)*. Courtesy Metropolitan Museum of Art, New York.

that something is wrong with Hogarth's married couple, that there is very little honey in the honeymoon. If we take the trouble to leaf through the entire series of the *Marriage à la Mode,* we find a continuous story involving a period removed from us in time, with differences of customs and costumes, but one still interesting as a valid human experience.

What is the difference between a set of such narrative pictures and, let us say, a set of drawings made for modern magazine illustrations? Although they have in common the function of entertainment, the earlier work also has esthetic value and a symbolic purpose, it has a universal truth to convey, concerning the behavior of men and women and the appropriate punishment for transgression. Both the eighteenth-century painter-printmaker and the contemporary illustrator draw their material from the life about them. The first distills from it something beyond the mere anecdote—a significant gesture, a symbolic movement or pose; the latter for the most part is satisfied to tell a story, to entertain. This distillation from a visual or emotional situation is what constitutes the difference between a photographic or reportorial rendition (or narrative for its own sake) and what we can begin to call the artistic experience. By singling out a particular aspect of life, by concentrating our attention upon it through artistic devices, the artist's superior technique has given it a new meaning, a new reality.

Not all narratives in art are so long and complicated as that in Hogarth's series of caricatures. We may choose many other types on the basis of the simple curiosity with which we started out. With a dramatic or poignant work like the *Execution of the Citizens of Madrid* by Goya (see Fig. 20, p. 33), we are drawn by its pathos and drama, by the sympathy we feel for the victims and our curious fear of the anonymous menacing invaders at the right.

As we have mentioned, another factor in narrative interest may be related to the question of familiarity. We recognize types of faces, costumes, buildings, with which we are acquainted through other sources. The value of this recognition factor lies in its putting us in touch, however tenuously, with a situation that we might have found strange because of our unfamiliarity with its technical aspects.

Let us look, for example, at a page from a late medieval manuscript, the prayer book known as *Très riches heures du Duc de Berri* (or *Very*

Fig. 20. FRANCISCO GOYA: *Execution of the Citizens of Madrid, May 3, 1808*. Madrid, Prado.

Rich Hours of the Duc de Berri, Fig. 21, p. 34) . Here are a sheepfold, a man leading a wood-laden donkey, people warming themselves at a fire indoors with their skirts raised, a man chopping wood outdoors, and a little cluster of houses in the background. In this work, as in the Goya or the Hogarth, part of our interest comes from the narrative itself (the tasks performed, the peasants drying themselves) , part from the recognizability of the circumstances in terms of human problems (the poverty of these long-gowned figures) , and part from the recognition of a familiar social or historical situation (the feudal aristocracy and its serfs) .

These reactions may not be specifically esthetic, but they have contributed to our appreciation of the particular work. They have been tinged by factors noted before: the emotional or sentimental, the physical (the sense of balance in the Goya and the charm of landscape in the manuscript page). They also involve, as we shall see later, certain symbolic elements which represent a higher level of understanding and appreciation.

Fig. 21. POL DE LIMBOURG: *Très riches heures du Duc de Berri* (February page).
Chantilly, Musée Condé.

Art as Religious Experience

In modern Western practice, religious art is far less important than in those earlier periods when it sprang directly from the needs of the time. Yet there are many religious groups today which turn to esthetic expression as a means of bolstering faith through modernized church structures, contemporary forms of religious painting, sculpture, and church ornament. The paintings by Matisse in the chapel at Vence and the Le Corbusier-designed chapel at Ronchamp (1955) are among the outstanding examples of this trend.

What does the religious art of the past mean to us today? For many, the churches and temples of the past have direct and positive meaning as symbols of faith; indeed their very forms, such as the cross-shaped church plan, are associated with sacred meaning and symbolism. We need not know very much about the Age of Faith that produced the Gothic cathedral represented at Chartres or Amiens (Figs. 22 and 14, pp. 35, 26) in order to respond to the lofty soaring quality, the mysterious impressiveness of shadowy vaulted interiors, the jeweled glow of stained-glass windows that absorb and reflect light in shimmering color patterns.

Fig. 22. Chartres Cathedral. View from southwest. Chartres, France.

Fig. 23. Hōryūji Temple. Nara, Japan.

We may wonder to what degree this imposing effect is the result of a conscious manipulation of parts by the designer and to what degree it is the natural result of a development of shapes, heights, and surfaces in response to the strong spiritual need of its time. This much is certain: whether or not we are of the particular faith represented by the cathedrals, we cannot deny the spiritual appeal of these structures and their accompanying sculpture, painting, and other ornament. Part of this feeling is, of course, associative, since many houses of worship have retained this basic form and we react—at least partially—as might be expected.

If we are confronted with a religious building out of an entirely strange culture, where we have no equivalent associations, our reaction may be different. The *Hōryūji Temple* at Nara in Japan (Fig. 23, p. 36) does not correspond to the average Westerner's idea of a religious structure, and he looks at it in an entirely different way from that in which he looks at a Gothic church. Let us establish in his mind, however, the fact that it is a temple, and he will begin to respond to it in religious terms, looking for the same kind of stimuli he received from the Chartres Cathedral. He will probably not find such stimuli in the structure itself unless the symbolism of the various parts is made clear, but the associated arts, such as sculpture and painting, will represent this feeling in a more obvious way.

In painting and sculpture, a tremendous body of material in both the Western and Eastern traditions offers an immediate nonesthetic but still spiritual satisfaction. In some cases the stimulus is as direct and obvious as that derived from a Madonna and Child, the representation of a martyrdom, or other holy scene, as in *Le Beau Dieu* of Amiens (Fig. 24, p. 37). Some works, on the other hand, have to show a label before we become conscious of their meaning.

A detail from the Sistine Chapel ceiling by Michelangelo, the *Jeremiah* figure (Fig. 25, p. 38), identifies itself through the artist's painted label. This fact established, we may think of the associations connected with the Old Testament prophet who, together with his fellows, is used by the painter to foreshadow the advent of a Messiah. Here is the prophet of disaster, sad and dejected at the sins of his people, the poet who in words of solemn beauty bemoans their sad state: "Oh that my head were waters, and mine eyes a fountain of tears, that I might weep day and night for the slain of the daughter of my people! . . . How long shall the land mourn, and the herbs of every field wither, for the wickedness of them that dwell therein?" The strong contemplative figure painted into a sculptural niche becomes a three-

Fig. 24. *Le Beau Dieu* (central portal trumeau). Amiens, France, Amiens Cathedral.

Fig. 25. MICHELANGELO: *The Prophet Jeremiah,* detail from Sistine Chapel ceiling. Rome, Vatican.

dimensional symbol of religious aspiration and purpose understandable to most of the Western world.

Admittedly, forms of this type, in which dejection and thoughtfulness are made evident by the downward movement of the shoulders, knees, and other parts, may still not communicate in religious terms to a Buddhist or other Oriental worshiper for whom the materials of faith have altogether different physical shapes. He might recognize the religious meaning of *Le Beau Dieu* with His hand upraised in an almost universal gesture of admonition or teaching. But other Christian representations might well be beyond him in content, although if he has been educated to the esthetics of Western art, he will appreciate the *Jeremiah* and similar works for artistic reasons.

Similarly, we may well recognize the high spiritual quality of the Buddha type of India or Indonesia (Fig. 26, p. 40), and readily associate it with religious meaning; but since the religious motives of the East are foreign to most of us, we cannot, untaught, appreciate to any serious extent that aspect of their art. With a little instruction and, just as important, with a certain amount of familiarity and exposure to these works, the Occidental observer may derive an altogether different kind of stimulus and pleasure—but this can be done only with the expenditure of some intellectual energy.

Since most religious art of the past necessarily stems from non-Judeo-Christian sources, it must be treasured by Westerners for its meaning as cultural expression as well as for its esthetic meaning. Both these areas can only be conquered or even approached through rational processes. Here we move beyond the immediate physical or emotional appeal with which we began.

Art as Visual History

Our initial experience with art has provided physical and emotional stimulation; we as spectators have brought relatively little to the process, rather allowing the works to act upon us. In most physical and emotional enjoyment of art, however, other types of reaction automatically come into play. The religious feeling, for example, is tied up with certain intellectually learned relationships as well as with the emotional overtones of the religious inspiration itself. In the physical and emotional areas it is almost impossible to separate from our responses factors of memory, learning, and the associative process. This points to the fact that the artistic experience is a totality of reactions.

One of the associative pleasures of art lies in its existence for us as a form of visual history. Here again we may appreciate a work of art for reasons not specifically esthetic, but which enhance its value for us immeasurably. Walking through any museum of antiquities, we meet objects such as ancient musical instruments of the Mesopotamians (Fig. 27, p. 40) a necklace or pair of earrings worn by a Greek matron, an intricate glass bottle used by a Roman apothecary, the belt buckle of a Merovingian warrior of the Dark Ages, the hope chest of a young girl of the Renaissance. All these things have, in addition to their form, color, and texture, an intriguing historical association that may add limitless interest for the spectator. They are the visible symbols of the past, the tangible remains of periods of time the only other surviving evidence of which may be such intangibles as poetry and philosophy. Such objects, first, lend support to literary and historical

Fig. 26 (left). *Buddha and Two Bodhisattvas.* New York, Metropolitan Museum of Art. Fig. 27 (right). Harp of Queen Shubad. Philadelphia, Pennsylvania, University Museum.

testimony from those periods or, where we have no readable literary relics, stand alone to tell their story.

A dramatic instance of the first type of visual history, support of existing written records, was the discovery in 1952 of the remains of a Greek vessel of the third century B.C., at the bottom of the sea outside the harbor of Marseilles. In this wreck divers found thousands of pieces of Greek pottery. These were of two main types: one made for commercial purposes as containers of the oil, wine, and olives exported by the ancient Greeks throughout the Mediterranean world; the other, a more carefully designed and decorated variety, made for general household purposes.

The ship itself, actually the property of a Roman merchant conducting his business from the Greek island of Delos, had worked its way along the eastern coast of Greece, through the straits of Messina, and up the west coast of Italy to Campania in the southern part of the peninsula, where many Greek cities existed. There the second type of pottery, the so-called Campanian ware, had been added to the cargo, and the ship had moved on into the Mediterranean, hugging the shore line as was the custom in those compassless days. Somehow it was wrecked off the southern coast of France outside the harbor of the Greek settlement known as Massilia (Marseilles).

Even if we do not see the pieces of pottery involved in this story, their historical function and meaning fascinate us. They offer firsthand corroboration of Rome's economic penetration into Greece, of the Greek commercial role in the ancient Mediterranean world, and of Greek settlements along that entire coastline from the Black Sea to eastern Spain. Here then, the object of art, now a Greek bowl or later a Merovingian buckle, confirms what we have already heard through other sources.

Sometimes, however, we must depend entirely on the object of art (whether commercial or fine art) for historical evidence. Certain cultures existed so far back in history that they had no writing; others, which had some written records, left us with no key to their language, so that the records cannot be deciphered. Prehistoric man is, of course, in the unlettered category. Such works as the wall and ceiling paintings in the caves of southern France and northern Spain (Fig. 28, p. 42) date back to the Paleolithic or Old Stone Age, around 25,000 to 10,-000 B.C.

The painter of prehistory, in an age occupied primarily with such fundamentals as food, shelter, and safety both from the elements and from wild animals, produced a primarily utilitarian art designed to help him achieve his purposes. The prehistoric representations of animals, vivid in their generalized realism and sense of movement, had a magical function. In painting them, the artist was trying to ensure the success of his wishes, namely, the capture of an animal for food or a defense against wild beasts such as wolves.

The pictorialization of wishes is a common human practice. From our knowledge of later, historical civilizations, we may form a judgment as to the meaning of pictures from a pre-literate period. In the time of the Early Christian catacombs we find images or "picture prayers" that project prayers for the dead. They recount the many ways in which the Lord has intervened to save people from difficult situations. Through this pictorial act the Early Christian hoped to strengthen his chance for salvation, to influence the Deity toward similar acts of saving. Another example of artistic wish fulfillment is the Christian votive

Fig. 28. *A Wild Horse* (cave painting). Lascaux, France.

object, a wax or clay form of an ailing part of the human body, made to be placed on a church altar for intercession purposes.

Among present-day primitive races in areas of the Caribbean world, the practice still persists of making an image of an enemy and driving pins into it to bring about his desired destruction. In the same way, among animal representations by prehistoric man we often find forms with spears or arrows stuck into them, similarly portraying the wish in tangible form. Old Stone Age objects or those of primitive man of later periods reveal many other aspects of prehistoric life. Indeed our whole conception of the character of prehistoric man comes from such studies.

We have had to rely on artistic sources for knowledge of even much later and greatly advanced cultural areas, such as ancient Crete— the island in the Mediterranean the development of which brought the rise of Mycenae and Tiryns on the Greek mainland, paralleling that of Troy in Asia Minor. Although Cretan civilization has left numerous evidences of a flourishing culture—complex buildings, elaborate and varied pottery forms, rich jewelry, delicate small sculptures, charmingly colored and suave wall paintings, and written records on clay tablets— we have only recently begun to decipher its writing. In other words, we have had to use such testimony as the paintings from the palace of

Knossos, like the *Cup-bearer* (Fig. 29, p. 43), for our knowledge of this whole civilization.

Reflected in these Cretan objects is a highly civilized urban life, with cities dependent on commerce and showing in many ways their cosmopolitanism and contacts with the outside world of their day. The general emotional tone of these works is far different from that of Egyptian objects with their stiff, unchanging formality (see Fig. 179, p. 318) or Assyrian ones with their emphasis on power and even cruelty (see Fig. 180, p. 318). The figure of the *Cup-bearer* is at once more elastic and yielding than either of the others and shows more consciousness of sheer physical existence in terms of movement and enjoyment.

We do not, of course, make elaborate deductions from only one work of art, but through an examination of various types of objects, we arrive at a general picture. From the different kinds of pottery we deduce everyday facts; the various layers of pottery remains, according to their thickness, even yield a way of measuring epochs of time.

Art as Intellectual Experience

In our enjoyment of the object of art as visual history, we have brought to bear our rational faculties; we have tried to discern one kind of

Fig. 29. *Cup-bearer* (copy of a fresco from the Palace at Knossos, Crete). New York, Metropolitan Museum of Art.

associative meaning in the work of art. The building, sculpture, or painting itself also offers an intellectual experience in the analytical sense when we set out to discover the formal or compositional elements that hold it together. In the attempt to calculate the system behind its construction or the relationship of various parts, we are going through a reasoning process, a challenge of the mind that yields not only deeper understanding but also a certain form of pleasure as we explore the artist's thinking.

Every work of art is the result of a certain amount of planning. The simplest way of visualizing this is to think of the artist as a man with a piece of paper and pencil working on a sketch or plan of what he seeks. We are accustomed to the notion of a building, for example, derived from an architect's drawings. It is relatively simple, therefore, to recognize that the work of sculpture or painting is also dependent on systematic thinking. Certain types of art, as we shall see, take less actual preparatory sketching than others; for instance, Chinese painting seems to stem primarily from a long period of contemplation by the artist and his attempt to identify himself with the subject. The Western artist, on the other hand, is basically a planner in the physical sense, working over his materials and their various possibilities of combination through experiments with lines, forms, and colors, until he knows in advance what he is going to do. To a limited extent it is possible for us to follow the path of his thought as we calculate (or try to calculate) the elements that tie together the various parts of the architectural, sculptural, or pictorial composition.

Let us try this with the façade, or exterior, of the Pazzi Chapel (Fig. 30, p. 45), an early fifteenth-century Florentine building. Here, as in most traditional Western architecture, we are dealing with relatively simple and geometric combinations of horizontal, vertical, and curved lines. The round dome above, the horizontal main bulk of the façade, and the vertical supporting columns constitute the three chief accents. The façade, as we can see, is actually a false one projecting out from the main shell of the building.

Dealing only with what can be seen directly, we may notice how the verticals of the cylindrical columns are repeated and varied as we move through the various parts of this false façade which precedes the actual building. Behind the columns are *pilasters,* flat columns attached to the building itself; doubled-up and half-length vertical pilasters come

Fig. 30 (*above*). FILIPPO BRUNELLESCHI: Pazzi Chapel. Florence, Italy, Cloister of Santa Croce. Fig. 30a (*below*). FILIPPO BRUNELLESCHI: Pazzi Chapel. Interior view. Florence, Italy, Cloister of Santa Croce.

directly over the columns (these alternate with simple single verticals) ; finally, under the cornice are free-standing posts that correspond in position to the doubled flat pilasters and the columns below.

Taking the horizontal accents, we begin with the long sections over each of the two groups of columns. This *architrave,* the section directly over the columns, consists first of a series of overlapping layers, then a wider area covered with circular medallions, and, at the top, a heavy projecting molding that acts both as accent and as termination, before the sweeping arch. The horizontal movements are continued in varied form in the little squares above, which transfer to a second band of overlapping layers, a broad section with wavy ornaments, and a heavier molding that repeats in continuous form the lighter moldings below. These protruding elements are summed up in the projecting cornice that caps the various two-dimensional horizontal forms.

The curved lines begin with the arch over the entrance doorway and the medallions along the architrave. Round-topped panels are visible on the building itself behind the free-standing columns of the false façade. If we could move in behind these columns, we would find above us a pair of three-dimensional barrel vaults parallel to the outer façade; their sweeping curvilinear movements give a new direction to the roundnesses of the façade. These vaults also add a third dimension that takes us from a simple two-dimensional surface decorated with geometrical ornament to the space-enclosing mechanism we call a building. We begin to feel this sense of space even though we have not yet come into the building proper (Fig. 30a, p. 45) in which similar horizontals, verticals, and roundnesses envelop the arrangement of the interior space.

Still considering the outside design, we assess the function of the three-dimensional dome, which carries the eye curvingly and sweepingly inward, varying the two-dimensional flat curves of the lower section as we now follow them inward in depth. The dome also moves up and down, repeating the lower-section verticals, and goes across at the base to reaffirm the lower-area horizontals. Finally in its summing-up function, the dome repeats the angle of the projecting cornice, and its little window openings follow the circular rhythm of the medallions on the architrave. Here, at the very top of the façade, the architect-planner has brought together all the linear forms of the lower portions in what we must regard as a self-conscious gesture of finality, a last and summarizing variation on the linear themes he has been developing throughout.

Can we apply this analytical method to other types of buildings, or is it pertinent merely to structures of this period? Will it apply to other art forms, such as painting and sculpture?

First let us recall the observation made above, that all art objects result from a certain amount of planning. This planning may be as self-conscious as in the Pazzi Chapel (architecture generally, because of its practical functions, must be planned) or as spontaneous as in certain modern paintings.

The second category may be exemplified by van Gogh's *Cornfield with Cypress* (see Fig. 222, p. 404). The painter arrives at a certain type of pictorial organization as a consequence of long familiarity with the tools of his craft, which leads him automatically to arrange what he has seen or felt. Like the pianist who has learned his keyboard and no longer has to look for particular notes, so the painter or sculptor of experience will spontaneously or intuitively fall into a more or less ordered sequence of forms, colors, and textures in response to certain visual or emotional stimuli.

In effect, the painter, like the musician, has mastered certain practices which enable him to put the various elements together in some sort of systematic way on either an intuitive, partially intuitive, or completely rationalized level. In such objects as the Pazzi Chapel we are concerned with the intellectual procedure followed by the architect, sculptor, or painter in composing his work of art, rather than with the intuitive responses he may make toward that end. The intuitive or spontaneous reactions of the artist are often as important, or even more important—just as those of the spectator may be; but for purposes of the present discussion, we may limit ourselves to the intellectual or rational processes involved.

The analytical method applied to an Italian Renaissance building may also be used with a modern structure like the *Savoye House,* built by the distinguished architect Le Corbusier (Fig. 31, p. 48). Here again is a reasoned combination of vertical, horizontal, and circular or spherical forms. The main concrete block of the building is a square buff-colored living portion raised on a grid of steel posts above a curved dark-green substructure, from which it is cantilevered out (see p. 114) and supported by additional metal shafts; this block constitutes the

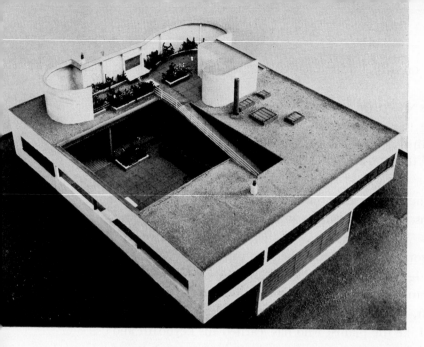

Fig. 31. LE CORBUSIER
(C. E. JEANNERET):
Model of Savoye House.
New York, The Mu-
seum of Modern Art.

primary horizontal mass of the building. Its mass is broken by the long narrow window spaces that are divided by regular vertical accents. The latter, in turn, are related to the verticals of the downstairs supporting columns spaced at parallel intervals to the window dividers and providing, as a result, a series of downstairs rectangular spaces. These spaces are repeated and varied in different ways by the main floor rectangles that create up-and-down and sideways movements.

The curvilinear forms in this structure consist of the tubular posts, the U-shaped green service area (the guest room–garage base), and the elegantly curved and open pink and blue wind-shelter above the main living quarters. These various curved areas stand in contrast to the straightness of the main rectangular portion, which acts as a powerful rigid space enclosure between the openness of the play space above and the service quarters beneath. Both the curved and the straight areas, however, have the highly polished symmetry of machined forms and convey some of this architect's expressed feeling that a house should be a "machine for living."

The relationship of the green lower area to foliage and grass, the reference of the pink and blue windbreak to the sky, and the cream to buff tones of the main section with its essentially everyday and practical purpose emphasize once more the rational nature of Le Corbusier's approach. At the same time they underline his belief that the esthetics, that is, the artistic quality of a building, is as important as its practical character.

Just as we have analyzed the components of a traditional and a modern façade, we investigate an older and a newer work in painting. Here also, as might be expected, we find the rational constructive planning mind of the artist at work, with at least enough of his planning evident to enable us to follow him part of the way. In the absence of the original painting, which deprives us of the all-important color and texture qualities, our judgment must of necessity be only partial. The obvious form qualities are manifested by lines, masses, and light and dark effects, but we should keep in mind always that there is far more to the story of painting than black-and-white illustrations are capable of telling us.

Although there are many older paintings that conform to the simple and rational symmetry of the Pazzi Chapel (for example, Giorgione's *Castelfranco Madonna,* Fig. 15, p. 27), in many other traditional works the related elements are not quite so apparent. By expending a measure of extra effort to understand them, we often find a proportionally added enjoyment. Vermeer's seventeenth-century Dutch painting showing a *Young Woman with a Water Jug* (Fig. 32, p. 50) offers a fairly complicated example of arrangement, but we may still ask the basic question: "What holds this work together?" and find a logical answer. Since the subject here—the act of grasping the pitcher and preparing to pour the water out of the window—is unimportant, however glorified by the artist's seriousness, we may concentrate on the form elements of the picture.

As with the two buildings already examined, we may think of this work as a combination of parallel vertical, horizontal, and rounded forms. The main curved form is represented by the woman, and subordinate curves by the pitcher and bowl and the cushion at the right. Balanced against these curved, spherical, and cylindrical shapes are the main squareness of the room itself and the subsidiary three-dimensional rectangularity of the table with its box. If we consider the woman merely as a curved silhouette against the wall, we may say that she stands in contrast to the rectangularity of the window, map, wall base, and chair at the right.

Actually, of course, the woman functions both as a silhouette and as a rounded form. She is related to the contrasting forms and shapes by

Fig. 32. JAN VERMEER: *Young Woman with a Water Jug.* New York, Metropolitan Museum of Art.

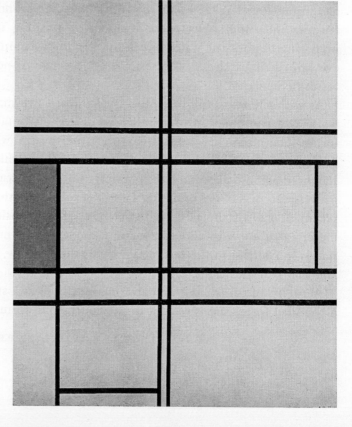

Fig. 33. PIET MONDRIAN: *Composition.* Courtesy Wadsworth Atheneum, Hartford, Connecticut.

the very fact of that contrast as well as by the physical fact of being tied to them. One arm touches the partially open window, her other the pitcher and bowl, while her neck is immediately adjacent to the flat wall map at the right, the rod of which points directly into the space between her shoulder and head. Thus the woman's body acts as a kind of hub or center from which radiate various connections with the rest of the room; the arms effect their contacts, as do the upper portions of her form, while the lower part of her body extends into the spaces of the room.

What other relating elements are here? One of the most apparent is the illumination streaming in from the window, the blue glass of which casts a light on the woman's face and on her white hood. Then the light travels further into the room, causing shadows to appear on the right side of the woman and reflections from the red and gold cloth to be seen on the undersurface of the silver bowl and pitcher. Similarly, the right side of the pitcher shows a blue reflection from the cushion at the right, adding to our feeling about the light as a vital and significant force within this room, causing shadows and relating the various objects to one another.

In the same way, as in most paintings, color is a unifying force. Blue is the most apparent color, proceeding from the window panes to the face and hood and finally to the reflection in the bowl. A heavier blue is found in the dress of the woman and the glass rod under the map, while an intermediate and related blue appears in the color of the cushion. In the original of this or other paintings we find comparable color repetitions and similarities, variations, and combinations of one or more colors that help to give unity to a work and thus betray the conscious intelligence of the planner.

Although for the purposes of discussion we have separated the various elements used by the painter, these elements are all part of the artist's logical filling of space through the movement of the arbitrarily constructed geometrical volumes, the light, and the color reflections. We have not yet examined any of these component forces for its possible creation of symbolic and other intuitive values. We shall come to this as a separate and added significance.

Before considering the symbolic approach, let us try another intellectual analysis, this time in connection with a modern work, Mondrian's *Composition* (Fig. 33, p. 50). As in Le Corbusier's Savoye

House, the elements in this painting are rigidly geometric, almost machined in character; its balance has the same dynamic and asymmetrical quality. This means that instead of the simple scale-balance arrangement of the Pazzi Chapel or Giotto's *Death of St. Francis* (see Fig. 176, p. 310), in which one part neatly balances another, we have in the two contemporary works a system of differently sized and shaped weights balancing each other, compensating for each other's pulls and tensions. What, then, is the skeleton framework of such a structure as the *Composition?* What gives it a sense of unity?

Since the spatial relationships are not as immediately apparent as in Vermeer's painting, we may concentrate first on the simple linear relationships. A rectangle is divided by sets of lines into six general portions (three vertical and two horizontal), with variation within three of the portions. No single section in this work is exactly the same shape or area as any other, so that as our eyes move across in either direction or up from the bottom or down from the top, the apparently flat areas seem to change slightly, creating perceptible surface tensions.

These two-dimensional, or side-to-side, tensions are accompanied by space tensions, that is, pulls from the outside in. Roughly, this means that there is a conflict between the flat picture surface (and its accompanying side-to-side movement) and inward-thrusting lines, forms, shadows, and other factors which tend to break this flatness. The simplest example of such conflict may be seen in Leonardo's *The Last Supper* (see Fig. 99, p. 159), where the powerful side-to-side movement of the table is opposed by the violent inward convergence of the other lines. Such a movement in Mondrian's work is effected through the backward movement of the small color area behind the black lines, the latter in their turn superposed on the large white spaces. Admittedly this is a much more limited space than appears in the far-reaching movement of the Vermeer or Leonardo picture. But as many modern paintings, the concentration of space which limits it to a shallow box, in which background and foreground are close together, is a desired and sought-for end; we shall see it many times again.

In both these factors (space and surface tensions) the painter plans very carefully and leads the spectator along a previously determined path. The same is true of balance, which is effectuated here through the movement of powerful vertical rectangles as opposed to equally strong horizontal movement. Each thrust in one direction is compensated for by an equally important thrust opposed to it.

We are not discussing here the moral or symbolic value of such painting, or whether it has the merit to exist side by side with more traditional painting—although it is as much a product of our industrialized society as Le Corbusier's Savoye House. What we are concerned with right now is the possibility of approaching the work from an intellectual point of view. That we have been able to do so is partly a result of the rational basis on which the work was organized.

Mondrian is not dealing with the same kind of emotional, symbolic, or intuitive values for which we turn to artists like Michelangelo and Rembrandt. Like a great many moderns, Mondrian is preoccupied with a "form experience," with the mental and physical excitement engendered by subtle balances, textures, movements, and color arrangements—in other words, with art for its own sake rather than for its more literary and associative possibilities.

Art as Symbolic Experience

A symbol in general is a visible sign of something invisible—such as an idea or a quality. It can be simply an emblem or sign, like % to represent percent or a lion to represent courage. These well-known symbol substitutions arise from conventional usage, association, and general relationship. But in poetry or art the symbol has a freer development. It transcends the everyday run-of-the-mill sign and assumes a new and fresh meaning, originating from a highly personal and even unique association born in the mind of the poet or painter.

The conventional type of symbol is not altogether absent from works of art. Such a well-worn symbol as the halo, a universal Christian feature, appears in Raphael's *The Alba Madonna* (Fig. 16, p. 28); the yoke-shaped *Arch of Titus* (see Fig. 164, p. 289) shows a form of building that was similarly pervasive in Roman society as a symbol of the triumph of a particular general or emperor. The use of these symbols requires no great intellectual initiative or intuition on the part of the artist, nor are they difficult for us to comprehend. On the other hand, the creation of a more poetic and ingenious form of symbolic representation requires an imaginative and sensitive personality, just as it asks for a deeper response from the spectator.

Fig. 34. MICHELANGELO: Tomb of Lorenzo de' Medici. Florence, Italy, New Sacristy, San Lorenzo.

Let us take, for example, the *Tomb of Lorenzo de' Medici* by Michelangelo, from the Church of San Lorenzo in Florence (Fig. 34, p. 54). This tomb and its counterpart on the opposite wall of the chapel, the tomb of Giuliano de' Medici, represent in a general way the dual conception of an active and a contemplative life. Lorenzo, who symbolizes the latter, was a less illustrious nephew of the famous Lorenzo the Magnificent. The nude male and female figures on the bases represent the idea of change, the passage of time, that is, mortality. On the tomb of Lorenzo are the figures of Evening and Dawn, while on that of Giuliano are those of Night and Day. This much information is directly gleaned from what Michelangelo himself said and wrote about them.

But the significant thing about the Medici tombs is that, before knowing the historical circumstances under which these works were executed, without knowing more than the general facts, we intuitively feel a kind of sadness, even despair, before the great nudes and a kind of futility and detachment from life in the effigies of the two Medici dukes. Although the tomb of Lorenzo is supposed to represent or symbolize the passive or inactive side of life, the artist's powerful expressiveness has carried it over into the realm of the tragic and the poignantly remote. This is due partly to the poetic personality of the artist himself, so vigorous that it reaches across time and materials to the spectator today, and partly to the sculptor's sensitive understanding of the tragedy of his times, from which the work ultimately sprang.

We cannot say that Michelangelo conveys these sentiments through the mechanical apparatus of the usual literary symbol, for these figures of Evening and Dawn are the artist's own, just as his conception of Lorenzo is unlike the usual portrait. On a purely intuitive and un-intellectual basis, we react to the sense of oppression, the fatigue of the brawny Evening and the misery of the magnificent Dawn. Intellectu-ally we may reason further, to think of the male as one who has worked hard and perhaps unrewardingly and the female as one who is unwilling to face the unpleasantness of the day ahead. Lorenzo him-self exudes a depressing quality and not merely the contemplative side of life, for his face seems deliberately in shadow and certainly negative in psychological character.

It is possible to infer, from the way Lorenzo and Giuliano are represented, that the artist was probably not too happy about his subjects. The Medici tombs express a quality quite different from the positive religiosity and spiritual strength of Michelangelo's earlier works, a result of the circumstances of the epoch as well as of the personal sense of futility which afflicted the artist. During the sack of Rome in 1527, the Florentine countrymen of Michelangelo expelled the long-ruling Medici family from their city. Some years earlier, the artist had undertaken to do the Medici tombs for Pope Clement VII— and so he found himself in the peculiar position of constructing fortifi-cations for his native city, which was soon under seige by the papal troops, while simultaneously working in secret on tombs memorializing members of a family for which at that time he had no particular respect. When Florence fell in 1530, those who fled (including Michel-angelo) were outlawed, and their possessions confiscated. When Mi-chelangelo was finally permitted to return, he took up the work on the tombs more in fear of the Pope than out of regard for Lorenzo and Giuliano, the subjects of the tombs.

Knowing this, in looking at Lorenzo we may now feel more strongly the quality of indecision that influenced this Medici's inglorious role in the history of his city, the restlessness of pose, and the impersonal anonymity of his face. Under his left elbow we see a rectangular box with an open-mouthed lion's head on its narrow end. This suggests the well-known "lion's mouth" box utilized by the later Medici to receive anonymous letters of denunciation, a symbol of their tyranny.

We may also recognize more rationally—as well as intuitively—the symbolic sadness of the four nude figures. When one of Michelangelo's contemporaries wrote a complimentary verse on the figure of Night from Giuliano's tomb, speaking of it as so lifelike that it would wake at a touch, the artist—speaking in the name of the figure—responded in the following lines:

> Dear is my sleep, more dear to be but stone;
> Whilst deep despair and dark dishonour reign
> Not to hear, not to feel is greatest gain;
> Then wake me not, speak in an undertone.[1]

Study as we will the figure of the virgin Dawn and the tired body of the Night, measure, assess, analyze their technical qualities as indeed we should, they are nevertheless an intangible summation of human spirit. Mastering the medium as did few men before or after him, the sculptor went on to sum up in visible form the invisible but mighty spiritual truths that for him were best symbolized by the attitudes or poses of the human body.

In the paintings of this great artist the purpose and effect are quite similar. Time after time in the many sections of the Sistine Chapel ceiling paintings, with their epic story of the Creation, the fall from grace, and the promise of ultimate redemption, we encounter this same grandiose expressiveness. Beginning with a fairly obvious idea, the artist adds a powerful sense of form and an even greater creative imagination to give new meaning to his material. A section of this gigantic complex of ceiling paintings, the *Creation of Adam* (Fig. 35, p. 57), illustrates how, through his manipulation of technical means, his new and imaginative disposition of the human form, and the projection of his own vibrant mentality, Michelangelo has transformed the basic idea into a poetic symbol.

[1] Translated in Charles Holroyd, *Michael Angelo Buonarroti*, N. Y., 1911.

Fig. 35. MICHELANGELO: *Creation of Adam,* detail from Sistine Chapel ceiling. Rome, Vatican.

In the Bible we are told: "And the Lord God formed man of the dust of the ground, and breathed into his nostrils the breath of life; and the man became a living soul." If we compare Michelangelo's interpretation of this moment with that of Ghiberti in his famous Paradise Gates (Figs. 35a, 90, 90a, pp. 58, 138, 139), we find that both avoid the literalism of the Biblical narration. Ghiberti shows the Creator helping Adam to his feet; Michelangelo gives an altogether new treatment to the story.

Michelangelo propounds once more the duality of existence in the forceful God and the passive Adam, symbolizing thereby the power of Deity and the relative unimportance of man. Through these contrasting figures the artist also suggests the idea of the strong versus the weak, the mature versus the young, the giver versus the receiver, as represented by the shapes and poses of the figures themselves. More than anything else, the recumbent Adam personifies potential power, while the flying form of God together with His surrounding seraphim articulates the creative force as His outstretched finger almost touches the limp finger of Adam and commands him into life.

Michelangelo has taken what is already a sufficiently poetic conception, breathing into man the breath of life, and by the use of powerfully opposing thrusts, weights, balances, and tensions (the form aspects of art), has transmuted it into a symbol fitting his own life and times. Ghiberti has not so effectively symbolized the original idea, with the

Fig. 35a. LORENZO GHIBERTI: *Creation of Adam*, detail from Paradise Gates. Florence, Italy, Baptistery of Cathedral of Florence.

result that the Biblical incidents shown in his gates become parts of a charming decorative pattern, though endowed with many outstanding virtues of their own: narrative drama, elegance of form, suave classical forms, deeply perspectivized views, and other effects.

One of the outstanding sources of symbolic reference for a painter or sculptor has been the field of literature: the Bible, Shakespeare, Milton, and, above all, the classics of Greek and Roman antiquity. Thus the *Primavera* (or *Spring*) of Botticelli (Fig. 36, p. 59), like the works of Michelangelo, reflects a contemporary and even personal quality expressed with the aid of certain literary references. Here the season of spring, the period of the earth's flowering, of the joy of growth, birth, and love, is expressed by a painting with poetic sadness as its chief mood. This mood is the result of the personality of the artist and his particular needs at the moment.

Botticelli's work first derives from reference to the Roman poets Horace, who described the three Graces dancing before the young god Mercury (at left), and Lucretius, who spoke of the arrival of Spring preceded by Flora, the goddess of flowers, strewing blossoms before the Spring goddess (blossom in her lips), who is blown forward by the spirit of winds (at right). In the center of the painting, head inclined to the left, stands the goddess of love, about whom most of the action

revolves without her active awareness. She appears dreamy and ab-
stracted, like the young Mercury, at whom a cupid overhead shoots
an arrow of love and before whom the Graces dance, all without effect.
Thus the allegory of spring, which we would expect to be joyous, turns
into a symbol of melancholy. Venus here represents beautiful young
Simonetta, married to a member of the Vespucci family (the same
family that produced Amerigo Vespucci), while Mercury is really the
ill-fated Giuliano de' Medici, in love with this lady; after her early
death he had fallen victim to a dagger-thrust in the famous Pazzi
conspiracy.

In painting this picture for the Medici family, the artist had these
facts in mind, just as Michelangelo had in mind other aspects of that
family's later history. Botticelli has in his own poetic and sensitive
fashion created a symbol of the futility of the love of Giuliano and
Simonetta Vespucci. He has portrayed it with a nostalgia and otherworldliness that are characteristic both of his art and of the end of the
early Renaissance. Lorenzo the Magnificent, another of the Medici
family, has described this feeling in one of his songs:

How lovely is youth, how fleeting always!
Who would be gay, let him, for to-morrow, who knows . . .

Fig. 36. SANDRO BOTTICELLI: *Primavera*. Florence, Italy, Uffizi Gallery.

馬
遠
松
陰
玩
月

Fig. 37. MA YÜAN (attributed to): *A Sage under a Pine Tree*. New York, Metropolitan Museum of Art.

The symbolic relationship between man and the world he lives in can nowhere be so well expressed as in the realm of landscape art, since nature itself is so clearly a symbol of that world. Let us compare and contrast an Oriental and an Occidental example of landscape art, each in its own way portraying a difference in approach and offering interesting symbolic references to 'man's attitude toward life. Ma Yüan was the thirteenth-century Chinese creator of *A Sage under a Pine Tree* (Fig. 37, p. 60), a painting done, like so many works of this type, in ink on silk. As characteristically Oriental, we may observe the medium (the material used) and the manner of painting, which relies not on sketches but rather on long periods of contemplation to achieve self-identification with a particular scene. The rapid execution of the picture is dependent on this feeling of identity and on a highly developed technique.

Like many Chinese landscapes, the painting consists of mountains and rivers which man is destined neither to dominate for his own purposes nor, in the manner of the modern Romantics, to use as a means for his own self-expression and importance. In the Zen Buddhist system, of which this art is a logical expression, man is only one of many equally important aspects of nature. He strives toward an intimate knowledge of this nature with which he constantly identifies himself and which gives him philosophical calm and peacefulness. Nature is good, and man can acquire goodness by trying to make this identification as complete as possible.

In this picture the tiny figure is the typical philosopher sitting before some impressive panorama, absorbed in contemplation of its meaning; in other pictures, a few tiny figures may move down-river in a boat beneath towering mountains or a traveler may walk alone. But always the relative insignificance of man before nature is symbolized both by the attempt of the painter-poet to let himself become lost in the vastness of the scene and by the tiny size of the human being: the philosopher, poet, beggar, or traveler.

It would be a mistake, however, to think that the scores of Chinese landscapes of this and other periods tell the same story or symbolize the same factors. True, they all indicate the identification of man with nature, and they all indicate the tremendous importance attached to the act of contemplation in this form of religious philosophy. But where Ma Yüan communicates the calm of an early morning scene with the mists rising out of the river, other works leave a sense of the lonesomeness of evening, the quietness of winter, or some other natural phenomenon in which the artist is absorbed.

While in China the art of landscape painting goes back at least as far as the tenth century A.D., in the Western world it coincides with the great development of the humanist ideal, beginning in the fourteenth century with the Renaissance. This ideal saw man as the measure of all things, and, therefore, man, rather than nature, became the dominant element, the overt vehicle for the expression of emotions. We do not necessarily mean that this way of symbolizing of the emotions is inferior to that of the Chinese masters—it is merely different.

El Greco's famous *View of Toledo* (Fig. 38, p. 62), confronts us with a landscape in which the approach is the very antithesis of the Chinese work. Here, through the distortion of form, color, and space, the artist sets up a sense of disturbance in the spectator, paralleling either the unhappiness felt by the painter himself or the unhappiness he feels it is his mission to convey. Where the Chinese artist distorts or changes the natural appearance of things in favor of a certain suavity of color and linear grace of design—summing up nature rather than representing it—the Spanish painter changes reality in order to emphasize his own intense feelings.

Fig. 38. EL GRECO: *View of Toledo*. New York, Metropolitan Museum of Art.

The appearance of the city of Toledo is altered as far as possible toward that end: the buildings are redistributed in an angular jerky fashion; the colors of the landscape turn from sharply delineated greens toward a gray-green, yellow, and bluish-green, the sky from its normal bright blue to a steely gray charged with greenish tonalities. Finally, the space becomes tightly compressed in an upward- rather than backward-moving conception, paralleling the tensions of the colors and the forms.

Toledo, the sunniest spot in the very center of Spain, is projected by El Greco as a place of misery. It reflects the unhappiness, the strain, and the morbidity of this period of the Inquisition and the spiritual

conflicts of the early-seventeenth-century Counter Reformation to com-
bat Protestantism. It would therefore be no exaggeration to look on
this work as a symbol of the artist's feelings and of the era. At the same
time we should mark the difference in approach between such artists
as El Greco, van Gogh, or even gentler souls like Constable (see Figs.
38, 222, and 107, pp. 62, 484, 177) and the Chinese painters as represented by Ma Yüan. The Western landscape artist is very much concerned with himself and his feelings, liking to stand away, as it were,
and contemplate his own misery, ecstasy, or other emotion, whatever it
may be.

Symbolic distortions of form, color, and space are also found in the
painting of van Gogh. His *Night Café* (Fig. 39, p. 63), also known as
Café at Arles, shows a typical third-rate provincial café late at night
with only a handful of people who have nowhere else to go, passing the
lonely hours here. Against the depressing purple and the frightening
reds and greens that fight with each other as did the artist and his
unhappy environment, the figures are isolated from each other.

In the upper left-hand corner sit a couple—together yet far apart—
while near them, unseen, a man sleeps with his head on the table, like

Fig. 40. MAX BECKMANN: *Departure*. New York, Collection The Museum of Modern Art.

the two derelicts on the right with their table-bed. For the price of a single drink one may spend the night in this spot which, in van Gogh's own words, was the kind of place where a man might go mad, even commit murder. The custodian of this mournful establishment, the white-coated waiter, stands near the lurid green, coffinlike billiard table and faces the spectator with the same air of blankness, symbolic of the meaninglessness of existence, as does the couple at the left. Each person exists in his own lonesomeness, although all are under the same roof at the same moment; each person bears in his soul the stigmata of modern man and on his face, in van Gogh's phrase, "the heartbroken expression of our time."

The awareness of the misery of the world, seen symbolically in the work of El Greco and van Gogh, is revealed in the work of a distinguished contemporary painter, the German Max Beckmann. His *Departure* (Fig. 40, p. 64) might be considered an allegory of modern man's reactions to the oppression of totalitarianism, but it is also Beckmann's symbolic expression of his individual reaction to the oppression with which he was confronted in Nazi Germany. Painted in 1937, just before the painter and his wife escaped to Holland, the large-scale triptych (three-part painting) deals with scenes of torture and a vision of spiritual liberation. This is no journalistic account, but rather a deliberate choosing of details, colors, and forms that will underline the painter's horror at what he has witnessed of his nation's degradation.

In the left- and right-hand wings are the physical and mental tortures which Hitler's Germany imposed. The man standing in the water barrel, the amputated hands, the woman about to be axed, all bespeak the physical side of that degeneracy. On the right, a wizened little figure beating the drum of war represents the propaganda of Dr. Goebbels, while the military figure with his eyes blindfolded may refer to the blind obedience and cooperation of the German army (the fish under its arm is a constant sex symbol of twentieth-century painting, and the reader may supply his own meaning). The man and woman tied to each other in an upside-down position are more difficult to explain readily, but they seem agonizingly united in this awkward posture, perhaps the Aryan married to a non-Aryan during that period.

From the tortures, killings, mutilations of these two side panels with their tense cluttered space, we emerge into the center panel with its limpid, blue, far-reaching background; here figures stand in a boat to make the "Departure." The king is the artist himself, the masked figure at the left is the inscrutable future, while the woman holding the child represents the hope and growth of a new life into which the painter feels himself moving. Different in symbolic elements from any traditional artist, the modern painter with all the individuality of his approach tries to make visible the invisible and, in this process, to leave us stirred by profound emotions. Thus he identifies himself with the basic function of art at all times.

Art and Reality

One of the chief functions of many works of art is the dramatization of reality or the heightening of meaning. Each work singles out a particular aspect of being and focuses our attention on it as forcefully as possible. The work may focus on a single attribute of the thing shown

—its redness, roundness, hardness—or on the general quality and meaning of the thing or moment observed.

Dramatization or concentration may be achieved through focusing light on a particular object, as in Rubens' *Descent from the Cross* (Fig. 17, p. 29) and Goya's *Execution of the Citizens of Madrid* (Fig. 20, p. 33), or through contrasting light and dark effects, as in Daumier's *Washerwoman* (Fig. 9, p. 22). Heightening of reality or intensification of meaning may also be achieved through elimination of detail, thus focusing attention on the monumentality, or other quality, of a given form, as in the Daumier. Size is another device for the focusing of attention, either through contrast with related figures in the same composition, as in Watteau's *Gilles* (Fig. 3, p. 9) and the Daumier, or through contrast with the picture space itself, as in Vermeer's *Young Woman with a Water Jug* (Fig. 32, p. 50). In the same way, directional thrusts augment visual and emotional interest, as in the curved diagonal of the Christ figure in the Rubens picture, the pyramidal climax in the Géricault work (Fig. 2, p. 8), or the violent inward pull in Leonardo's *The Last Supper* (Fig. 99, p. 159).

These focusing devices which dramatize aspects of reality often take liberties with the so-called "facts" of nature, distorting color, space, proportion, and texture, or rearranging their relationship to each other as the new artistic truth demands. In such representational works as we have just examined, the artist heightens what needs to be heightened and subordinates what needs subordinating.

In such nonrepresentational works as the Mondrian (Fig. 33, p. 50) or the Kandinsky (Fig. 109, p. 181), this heightening of meaning is not so easy to perceive, but it is nevertheless present. Neither of these works would appear to have any basis in ordinary reality, yet they are the reactions of human beings to a given visual or emotional situation, each exaggerated in its own way to convey certain sensations. In the Mondrian work the artist *saw* an outline and bulk which interested him and which he proceeded to reduce to the geometric simplifications that are his system. The Kandinsky painting, on the other hand, is the result of what the artist *felt* at a given moment, a feeling of excitement or exaltation transmitted through the sparkling outward movement of angular forms and of colors reaching climax after climax as they burst out of the picture. In this work we have a series of purely imaginary forms and colors brought together in an arbitrary relationship the purpose of which is the establishment of a mood.

Whichever path we take to the art object of the many suggested in this chapter; whether we deal with the representational forms of traditional art or the nonrepresentational arrangements of more contemporary styles, we are always aware of the work of art as agent in the creation of a new and more exciting reality.

▶PART II
The Varying Techniques
of Art

▶3

Drawings: Their Methods and Meanings

WE MAY TURN now to the ways in which various types of art are created. In the next few chapters we shall make a simplified approach to the techniques of each art, considering the advantages and limitations of each technique as well as its history. This will give us some understanding of actual physical problems and further insight into how the artist thinks, what he must know before he can create.

We begin with drawing, since this skill is basic for so many, if not indeed for all, other techniques. Drawings stand as visible evidences of the artist's thinking and planning in every field of plastic creativity. But as we shall see, this does not by any means exhaust their artistic importance and function.

Drawings may be considered under three broad headings. On the simplest level, they are notes made of a particular object or situation at a specific moment of interest. Secondly, drawings may exist as works of art in themselves. Finally, they function as studies for some eventual painting, sculpture, or other work.

The Drawing as a Notation

In the first category is the so-called sketch of something seen at a given moment in an accidental arrangement of clouds, people, or other forms that catch the eye. The artist walking in the country, riding in a train,

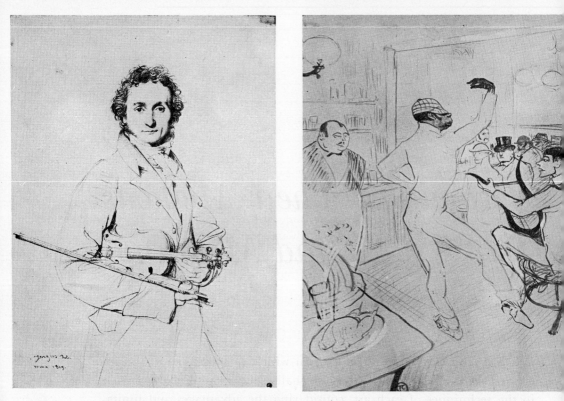

Fig. 41 (*left*). J. A. D. INGRES: *Nicolò Paganini*. Paris, Louvre. Fig. 42 (*right*). HENRI DE TOULOUSE-LAUTREC: *Chocolat Dancing* (Chinese ink). Albi, France, Albi Museum.

or sitting in the theater will encounter many situations and effects that seem worthy of recording. These notes, sketches, brief linear indications in a kind of visual shorthand, may or may not figure in any final work. They may serve merely as practice, as play, or as a kind of self-expression.

The Drawing as a Complete Work

The second type of drawing exists as an end in itself. It is generally a finished picture rather than a sketch of the subject and more often than not is a portrait, such as the works by Holbein, Degas, or Ingres. Such works as Ingres's portrait of the youthful *Nicolò Paganini* (Fig. 41, p. 70) exemplify the finished work, the complete statement in itself without reference to any future painting. Ingres did a whole series of portrait drawings, as did Degas. These represent clear-cut cases in which, so far as we can see, the painter had no intention of going beyond the drawing; but many other drawings could serve either as works of art in themselves or as possible bases for later developments. The Lautrec drawing *Chocolat Dancing* (Fig. 42, p. 70) is a typical study of the lithe movement that intrigued the crippled painter; here it is an affected and mannered motion almost ceremonial in its solemnity. The dancing figure stands out between the eager expression of the delicate young man with the lute and the heavy-set phlegmatic waiter on the other side. This does not have to be carried any further as a work of art; it is as complete a statement as the restrained and flowing beauty of the Ingres drawing. But it is so improvisatory in form, so "impressionist," that we might look for its further use in a lithograph or painting—although it was never so used.

The Drawing as a Study

The third category of drawing is that in which the sketches are made as studies for some subject or theme, eventually finished as a painting, sculpture, or building, or in which the sketches serve as a means of ex-

Fig. 43. MICHELANGELO: Studies for *Libyan Sibyl* (red chalk). New York, Metropolitan Museum of Art.

ploring a particular problem in movement, in drapery, in form, or in emotion.

A sketch in red chalk shows Michelangelo's thinking in connection with a figure that was to represent the Libyan Sibyl in his Sistine Chapel frescoes (Fig. 43, p. 71). A drawing of this kind exemplifies Goethe's well-known remark: "Drawings are invaluable not only because they give in its purity the mental intention of the artist, but because they bring immediately before us the mood of his mind at the moment of creation." Here we see the mind of the artist at the moment of conceiving this heroic figure; then we follow him along the various paths he took while solving the problems posed by the figure and its movement (Fig. 43a, p. 72).

We see how the sculptor-painter visualized everything in terms of the nude human body, how he originally worked on the sibyl (a female prophetess) as a male figure and made the final change to indicate its proper sex. The change appears in the nature of the face, which is modified from the quiet masculine force of the head on the body to the gentler, even sweet, expression of the trial face at the left. This face, like the three successive sketches of the big toe on the pivoting left foot, shows the actual experimentation, the path of Michelangelo's reasoning. There is also, on this same single sheet of paper, additional evidence of his approach to the twist of the body itself and to the way the left hand would hold the enormous volume he intended to use. This is not a particularly "sketchy" sketch, because of the artist's strong desire for three-dimensional articulation of the figure, which he always visualized as a piece of sculpture rather than as a section of painting.

Modern artists, too, often use the preparatory drawing as a basis for painting or sculpture, as in Orozco's dramatic study for the central figure from the cupola of the Hospicio Cabañas in Guadalajara (Fig. 44, p. 73). In fact, as already remarked, the drawing may be a preparation for almost any kind of designed work in the fine or applied arts. Although some may rebel at the idea of drawing as the "mother of the arts," every work of art, by definition, is planned by an artist, on whatever level he may be operating. Further, an artist generally thinks through the medium of a sketch of some sort, whether he be painter, sculptor, architect, or designer of automobiles, packaging, posters, typography, pottery, prints, or anything else.

A partial exception to what seems a universal rule is found in

Fig. 44. JOSÉ CLEMENTE OROZCO: *Legs* (charcoal, 1938–1939; study for *Man of Fire* in Hospicio Cabañas, Guadalajara). New York, The Museum of Modern Art.

sculptors who, instead of making sketches on paper, will build up little clay models on which the final work will be based. Other sculptors, however, will draw on the wood or the stone, or will make one or many drawings from which the sculpture will be evolved. It is surely not accidental that sculptors like Michelangelo, Rodin, and Henry Moore are among the great draftsmen of their respective generations.

As for architecture, there is obviously an ever-present need for layout, planning, and design, in both plan and elevation, in the general disposition of parts and the character of the individual section or ornament. The drawing is the basic requirement, and not one drawing but many drawings.

In painting, the vast majority of pictures, especially the traditional ones, have relied in some measure on a sketchy drawing or a finished and elaborate cartoon drawing. There are some exceptions, even for art of the past and certainly for more recent painting. The pictures of Hals (Fig. 12, p. 24), so immediate and spontaneous in mood and effect, do not seem to have been based on preliminary drawings—at least no such drawings have been found. By the same token, the Impressionist paintings of the 1870's, particularly those of the outdoor painters like Monet, Pissarro (Fig. 11, p. 24), and Sisley, did not need linear preparations; these works were intended to be primarily atmospheric in quality. Degas and Lautrec, on the other hand, are basically linear in their approach and to that extent more traditional in this respect.

The preparatory drawing is not necessarily old-fashioned in connection with paintings, for many works in our own century have been preceded by sketch after sketch. From Seurat's *Sunday Afternoon on La Grand Jatte* (Chicago Art Institute), with its many drawings and sketches in water color and oil, through Picasso's *Guernica* (see Fig. 234, p. 438), the development of the modern movement is filled with drawings designed as sketches for finished works, whether in painting or sculpture. Only in the most spontaneous varieties of contemporary Abstract Expressionism (intuitively expressed without recognizable objects, see Fig. 126, p. 209) will the artist produce paintings without previous planning; such practices as the splatter technique would seem to dispense with the preliminary sketch.

Similarly, it is safe to say that for the most part the contemporary sculptor still plans his work to some extent with the aid of drawings,

Fig. 45. LEONARDO DA VINCI: Cartoon for *Madonna, Child, and St. Anne*. London, Royal Academy of Arts.

although here also the existence of certain spontaneous and accidental effects might make the drawing little more than a general guide. Even completely "free-form" sculptors will express an idea with a small sketch which may or may not be closely followed in the finished work. We must, of course, recognize that there is no law compelling an artist to stick to a set plan, especially when the set plan is his own. Thus there is a difference between the cartoon for Leonardo's *Madonna, Child, and St. Anne* (Fig. 45, p. 75) and the final painting in the Louvre (Fig. 46, p. 76). The painter went to considerable trouble to work up the magnificent drawing, but he later changed his mind on certain details—and not necessarily for the better. Too much reworking has resulted in a certain dryness of effect, in a loss of the original freshness.

We may perhaps generalize that in older times, when the obligation of the artist to the client was a more direct one, a deviation from the final and accepted sketch might have been a rather serious matter. Today, the artist, independent, feels greater freedom in changing his plan as he goes along.

Fig. 46. LEONARDO DA VINCI: *Madonna, Child, and St. Anne.* Paris, Louvre.

In spite of exceptions, we may assume that in the Western tradition the drawing is frequently the necessary preliminary to a finished product in any medium. In the Orient, however, we know that the artist works neither from perception of the object itself nor from the perception gained from many drawn studies of that object. He works rather from a process of self-identification with the object, person, or scene, which enables him—after a lengthy period of meditation on its quality and essence—to set down in rapid fashion its essential form elements in a typically summary and ideographic (picture-symbol) manner.

Expressive Uses of Line

The drawing, like the print (see Chapter 7), makes certain demands on the spectator. Since most drawings are monochromatic, they must make their effect as line and nothing else. With this line alone the artist has to express bulk in the body, in drapery covering the body, in nature, and elsewhere. The delicacy of Ingres's folds of cloth in the violinist's sleeves suggests the bending of the heavy material; the slightly heavier line in the clothing of Chocolat in the Lautrec drawing suggests the musculature beneath the clothes, while the strongly ac- cented line in the chin of Michelangelo's sibyl conveys the sensation of flesh. Where shadow is necessary, the artist groups lines together in parallel form (see face at lower left in the Michelangelo drawing) or brings them even closer together, as on the body of the sibyl, or makes them much heavier than other lines, as in the legs of Orozco's flying man figure. In the last-mentioned drawing we also see that in such media as charcoal (and pencil or chalk) it is possible to give the effect of shadow by smudging with the finger.

A drawing may run the gamut from the representational quality of the Michelangelo example to the relative abstraction of the Ingres. The former leaves very little to the imagination; the latter, with only a few linear suggestions in its lower section, leaves us to imagine the form of the body. In predominantly linear drawings of the Ingres type, the effect springs primarily from the suggestibility of line; in the Michelangelo work, the lines grouped together to form areas of shadow give a *chiaroscuro* effect of modeling the figure, which comes to life in terms of this contrast between light and shadow.

Another type of drawing combines linearism with the shadowy effect of a wash of color, as in Rembrandt's *Man Seated on a Step* (Fig. 47, p. 78). Here the form suggestions of the ink line are reflected in an almost mysteriously effective way by the emergence of the wash area as shadows cast by the actually nonexistent forms. Finally, there is a type of drawing in which line as such no longer exists and the forms appear as a result of working charcoal into the paper in areas, almost like painted silhouettes (*cf.* Seurat, *In the Theatre*, Fig. 48, p. 78).

Drawing in Past Ages

The ability to sum up the character of a given form by means of an outline is not confined to artists of recent historical times. As far back as the Old Stone Age, we find artists with a highly developed, magic- impelled, naturalistic sense of silhouette, as shown by the animal paintings of southern France and northern Spain (see *A Wild Horse*,

Fig. 47 (*left*). REMBRANDT VAN RIJN: *Man Seated on a Step* (ink and wash). New York, Metropolitan Museum of Art. Fig. 48 (*right*). GEORGES SEURAT: *In the Theatre* (charcoal). New York, private collection. (Photo courtesy Lilienfeld Galleries)

Fig. 28, p. 42). Primitive peoples living on the Stone Age level of civilization even in our own times, such as the Bushmen of Africa, have shown similar talent. In the New Stone Age, during the first age of husbandry and the development of a more decorative and abstract viewpoint, line was used in the so-called geometric style, the non-realism of which was operative in the Mediterranean world for millennia, as in the art of Egypt and Mesopotamia.

With Greek art we come once again to a viewpoint naturalistically oriented but tempered by the idealism characteristic of Greek expression. In the Panathenaic amphora (Fig. 49, p. 79), with its representation of Pankration (a mixture of boxing and wrestling), we see the amazing linear skill of the Greeks of the fifth century B.C. The black figures are outlined on a red background, primarily to fill the space on the vase in a decorative manner, so that they curve outward to meet the gentle swell of the vessel. Both this kind of black-figured vase and the red-figured type are famous for their skillful line drawing. Of particular delicacy are the individual lines visible here as white lines on black, their actual colors, and done with a single unfaltering bristle of the brush. This represents one of the finest types of draftsmanship in existence.

During the medieval period, draftsmanship varied from the austerely

elegant—as in Byzantine manuscript illumination—to the expressionistic, evocative of emotional states—as in Carolingian, Ottonian, and
Romanesque manuscripts. The nervous jagged style of drawing typical
of much of the pen-and-brush combination of Carolingian illumination (Fig. 50, p. 79) is a spiritual emanation of a highly religious age,
just as the Greek drawing expresses an altogether more serene and
self-confident spirit in the clarity and precision of its line.

With the Renaissance and the introduction of paper to replace the
expensive vellum of the Middle Ages, the artist was in a better position
to make the many studies demanded by his particular method based
on knowledge and experimentation (cf. sketches for the *Libyan Sibyl*,
Fig. 43, p. 71). The pen and brush continued as the favorite instruments, and drawings were often done on tinted paper with the lines in
ink and the highlights put in with touches of white.

Fig. 49 (*left*). Kleophrades Painter:
Panathenaic amphora (*c.* 490 B.C.). New
York, Metropolitan Museum of Art.
Fig. 50 (*right*). Evangelist Page from
Ebo Gospels (pen and brush drawing)
Épernay, France, Municipal Library.

Fig. 51. LEONARDO DA VINCI (attributed to): *Head of a Woman* (silverpoint with white on bluish paper). New York, Metropolitan Museum of Art.

Development of Other Methods and Materials

Silverpoint. One method developed during the Renaissance was the silverpoint drawing, used when special delicacy of effect was desired. A silver-pointed instrument was drawn over a sheet of paper which had first been prepared with zinc white. There resulted the fine clear grayish line we see in such drawings as the *Head of a Woman* (Fig. 51, p. 80) attributed to Leonardo da Vinci. The delicate dreaminess of this head, typical of the smoky, hazy quality of Leonardo's art, emerges from the bluish glazed paper heightened with white; it is created by the feather-light touch of the silverpoint itself.

The High Renaissance proper, climax of a long period of experimentation with human anatomy and linear perspective, seemed to enforce a more vigorous method. The lyricism of silverpoint gave way before the vigor of red or black chalk drawing or pen drawing. It was in these more than ever before that a sense of immediate moment, of creative urge, was conveyed from artist to spectator. Whether we are looking at the magnificently muscled, determined forms of Michelangelo, directly and vigorously applied in red chalk to the surface of the paper, or at the more overtly emotional forms of Tintoretto in the same medium, we are in direct touch with the artist's first impulses.

By comparison with these sketches, painted works by the same masters often have an indirect and oblique quality.

Chalk. Many masters of the High Renaissance used the chalk drawing: Leonardo, Correggio, Raphael in Italy; Dürer and Holbein in Germany. It was also used by later artists in other countries: Rubens and Van Dyck in Flanders; Watteau in France; Gainsborough in Britain. The range of the chalk medium can readily be estimated when we consider the differences between the red chalk sketches for the *Libyan Sibyl* (Fig. 43, p. 71) and Watteau's *Seated Lady* (Fig. 52, p. 81).

In the first drawing a firm application of the chalk gives a forcefully outlined form, while a sharpened point gives precision to the little cross-hatched lines that constitute the shadows delimiting the figure. The total impression is of a strong softness—strength emanating from

Fig. 52 (*left*). JEAN ANTOINE WATTEAU: *Seated Lady* (red, white, and black chalk on paper). New York, Metropolitan Museum of Art. Fig. 53 (*right*). EDGAR DEGAS: *Portrait of Manet* (lead pencil). New York, Metropolitan Museum of Art.

the contour lines and the muscles, and softness from the warm texture of the chalk itself—a duality of effect typical of Michelangelo's works (*cf. Creation of Adam*, Fig. 35, p. 57).

In the drawing of the *Seated Lady*, by the greatest master of the chalk medium, we have a subtle and sensitive combination of red, white, and black chalk applied with breadth and smoothness by the side, rather than the point, of the chalk. The lyrical delicacy of Watteau's general style seems admirably suited to the use of this medium with which he succeeds in achieving soft, effective coloristic quality.

Pencil. Of post-Renaissance materials employed for drawing, perhaps the most common is the lead pencil, used very widely as early as the seventeenth century, when Dutch artists made it a foundation for their water-color paintings and British artists for their miniatures. For a long time the practice of using pencil under water color was widespread, but in the nineteenth century the possibilities of the pencil as a medium in its own right became clear. First, it was convenient for setting down rapidly the immediate impressions of a given situation or form, eliminating the need for any other materials. Second, and more important, artists became aware of the fact that the pencil had a potential delicacy which could be approached only by the silverpoint drawing.

The many fine portrait sketches done by Ingres during his youth in Rome frequently have a softness and evanescence as refined as the effects in Leonardo's *Head of a Woman*. Ingres's sketch of *Nicolò Paganini* (Fig. 41, p. 70) has been indicated as an instance of the drawing as a finished work. It demonstrates the range of possibilities of the pencil medium, from the almost disappearing lines of the lower extremities to the slightly stronger arms, the soft but firmer violin and bow, and the detailed and firmly drawn head.

If the Ingres drawing in some respects suggests earlier techniques, Degas's *Portrait of Manet* (Fig. 53, p. 81), also done in lead pencil, does not. Here the sketchy essence of the pencil drawing is preserved in the left-over lines that indicate earlier trials for the legs, the hat, and so forth. The lines themselves are the typical soft-textured symbols that characterize this medium at its best.

Although the pencil drawing is among the most effective means for a quick sketch or small sketch, its suave texture does not lend itself to large-scale drawings, where it has a too perceptible sameness of effect. Where, however, the artist is interested in soft or atmospheric effects and is willing to give up the crisp sharp line of pen and ink, he will turn to such media as charcoal and pastel. The pastel will be considered under our discussion of painting, as a more elaborate and intricate technique (see Chapter 6).

Charcoal. Charcoal is especially useful in representing broad masses of light and shadow, as in the exciting flying figure which Orozco sketched (Fig. 44, p. 73). Some critics feel that its use is too facile and therefore dangerous, since its results appear to be obtained with relatively little trouble; but the fact remains that it can be, as here, one of the most dramatic and effective of media.

The range of the charcoal drawing is indicated by the difference between the direct three-dimensionality of the Orozco and the quiet and romantic atmospheric effect of Seurat's drawing, *In the Theatre* (Fig. 48, p. 78). Seurat's method is to absorb the charcoal into the fabric of the paper so as to suggest something spiritual and disembodied passing through the solid substance of the paper itself.

Ink and ink with wash. Among drawing methods the ink and the ink with wash are of great importance. There is an immediate crispness about a pen line (either by itself or in combination with wash) to which many artists readily respond. As early as the Middle Ages we find the pen used, often as accent-maker in drawings done with some other medium. By the seventeenth century, artists like Rembrandt (see *Man Seated on a Step,* Fig. 47, p. 78) and Claude Lorrain gave the pen drawing a new function by using it as a base or in combination with washes of brown or India ink.

The contrast possibilities in such works, as between the almost finicking delicacy of the thin and sketchy ink line and the soft shadowy quality of the wash background, are great. They range from the strong differentiations in the Rembrandt, where a suggested form throws a rather substantial shadow, to the wash drawings of artists like Claude Lorrain, whose lines literally melt into the brown wash which constitutes the chief part of the drawing. Rembrandt is mainly a draftsman, and his pen-and-wash shows that fact. He uses the medium effectively in many ways, from a casually noted study sketch to an important and serious design. Very few drawing media offer the potentialities of the pen-and-wash, which can be both strong and delicate as here, and yet

Fig. 54 (*left*). LYONEL FEININGER: *St. Mary's Church* (pen and ink). Formerly New York, Curt Valentin Gallery. Fig. 55 (*right*). FRANCISCO GOYA: *They Make Themselves Drunk* (brush drawing). New York, Metropolitan Museum of Art.

give a sense of spaciousness and mystery in its washed-in shadows and atmospheric quality.

Ink by itself also has a considerable range, as we can see upon comparing the drawing in Chinese ink by Toulouse-Lautrec (Fig. 42, p. 70), with its lacquerlike black effects, and *St. Mary's Church* (Fig. 54, p. 84) by Feininger. In the former we move through the tonal range from delicate gray to deep rich black; in the latter, it is as though the artist has chosen to dematerialize form and allow space to percolate through it. Lautrec's forms keep their solidity and movement throughout; those of Feininger are almost painfully still, dissolving before our eyes while we look.

Finally we may cite the brush drawing, a medium close to painting and sometimes, notably in Oriental art, identical with it. Like the artists of the Renaissance in western Europe, Oriental artists used ink with the brush to give a careful and beautiful precision of outline. During the seventeenth century, however, European artists like Rembrandt began to use the brush with new freedom and improvisatory strength of movement, as though it were a pen. Such artists, especially the great Spaniard, Goya (*They Make Themselves Drunk*, Fig. 55, p. 84), achieve effects of light and shadow through touches of the drawing brush. Form is given to a figure through an indication of the swelling of a haunch or the rounding of a shoulder. The fact that the artist is not utilizing color as such, that he is working in a monochromatic medium, brown wash, and in a sketchy improvisatory manner, enables us to classify this brush picture as a drawing. Moreover, many of Goya's drawings were preparatory sketches for his *Caprichos* series of aquatint prints.

In this brief outline we have seen some drawings that were made for their own sakes, as finished works of art, and some done as sketches. Others have been associated with the preparation for later pictorial works or such other types of objects as vases, books, or armor. In the art forms into which we proceed now—architecture, sculpture, painting, the various kinds of prints, and the industrial arts—we shall find that the one thing held in common is the drawing, the visual plan without which most objects of art would not have come into being.

▶4

The Nature of Architecture

OF ALL THE ARTS, architecture has the most social direction and economic basis. However beautiful in its final impact on us, its basic objective is utility; it is made to serve some concrete purpose for an individual or a community. It is almost impossible to visualize a building that would not be useful socially, even if only in a limited way.

On the other hand, many forms of painting and sculpture have as their prime reason for being a sense of beauty, the uses of which go no farther than stimulation of the senses, the mind, and the emotions—exciting and rewarding though this may be to the creator and the viewer. This does not mean that painting and sculpture are inferior to architecture; if anything, they are perhaps purer forms of art. It merely means that from the social point of view, architecture has a more immediate and everyday usefulness.

First there is the need for a dwelling for living beings, earlier expressed in the cave and then in edifices such as the hut and the house. Almost parallel is the necessity for a dwelling for the dead, from the simple grave in the ground to structures such as the tomb, the mausoleum, and the pyramid. Other types of necessities include shelters for the gods, such as temples and churches, and shelters for rulers, such as palaces.

We may say, then, that architecture concerns man-made structures of solid materials arranged so as to enclose a definite space for some useful purpose and in an artistically designed manner. Its aim is ". . . to build structures at once commodious, strong, and satisfying to the artistic sense." In this second statement we add the idea of comfort and the feeling of strength to our original description.

We can appreciate a picture by standing before it and a piece of sculpture both by standing before it and by walking around it, but architecture must be entered in order to make its full effect. By going into a building, we bring into play a sensation of movement and a feeling of extension into space that no other art can equal. Architecture may endow us with a spirit of exaltation by its up-thrusting spaces, as in Gothic churches (Fig. 22, p. 35), or a sense of poise and dignity through its horizontal and vertical balances, as in Greek or Renaissance buildings (see Figs. 62a and 30, pp. 97, 45). We move our heads about, bend back our bodies, move around in the act of experiencing the building.

Architecture may be more or less useful in the social sense; it may be more or less satisfying in the esthetic sense. We may say, for example, that a tomb is less useful, in the long run, than a city hall or a residence. Similarly, certain types of useful buildings, such as warehouses or suburban garages, may be less satisfactory esthetically than libraries, museums, or similar forms.

We may distinguish between man-made structures and such nature-made habitations as caves, nests, or groups of trees. These latter are not art, since they were not planned by human beings but exist as the result of natural accident or of the instinctive reactions of animals. In some areas, nature provides either such ready-made shelters or else the physical means and material for easy building. In the tropical climates shelter does not pose a serious problem, for even primitive man can put together branches, rushes, fronds, and so on, into a temporary refuge. On a somewhat higher level of civilization, he will build with sun-dried or oven-baked brick, perhaps made of river clay, a structure that can also be replaced or abandoned. In temperate climates, available materials, sometimes worked in more complicated ways, include wood, stone, and clay. Finally, in frigid areas, primitive man will build with ice blocks, as in the Eskimo igloo.

The more civilized the era the more effort is made to secure conventional materials and to devise newer, and perhaps better, materials. In the highly developed society of ancient Egypt, large blocks of stone were hauled long distances for the building of temples and tombs such as the Pyramids. In Assyro-Babylonia, men worked to fabricate such surfacing material as the glazed tiles on the outside of palaces and temples. The Greeks quarried nearby marble for their structures, which they then embellished with complex sculptural arrangements (see Figs. 62 and 62a, pp. 96, 97) and significant color backgrounds. Rome, in turn, built first of brick, later faced with slabs of marble, and then of concrete faced with various materials.

In most later cultures, similar efforts to give architecture a special character through the careful choice and working of materials were limited by the materials themselves—wood, stone, baked clay, and the like. During the twentieth century, however, as technology has moved forward, we find the modern architect availing himself of such metals as steel, wrought iron, copper, and various alloys, of such stone materials as onyx, of glass brick, fiberglass, neon tubing, reinforced concrete, and many other substances never before used architecturally (see Savoye House, Fig. 31, p. 48; Tugendhat House, Fig. 64, p. 101; R.C.A. Building, Fig. 58, p. 92; the *Seagram Building*, Fig. 78a, p. 120; the General Motors Research Center in Detroit, the Massachusetts Institute of Technology Auditorium).

Types of Architecture

Residences. Residential buildings can be divided into two broad types: individual homes and group residences. In modern times the Savoye House, the Tugendhat House, and the California Johnson house (Fig. 56, p. 89) exemplify the individual dwelling, and the *Gratiot-Orleans Housing Project* in Detroit (Fig. 57, p. 90) exemplifies the group dwelling. Just as the Tugendhat House and Savoye House represent rather expensive private residences, the category of individual homes may also include the palace, from the relatively small Palazzo Farnese to the elaborate form of the Louvre and the Palace of Versailles (see Figs. 155 and 156, pp. 275, 276).

Funeral and commemorative structures. Funeral and commemorative buildings include the Pyramids of ancient Egypt, Grant's Tomb in New York City, the Lincoln Memorial in Washington, D. C., and the Panthéon in Paris. Some, like Grant's Tomb, are meant to be both tomb and memorial; others, like the Lincoln Memorial, are commem-

Fig. 56. HAR-
WELL H. HARRIS:
Ralph Johnson
House (1951).
Los Angeles,
California.

orative only. These two overlapping types are socially useful because
they both afford a gratification of national pride and honor the great
men of a country; the Panthéon has inscribed on its façade: "To its
great men a grateful fatherland."

Some commemorative structures may be regarded as in a fringe or
borderline category, since they may neither enclose space nor be occupied or occupiable. Such a structure is the arch of triumph commemorating the conquest of a Roman general, for instance, the Arch
of Titus (see Fig. 164, p. 289). This partially encloses a given space
for a once-useful commemorative purpose. Another such structure is
the obelisk or memorial column that memorializes the achievements
of a great figure, for instance, the Vendôme Column of Napoleon in
Paris or the Column of Trajan in Rome. The latter monument was
even designed to hold Trajan's body within its base.

Religious edifices. One of the most important types of architectural
art is the religious. This has been practiced since time immemorial and
is represented by examples from every known religion of civilized and
primitive man. Among Western illustrations are Early Christian (see
Fig. 178, p. 313), Byzantine (see Fig. 68, p. 109), Romanesque (see
Fig. 190, p. 333), Gothic (Fig. 22, p. 35), Baroque (see Fig. 214, p.
388), and many other Christian churches including contemporary ones
built in the modern idiom. We also have Oriental temples, like *Hōryūji*
at Nara in Japan (see Fig. 23, p. 36), and pagan temples, like the Parthenon (see Fig. 62, p. 96). There also exist Jewish synagogues, Buddhist shrines, Mohammedan mosques, African ritual houses, Oceanic

Fig. 57. GRUEN, YAMASAKI, AND STONOROV:
Housing project from Gratiot-Orleans Re-
development Project, Detroit, Michigan.
(Photo by Lens-Art, Detroit)

temples, precolonial Aztec, Maya, Inca, and other Central and South
American forms.

Official and commercial buildings. The official building encompasses
many varieties, both traditional and contemporary. In ancient
Greece were included those of the agora or town square, the council
house, and the treasury. In Rome we find the basilica, the commemorative arch or column, the forum. During the Renaissance, with the
growth of town life, the city hall became important as an expression
of the business-involved community. At the same time the palace (or
palazzo or château) became both an outstanding residential form and
a building with certain distinctly official functions. The already mentioned Palace of Versailles was the actual seat of the French government as well as the residence of King Louis XIV.

With the rise of modern democratic society, official buildings of new
types came into being: houses of parliament, courts, chancelleries, and
other administrative units; prisons, hospitals, and other edifices sponsored or partially sponsored by government. Schools, theaters, and
museums were now open to all people. Theater and museum architecture have played an important role in these changes: the Opéra and
the Comédie Française in Paris, the British Museum in London, the

Museum of Modern Art and Carnegie Hall in New York, St. George's Hall in Liverpool, all exemplify new varieties. Such buildings may now be considered as public-service buildings, whereas previously, under older governmental authorities, the public to which they appealed and which they admitted was very limited.

Earlier ages, however, had not been without public-service buildings. Greek and Roman life illustrate this contribution in the Greek stadia, theaters, concert halls, and libraries, and the Roman amphitheaters, stadia, baths, theaters, and basilicas. All these types of public-service buildings have come down to us today in one form or another and have been supplemented by more modern developments.

Modern times have brought into being a host of communications buildings which are actually commercial structures but which play a special role in our commercial world. These include telephone exchanges (New York Telephone Building), radio and television centers (R.C.A. Building, Fig. 58, p. 92; and Broadcasting House, London), and domestic and overseas telegraph buildings. Although the administrative centers of these industries may be characteristic of any modern large-scale business building, the actual sending structures have special forms. Another and allied type stems from the development of modern travel facilities—railroad and subway stations, airport terminals, docking sheds and terminals, each with its distinct problems of function, each with its separate design resulting from those functions.

Commercial buildings proper include office structures, department stores, shopping centers, markets, banks, stock exchanges, fair buildings (especially the elaborate state or world's fair building). The materials on which the activities of these buildings are based come from factories of various kinds—industrial rather than commercial buildings, with forms more specialized for their own work. Some factories have problems of safety that influence design; others have problems involving heavy materials, flow of parts from one area to another (as in the belt-line production system), disposal of waste matter, and a host of other practical factors that influence the ultimate form of the building. While the simple office building may contain administrative and sales headquarters for a thousand different products, the places where those products are made may necessitate myriad details of difference in design, owing to the specific nature of production problems (see below, Industrial Art, Chapter 9).

Fig. 58 (*left*). R.C.A. Building (1932). New York, Rockefeller Center. Fig. 59 (*right*). CASS GILBERT: Woolworth Building (1910–1913). New York.

New demands of modern times. All this points to the fact that the function of architecture in modern society is not quite so simple or static as in the past. For a long time, and as late as the end of the nineteenth and the beginning of the twentieth century, official and semiofficial architecture such as the Lincoln Memorial and various museum buildings were planned in terms of traditional design elements. That is to say, their architectural vocabulary in both outline and ornament was borrowed from the Renaissance, the Middle Ages, and other eras. This borrowing was possible especially since the function of these buildings was not radically different from that of earlier ones. Many museums took their cue from such structures as the Louvre, in itself a former royal palace, or from formal buildings erected during the nineteenth century. Memorials, like many comparable edifices, demanded the dignity of traditional ideas; they had to suggest the past and a respectability which could only be conferred by old and accepted ideas.

With the beginning of the twentieth century, the pressure for new types of buildings to fill new social and economic needs became irresistible. Although traditional ideas were still adopted (see the *Woolworth Building*, Fig. 59, p. 92, finished 1913, for a medieval-influenced structure), a change was needed both in function and in the means of expression of that function. There were so many new needs that could not be satisfied by the old layout and form of buildings that architecture inevitably moved onto a new plane of existence. How, for example, was one to shelter machinery or to house the increasing number of workers drawn from the country to form the great cities of our time? Could these problems be solved through the traditional eighteenth-century residence plan or the traditional official building? Obviously not—and at the outset many of the new problems were solved by engineers rather than by academy-trained architects.

As time went on, this practical emphasis was tempered by the design factor, and the transition was complete. New esthetic doctrines arose in architecture, just as in painting and sculpture. "Form follows function" was the credo of the forward-looking American architects inspired by the innovations of Louis Sullivan (the teacher of Frank Lloyd Wright) during the early years of the century. Later, after World War I, new beliefs like that expressed by the Swiss architect Le Corbusier, that a building should be a "machine for living," grew and spread.

Two important concepts are involved in this new functional architecture: first, that the building should look like what it is designed to do; second, that the materials used should act in accordance with their own properties and not like other substances. The first principle is illustrated in reverse by a railroad station that looks like a church, a courthouse that looks like a medieval castle, or a modern bank that looks like a Greek temple. Obviously these buildings do not look like the task for which they were presumably built.

The second principle may be shown—again in reverse—by the interior of the *Bibliothèque Ste. Geneviève* (Library of St. Genevieve) in Paris (Fig. 60, p. 94), where the cast iron columns and vault ribs embellished with Renaissance ornament imitate a traditional stone-vaulted interior. Here the material is used in a way inappropriate to itself. In all these examples, architects faced with the demand for railroad stations, courthouses, and banks timidly held on to the styles of the past instead of trying to develop styles expressive of the new

needs. With the library, the architect had iron with its special properties made available to him, but instead of developing those properties, he forced iron to act like stone.

Materials and Their Uses

The materials of architecture range from the most primitive to the most complex and civilized. Among primitive groups, ice and snow or skins and cloths may be used; on a slightly higher level we find brick and earth, used separately or together. The use of wood—another simple material—is widespread, from Scandinavia and Russia to New England. Sometimes the wood used at an early stage of a given culture is later replaced by richer and more elaborate materials such as marble, as in the temples of ancient Greece.

Stone in its various forms has a long history. Concrete, although originally used by the Romans, disappeared for a long time, and its use was revived during the nineteenth century in a special reinforced form. The use of metal in architecture dates from the mid-nineteenth century, progressing from cast iron to wrought iron and steel and from a relatively modest function to a fundamental and important one, serving today, together with concrete, as the structural basis of most large buildings.

Glass (both transparent and translucent), glass tubing, glass brick, heat-treated and glare-treated glass, colored brick, aluminum sheathing, plastics (as in screening), all are among the wealth of new materials utilized by contemporary architects for decorative and structural purposes. Some of the materials of the modern architect are traditional—wood, concrete, glass, brick, and stone. Yet even the traditional materials have been given new meaning by being combined with each other and with the newer ones listed above, as in the bronze, glass, and concrete Seagram Building (Fig. 78a, p. 120).

At the same time, there are startling new variations in the old materials, each appearing in colors, textures, and consistencies never seen before. Glass, for example, with its sole traditional function the admission of light, can now be treated so as to deflect both heat and light rays. Concrete is given wider range through the addition of iron and steel as internal or external reinforcement. Glass brick and glass tubing substitute for brick and also fulfill the function of translucent lighting, as in the Administration and Research Center of the Johnson

Fig. 61. FRANK LLOYD WRIGHT: Reception room, Johnson Wax Company Administration and Research Center. Racine, Wisconsin. (Photo courtesy S. C. Johnson and Son, Inc.)

Fig. 62. Model of Parthenon, restored. View of interior. New York, Metropolitan Museum of Art.

Wax Company (Fig. 61, p. 95). Stone is used not only in its traditional function but also as internal decoration or in other new variations. In general, the modern architect, freed from the bonds of traditionalism, is no longer deterred by academic or text-book limitations of the functions of material, as were the architects of the immediate past.

Traditional and modern applications. The use of architectural materials with their limitations and functions may be regarded in two ways: traditional applications and modern ones. In general, sharp limitations were imposed in the past by the availability of certain materials, restricting what the architect was able to accomplish in stability, fireproofing, height, or span of roof. In the Parthenon interior (Fig. 62, p. 96) the method of roofing the relatively broad space of an official temple was largely determined by the fact that a marble slab placed horizontally across upright walls can be only so long. Marble, like all stone, is crystalline in quality as well as heavy. When used in such a position across a fairly wide space, it is affected by its own weight, which, beyond a certain point, will cause it to break. The Parthenon, therefore, has a relatively narrow interior.

Contrariwise, a wooden beam has a tensile strength, or bendability, that would remedy this defect, but wood is limited in its available lengths and, even more important, is subject to burning. For a simple residential house, however, wood (and brick) has proved over the years a cheap and effective material.

In many countries, especially in the Near East where wood is relatively scarce, brick has long been a favored material. With various types of either sun-baked or kiln-baked brick, it is easy and cheap to erect the walls of a building by laying courses (continuous rows) of bricks. The nature of this material, however, with its small units, rules out its possibility of achieving a horizontal roofing, as with a marble slab or wooden beam. For this reason, Near Eastern peoples evolved the vault, which may be described as a series of arches laid together in the form of a canopy (see Fig. 190, p. 333), and the hemispherical dome (see *Hagia Sophia,* Fig. 68, p. 109).

Stone is stronger and more permanent than brick and enables the builders to erect such impressive and long-lasting monuments as the Parthenon (exterior view, Fig. 62a, p. 97), the cathedrals of the Middle Ages (Fig. 22, p. 35), and the palaces of the Renaissance and post-Renaissance periods (see Fig. 155, p. 275). In all these types where a broad space is to be roofed, the vault form is used, unless the

Fig. 62a. Parthenon. View from northwest. Athens.

architect is willing to compromise by using posts or columns in the middle of his floor space to support the roof.

The modern revolution in materials is illustrated by steel which, usable in any type of building, enables the architect to overcome the spatial and weight limitations (the load capacity) of earlier materials. With its tensile strength and the possibility of riveting one length of steel to another, we can bridge wider spaces and maintain the safety factor without trouble. Moreover, we can attain heights never before possible (see R.C.A. Building, Fig. 58, p. 92). In a Romanesque church, for example (see Fig. 190, p. 333), the height of the building was maintained by immensely thick outer walls that, however thick, had a definite limit beyond which it was not safe to build.

In Gothic churches (Fig. 22, p. 35) this limit was raised by a skillful system of dynamic and opposing weights, so that both height and width were considerably increased. Yet in this system also there was a point beyond which it was not safe to raise the building, first, because the foundation was not sufficiently strong, and second, because the vaults finally became so heavy that their own weight was enough to collapse the building in spite of the elaborate buttressing system. With the use of steel, however, a new type of building has come into being. Steel girders, tied together both vertically and horizontally in a flexible and powerful arrangement, support the weight of the floors and roof, while walls, now reduced to the subordinate role of enclosing spaces, are of uniform thickness all the way up and are both easy and cheap to erect.

While the steel skeleton is the necessary basis for a skyscraper (office, apartment, or hotel), reinforced concrete is more suitable for industrial structures such as bridge supports, power plants, factories, and dams. This latter medium has the double virtue of compressibility (strain-bearing) and tensile strength. The concrete may be poured into almost any desired form and, when allowed to harden, will safely undergo the greatest compression; iron rods reinforcing the concrete will absorb shocks and vertical and horizontal strains. In a bridge, the great weight of the steel superstructure has to be borne in part by concrete piers, the iron reinforcements of which permit the structure to sway safely in the wind. In such a skyscraper as the R.C.A. Building (Fig. 58, p. 92), the concrete foundation must bear the compressive

Fig. 63. TABLER & STOJOWSKI: Statler-Hilton Hotel. Dallas, Texas. Sculpture, JOSÉ DE RIVERA: *Construction* (1955).

weight of the entire building as well as the strain from the sideways swaying caused by high winds.

Apart from the steel skeleton and the concrete foundation, one other element has helped to make possible the mighty skyscrapers of our period. This is the high-speed elevator, brought into being by the invention and development of electricity. Without it, a many-storied building would be unwieldy, even useless. In the days of the lower building it was possible for office structures up to a height of ten or a few more stories to function with the aid of the hydraulic elevator, a device which looks fairly clumsy in retrospect but was a great advance in its time. In the operation of the gigantic buildings initiated by the Chicago and New York skyscrapers and their contemporary descendants, however, safety and speed have been major considerations in moving people from one level to another. These factors are satisfied by the new high-speed self-stopping elevators.

One of the many innovations of the modern building, especially in

MATERIALS AND THEIR USES   **99**

the skyscraper—although elsewhere as well—is the increased use of glass. Indeed, many façades seem to be made up not of solid walls but of glass with little or no additional material. The R.C.A. Building and the Philadelphia Savings Fund Society Building begin to convey this feeling quite clearly. Smaller residential structures such as the Savoye House (Fig. 31, p. 48) and the garden façade of the Tugendhat House increase this impression (Figs. 64 and 64a, pp. 101, 102). Recently, both the skyscraper and the modern residence have carried it to a high point, as in the Statler-Hilton Hotel (Dallas, 1955, Fig. 63, p. 99) or the United Nations Secretariat, New York (Fig. 65, p. 104). On the slab-shaped Secretariat, green-tinted heat-resistant glass is the dominant external note, reducing the function of the other verticals and horizontals.

Another important factor making the modern tall building possible (besides steel, reinforced concrete, electricity, high-speed elevators) is mass production. In modern times the ability to mass-produce such elements as steel girders, aluminum bars and strips, large panes of glass, and many other necessary materials is in itself an absolute prerequisite of our new buildings.

Elements of Structure

In discussing the materials used in construction, we have also been considering many of the elements of architectural construction such as walls, columns (or posts), beams, openings (windows and doors), roof covering, arches, vaults and domes, and steel skeletons. Both the materials used and the elements of construction were clearly associated with the practical function of each building. And to these three factors (function, materials, and structural elements) we must add that of design or planning to complete the components necessary for architecture. This architectural design or plan relates the layout of the building to the superstructure and the latter to the various spaces enclosed (or inferred), and these to the surrounding or enclosing walls and their decoration.

The wall. The enclosing or limiting wall has already been treated to some extent. As an architectural element it may vary in thickness, height, shape (curved, straight, elliptical), completeness, manner of construction, basic function, and ultimate esthetic purpose and effect.

Fig. 64. MIËS VAN DER ROHE: Tugendhat House (1930), garden façade. Brno, Czechoslovakia.

In some styles of architecture, the wall as a wall is more important than in others, either for decorative or for functional reasons. We may contrast the purpose of the façade of the Pazzi Chapel (Fig. 30, p. 45) with that of a modern building, the Savoye House (Fig. 31, p. 48). In the chapel, the false wall is an area to be covered with ornament and is otherwise relatively functionless. In the house, the wall is a partly limiting, partly liberating surface, without ornament of any kind and far more transparent in quality and effect. Although this wall delimits in a physical sense the space of the interior, it also permits, because of its transparency, a flow of vision from the interior to the exterior and vice versa. Many subsequent buildings, among them the well-known Philip C. Johnson house in New Canaan, Connecticut, have been influenced by this point of view.

In some styles of architecture the wall is more important as a "bearing" or carrying element, that is, for functional reasons. This is seen in Romanesque (see Fig. 190, p. 333), Egyptian, Renaissance (see Fig. 155, p. 275), and many other traditional styles where the walls *are* the building, carrying themselves as well as the floors. They are far less important, however, in the Gothic (see Fig. 14, p. 26) and in most modern styles (see Fig. 64, p. 101). The latter category includes a method of building in which the wall, often of glass, has as its purpose the creation of a continuity between inside and outside

Fig. 64a. MIËS VAN DER ROHE: Tugendhat House (1930), living room. Brno, Czechoslovakia.

rather than the support or containment of window and door openings or use as a screen for ornament. The weight is then carried by skeletal frame construction of steel, with the walls hung as a curtain on this framework.

Ornament, in the traditional sense, is almost completely absent from the modern building, which relies on the texture and color of its walls and similar elements for decorative embellishment. Thus, in the sparely designed Savoye House, the various large blue, red, and green areas take the place of the applied ornament seen on buildings like the Pazzi Chapel.

The modern wall, in addition to its delimiting quality and its function as a transparent curtain between inside and outside, also has a mobility previously envisaged only in Japanese architecture. Japanese walls are not only translucent to admit light, but also movable to admit both light and air and to make the garden and house part of the same space area. In contemporary Western architecture we have new treatments of both interior and exterior walls.

Within a building, for example, Tugendhat House (Fig. 64a, p. 102), the walls do not necessarily extend all the way from one side to the other to make completely enclosed areas. A wall may run part of the way across a room and sometimes only part of the way up to the ceiling. The architect avoids the interruption of the free-flowing space he deems essential, and the inhabitant of the building moves freely in a continuous space which carries him both physically and visually from one room to another and, finally, to the outside wall, where large windows perform the delimiting function. These deliberately incomplete interior walls may sometimes be moved from one position to another, giving an additional and useful flexibility to the interior, which may be changed with the needs of the family.

Exterior walls also have acquired a new mobility in hot climates, where they may be made up of movable louvers or units. Somewhat similar to Venetian blinds, these can be manipulated from different points to assume the angle most conducive to shade at the necessary times of day.

Windows and doors. Windows and doors constitute the two chief types of openings. Their purpose is to afford ready access of light, air, and entry for the occupants. Different climates and purposes naturally require different types of windows and doors. Even in traditional architecture it was evident that whereas it was desirable to admit light in northern buildings where there was relatively little sun, in southern buildings it was far more advisable to keep sun out. Such northern churches as the Gothic cathedrals of the île de France (see Fig. 14, p. 26), with their aim the admission of as much light as possible, are in contrast to the cool dark churches of Italy or Spain.

The most striking thing about windows in the history of architecture is their increasing use as we come down into modern times—because of a growing concern with efficiency, health, and comfort. To see the distance we have come, we may contrast the eighteenth-century American house, *Royall House* at Medford, Massachusetts (see Fig. 172, p. 302), with the economically comparable twentieth-century Savoye House by Le Corbusier (Fig. 31, p. 48). Today most factories, apartment houses, schools, stores, and other buildings use glass to the maximum so that people working and living in them will be happier and more healthful. We can imagine that the reactions of a worker in a wall-enclosed factory will be quite different from those of a man working in a building where glass gives him a view of the outside and a consequent sense of ease. By actual test it has been found that the latter worker is more efficient; he produces more for his employer and for himself as a result of this intelligent planning (Fig. 65, p. 104).

Fig. 65. United Nations Headquarters (Secretariat, Conference, and General Assembly buildings). New York.

Windows and doors, whether traditional or modern, are also important elements in the decoration of the building and its design qualities. In traditional buildings like the Palazzo Farnese (see Fig. 155, p. 275) the windows afford a rhythmic vertical movement against the predominantly horizontal effect of the palazzo (see *Principles of Design,* Chapter 10). In a more dramatically conceived building, *San Carlo alle Quattro Fontane* (see Fig. 214, p. 388), the windows, like the doors, are part of an allover arrangement of darks and lights, increasing the movement in and out as well as the emotional interest.

In such modern structures as the R.C.A. Building (Fig. 58, p. 92), the Philadelphia Savings Fund Society Building (Fig. 73, p. 114), and others, the very nature of the functional problem—to repeat an almost infinite number of openings for small office cubicles—results in far more regularity in the layout of windows. Yet the designer's incorporation of the movement of the windows with that of the piers running vertically and horizontally is significant. In the R.C.A. Building, the masonry piers thrust upward in a functional sense that repeats the basic form and vertical movement of the building itself. Within this forceful movement the windows become mere sparkles of light, playing a minor role in the totality. In the Philadelphia building, however, where height is less important and where the building moves sideways as well as upward, the windows are set back slightly from the surface of the structure and help to balance the upward thrust with a sideways movement.

Doorways are also part of the esthetics of a building. In some buildings their effect is far less than in others—deliberately so. The relative lack of doorways in a typical Romanesque building of the twelfth century (see Fig. 190, p. 333) contrasts with the wide open, inviting, and relatively numerous doorways in the typical Gothic building (see Fig. 191, p. 335). In traditional architectural forms, doorways often have a ceremonial purpose associated with a religious or royal procession and therefore carry importance in the architectural scheme together with their symbolic meaning. Thus the main doorway of the Gothic cathedral is related symbolically to the aspirations of Gothic life. As part of the symbolic orientation of the church, the altar is in the east end, toward the rising sun. The main doorway is on the west side toward the setting sun, and its sculptures show scenes of the Last Judgment at the end of the world. In a modern building where the main function is utilitarian, the doorway is related to the design of the whole but usually is otherwise unobtrusive.

The post or column. Another basic element in buildings is the post or column, used primarily as a support either for superstructure, as in the Parthenon (Fig. 62a, p. 97), or for interior roof support, as in Egyptian temples and Christian churches (Chartres Cathedral, Fig. 22, p. 35). In proportions and surface quality the column offers a great variety of shapes and decorative motifs, varying from the gigantic and highly decorated Egyptian column to the more delicately proportioned and comparatively severe Greek or Renaissance column.

In modern times the column or post, sometimes of metal, sometimes of concrete, is often austerely simple, as in the spare slimness of the posts on the exterior of the Savoye House (Fig. 31, p. 48). The arrangement of the columns may be in one place, as here, or may be a more elaborate part of the interior space arrangement, as in the

Johnson Wax Company Administration and Research Center, with
its mushroom-topped cast concrete columns. But this arrangement is
always part of the esthetic meaning of the structure (Fig. 66, p. 106).

The column generally does not exist by itself; most often it is in the
building as part of a vertical and horizontal combination known as a
post-and-lintel element, which in its most basic form is represented by
the doorway, as on the Parthenon façade (Fig. 62a, p. 97). Although
there are disadvantages in the post-and-lintel system—the lintel may
break because of its own weight, because of weight applied from above,
or because of shearing off at the point of contact—it is the simplest
and the most widely used. Using stone, it gives us a relatively narrow
vertical arrangement because of the breakability of the material. Using
wood, as in Oriental architecture (see Fig. 23, p. 36), it forms a horizontal rectangle, because a relatively thin wooden column can support
a fairly long beam and therefore a wider opening.

Arches. A basic architectural element is the arch. This consists of
one line of regular and relatively small wedge-shaped units placed in
a semicircle, a horseshoe shape, a pointed arrangement, a flattened
curve, or any other form that will hold together as the wedges press

against each other. The wedge-shaped blocks, or *voussoirs*, slide into position, their narrow ends facing down and holding each other in place, the totality of the arch locked finally by the central keystone.

Since the pressure is from above, the arch generally tends to bulge outward at the sides unless given compensating support of some kind. Generally speaking, the arch is part of something else, like a vault (see below); used by itself, it appears in such forms as the Roman aqueduct, where the continuous series of arches support each other, that is, keep each other from bulging out and therefore falling down, and are hooked onto a strong cement pier at the beginning and the end. In modern architecture, arches may also be formed of wood or metal, each offering special advantages of economy, lightness, flexible strength, and mass production.

Roofing. The relative advantages and disadvantages of materials used in building are nowhere as clearly demonstrated as in roof coverings. We have already seen how the availability of a particular material in traditional architecture influenced the question of whether the roof would be covered with a wooden *truss,* a brick *vault,* or a stone *dome.*

One of the simplest types of building, the rectangular structure covered with a gabled roof, generally uses the *truss* ceiling. This consists of an arrangement of diagonal beams running along the slope of the ceiling like the two arms of a triangle; the base is formed by a horizontal ceiling beam stretching from wall to wall. Between the diagonals and this horizontal, there is a short vertical beam at right angles to the horizontal, as well as a pair of short diagonal struts from the base of the short vertical member to the long diagonals directly above, thus:

Of this truss arrangement, which may be erected in metal as well as in wood, only the horizontal ceiling beam is visible from the interior of the building; the other five members are generally masked by the covering of the ceiling, except in barns and other simple structures.

The distance between walls may also be spanned by a *vault.* This can be described as a series of arches placed side by side to form a continuous canopy or tunnel of stone, brick, or other material. The simplest form of vault is in this canopy shape and is known as a barrel vault. It is found in many Assyrian and medieval Romanesque buildings (see Fig. 190, p. 333).

More complex shapes occur in Romanesque buildings in which two barrel vaults cross each other to form what is called a groin vault. This appears even more frequently in Gothic architecture (see Fig. 14, p. 26). Here the vault moves toward a pointed, rather than a rounded, top, as is also true in a number of Middle Eastern variations of the vault shape, as in the Moslem architecture of Persia.

Although the vault has a tremendous decorative and functional value, it is necessarily limited in scope by the weight and nature of the materials used. Thus, in Romanesque architecture, the weight of the stone vaults in the nave or center of the church was so great that the supporting walls had to be thickened, as well as deprived of window openings, in order to maintain their strength. Even where it was possible to do away with the immensely thick walls of the Romanesque church, as in the following Gothic style, the weight of the stone always remained a factor that limited the height of the building; Gothic builders could go so far and no farther in a vertical direction.

The vault, moreover, like its constituent arches, is constantly exerting outward thrust as a result of the weight imposed upon it as well as of its own weight—a thrust that would cause it to burst unless the strain were relieved in some fashion. A more pointed shape, as in Gothic architecture, tends to relieve this strain. Of more help, however, the outward thrust of the typical traditional vaulting system is counteracted by counterthrusts from adjacently placed half-barrel vaults, as in Romanesque architecture (see Fig. 190, p. 333), or from external struts known as flying buttresses, as in Gothic (see Fig. 14, p. 26). A third means of relieving strain is to place so-called ribs along the underside of the vault, ribs running parallel to the narrow side of the vault and carried down along the lower wall to the ground.

The *dome* presents many similar problems and limitations. While the vault is used to cover a rectangular building, running lengthwise above the walls, the dome is employed to cover either a circular or square building. Interesting variants of this hemispherical vault, or dome, may be seen in the Roman *Pantheon* (Fig. 67, p. 109) and in the Byzantine church of Hagia Sophia (Fig. 68, p. 109) in Istanbul. In the first, a squat cylinder, to which a portico has been attached, is capped by a hemisphere of concrete. This monolithic (one-stone) top

Fig. 67 (*above*). Pantheon. View of exterior. Rome. Fig. 68 (*below*). Hagia Sophia. View from southwest. Istanbul, Turkey.

was formed by pouring the concrete into a framework of brick squares and allowing it to harden. Once the hardening has occurred, there is no likelihood of the dome bulging outward and destroying itself, but the problem of the downward-thrusting weight of the mass is still there, and is solved by the use of very thick walls in the stubby cylinder below.

Fitting the top of this cylinder to the lower portion of the hemisphere presents no difficulty since both are circular in shape (Fig. 69, p. 000). There are many instances, however, in which the lower part of a building is square. To provide a complete and enclosed roof for it, the circular dome has been used, and special architectural devices have had to be developed to fit the two shapes together. The most important of these devices is the *spherical pendentive,* as seen in Hagia Sophia (Fig. 70, p. 111).

Here the transition from a square plan to the circular base of the dome is made by throwing an arch from the heavy piers defining the four corners of the square—making four arches. From each of the piers and between the curved surfaces of the incoming arches, the mason begins to build row upon row of stones, proceeding from a tiny pointed area to a wide curving area on top and thus forming a triangular section of a sphere, which is the spherical pendentive. The top of each of these pendentives constitutes a quarter of a circle. When the four quarters are joined, we have the complete circle necessary for the base of the dome, which is then built up from that point.

However light such a dome may be (and often special efforts are made to limit its weight), it still constitutes a formidable weight for the walls to support. In Hagia Sophia, two sides of the building (Fig. 68, p. 109) are buttressed, or supported, externally by the addition of pairs of heavy stone piers which lean their weight against the walls. The other sides are reinforced by placing a smaller half-dome below the main dome, and then pairs of still smaller half-domes below this single one. From here a number of lower vaults take over the weight, until it is finally grounded at the base of the wall.

Another method of transiting from the square base to the round dome is provided by a device known as the *squinch.* In essence this is a member (straight or curved) that is thrown across the angle of the square in order to form a shape close to an octagon, on which it is much easier to set the dome. The simplest form of squinch is merely

Fig. 69 (*above*). Pantheon. View of interior. Rome. Fig. 70 (*below*). Hagia Sophia.
View of interior, looking toward apse. Istanbul, Turkey.

Fig. 71. Terminal Building. Lambert–St. Louis Municipal Airport. St. Louis, Missouri.

a straight beam thrown across each of the four corners to make the required octagon. Another is an arch thrown across the ground piers, as in Hagia Sophia—arches above which square walls are erected. Across the corners of these square walls are erected smaller arches, which convert the square into an octagon for the placement of the dome.

All of these general roofing methods must also be characterized in terms of the possible difference between the shape of the ceiling inside the building and the form that is visible outside. That is to say, externally gabled buildings may have interior barrel vaulting, as in Romanesque architecture, or interior pointed vaults, as in Gothic.

The functional motivation of the various types of external roofing often depends on climatic conditions. Snow makes a gable necessary so that the roof may shed its burden and not be broken down or otherwise spoiled. In hot climates, on the other hand, a flat roof is desirable so that people may sleep outdoors or sit under an awning during the day.

The need for stone vaulting arises either from a desire for monumentality and space, as seen, or from considerations of safety, important during the Middle Ages when fire was a constant hazard. Chartres Cathedral (Fig. 22, p. 35) was burned down twice during the twelfth

Fig. 72. EERO SAARINEN: Water tower (stainless steel; capacity, 250,000 gallons). Detroit, Michigan, General Motors Technical Center.

century; earlier medieval buildings were frequently burned by Norse and Magyar invaders.

In most, if not all, of the traditional roofing methods described, the controlling factor in construction is the limitation of the material itself: the weight of stone, the pliability of wood, and so forth. With modern materials, however, roofs of impressive proportions and unusual shapes may be designed and constructed. Cast concrete makes possible the three sets of intersecting cylinders that form the roof of the *Lambert–St. Louis Municipal Airport Terminal Building* (Fig. 71, p. 112). Eero Saarinen's Trans World Airlines terminal at Idlewild Airport, New York, (1958–1960) involves a thin concrete shell of four domes, 300 feet long. In the interiors of railroad terminals, a steel framework permits us to span spaces that were hitherto impossible to cover without piers to support heavy brick or concrete vaults, as was done in ancient Rome. Another new method of achieving such continuous rounded surfaces is through "stressed skin" construction, in which sheets of metal or materials such as plywood are bent under stress into the required continuous form, as one finds in gas storage tanks or water tanks, like Saarinen's stainless steel *Water Tower* in Detroit (Fig. 72, p. 113). Shapes of this kind need no skeletal framework; the skin and skeleton are one.

Fig. 73. HOWE AND LESCAZE: Philadelphia Savings Fund Society Building. Philadelphia, Pennsylvania.

The cantilever. Related to the standard modern skeletal steel framework is the structural element known as the cantilever. An extension of that framework, the cantilever permits the builder to bring forward a series of horizontal beams supported only at the point where they leave the side of the framework. These horizontal beams are strong enough to carry both floor and exterior wall, but allow the designer to eliminate the street level wall—an advantage when space is at a premium and an interesting way of avoiding the sometimes monotonous repetition of vertical supporting members.

Loads may not only be placed on the cantilevers, but they may also be hung from them. Continuous rows of windows are thus made possible in the Philadelphia Savings Fund Society Building (Fig. 73, p. 114). Other instances of the same approach are found in the work of Frank Lloyd Wright, whose residences—Robie House, Kaufmann House (Fig. 74, p. 115), and others—use the cantilever most effectively for purposes of design. An extension of this method is found in

114   THE NATURE OF ARCHITECTURE

suspension construction in which the entire edifice, like the Johnson Wax Company Laboratory Tower (Fig. 75, p. 116), is hung from a high central mast, each floor cantilevered out from the center. Under certain light conditions one can see the divisions into separate laboratory sections marked by the floor areas beyond the translucent shell of the building. The tower itself rises 156 feet into the air, yet it is supported at its base by a unit that is only 13 feet in diameter at its narrowest point (Fig. 75a, p. 116). Because of the contrast between the tower and its supporting column, this structure appears to float in the air.

Planning and Design

When we come to the elements of composition or planning, we must recognize that virtually no building is erected without some form of drawn plan. The shape called for by a plan may vary from an elementary one such as the rectangle of a garage to the symbolic design of the typical church or the otherwise complicated layout of a modern factory. The superstructures are invariably dependent on the nature of their respective plans.

Such superstructures may be considered as three-dimensional solids in either elementary or complex relationships. The simpler the geometric solid represented by the building, the more immediate its impact and satisfying its effect. Such simple geometric solids include the

Fig. 74. FRANK LLOYD WRIGHT: Kaufmann House ("Falling Water"). Bear Run, Pennsylvania. (Photo courtesy The Museum of Modern Art)

Fig. 75 (*left*). FRANK LLOYD WRIGHT: Johnson Wax Company Laboratory Tower (1949). Racine, Wisconsin. Fig. 75a (*below*). Base of Tower. (Photo courtesy S. C. Johnson and Son, Inc.)

pyramid form, appearing in Egyptian architecture; the cube, appearing in the modern home and Pueblo Indian dwelling; the cone, appearing in the primitive hut and the top of a medieval tower; the cylinder, appearing in the modern grain silo and the medieval bell tower (Tower of Pisa); and the hemisphere, appearing in the igloo and some Near Eastern buildings.

These same geometric solids also exist in combinations. We may speak of a combination of cube shapes in the modern building or the Pueblo houses, a cube plus hemisphere in the Byzantine Hagia Sophia (Fig. 68, p. 109), a cube with cone cap or one or more cubes with a hemisphere in the bell tower, a cylinder with a hemisphere in the silo, a half-cylinder with a hemisphere or half-cone in the church apse form, and other increasingly complex arrangements.

Mass. Superstructures with either simple or complex geometrical solid construction confront the spectator with their mass or bulk, which may be visually effective through simplicity or some monumental quality. Where mass consists of the simple geometric shape, in any of the forms above, the esthetic effect is relatively simple and immediate. Where, however, there are many masses involved in one structure, the effect is not quite so simple.

In Hagia Sophia (Fig. 68, p. 109) the basic shapes are those of the hemisphere and the cube. But a second look at this building reveals additional masses: the heavy piers on the north and south sides, and the half-domes and other elements on the east and west sides. These all form an important esthetic relationship in their repetition of the rectangular form of the cubic base and the roundness of the spherical dome. The masses of material which here impress the eye with their bulk have the effect of balancing each other as well.

Furthermore, the mass (or masses) of a building may be related in an even more dynamic manner. This may be seen in the asymmetrical arrangement of such a structure as the R.C.A. Building (Fig. 58, p. 92) or the Woolworth Building (Fig. 59, p. 92). The latter shows a relatively simple dynamism; the two base masses, arranged about an open space like the top half of an "H," support a continuation of themselves in the form of the vertical thrusting tower.

In the R.C.A. Building the arrangement of masses is made more asymmetrical as it forms part of a constantly moving pattern of buildings, of which it is only one of the large elements. Within itself, however, this building has an interesting pattern of block forms. On the narrow side (main entrance) a powerfully upthrusting main mass is flanked by smaller subordinate sections. These are affected in part by the city zoning requirements, which necessitate setbacks at intervals, as well as by the logic of the design and the building's function. The wider sides of the buildings give the appearance of large rectangular pieces sawed out of the mass in a series of regular steps from the bottom to the top.

By comparison, the masses of the much smaller Philadelphia Savings Fund Society Building are more varied than either of the preceding examples. The masses in this building may be identified as the horizontal base with its varying curved cornice, the dynamically vertical elevator structure attached to the side of the building, and the main section. The latter is a variant of the elevator mass, but compromises between its own verticality and the horizontality of the base through a contrast between the vertical direction of the piers and the horizontal movement of masonry areas dividing the windows.

Volume of space. The mass of a building does not always correspond

Fig. 76. The Pyramids and Sphinx. Gizeh, Egypt.

with the volume of interior space it encloses. The most obvious example and the simplest illustration of possible disparity between inside and outside is seen in the Egyptian Pyramids (Fig. 76, p. 118). These gigantic masses of masonry (average height about 275 feet) each contain but three relatively small rooms, the largest of which is 34½ feet long, 19 feet high, and 17 feet wide. This and the other two even smaller chambers constitute the total of enclosed spaces; the rest is solid stone bulk.

Although the Pyramids show extreme disparity between mass and volume—resulting here from the desire for monumentality, permanence, and secrecy—other structures are surprising in their own way. Hagia Sophia in its powerful and massive external bulk offers a dramatic contrast to the extreme openness of its interior. The architect, given the initial desire to achieve a high and wide internal volume of space, had little choice but to provide these external supports.

The greater interior space in the Christian building as compared with the earlier Greek temple (Fig. 62, p. 96) is impelled by definable social and practical reasons. In Greek religion the congregation did not enter the building, preferring rather to approach the building as a complex of sculptural religious symbols, but were met by the high priest who would perform the necessary rites, accept gifts, and retire to the interior of the temple to place them at the foot of the god's statue. This statue occupied much of the interior space in the Greek temple, and since only the priest and his aides entered the temple, to place the gifts and to visit the treasury room in the rear, there was no social need for more space. With Christianity, on the other hand, there is the actual congregational need for space to worship, the elaborate rituals performed by walking around an altar, and so on.

Those needs in the Early Christian period were satisfied by such buildings as Santa Maria Maggiore (Fig. 77, p. 119). The same spirituality that led Early Christians to decorate the interiors rather than the exteriors of their basilicas (emphasizing the soul rather than the body) led them to regard space as a means of achieving a sense of unity with God. In such buildings as Hagia Sophia (Fig. 68, p. 109) space was an evidence of the pervasive spirituality of the time, an earnest of the existence of God, a symbol of man's striving to meet Him on a plane higher than the merely earthly. This sense of aspiration and striving is felt even more strongly in such typical Gothic churches of the thirteenth century as those at Chartres, Paris, and Amiens (Fig. 14, p. 26).

The interior space of the Gothic cathedral introduced a quality, however, that is of great importance, especially to modern architecture. Its openness of structure, which permitted the architect to pierce the walls with stained-glass windows, also created a sense of continuity between the inside and outside of the building that had seldom, if ever, been felt before. Where earlier examples emphasized the contrast between inside and outside or, in our present terms of reference, between mass and volume or space, the Gothic structure seems planned to show a correlation between the building's mass and the space enclosed.

In modern buildings such as the Tugendhat House (Figs. 64 and

Fig. 77. Santa Maria Maggiore. View of interior looking toward apse. Rome.

Fig. 78 (*left*). SKIDMORE, OWINGS, AND MERRILL: Lever House (1952) New York. Fig. 78a (*right*). MIËS VAN DER ROHE AND PHILIP JOHNSON: Seagram Building (model; 1958). New York.

64a, pp. 101, 102), there is a similar sense of continuity between indoors and outdoors. The volumes of space enclosed by this structure are not arrested by interruptive walls; they are, rather, allowed or even urged to continue through the large areas of window facing the outside. Similarly, upon looking in from the outside, we also get the feeling of continuity. This sensation resembles that inspired by the Japanese home with its movable and often translucent walls, sparse furnishings, and other functional features. It is amplified by the flexibility and fluidity of the interior spaces and their relationship to each other. In the interior of the Tugendhat House, as noted earlier, the continuously flowing space is quite different in esthetic effect and social meaning from the carefully and permanently laid-out space enclosures of the traditional Western house or apartment.

Interior spaces, like exterior masses, are also subject to artistic analysis and must fit into the total esthetic pattern that makes the building a piece of architecture. In the Savoye House (Fig. 31, p. 48) the interior is laid out in a series of rooms or enclosures around an open courtyard, in a relationship that balances the proportion of rooms against the amount of completely open space. This necessity for balance applies to any interior, even a traditional one. The Pazzi Chapel, for example, encloses a domed square space, with two sub-domes that balance the large one and cover miniature rectangular areas of their own.

It is even possible to consider space as an attribute of some exteriors as well. Looking at a building like *Lever House* or the Seagram Building in New York (Figs. 78 and 78a, p. 120), we find that the architects have been at some pains to create not only a proportional relation between the upstanding main section or slab form and the subordinate rectangular areas, but also a connection between the filled areas or masses represented by these two and the open space above either the substructure or platform. In other buildings, too, this relation of the masses to the voids is deliberate. It may be seen in the often cited Philadelphia Savings Fund Society Building (Fig. 73, p. 114), the R.C.A. Building, and many others, and should be counted as one of the means of creating artistic unity within the structural design.

Not only can the masses and voids be harmoniously related; in addition, the masses and the silhouette they create can be combined effectively. They may be altogether integrated, as in the R.C.A. Building, where the subordinate masses are so solidly united to the main emphasis that they create a tight, sharply felt outline or silhouette as well as a feeling of space-filling masses. On the other hand, over-ornamented buildings of the nineteenth century in the then-popular eclectic styles, like the Paris Opéra, may have a silhouette, even an interesting one, but it seldom shows a clear or integrated relationship to the main masses.

Layout and circulation. One of the many ways in which one judges architecture is through the eminently functional element of circulation. Does the building work? Do its entrances fulfill the function of getting people in adequately? Do its elevators move fast enough to get crowds off the main floor and distributed among their respective offices; do they perform well at the end of the working day when everyone is clamoring for elevator space and exit room? From this point of

Fig. 79. GRUEN, YAMASAKI, AND STONOROV: Model for Gratiot–Orleans Redevelopment Project. Detroit, Michigan.

view we may compare a building like the R.C.A. or the Seagram Building and its gigantic tasks with some of the more old-fashioned office buildings in any big city.

The older structures, built for a time and tempo that have been left far behind, are often unable to keep up with the additional pressures of contemporary living; their elevators are too slow, too few, and poorly placed. On the other hand, the R.C.A. type of edifice enjoys the benefits of a large bank of express and local elevators, carefully placed a good distance from the multiple entrance doors and arranged so that they divide the job by vertical areas in the building—one set going up only as far as a certain floor, another set to a group of higher floors, and another still higher. Although the layout or circulation of the individual floor may seem a routine matter, this too can be handled inadequately when one has to walk endless yards from the point of disembarking from the elevator to one's destination.

What is true for a colossus like the R.C.A. is just as true for a smaller office building or for a relatively very small individual residence or apartment, old or new. The Palazzo Farnese and even the Louvre (see Fig. 171, p. 301) show conspicuous defects in circulation, since there is often no way of entering certain rooms except through others or by going outside into an open patio or public corridor. Modern residences overcome this defect by planning the rooms around an entrance hall or other neutral chamber, so that people may be undisturbed by others passing through.

It may be argued in regard to buildings like the Louvre that the need for privacy, brought about by today's multiplied pressures, did not exist to the same degree under the ceremonial arrangements of kingship, which made almost all the monarch's activities public. Where today we consider it a serious problem if our administrative officials are not able to be alone, such privacy for a monarch like Louis XIV was almost undreamed of. The ceremonial levées, dinners, parties, and other functions made the monarch subject to constant display. Yet from the viewpoint of ready access to rooms, it was generally possible for the servants, for example, to use back stairs or narrow staircases in the walls of a palace or castle—emerging in a particular room through what to all intents and purposes was a secret entrance; otherwise any visit was a public act through a public thoroughfare.

Traditional buildings like the Louvre, Versailles, and the Farnese differed not only in their layout or circulation from modern buildings like the Gratiot-Orleans or the Williamsburg Housing Projects, but actually in the social orientation that made them possible. The older buildings reflected the desire of an individual for glory and were dedicated primarily to his welfare. However many others might be housed in the same structure—and at Versailles there were hundreds —the fact remains that, either socially or physically, these people were there to serve the king.

In a modern housing project (see Fig. 79, p.122) we have the antithesis of the older palace, a building to serve the interests of the community. Essentially the same is true of business offices, banks, railroad stations, schools, hospitals, and other public-service buildings. These are all the products of the newer democratic needs of modern society. To that extent they pose new problems of both design and utility—that design and utility which together constitute the basic elements of architecture.

▶ 5

The Meaning of Sculpture

BY ITS VERY NATURE, sculpture differs in artistic character from the two-dimensional art of painting. As sculpture is already three-dimensional, its function is to become effective in terms of form sensation, movement into open and filled spaces, and spaces penetrating each other—as well as texture and color. All sculpture, old or new, offers us opportunity for enjoyment not only through sight but also through touch, balance, and actual physical movement.

In the process of examining a piece of sculpture, we respond to its immediate visual stimuli of form, color, and texture, movement into space, and other obvious appeals. Then, usually, we move around the work; this creates new visual sensations of form, color, and the rest, as new views appear, illumination is changed, and other factors differ. Such an experience reveals an endless process of change, whether in traditional representational sculpture or the more abstract contemporary type. Greek sculpture, for example (Fig. 80, p. 125), exists in terms of its various silhouettes. One can walk around the *Hermes* by Praxiteles or the *Aphrodite of Cyrene* indefinitely, each step offering to the eye a new and interesting outline.

A second pleasure concerns our sense of touch. Certain materials in sculpture, such as polished marble, wood, steel, invite the touch of the fingers. Not only the "skin" of the object, but its very lines may call on this sense: the glistening black granite *Javanese Panther* (Fig. 81, p. 126) by Mateo Hernández has been stroked by thousands of schoolchildren and adults. The sculptor creates through the actual

124

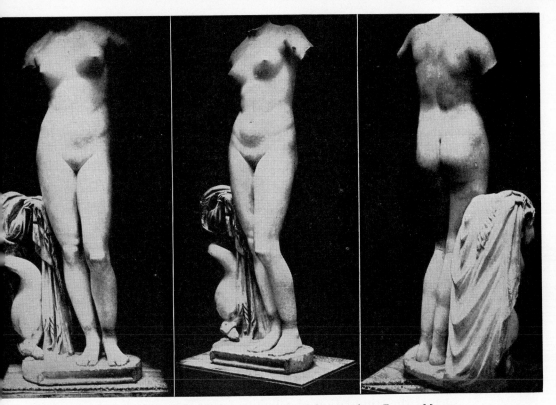

Fig. 80. *Aphrodite of Cyrene*. Front, three-quarter, and rear view. Rome, Museo delle Terme.

physical manipulation of clay, stone, or other substance. He models with his hands the clay that ultimately is cast in bronze, terra cotta, or other material; and in the direct carving of wood or stone, his fingers are as useful to him as his eyes. The sculptor's original handwork evokes in us a tactile as well as a visual response.

A third special appeal of sculpture, especially in the contemporary world, is to our sense of balance. Although this sense is also engaged in the appreciation of architecture and to a more limited extent in painting, certain examples of modern sculpture (by Reginald Butler, Mary Callery, Jacques Lipchitz, Constantin Brancusi, and Theodore Roszak, Fig. 82, p. 127) project themselves violently toward a new imaginative space area well outside the actual physical limits of the works themselves. This projection forces an almost physical adjustment in our visual movement and a strong shifting of the path of visualization (and hence balance) that may perhaps be compared in a rough way to the effects of certain types of Baroque sculpture, such as *Ecstasy of St. Theresa* by Bernini (see Fig. 98, p. 153).

Fig. 81. MATEO HERNÁNDEZ: *Javanese Panther* (diorite; 1922–1925). New York, Metropolitan Museum of Art.

Again, we may observe that traditional art often achieves certain esthetic effects (here, movement into space) comparable to those of modern art; but in traditional works an underlying functional reason, such as the stimulation of religious fervor, accounts for these esthetic effects. Modern sculpture may sum up the sense of movement for its own sake; indeed it *is* movement, and the sensation it imparts is valid within a framework of its own, the world of art. What does a Calder mobile (Fig. 83, p. 128) try to "convey"? In the old sense it means very little, perhaps nothing. In the modern sense, however, Calder embodies in all his creations (as do many others today) the very idea of motion, carrying us visually and physically into other spheres, offering us a movement sensation, a balance sensation, and the usual form sensation as well.

In comparing a contemporary product with the motion-filled work of the Baroque artist, we may note that the latter is still mainly preoccupied with space-filling problems, although his space moves by implication beyond the original limitations of the design itself. But in traditional sculpture we are always conscious of these limitations, whereas in a contemporary work they seem of far less consequence. The traditional primary interest in space-filling forms (see Michelangelo, Fig. 34, p. 54) differs sharply from the contemporary increasing interest in either the alternation of open and filled spaces (see Lipton or Rivera, Figs. 63 and 85, pp. 99, 130), the use of space-penetrating planes (see Pevsner, Fig. 84, p. 129), or form movement for its own sake (see Roszak, Fig. 82, p. 127).

In sculpture, as we shall find in painting, a whole new series of esthetic ideas now exist to challenge traditional values. Although for many people the new sculpture seems more dynamic and space-conquering than the old (moving outside the boundaries of traditional sculpture, whose tensions remain within the work), this does not invalidate the older art. Similarly, the standard values of earlier days should not prevent us from appreciating sculpture in our own time.

The Uses of Sculpture

Historically the most important and consistent use of sculpture has been in religion, as in Bernini's *Ecstasy of St. Theresa* (see Fig. 98, p. 153). Another important function lies in commemorating individuals or groups, as in the Arch of Titus (see Fig. 164, p. 289) honoring the triumph of Rome over the Hebrews. Portraits constitute another

Fig. 82. THEODORE ROSZAK: *Cradle Song* (steel, bronze, and silver nickel; 1953–1956). Courtesy Pierre Matisse Gallery.

Fig. 83. ALEXANDER CALDER: *Pomegranate.* New York, Whitney Museum of American Art.

notable use, as in Houdon's *Voltaire,* Donatello's *Gattamelata,* Verrocchio's *Colleoni* (see Figs. 165, 199, and 200, pp. 291, 347, 349), and many similar works. Sculpture may also record everyday subjects, describing life and customs at a particular time, as in the charming little terra-cotta figurines of Hellenistic times. Literary expression finds a place, too, as in the famous *Laokoön* inspired by a story of the Trojan War (see Fig. 187, p. 325).

The genre, or everyday, subject and the literary theme are more limited than other sculptural uses; they are concerned with the satisfaction of an intellectual need rather than a historical, social, or commemorative purpose. They are primarily artistic products as in twentieth-century sculpture. When no temples or sculpture-decorated cathedrals are being built, when public monuments have reached an abysmally low level, when sculpture no longer has a place in the small modern home, it is pushed out of doors into the garden or remains in the museum. This lack of function has contributed to the ultimate turning of modern sculpture toward a complete art-for-art's sake ex-

expression. The Pevsner sculpture (Fig. 84, p. 129) illustrates the highly individualistic styles achieved by contemporary sculptors, styles which are acceptable to a limited number of art lovers. The Lipton work (Fig. 85, p. 130), inspired by religious considerations and with a particular building location in mind, is within the compass of modern expression and yet addresses itself to specific needs in the older way.

Size and Dimension

The various dimensions of sculpture range from very much larger than life-size to a tiny format that approaches the miniature, as in a coin less than one inch in diameter. From ancient Egypt we have gigantic sculptures such as the Sphinx (over two hundred feet high), and on a lesser scale are many other larger than life-size works. Michelangelo's *Moses* (Fig. 87, p. 133) represents a larger-than-life conception frequently found in traditional sculpture, especially when associated with architecture. Myron's *Discobolus* (Fig. 86, p. 132) is a slightly larger than life-size figure typical of certain classes of Greek sculpture, while Houdon's *Voltaire* (see Fig. 165, p. 291), Bernini's *Apollo and Daphne* (see Fig. 177, p. 311), and many other works of

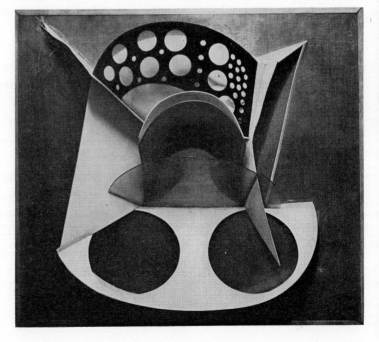

Fig. 84. ANTOINE PEVSNER: *Bust* (metal and celluloid: before 1926). New York, The Museum of Modern Art.

Fig. 85. SEYMOUR LIPTON: *Eternal Light* (nickel silver). Tulsa, Oklahoma, Temple Israel.

various periods can be taken to illustrate the life-sized sculptural dimension.

We should note, however, that this quality of being larger than life-size or life-size is not important in itself except as it may reflect something of the artist's purpose, as in the implied monumentalization of the *Khafre* (Fig. 88, p. 133) and *Moses* and the far greater humanization of the *Discobolus* and *Voltaire*. More important, size alone cannot lend monumentality and impressiveness. There are outsize sculptures of the late Roman period which are merely blown up and do not effectively ennoble their subject.

Conversely, smaller than life-size figures often demonstrate that largeness of conception rather than largeness of size is what makes a monumental effect. This is made clear by the famous Louvre *Gudea* (see Fig. 181, p. 320), which is approximately 3½ feet high, by the Cretan *Snake Goddess* (see Fig. 182, p. 320), which is seven inches high, and by the finely designed Greek coins of antiquity (see Fig. 138, p. 225), which are approximately the size of our own modern coins. All these, in spite of their diminutive size, achieve a real effect of majesty.

One of the chief determinants of size (though not the only one) is function. The architectural—and social—function of the *Khafre,* a monument to the greatness of a pharaoh, or the *Moses,* part of the unfinished monument to Pope Julius II, influenced the size in which the artist projected his work. A sculpture designed to be seen by many people as part of a building, enclosure, or city square will necessarily be large. The *Gattamelata* of Donatello (see Fig. 199, p. 347) is set on a high pedestal before the Church of St. Anthony in Padua and had to be large in order to make sense visually.

The *Athena Lemnia,* the *Doryphorus* (or *Lance-bearer;* see Figs. 183 and 185, pp. 322, 324), and other examples of Greek sculpture, even when not actual parts of a temple structure, have a basic monumental function and are therefore presented in larger than life-size. Here the idea of glorifying the human being is also operative and is probably part of the reason for enlarging the figure. In contemporary society when there is a political need for glorifying a head of government, the same thing happens. This is illustrated by the huge statues of Stalin, Hitler, and similar political figures.

When the function of the sculpture is more limited, either created for personal pleasure on the part of the artist or made for someone's home, we may expect to find a more modest size. Eighteenth-century Rococo sculptors, such as Clodion, designed their work for the cozy boudoirs of the time. Similarly, many sculptors today realize that outside of the museums and conventional government commissions there is little place for monumental sculpture, and they are turning to smaller pieces that can be bought for the home.

Finally, the degree to which the contemporary sculptor has become dissociated from actual work for the state, the church, and other types of traditional patronage is also the degree to which he no longer need produce large-scale pieces. He now works for himself within the modest physical requirements of his studio and the equally modest financial limitations of his profession, which make monumental sculpture financially prohibitive. There are sculptors working in stone whose creations do not sell and who at the end of each year find they have spent an enormous amount of money on materials with no likelihood of return.

Free-standing Figures

Sculpture may be considered as belonging to one of two categories: free-standing or relief. Free-standing figures, which may be of many varieties, can be seen from all sides and must be walked around to be

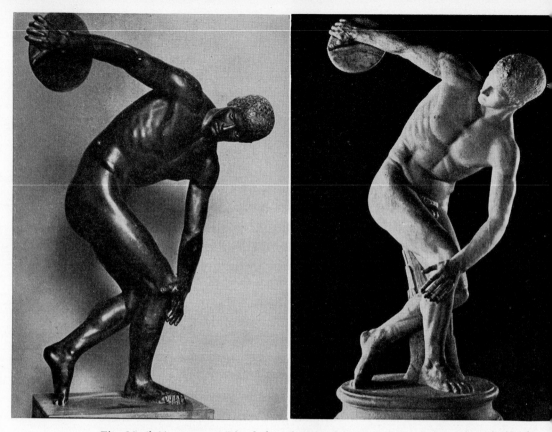

Fig. 86 (*left*). MYRON: *Discobolus* (bronze reconstruction). Rome, National Museum. (Fig. 86a (*right*). MYRON: *Discobolus* (Roman marble copy). Rome, Palazzo Massimi.

appreciated. A simple example is Myron's *Discobolus* (Fig. 86, p. 132), created as a three-dimensional form independent of architecture. As it was not to be seen against the background of a wall or pediment (*cf. Khafre* and *Lapith and Centaur,* Figs. 88 and 96, pp. 133, 152) and as it was undoubtedly set out in a space where it could be viewed from all sides, it had to be planned so that each view would be significant.

Michelangelo's *Moses* (Fig. 87, p. 133), on the other hand, was not designed for any such purpose but rather as a corner figure on a gigantic tomb. While scholars have seen photographs of the rear view of the *Moses,* for most of us it remains a front-viewed object set into an artificial niche in a later architectural composition. Yet the photographs show quite clearly that the work was meant to be seen from more than merely the frontal position. Within the framework of its original purpose, it would have been approachable from the sides as well, and therefore the artist would not think of it in the terms used by the sculptor of the *Khafre* (Fig. 88, p. 133).

The *Khafre* (one of a series) was made to be put against the wall of a tomb, and the artist had to concern himself only with the frontal view. Since figures were arranged fairly close together against that wall, even the side view did not matter too much, although the work is finished there as well. The *Khafre* is not part of the building in the same integrated sense as is *Le Beau Dieu* of Amiens (Fig. 24, p. 37), which was made for a particular niche and therefore physically connected with it. The Egyptian work, however, must be considered architectonic in function. For this reason as well as for reasons of permanence, impressiveness, unchangeableness (see under *Ancient Art*, Chapter 12), the Khafre figure takes on a blocklike form that is entirely geometric in quality.

Every element in this form is controlled by the geometrical con-

Fig. 87 (*left*). MICHELANGELO: *Moses* (marble). Rome, San Pietro in Vincoli.
Fig. 88 (*right*). *Khafre* (diorite). Cairo, Egyptian Museum.

cept; the arms, legs, and torso are related to parallel lines within the rectangular block from which the figure was carved. Moreover, none of the parts of the figure project beyond the limitations of that original block, and to that extent they are controlled by it. In works of this type the back is parallel to the rear line of the block, the thigh to the bottom line, the upper arm to the rear line, the lower arm to the bottom line, the feet to the bottom line, and so on. The artist is careful to keep all these elements within the imaginary but very exact limitations of a three-dimensional rectangular block which can be projected around the figure.

As for free-standing quality, we notice that whereas the *Moses* and the *Discobolus* are clearly meant to be walked around, the *Khafre* is not. And yet the latter is almost completely disengaged from its background, so that it serves as a transitional example of a figure between the free-standing state and the relief.

Moving from the hard diorite of the Egyptian sculpture with its need for permanence, generality, and almost inhuman dignity and impressiveness, we come to the softer marble of *Moses*. Here also a tight concentrated form is limited by the still perceptible original lines of the rectangular block. But the requirements of High Renaissance art were quite different from those of Egyptian art, and techniques had changed enormously. In spite of the block form, there is a feeling of real movement within its scope.

The Egyptian sculptor had arrested movement by bringing all the lines into a parallel relationship with the ground so that eyes, shoulders, hips, and feet were in planes parallel to each other (what is known as frontality) ; but the Renaissance artist, while retaining the integrity of the block and not venturing beyond it, was interested in communicating movement. Arms cross each other, the head is turned away from the body, and the legs are drawn back from the front line of the block to differing degrees. Moreover, the elements are so arranged that, instead of the static frontality and parallelism of the Egyptian, they have a dynamic spiral movement characteristic of Michelangelo's work.

Beginning at the lower left and moving right, up and around again to the left in a continuous counter-clockwise fashion, the movement is carried along the left arm, left across the back, through the right hand up into the beard, and finally out into space by way of the head.

This procedure conveys not only movement in general but psychological release from the self-imposed restrictions of the block. It also projects a state of tension in resolving the conflict between the block and the spiral movement. The tightly integrated form used by Michelangelo has been adopted by many later sculptors and is still in favor today.

As for considerations of the medium and its influence, for the Egyptian sculptor the hard diorite almost imposed a generalized form and a lack of detail. The softer marble used by the Italian enabled him to achieve his desire for greater naturalism, for psychological quality and detail of feature and clothing.

The *Discobolus,* another example of free-standing sculpture, was originally made of bronze, which enabled the artist to attain freedom of movement and loosening of the figure. Greek artists of the fifth century B.C., feeling the need for greater liberation of form than their predecessors had used, developed a freer medium. This work is an example of the increasingly esthetic interests of the ancient Greeks. In addition to their primarily functional religious and commemorative art, they also created much of what we would call today "art for art's sake" (see below, *Bronze and other metals*).

The really important difference between a work like the *Discobolus* and the two other figures discussed lies in the abandonment of the block form, which frees the figure to express movement. Where the Egyptian figure signifies permanence and power and the later Italian figure the frustrations of the artist and the age itself, that of Myron symbolizes an abstract quality which we can call motion. What concerns the Greek master is the general sense of movement and the way the human form, by being presented in a certain manner (here in a continuous arc), may express this sense. Toward that end, the violation of the block, seen in the way the figure leans far outside it, is actually helpful.

Figures of this type—and classical Greek and Roman art abound in examples—emphasize the silhouette of the sculpture rather than the block form or the violent tensions stressed in other categories. From whichever angle we look at a piece of classical sculpture, it presents, or should present, an interesting silhouette or linear movement for the eye to follow. In the *Discobolus,* the chief linear arrangement is through the right arm—shoulders—left arm—left leg. A countercurve

Fig. 89. *Horsemen* (marble), detail from Panathenaic Frieze of Parthenon. London, British Museum.

is offered by the silhouette going through the head—torso—right thigh, thus effecting an interesting stabilization of forces as one curve moves around to the right, the other to the left.

Relief Sculpture

Traditionally we distinguish between free-standing sculpture like the *Discobolus* and *Moses* and relief sculpture. This involves figures that are part of or sunken into a background. To express it somewhat differently, we may consider relief sculpture as projected or raised from a background against which it is seen "in relief." Two well-known examples of this art are the *Panathenaic Procession* from the Parthenon in Athens (Fig. 89, p. 136) and the so-called *Paradise Gates* from the Baptistery of the Cathedral of Florence (Figs. 90 and 90a, pp. 138, 139).

These two works exemplify the range of dimension of relief sculpture in actual feet and inches as well as the range of relief, or detachment from the background. The Parthenon relief is 4 feet 4 inches high, while the panels of the Baptistery doors are each 2 feet high and the entire doorway is 18½ feet high. These examples, of course, do not begin to exhaust the possibilities of dimension for relief sculpture, but they give a fair idea of the fact that, like free-standing sculpture, relief sculpture is to a certain extent controlled by the needs of the moment.

As to the height of relief, the degree of projection from the background, the Greek work is far less detached than the Italian, in which some of the figures are almost completely disengaged. Furthermore, in the Greek work the figures tend to be more or less on the same level of relief, while in the Italian there is a range from very low to medium and high which sums up the possibilities in this direction. We generally speak of low relief, medium relief, or high relief. All of these are illustrated here and indicate the nearness of figures shown in high relief, the relative distance of figures seen in middle relief, and the far removal in space of figures carved in low relief—which are the most difficult to see clearly. There is one further type, not illustrated here, known as hollow relief, or intaglio, where the forms are either incised into the surface or, better, sunk below the surface in reverse relief.

Both the Greek and Italian works are parts of buildings and are designed for that purpose, the former for the wall behind the outer columns of the temple, the latter for one of the entrance doors of the Baptistery of Florence. This is the traditional role of the relief sculpture; it has until very recently played a functional part. Today, however, such artists as Matisse and Arp (Fig. 91, p. 140) and many others create relief sculptures for esthetic purposes alone, without reference to architecture.

The two traditional examples we have discussed differ in their esthetic quality rather than in their function. The earlier one reflects the relatively nonspatial character of Greek art with its neutrality of atmosphere. The far greater spatial naturalism of the gates is due to the increasing humanistic needs of fifteenth-century Italy with its accentuation of realistic anatomy, perspective, and other such developments.

Fig. 90. LORENZO GHIBERTI: Paradise Gates (bronze). Florence, Italy, Baptistery of the Cathedral of Florence. (Photo courtesy Italian Tourist Information Office)

Modern Concepts of Sculptural Form

Although one could perhaps retain the categories of free-standing and relief for contemporary works, this distinction has now become somewhat meaningless, more in the three-dimensional, free-standing form than in the relief form. The modern relief of the Nicholson, Arp, Matisse type is still for the most part a relief. But the concept changes in the so-called free-standing sculpture of such artists as Lipchitz, Moore, Gabo, Pevsner, Callery, Calder, Lassaw, and Roszak (see Figs. 82–85, pp. 127–130). Although we can undoubtedly walk around most of these works, we can also (at least visually) go *through* them. In addition, they are so conceived that their various parts often penetrate or move to penetrate each other, seriously transforming the nature of the space that is filled or partially filled. It is in such works that we see how traditional attitudes toward sculpture have been changed by the artists themselves and that consequently the spectator's attitude is also subject to change.

Fig. 90a. LORENZO GHIBERTI: *The Creation,* panel from Paradise Gates. Florence, Italy, Baptistery of the Cathedral of Florence. (Photo courtesy Italian Tourist Information Office)

Fig. 91. JEAN ARP: *Relief,* 1930 (painted wood). New York, Collection Mrs. George Henry Warren, Jr. (Photo courtesy The Museum of Modern Art)

The Materials and Techniques of Sculpture

Terra cotta. As an art medium, terra cotta was one of man's earliest vehicles of expression, appearing in prehistoric times, and the Egyptians, Greeks, Chinese, and peoples of India later brought its use to a high artistic level. The term itself describes various types of baked clay which have been shaped into a desired form. Popularly known as pottery, terra-cotta ware may be finished with lustrous glazes or left unglazed. It has been produced in both ways during ancient times (we should note especially the brilliant works of the Chinese Sung dynasty) and more recently, as can be seen in the works of the sentimental fifteenth-century Della Robbia family in Italy (Fig. 92, p. 141) and the charming eighteenth-century Frenchman Clodion. In the more decorative early twentieth-century productions of the Wiener Werkstätte in Austria, and in the contemporary imaginative creations of Picasso (see Fig. 236, p. 439), we find further examples.

The advantages of terra cotta have kept it in use through the ages. First, in an art the materials of which are generally difficult to handle, terra cotta is easy to manipulate—the original clay is built up on a metal framework, or armature, and then baked inexpensively. Secondly, after it is baked, it becomes one of the most durable media, not subject to decay, erosion, or cracking, although of course it can be broken readily by shock.

A third advantage lies in the color possibilities of terra cotta—consider the delicately toned Della Robbia reliefs and the vividly colored Picasso birds. These color effects may be attained either through the use of different colored clays or through the addition of a coating of differently hued glazes, baked into the surface of the sculpture during a second firing process in the kiln, or baking oven. The final advantage is in the reproduction potential of this medium, which makes additional copies available from the original model. A reverse hollow mold is prepared from the original object, and subsequent pressings made

Fig. 92. ANDREA DELLA ROBBIA: *Annunciation* (glazed terra cotta). La Verna, Italy, Chiesa Maggiore.

from it are in their turn put through the kiln—to be fired, glazed, or treated in any way the sculptor wishes.

The colorful and decorative possibilities of terra cotta made it attractive to architects for use on the exteriors of buildings, especially in the ancient Mediterranean world. In modern times it has enjoyed a strong revival, and many American sculptors today are using this medium. Our own period, with its reduction in the size of dwellings and apartments, has made the small terra cotta and the equally small bronze the only two types of sculpture feasible for the home.

For the sculptor, terra cotta offers perhaps the greatest advantages of all materials in its color, texture, price, reproduction, and size. Its range may be appreciated by contrasting the smooth limpid softness and charm of a Della Robbia plaque with the deliberately rough texture and expressive vigor of the Picasso bird figurine. It may also be seen in the contrast between small graceful T'ang statuettes and monumental architectural reliefs, such as those produced in antiquity or the modern example on the pediment of the Philadelphia Museum of Art.

Bronze and other metals. Another method in which the sculptor works from a clay model to a furnace-treated final form is bronze casting. This material came into use long after the various types of clay, but its history goes as far back as the Bronze Age itself (*c.* 3000–1000 B.C.). Ancient China, Crete, and Egypt as early as the third millennium B.C. had mastered the technique of bronze sculpture. Bronze was widely used during the classical Greek period (see the *Discobolus*) and was also utilized by the Etruscans in Italy and other ancient folk. Through the Middle Ages, the Renaissance, and modern times it has retained its agelong popularity (see Gates of Paradise, Fig. 90a, p. 139).

As with terra cotta, the sculptor can make his original model in clay, from which a casting is made in bronze metal by a not too difficult process. Moreover, the casting may be reproduced almost perfectly and in quantity. The greatest and most apparent advantage of the metal lies in its tensile strength, its ability to be subjected to shock, bending, or other strain without cracking or breaking. This quality has the further and more significant benefit of permitting the sculptor to arrange his figure in poses that would be impossible in terra cotta, stone, or other brittle materials. The most obvious application of this is in the execution of figures in bent or otherwise straining postures: a leaping animal, a dancer on her toes, an athlete throwing a ball. In such works the figure is necessarily out of balance; in marble or terra cotta the strain of its weight might be too great, whereas the tensile strength of the bronze is more than sufficient to bear the extra burden.

In Remington's *The Bronco Buster* (Fig. 93, p. 144), where the horse rears on its hind legs and the rider leans forward, we might imagine that an almost impossible amount of imbalance and strain would be involved. Yet the fact is that the largest element—the horse's body—is hollow, as is the figure of the man, so that the weight is not nearly so great as it seems. The points of worst strain, the hind legs of the horse, are reinforced, or "loaded," with an extra amount of metal in order to bear what is required of them. Thus weight is taken away from those areas where it would potentially do the most damage and added where it will do the most good.

Another and even more striking technical advantage of the bronze medium is demonstrated in the *Discobolus* (Figs. 86 and 86a, p. 132) by Myron, Greek sculptor of the fifth century B.C. The creation of such figures became possible in the first place because of the development of the bronze technique, which liberated the human form and allowed it to move freely in various directions, to bend and twist without endangering the sculpture. Interestingly enough, since most of our knowledge of ancient Greek sculpture comes from later Roman copies in marble, we find the *Discobolus* executed in that material, for which it was never intended. The copyist who used marble because it was fashionable at the time was forced to reinforce the figure with a tree-trunk section at the base—manifestly absurd for discus throwing but necessary inasmuch as great strain is imposed at that point and marble is a brittle material. Copies of this type also show props inserted between arms and bodies and elsewhere. We shall see how the method of making the bronze sculpture overcomes the limitations of marble and other such materials.

Another advantage of bronze is that since it is finally cast from a clay original, as many details as desired can be worked into that original in a perfectly natural way as the figure is modeled. The final point of gain is the wide range of color finish permitted, extending from a pale but intense gold through a series of browns, reds, and greens. These patinas or finishes can be formed artificially with the aid of

Fig. 93. FREDERIC REMINGTON: *The Bronco Buster* (bronze). Courtesy James Graham & Sons.

acids or will form themselves with exposure to the air, which causes oxidation or other chemical reactions in the metal.

Bronzes are cast from a clay model that is generally built up around a metal armature, or skeletal framework, which supports the weight of the clay. The model is then prepared for casting by making a negative, or reverse, mold of it in a material such as plaster or gelatin. This is done by painting the outside of the model with the plaster or gelatin, which then takes on all the details of the original model in reverse. The negative is removed and split, and on its inner surface a coating of molten wax is brushed in successive layers until it reaches the thickness the artist wants for his final bronze. The artist can work on this still soft wax for last details.

Then the inside and the outside of the hollow wax figure are covered with a mixture of quickly hardening, fire-resistant materials such as silica, plaster, and other chemicals—or plain pipe clay. Between the inner and outer layers of this fire-resistant material lies the easily meltable wax. The model is put in the oven and the wax is drawn off

144   THE MEANING OF SCULPTURE

through a previously prepared series of gates and vents attached to the model. After the wax is melted out, the resultant hollow space is filled by molten bronze which, as it pours into each area, replaces the wax in exact detail and is held in shape by the fire-resistant inner and outer sections.

After the bronze has cooled sufficiently, the inner and outer sections are removed, and the bronze is cleaned in an acid bath. At this point it may be given an artificial patina or finish. The method we have just described, the one most generally used in bronze casting, is known as the *lost wax,* or *cire perdue,* method, from the fact that the wax has been melted away or lost.

Although bronze has been the most popular metal used in sculpture and has the longest history, other metal media have also been utilized traditionally. Among these we find brass, mentioned in the Old Testament and used in classical antiquity as well as in the Middle Ages. In times past it was beaten out in sheets; today it is made in cast form. The cleanliness of its traditional high polish is one of its most attractive features, although it tarnishes rapidly if not kept in condition.

Copper, too, is known to have been used in prehistoric times, then by the Egyptians and the Mesopotamian peoples, all of whom found its high malleability advantageous. It is softer than brass and more readily worked, possessing at the same time great strength and resistance to corrosion in the air. Although it does not flow in its molten state as readily as does bronze, it, together with tin, forms the basis for all types of bronze as well as of brasses and many other alloys. It is best used when sheets of the metal are to be hammered, twisted, or pressed into the required form. In the same way gold, lead, pewter, and tin may be handled in sheets and fashioned into three-dimensional as well as relief forms, each with its own coloristic and textural qualities.

Iron also may be hammered, particularly when it is heated. Handled in this way, it is spoken of as wrought iron. Modern sculptors, increasingly aware of the possibilities of this medium, have wrought in iron with the aid of the welding torch a variety of expressive and powerfully imaginative abstract forms, such as the work of the American David Smith.

Sculptors in the new Abstract Expressionist or Abstract Surrealist mode have also utilized steel, aluminum (Calder, Rivera, Roszak), plastic metal (Lassaw), nickel-silver (Lipton), and other metals (Figs. 63, 82, 83, and 85, pp. 99, 127, 128, 130). The addition of many new media in the metals has enriched the possibilities of sculpture. These developments remind us that we are living in a highly technological century—one that has produced many new materials that can be used to express the dynamics of our age.

There is another series of newcomers, some unheard of in the past: plastic wood, plywood, molded glass, and a host of synthetic substances known as plastics, which—either singly or in various combinations— have been used successfully for sculpture, as in the work of the Russian-born artists Gabo and Pevsner (Fig. 84, p. 129). This group of new materials, however, has found its greatest application in the field of industrial design, which will be discussed later.

Stone. Stone as a sculpture medium can be carved, chipped, or cut and has its own advantages as well as liabilities. It is more difficult to work with than clay, which is easily molded and cast, but it is more permanent than terra cotta and more translucent and grainy than bronze. In addition, many sculptors find the actual physical resistance of stone an exciting and stimulating feature.

This very quality of resistance makes it necessary for the artist to have a clearly defined idea of what he wants, since he cannot improvise in stone as he does in clay. This quality, furthermore, may give stone sculpture an impressive austerity of form, as in Egyptian statues of basalt or granite. Stone also has the advantage of associating itself readily with stone architecture, and thus through the ages (in Egypt, Greece, medieval Europe) its use has found high favor.

The color characteristics of stone may differentiate it from other sculptural media. For instance, the whiteness of marble, as well as its softness of texture, makes it admirable for portraiture, especially of women and children, for whose soft faces darker bronze or wood would not be nearly so appropriate. When we look at the edge of a marble against the light or out of doors, we see a translucency or glow that is very affecting (see *Hermes,* Fig. 136, p. 223). The whiteness of marble is well suited to garden sculpture, where the contrast is striking between the white of the stone and the greenery—a contrast not possible with bronze, which often turns green out of doors, or wood, the darkness of which makes it less visible.

At the other extreme from marble, coloristically speaking, is the black *Javanese Panther* (Fig. 81, p. 126) by Mateo Hernández, a modern Spanish sculptor. Here the color as well as the texture of the stone lends considerable authenticity to the feelings of sleekness, power, and menace the artist wishes to convey.

Stone varies in color so that we may find a gray or black granite (the latter illustrated in William Zorach's well-known *Head of Christ*), a gray or red sandstone, a black or white marble. Other color effects in stone are supplied by such materials as bluestone, brownstone, and onyx, or by the actual application of color to the stone. This latter method was widely practiced by ancient and medieval craftsmen and is being followed again today by artists like Eric Gill.

Just as marbles achieve part of their effect by smoothness of texture, other types of stone transmit different stimuli: the matte quality of limestone, the harshness of granite, the roughness of sandstone.

Stone sculpture always uses a carved rather than a modeled or shaped technique, unlike clay and its variants. The actual process of carving the stone may be indirect or direct. In the indirect method the artist prepares a full-scale model in plaster of Paris cast from a clay figure. This plaster model becomes the basis for exact measurements that are transferred to the marble or other stone block from which the final figure is to be carved. The measurements are transferred by means of a pointing machine—an upright bar with a series of adjustable horizontals swinging from it crosswise. With these cross-bars a given section is measured on the model, and its dimensions are transferred mathematically and proportionately to the final block.

Since this is a relatively mechanical process, it generally happens that the "pointing" and much of the later carving itself can be done by artisan carvers rather than by the sculptor himself. In addition to the potential loss of spontaneity inherent in such a method, there is the problem of adapting the marble or other stone to an expression first articulated in plaster. On the other hand, this indirect method is economical and safe—economical in its distinct saving of effort for the sculptor and safe in that the possibility of mistake, so great in the direct method, is almost completely eliminated.

The direct method involves the sculptor in a series of drawings and models, the fruit of which are transferred to the stone. The artist may draw directly on the block (as also on wood) for his proportions and

THE MATERIALS AND TECHNIQUES OF SCULPTURE 147

general form indications, but as he goes along, the details and actual feeling of the work develop, so that there is a direct and permanent contact between the artist's idea and the finished result. In this direct method we are also keenly aware of the nature of the medium, which is the direct carver's primary interest. He is always concerned with the texture of the material and even with the shape of the block from which his figure is basically derived. The shape of the block may determine and will certainly affect the result.

The direct artist uses relatively few tools. He blocks out his forms in a general way, working carefully as he removes the excess material so as not to take away too much, a mistake which could not be remedied except by altering the design. While the possibility of making an error in this direct process may appear frightening, it has the virtue of forcing a certain spontaneity on the sculptor.

As in most types of oil painting, the direct carving already exists as an organic entity at the very beginning of the work. It moves along the various steps as a whole, that is, the entire production develops from the first to the second to the third stage. The artist is constantly working on the whole piece, keeping the various parts on a level with each other.

This method is represented by the carvings of Michelangelo (see Fig. 87, p. 133), a sculptor noted for his direct attack on the marble and for his awareness of the nature of the material and the very shape of the block itself. In some works we find this sculptor purposely leaving certain portions of the figure roughed-out, the small details remaining unpolished, as in the head of the Evening figure on the tomb of Lorenzo de' Medici. In other cases, like the David, the work is conditioned by the enormous and long shape of the marble block. There is a passage in one of Michelangelo's sonnets in which he says that the sculptor does not invent anything that is not already inherently in the marble.

In the post-Renaissance and modern periods up through the nineteenth century, the spontaneous and direct carving method gradually gave way to the indirect method. Especially useful in creating large areas of architectural decoration, the indirect method, applied even to individual figures, prevailed until very recently. Within the past generation, however, the direct method has come back into favor.

Wood. Wood is a relatively perishable material, subject to splitting from temperature changes, warping from moisture, and disintegra-

Fig. 94 (*left*). ERNST BARLACH:
Freezing Girl (wood). Hamburg,
Germany. Reemstma Collection.
Fig. 95 (*below*). Top of a Mirror
Case (ivory). New York. Metropoli-
tan Museum of Art.

tion from the attacks of termites. It is further limited by its grain,
which enforces a certain type of cutting and thereby curtails the artist's freedom. On the other hand, the variety of woods available to
the sculptor is almost endless in texture, color, and degree of hardness.
A well-known handbook on sculpture lists eighty-five separate and distinct types of wood with subvarieties under pine (forty varieties),
oak, mahogany, macaya, ebony, and others.

On the positive side, wood is usually much lighter than stone, varies more in hardness, offers a high degree of workability, and lends itself to application of external painting and gilding. Finally, it enables
sculpture to exist in areas where stone is neither readily accessible nor
sufficiently cheap. Its grain offers certain special esthetic stimuli, particularly along the lines of roughnesses and smoothnesses (see Barlach,
Fig. 94, p. 149). This grain can be incorporated into the artist's design as a series of concentric curves, parallel linear indications, or in
other ways.

Whereas in traditional stonework—by Michelangelo, Egyptians, and so on—we are aware of the block form from which the artist started, in wood the log, with which the carver usually begins, gives the work a generally cylindrical quality. Wood sculpture, like stone, is basically a subtracting process, with large masses of material cut away to bring forth the final form. As in stonework, there is a sensation of the figure having been torn from the original piece of material.

Ivory. Although today so-called "ivories" are for the most part commercial souvenirs and not really made of ivory, in centuries past this material produced a number of interesting art forms: the book covers and cosmetic boxes of the Middle Ages and the figurines of the ancient Mediterranean and the Far East (see *Snake Goddess,* Fig. 182, p. 320). Like wood, ivory is vulnerable to temperature changes and must therefore be cared for with this frailty in mind.

As a rare and expensive material, traditional ivory (the tusks of elephants and often of walrus or hippopotamus) was used for such items of luxury and prestige as the charming religious objects of the fourteenth century or the jewel and cosmetic boxes of that time (Fig. 95, p. 149). This material also looks the part of an aristocratic substance —chaste, pure, and remote in its white surface, customarily small and elegant in the forms it produces.

As with wood, its grain must be followed, a limiting factor in many ways. Also as in wood, its relatively unstable structure leads to cracking and warping; this, as well as its cost, makes the sculptor limit its use to relatively small and compact compositions.

Sculpture and the Other Arts

It is customary to make sharp distinctions between the various arts, if only for purposes of classification; but the fact remains that in both quality and function the arts are closely related. Architecture may have a flowing or decorative and hence more pictorial character, as in the Moorish mosques and palaces which are primarily surface ornament and color rather than structure. In the same way, architectural emphasis on light and dark modulations, as in the church of *San Carlo alle Quattro Fontane* (See Fig. 214, p. 388), is sculpturesque in quality.

Painting can also partake of the qualities of other arts. Such works as Michelangelo's *Creation of Adam* (Fig. 35, p. 57) are distinctly sculpturesque in character, emphasizing three-dimensionality and giving the illusion of sculptured forms. Paintings like Mondrian's *Composition* (Fig. 33, p. 50), emphasizing structural values and constructional interests, may be called architectonic. Sculpture, too, may be related to the other arts—it may be either pictorial or architectonic. It may also be used in conjunction with either or both of those arts. Sculpture and architecture have made a traditional combination throughout history, sometimes adding painting as well in wall, dome, or altar. In the modern world, as a result of the presumable need for keeping the line of the building pure, this functional relationship has been much less stressed, eliminating an important outlet for the modern painter and sculptor. In buildings like the Greek temples and Gothic cathedrals, the integrated relationship and functioning of architecture and sculpture reach a high point.

In the Parthenon, for example (Fig. 62a, p. 97), there were four distinct types of sculpture: the monumental inside statue of Athena (Fig. 62, p. 96), the larger than life-size figures of the pediments (see Fig. 184, p. 322), the smaller than life-size figures in the metopes, or square spaces over the columns (Fig. 96, p. 152), and finally the frieze (Fig. 89, p. 136) set on the outside of the enclosing wall of the temple. All four varieties of sculpture were made for particular spots in the building, each being given a size, height of relief, color background, and so forth, in keeping with its function. In the Parthenon frieze the relief varies in height of modeling; the top is in higher relief than the bottom, since the lighting, coming from below through the spaces between the columns, would leave the upper portion less lighted and needing more visibility. Yet the frieze in general, alone on the wall, is in low relief, since there is nothing to distract the spectator.

The metope reliefs, however, which are set among distracting architectural details, show a degree of relief considerably higher. The pedimental figures (as the *Theseus*), the most important part of the external sculptural decoration, were made larger than life-size both because of their symbolic importance and because they had to be visible at a considerable distance from the ground. In addition, the brilliant reflective quality of the marble was overcome to a certain extent by tinting the individual figures, which presumably were placed against a blue-black background that would make them more visible.

Another excellent example of sculptural integration with architecture is in the Gothic cathedrals of the thirteenth century. *Le Beau Dieu* of Amiens (Fig. 24, p. 37) was made for the particular spot on which it is now found. It was carved apart from the building and put into place on the pedestal left for it, under the little canopy planned for its ultimate appearance. Gothic sculptures of this type are perhaps more integrated with their buildings than those Greek works that have an appeal and importance even apart from the building. The Parthenon metopes and reliefs, and even the *Theseus,* can be enjoyed for themselves, while *Le Beau Dieu* with its straight up-and-down rectangular form seems to be comfortable only in the niche—which, in its turn, looks like a gaping tooth space without the sculpture.

Seen apart from their destined places, many Gothic sculptures give this feeling of incompleteness. We know that the integration was consciously designed, because we may contrast an earlier example of cathedral sculpture, the façade of Chartres Cathedral (Fig. 97, p. 153), where the architect-sculptor has tried to affix the figures to the face of the building. His idea was to attach the sculptures to the columns without benefit of niches or canopies and to elongate and flatten the forms accordingly. A simple comparison of the style of the Chartres and the Amiens figures shows a movement toward naturalistic proportions, solidity of form, and three-dimensionality.

By the time of the Renaissance, however, the integration of sculpture with its architectural background gave way before the creation of a considerable number of free-standing figures, usually the product of an individual artist (rather than a group) for an individual patron. Although there were still works like the Della Robbia plaques (Fig. 92, p. 141), made for a particular place in a church or other public building, the tendency was in the other direction. The Renaissance also placed great emphasis on the difference between the various arts, even though most of its great men (Leonardo, Michelangelo, Raphael) were proficient in several fields.

During the Renaissance an increased interest in naturalistic effects of perspective and anatomy was reflected in a more pictorial type of sculpture that concerned itself less with simple volumes, as in classical and medieval art, and more with sensations of movement in depth and illusions of reality. The Gates of Paradise by Ghiberti from the Bap-

Fig. 97 (left). *Saints and Royal Personages,* Façade of West Portal. Chartres, France, Chartres Cathedral. Fig. 98 (right). GIOVANNI LORENZO BERNINI: *Ecstasy of St. Theresa.* Rome, Santa Maria della Vittoria.

tistery of Florence (Fig. 90a, p. 139) illustrate a pictorialism not usually associated with sculpture. Each panel on this bronze door suggests a framed picture in its clearly marked and accentuated feeling of physical recession. The lines converge toward the horizon in linear perspective, and the figures fade into the background, changing from high relief in the foreground to middle relief and finally to low relief for those figures that are supposed to be far away from the spectator.

Another noteworthy pictorial sculpture is the famous *Ecstasy of St. Theresa* (Fig. 98, p. 153) by Bernini, where the operatic tendencies of the Baroque reach a logical climax (see Baroque and Rococo art, Chapter 16). The mass and weight of the Renaissance figure (see Donatello, Fig. 199, p. 347) give way here before a dematerialized— that is, spiritual rather than material—concept. The draperies in motion hide the solidity of the form, open the contour lines of the earlier sculpture, substitute indefinite for definite impressions, accentuate startling light and dark contrasts, and stress the emotional at all costs. The saint and the angel are placed on a formless cloud, floating in insubstantiality, bathed in the supernal golden light descending from above, as divine love pours down on the ecstatic saint. White marble, Bernini's special medium, is warmed by the golden pictorial effects of the rays of light and the colored columns behind the group.

The entire complex is set within an architectural framework of luxurious columns arranged under a broken and backward-bending pediment on which the elements of architecture are used brilliantly, if unconventionally. The mixture of sculpture, pictorial character, and architecture is indeed unconventional, but no more so than in other arts of the time. The grand opera mingles instrumental music, vocal music, the dance, painting, and architecture in what may be a "bastard art" but is nevertheless as genuine a manifestation of the period as is the *Ecstasy of St. Theresa*.

The question of the relationship of the various arts arises again in modern times. As noted elsewhere, the more advanced architects have tended until recently to exclude sculpture and painting from their calculations. During the past few years, however, there has been a change in attitude, resulting in such works as the José de Rivera steel *Construction* for the Statler-Hilton Hotel in Dallas (Fig. 63, p. 99), the Lipton sculptures for synagogues (Fig. 85, p. 130), and the Gottlieb stained-glass window in a synagogue in New York. In painting—

sculpturesque, architectonic, or purely pictorial—we find as ready a crossing of lines as before.

Jacques Lipchitz, the distinguished contemporary sculptor, has said: "To me there is no difference between painting and sculpture; they are like two different musical instruments. For instance, a violin and a piano. Naturally each has a different sonority, and different techniques are required to master them. But the important thing is the music they produce." This is surely a far cry from the belief attributed to Michelangelo concerning the superiority of sculpture over painting. It is perhaps a reflection of the more fluid attitude of the modern artist toward the materials of art—an attitude felt especially in the work of our contemporary sculptors where, for various reasons, it is often difficult to believe that we are dealing any longer with the traditional art of sculpture.

Painting and Its Techniques

▶ 6

THE ART OF PAINTING, lacking the obvious practicality of architecture or the inherent three-dimensionality of sculpture, makes a special appeal to the sensitivity and application of its audience. This appeal is quite different from that of architecture, where the mundane function of a building, its understandable machinelike quality, its interior spaciousness, and other factors are easily absorbed; and it is different from that of sculpture which may interest us through its mass, monumentality, physical balance, or violent projection into space.

Technically, painting is the art of spreading pigments, or liquid color, on a flat surface (canvas, panel, wall, paper) to produce the sensation or illusion of space, movement, texture, and form, as well as the tensions resulting from combinations of these elements. It is understood, of course, that through these technical devices are expressed the intellectual, emotive, symbolic, religious, and other subjective values presented elsewhere in this book. Sometimes it is difficult to mark the line between painting and drawing, because both arts apply colored materials to a surface of a different color; but painting usually involves the use of a brush and of fluid color.

From the beginning of recorded time, painting has been associated with religion, as in the prehistoric cave paintings of southern France and northern Spain (see Fig. 28, p. 42), Egyptian tomb painting, and other examples. During the Greco-Roman period, its scope was broadened to include everyday subjects of various kinds, landscape, and

156

commemorative portraits; but the end of the Classical age brought about a sharp decline in the functions of this art. During the Middle Ages painting was confined to use as decorations on church walls and illustrations for religious texts on the pages of manuscripts (see Fig. 50, p. 79).

With the Renaissance and the growth of humanistic interests, however, portraits and depictions of pagan subjects and historical references appeared in quantity (Figs. 8, 20, and 43a, pp. 21, 33, 72). By the seventeenth century the art of landscape emerged once more, and genre (everyday) material was more important than ever (Fig. 32, p. 50). Since the nineteenth century, painting has added to its already extensive repertoire a whole series of purely esthetic or artistic subjects, as "art for art's sake" has become one of the chief motivations for pictorial creation (Fig. 33, p. 50). Continuous experimentation with form, space, and other purely artistic sensations or values has led to new concepts of painting that are frequently at great variance with traditional notions. Yet these changes have occurred within an art the techniques of which remain substantially what they were centuries ago. Conversely, the only area in which important technical changes have been made is Mexico, where synthetic paints have recently been developed but where the stylistic changes are not extreme.

An important modern viewpoint on painting is expressed by Maurice Denis in *Theories,* in which he says: "One must remember that a painting before being a warhorse, a female nude or some sort of anecdote, is essentially a flat surface covered with colors that are assembled in a certain order." Although Denis belonged to a late nineteenth-century school that was still interested in subject matter, the important point he makes here—and it is suitable to much subsequent modern painting from Cézanne on—is that painting is primarily an affair of arranging colors in a certain way. We may appreciate the possibilities of such arrangement when we recognize, among other things, the significance of light and shadow in creating roundness and form, or the forward movement of warm colors and the backward movement of cool ones.

The Painter Creates an Illusion

Movement and depth. The effects of painting, as our definition implies, are *suggested;* its tensions do not result from one mass actually coming into conflict with another, as is often the case in sculpture, but rather from an implied visual contrast that is not always immediately apparent. To illustrate, let us look again at the conflict between the block from which the Michelangelo *Moses* (Fig. 87, p. 133) was cut and the tight spiral movement within the figure as it moves from left to right, rising from the bottom—up, around, and out. This piece of sculpture stands surrounded by its own three-dimensionality, independent in form and clear-cut in direction. Once the movement is indicated, it is fairly easy to see, especially in the absence of distracting stimuli.

If we take a comparable painting, the same artist's *Jeremiah* (Fig. 25, p. 38), we find that we are looking at the additional element of color as well as at smaller figures in the background and architectural enframements. More important, since the artist as painter works from an absolutely flat surface, he (and we) must work harder to realize the three-dimensional effect of tension. Whereas in sculpture the effect of a withdrawn foot is quite direct, as it would be in real life, in painting the artist has created an *illusion* of that effect by foreshortening the legs so that they appear to be withdrawn.

An extreme instance of the necessity for understanding the language of painting is shown in Mondrian's *Composition* (Fig. 33, p. 50) where the backward and forward movement is abetted by the colors used. A less extreme example is the *Descent from the Cross* by Rubens (Fig. 17, p. 29) where the conflict of masses is much clearer. But here also, beyond the mere straining of muscles, we have special tricks of color and lighting that help the artist and the spectator to realize the required tensions.

In the Rubens painting, as in the Michelangelo sculpture, there is a similar tension between the shape of the frame and the curved diagonality of movement—here crossing from upper right through lower left. The painting also shows a Michelangelesque straining and power due to influence from the earlier artist, direct and indirect. Yet to achieve its full force, the Rubens painting flares out at the corners, adding another source of tension. There is also a backward and forward motion of individual figures, who palpitate continually in a typical Baroque manner that is far more complex than the relatively concentrated movement of the *Moses*.

We must also consider the function of light in creating the illusion

Fig. 99. LEONARDO DA VINCI: *The Last Supper*. Milan, Italy, Santa Maria delle Grazie.

of movement and depth. In sculpture the effects of light are immediately perceptible to the degree that they are reflected from a surface of stone, metal, or wood. Light in painting works in a less obvious manner. It may be reflected back into the eyes of the spectator as in the *Malle Bobbe* (Fig. 12, p. 24), but even here the action is more subtle than in sculpture. By the very nature of the oil medium, here, or in the *Descent from the Cross,* light is controlled by the painter; he may cause it to fall on opaque surface color and to be reflected at once or allow it to penetrate a transparent surface color and become absorbed by the dark underpainting. On the one hand, we see a bright surface; on the other, a relatively dark one. (See below, *Oil,* pp. 170–179).

Spatial devices. The attempt to simulate the third dimension, which in sculpture and architecture is an actuality, has evoked through the ages a whole series of spatial devices. In older art—Michelangelo's *Creation of Adam* (Fig. 35, p. 57) and *Jeremiah;* Vermeer's *Young Woman with a Water Jug* (Fig. 32, p. 50) —such devices can easily be seen. In the reclining figure of Adam, Michelangelo gives us the illusion of a forward-moving right forearm by the device known as *fore-*

shortening. That is, by an abrupt convergence of the lines of the arm, that member is made to thrust forward toward us.

Similarly, in the Vermeer painting there is a related device known as *linear perspective* in which convergence of the lines makes the table assume its naturalistic appearance of moving away from the front line to the rear. Perhaps the best known and most dramatic instance of the working of linear perspective is the *Last Supper* by Leonardo da Vinci (Fig. 99, p. 159) where a tremendous pull backward to the head of the Christ is caused by the converging lines of the table, ceiling, and walls.

The two chief purposes of perspective are to give a sense of movement into the picture space and to make visually credible the fact that figures farther away are more difficult to see. This phenomenon, which we have all experienced, is a matter of diminishing both size and clarity. The former is diminished through linear perspective, which reproduces on a flat surface what happens when the rays of light from a distant object come into the eye. If we trace lines from the top and bottom of such an object through the diagramed lens of the eye and onto its retina, we find that those lines will measure a smaller image on the retina when the eye is farther away than when it is nearer.

The diminishing of clarity occurs in nature because the distant object viewed is out of focus so far as the capabilities of the eye are concerned. In painting this is reproduced by *aerial perspective,* lessening the color strength of objects that are supposed to be farther away. If we look at Raphael's *Alba Madonna* (Fig. 16, p. 28), we find a difference in color quality from foreground to middleground to background, each area becoming successively lighter and more difficult to see as it moves away from us. Other examples of this device are to be seen in the Giorgione *Concert Champêtre* and the Constable *The Hay Wain* (see Figs. 175 and 107, pp. 308, 177). Additional spatial devices will be discussed in Chapter 14.

Forms. The illusionistic devices considered so far have dealt primarily with the existence of forms within the space delineated by the painter. The three-dimensionality of the forms themselves often results from the functioning of *chiaroscuro* (literally, "light-dark"), the creation of form through either a gradual or a sudden transition from light to shadow in a painting or drawing, the change which presumably takes place in nature but which we do not always see there in such detail.

In the Leonardo *Madonna, Child, and St. Anne* (Fig. 45, p. 75)

160   PAINTING AND ITS TECHNIQUES

or the *Expulsion from the Garden* by Masaccio (see Fig. 193, p. 338) we notice the highlights on the one side of the figures, with a gradual change to a medium light and then to shadow at the other side. Most painters of the Renaissance and post-Renaissance European tradition followed this method, until the late nineteenth century when more abstract means of representation began to take its place. In the Orient, however, (see Fig. 37, p. 60) the roundness of the figure or the spatial quality of the picture as a whole do not depend on such devices, leaving the spectator a greater role in the comprehension of volume and space (see below under *Water color*).

Texture. Whereas in sculpture the realization of form and space may involve the senses of balance and touch as well as actual physical movement, in painting the impulses come into the eye, the only source of stimulation. Many paintings, for example, have pronounced textural quality, but seldom, if ever, does the occasion arise for us to touch the surface of a painting. Let us look, for instance, at Rembrandt's *Man with the Golden Helmet* (Fig. 104, p. 174). To create an impression of the richness of gold in the helmet, the painter has worked the surface up to a point where in some areas the pigment is as much as three-sixteenths of an inch above the canvas. The fact is, however, that we respond to this texture purely visually, as with any other type of textural experience in this art.

The satiny texture of the Vermeer *Young Woman with a Water Jug* (Fig. 32, p. 50) or the Terborch *The Concert* (see Fig. 237, p. 446) creates such a powerful illusion that our sense of touch responds to it without actual contact. Similarly, Impressionist and Expressionist paintings have a textural quality designed to stimulate visually certain responses from the spectator. In the case of the former (see Pissarro, *Peasants Resting,* Fig. 11, p. 24), the looked-for response is a feeling of twinkling and delicate movement across the surface. The Expressionist type of picture, on the other hand (see van Gogh, *Night Café*, Fig. 39, p. 63), gives a violent and spasmodic sensation of movement through its texture, in accord with the more powerful emotion the artist wishes to express.

Uses of Color

The Impressionist and Expressionist works also achieve their aims through the medium of color, perhaps the most important aspect of painting. Color can impart many things. The shift from warm to cold colors will give inward movement, while the manipulation of color strength will lend an illusion of aerial distance. Color can convey a sense of motion in itself, as in the sparkling and harmonious tones of the Impressionists or the more clashing and purposely inharmonious hues of the Expressionists.

Color may also have a symbolic intent and effect. Blue, for example, as often used by van Gogh, may signify the largeness of the universe. In earlier periods, when religion was a dominant factor in art, blue might symbolize Heaven, as in the *Alba Madonna* of Raphael. Red, on the other hand, is associated with violence and suffering as in van Gogh's *Night Café*, or, more specifically, in earlier periods with the sufferings of the Virgin, who is generally shown in a blue cloak with a red undergarment to combine the elements of Heaven and suffering in her person.

The symbolism of medieval or even Renaissance paintings is sometimes rather mechanical, but that of modern art is more subtle. Moreover, it is quite personal in character, so that a yellow used by one artist may have an altogether different function in another's work. The blue of Beckmann in the central panel of his triptych *Departure* (Fig. 40, p. 64) is a gentler and more lyrical blue than that of van Gogh. Here it represents the idea of distance, elapsed time into the future, and—most important—release. Whatever the painter meant at the moment of creation, some of these reactions will emerge for the spectator who is willing to extend his understanding of the picture.

The depressing greens of Lautrec, van Gogh (*Night Café*, Fig. 39, p. 63), El Greco (*View of Toledo*, Fig. 38, p. 62), Munch, and other artists represent another use of color as symbol that is certainly not accidental and that must be understood for our full appreciation. Although color plays an important part in certain types of sculpture and architecture, its use in painting is more complex, offering much more to the spectator and rewarding him accordingly.

Color in painting can also establish or help to establish tensions that are more directly important to the modern artist than to the traditional painter, although in traditional works, too, we ultimately find similar values unconsciously embodied. In the Mondrian *Composition* and the Matisse *The Young Sailor* (see Fig. 225, p. 407), certain colors are used to give the sensation of forward movement, others to give the feeling of backward or inward movement, thus setting up the conflict of opposing forces. This use may be seen in an El Greco (Fig. 38, p. 62) or a Gainsborough, but there it is secondary to the content.

Traditionally we have thought of color as an adjunct to the figures and hence to the content or story of the painting, as in the *Alba Madonna* (Fig. 16, p. 28), but this does not hold for many modern works. Very often, as in the work of Matisse (see Fig. 225), the color use will be purely esthetic or artistic, having little or nothing to do with the problem of description or the attribute of naturalism. This is not willful disregard of the facts but rather a feeling on the part of the artist that the motif or theme is merely a starting point for an exercise in form-color-space expression. His obligation, therefore, is not to tell the story of the *Bathers* or *The Young Sailor* (see Fig. 225, p. 407) but to build up a satisfying arrangement of forms, spaces, or —in Matisse's case—vivid blue, lavender, green, and red colors to convey a feeling of aliveness and movement, of visual excitement.

Although one must always realize the importance of drawing in the planning of both traditional and contemporary painting, the fact remains that the very essence of painting is color. In most of the painting media we shall investigate here, this pre-eminence remains. It is color that gives a special character to fresco, oil, tempera, water color, and other methods of painting. To fresco it gives a certain simplicity, to oil a depth, to tempera a crispness, to water color a transparency, and to other media whatever visual and symbolic quality they may possess.

Social Functions of Painting

Today most paintings are the product of studio thinking, moving from there into the home or the museum as objects of art; paintings of the past, however, had a much wider function in the life of the community. They decorated houses of worship, tombs, residences, as well as various types of public buildings such as city halls and courthouses, the modern counterparts of which are often decorated meagerly and perfunctorily. Paintings have been utilized as wall or ceiling decoration, a form of art still practiced today and known as mural painting. This term, derived from the Latin word for *wall*, has nothing to do with the actual medium used; generally speaking, mural painting in the past was done in fresco—water color on fresh plaster. A mural may also be painted on a dry wall, in oils, or in any other medium that lends itself to application on a flat surface; see, for example, Leonardo's *Last Supper* (Fig. 99, p. 159), done in oils on a special surface.

Another category is easel, sometimes also called panel painting. While the mural is fixed by definition to the wall—with the specific exception of the portable wall painting—the easel picture is made to be moved from room to room and from residence to residence. Except for fresco, which has been limited to walls, easel painting uses almost all media: oil, tempera, water color, oil and tempera mixed, as in van Eyck's *Arnolfini Marriage* (Fig. 8, p. 21), and many others.

Sharing characteristics of the portable and the fixed painting is the altarpiece, which may be moved but is generally made for a particular permanent spot, for instance, *Adoration of the Lamb* (see Fig. 103, p. 172). The altarpiece may vary considerably in size. The same is true of mural paintings, the size of which varies in accordance with that of wall or ceiling, and it is true of portable pictures, which range from miniatures to large-scale oils.

Techniques of Painting

Fresco. Let us look first at fresco, a medium with a long and far-reaching history. Although the term *fresco* comes from the Italian for *fresh* and therefore implies painting on a fresh or wet surface, there have been two types of fresco: the *fresco secco,* or dry fresco, and the *buon fresco.* The latter is the process generally described in books and was used by Giotto (Fig. 176, p. 310), Michelangelo (Fig. 35, p. 57), Masaccio (Fig. 193, p. 338), and Orozco (Fig. 207, p. 363), who painted on wet lime plaster with paints mixed with water or with water and lime. The *fresco secco* artists worked on a relatively dry wall and used, according to some authorities, paint mixed with egg and therefore closer in quality to egg tempera.

In the *buon fresco* method the limewater in the mixture forms a layer of calcium carbonate, acting as a binding medium between the pigment on the outside and the plaster wall. The permanence of this medium is proved by the survival of ancient frescoes such as those at

Knossos in Crete (see Fig. 29, p. 43) and the Roman *Theseus* (see Fig. 208, p. 365).

The *buon fresco* method, revived during the early Italian Renaissance by such painters as Giotto, is described in the famous handbook, *Il Libro dell' Arte (The Book of Art)*, by Cennino Cennini. Whereas in *fresco secco* the pigment is carried by egg and diluted by water, here the pigment is carried by water alone and applied to a wall that has had at least two coats of plaster.

According to Cennini, the painter was to apply the first coat of plaster, allow it to dry, then draw his design on it. Over this design would be applied another coat of plaster, or *intonaco,* through which the design could be seen and which would serve as the final wet base for the water-suspended paint. This process has been clarified for us by the damage done to the frescoes in the Campo Santo at Pisa during World War II.

Cennini's early-fifteenth-century formula was elaborated in the later fifteenth and early sixteenth centuries. Frescoes like Michelangelo's (Fig. 35, p. 57) received more than two coats of plaster; moreover, the designs or preliminary drawings were applied directly to the last coat of *intonaco*. Individual cartoons for each figure were transferred to the wet *intonaco* coat by tracing their lines through the paper, thus indenting them on the still moist plaster, or by pricking tiny holes through the outlines onto the wall, leaving the cartoon in place, and shaking some charcoal dust through the holes to give an outline. These outlines then remained, to be gone over with color.

Fresco painting is carefully and systematically planned and laid out, section following section with a precision that leaves little room for alteration or inspiration. The artist prepares his cartoons and lays out in advance as much of the wall as he knows through experience he can paint in one day. This section is given the final coat of *intonaco* by a plasterer, and the appropriate full-size cartoon is outlined on the wall by the painter. After finishing the actual painting of that area, he allows the section to dry. The following day, another section of plaster is prepared, and the same procedure is followed.

Progress from one day's work to another can often be traced by the joins between the various days' plastering. In *The Creation of Adam,* there is a join where the neck fits into the top of the chest and another at the hip bones across the body. From this we deduce that the 12-foot-long figure was painted in three sessions.

There are relative advantages and disadvantages to the fresco method. On the positive side, it is an almost permanent medium suited to the needs of architecture, lasting as long as the building itself, having a monumentally broad, usually undetailed, and simple effect that can be seen from considerable distances. Its lightness of color and charming decorative quality are illustrated by the Giotto frescoes in Padua or Florence, with their large areas of blue, red, and yellow-gold —especially the cerulean blue that so often serves as background for the mural panels. The surface is dry and somewhat flat in color, although the generally sculpturesque approach of such Florentine masters as Giotto and Michelangelo results in a powerful three-dimensional appearance.

The very nature of the medium makes it advisable not to work on details but to concentrate on large simple areas that add to the basic monumental quality. This is customarily enforced by the architectural requirements of distance viewing, and also by the relatively quick-drying plaster that forces the artist to finish his work on each section in one day.

As for drawbacks, the same quick-drying plaster that impels the artist to be sure of himself and generalized in his painting also makes it impossible for him to correct any mistakes or to change his mind without chopping out the offending section, an arduous process that would leave marks where new plaster was added. Also, the joins from one day's plastering to the next are almost invariably visible, although by skillful planning the artist can often arrange to have them blend with the outline of the figure or its parts.

The lack of detail is not so much a disadvantage as a characteristic of the medium, as is the somewhat limited color range (as compared with oil). More serious are the actual technical difficulties involved in getting wall, plaster, and paint into a functioning and significant combination. The amount of wetness for the plaster, particularly for the final coat, is decisive, controlling as it does the degree of adherence of the coat to the wall or the extent to which the colors will hold or will run.

During the nineteenth century, when fresco painting was still being practiced in Europe—but long after the Renaissance tradition had

Fig. 100. JOSÉ CLEMENTE OROZCO:
Miguel Hidalgo y Costilla, detail
of staircase mural in Guadalajara,
Mexico, Palacio del Gobierno.

run dry—technical procedures became very bad. In the twentieth century, the techniques of the Renaissance were revived by the Mexican school, as in Orozco, *Miguel Hidalgo y Costilla* (Fig. 100, p. 167), through actual reference to Cennini, Vasari, and other early writers. Although the modern works have achieved a remarkable artistic quality in their decorative effect, monumentality, and basically sound architectural function, the actual material procedures are not always satisfactory. It is questionable whether the Mexican works done in fresco will last as long as those of the Italian Renaissance. (The Mexicans have, however, developed lasting synthetic paints for murals.)

Owing to the tendency of the plaster to absorb water, true fresco cannot be used safely in wet climates; it is seldom found in northern Europe. Exposure to weather is also damaging because of the sulphur often present in a city atmosphere, which can convert the binding calcium-carbonate layer to calcium sulphate and hasten disintegration. Another problem rises from the limited number of pigments that will not change after the work is completed. This demands the simplicity of color effects by which fresco painting is characterized and differentiates it sharply from oil. The oil has an extensive color range, possibilities of sharp dark and light contrasts, brilliant color contrasts, and can easily take added pigment (impasto) for additional enrichment—all in contrast to fresco.

Tempera. The term *tempera painting* is generally reserved for works done with pigments tempered or carried by egg yolk (with or without the white), hence the frequently occurring phrase, *egg tempera.* Where in fresco, since the paint was absorbed into the ground, the distinction between the paint itself and the ground was practically nonexistent, tempera, like oil, necessitates the preparation of a special ground or base on which the pigments are applied as a separate layer. During the medieval era, tempera on wooden panels was the most frequently used medium for easel paintings, or transportable works, while fresco was used for wall or permanent paintings. During the later fifteenth century, oil gradually displaced tempera, first in northern and then in southern Europe, that is, Italy.

Since the majority of the famous Italian altarpieces and panel pictures of the fourteenth to fifteenth centuries (as *Birth of Venus* by Botticelli, Fig. 101, p. 169) were done in this medium, much information again comes from Cennino Cennini's handbook. The beginning of the process, we learn here, involves the preparation of the wooden panel. Because of its tendency to warp and crack, this panel must be carefully seasoned, sometimes for as long as a year, so that all moisture is taken out. Then it is polished down and sanded, and a background or base that will receive the tempera pigments is prepared. The base consists of a white gelatinous substance known as *gesso,* a mixture of plaster of Paris and size (highly refined glue), applied in a series of thin, alternatingly rough and smooth coats. Although other substances can be substituted for plaster of Paris, for instance, chalk, the plaster offers the best kind of ivory-smooth and hard surface for the pigment.

Before the actual painting can be done, the usual number of preparatory drawings must be made and a final detailed drawing prepared to correspond with the space on the panel. The drawing is then trans-

Fig. 101. SANDRO BOTTICELLI: *Birth of Venus*. Florence, Italy, Uffizi Gallery.

ferred to the surface of the smooth gesso by a pricking method similar
to that followed in fresco, after which the indentations are filled and
connected with a painted outline. In the tempera method, the paint
itself is built up by a series of layers, often spread on a base of greenish
ground color. At first the layers or washes are light, and then they are
strengthened as the painter proceeds to the final outside layer.

Gelatinous in substance because of the egg tempering or carrying
them, these colors are relatively difficult to manipulate. Even when
diluted with water, tempera pigments dry rapidly (just as a bit of egg
hardens immediately on our clothes). For this reason, as well as because its transparency is greater than that of oil (although less than
that of water color) and does not allow anything beneath it to be con-
cealed, any changes or corrections are almost out of the question. The
painter has to be very sure of what he is doing and very careful while
doing it, a condition that makes for neither ease of manner nor elasticity of execution.

We may contrast the quality (even in black and white) of Botticelli's *Birth of Venus* (Fig. 101, p. 169) with that of typical oil paint-

TECHNIQUES OF PAINTING   **169**

ings which we shall examine below. We notice that in tempera as in fresco painting, the presence of a white underpainting or base gives a certain clarity and glow to the picture. We see also that the painting is made up of tightly worked outlines rather than color and tonal modifications as in oil. On both counts this differentiates the tempera from the average traditional oil picture, in which the background is relatively dark and the forms are made up of patches of color and their gradations. Although it is difficult here to indicate actual coloristic distinctions between the clarity of fresco and the clarity of tempera, we may point out the difference between the relatively rough-grained plaster base for fresco and the highly polished, smooth base for tempera work; and the matte dull finish of fresco colors as against the delicacy (here grayish pink) of such pictures as the *Birth of Venus*.

In addition to the general difficulty of working it, tempera offers other problems. The presence of sulphur in the albumen of egg tends to darken certain colors, which therefore cannot be used, thus limiting the palette of the tempera painter. Although the tempera range is wider than that of fresco, it still does not approach that of oil. On the other hand, it has a special luminosity and a delicate charm that make it uniquely beautiful and suitable for subjects like the lyrical *Birth of Venus* and other imaginative themes. Modern painters often use it in connection with the dream effects of Surrealist painting. A further advantage of tempera is its durability, in which regard it appears far to surpass oil. With its final protective coat of varnish (which also enriches the colors), the tempera medium or vehicle protects its pigments as fresco and oil do not, since they suffer from changes in tonality caused by disintegration or decay.

Oil. The first thing that strikes us about oil painting—and we have only to walk through any picture gallery to see it—is the tremendous variety of expression this medium makes possible. It has been pointed out that the mention of such techniques as fresco, tempera, or water color immediately evokes a particular type of image, but oil painting does not. From among the oil paintings pictured in this book, we may choose such diverse examples as the sixteenth-century work by Leonardo da Vinci (Fig. 46, p. 76), the seventeenth-century picture by Vermeer (Fig. 32, p. 50), and the nineteenth-century works by Pissarro, van Gogh, and others (Figs. 11, 39, pp. 24, 63). Although oil

Fig. 102. GIOTTO: *Madonna and Child Enthroned* (altarpiece). Florence, Italy, Uffizi Gallery.

is the vehicle or carrier of the paint in all of these examples, the nature of the final works, their benefits from the use of oil, are quite different. The first example stresses the dark and light possibilities, the second the transparency of the medium, the others its potential spontaneity and sketchiness.

The purpose of the oil used in painting, most often linseed oil, is as a vehicle and as a drying mechanism. Before the fifteenth-century development of this new medium, oil-varnishes of a slow-drying nature had been utilized to make permanent the tempera pigments in panel pictures, as in the Giotto *Madonna and Child Enthroned* altarpiece (Fig. 102, p. 171). If we compare this work with its limited color range to a painting by the van Eycks, such as the *Adoration of the Lamb* (Fig. 103, p. 172) with its luminously glowing and rich tones,

Fig. 103. HUBERT AND JAN VAN EYCK: *Adoration of the Lamb* (Ghent altarpiece, lower central panel). Ghent, Belgium, Cathedral of St. Bavo.

its subtle transitions from light to dark, its more intricate detail, we have a measure of the change wrought by the fifteenth-century Flemish improvements in oil.

From use of a thick, dark, and slow-drying oil-varnish which acted primarily as a protective agent, the Flemings changed to a clear, quick-drying, varnish-mixed oil. Applied in final glazes over their original tempera painting, this yielded new flexibility, depth, and durability. The transparency of the van Eyck background as compared with that of Giotto or Botticelli is quite apparent, as is the greater and evidently more easily worked-in detail throughout the picture. Most important, however, are the glow and depth of the various colors, their richness of surface, their reflections back and forth from each other.

Although the Italians of the fifteenth century soon adopted the technique of using oil glazes over tempera, oil by itself did not come into general usage until the end of that century, and canvas replaced wood panels only in the early sixteenth century. The new oil medium was applied to the canvas not on a gesso background—since that absorbed oil—but on a ground containing whiting, china clay, and other non-oil-absorbent materials, which also kept the canvas flexible and prevented cracking.

Among the chief advantages of the oil medium is its range of tone, that is, the range from light to dark within each color. This is illustrated in such a painting as the Vermeer *Young Woman with a Water Jug* (Fig. 32, p. 50) with its wonderful variety of blues, as also in the famous *Blue Boy* by Gainsborough. A second advantage lies in the large number of actual colors or hues that can be employed because of the additional protection given by the medium. (Tempera, as we have seen, tends to change certain colors, which consequently have to be omitted.) Third, the oil can be worked over and over and therefore can be corrected, even after a long time. In this way, the idea behind the painting may be developed and varied as the artist progresses; he need not predetermine every aspect as he must with the immediately drying and immutable tempera technique.

In the oil painting that began around the time of the Renaissance, the groundwork, or priming, exemplified by the dark underpainting of a Titian or Rembrandt (see Figs. 196 and 152, pp. 342, 271) or the light underpainting of a Fragonard (see Fig. 214a, p. 392), became of overwhelming importance. The reason for its primacy is that after a number of years, the painting tends to go more and more in the tonal direction of the original priming, which ultimately becomes the determinant of the painting's quality. This is demonstrated in the deterioration of some paintings by men like Poussin, whose brown underpainting has won out over the subsequent colors, or Reynolds, whose gray underpainting finally became the dominant note of the work. This change can be avoided by combining in the underpainting all the colors necessary to the final work, working glaze by glaze from the initial groundwork to the final surface effect.

During the period between the Renaissance and the early nineteenth century, two general methods of oil painting were dominant: one group of artists began on a light ground and the other on a dark ground. Michelangelo, a representative of the Florentine method, illustrates the first tendency (Fig. 35, p. 57) and Titian, the great Venetian painter (Fig. 196, p. 342), the second. By and large most painters during this period followed the same general principles in their approach to oil painting, the application varying with the individual. During the eighteenth century, for example, some artists (especially in Britain and the United States; see Gainsborough, Fig. 170, p. 300) worked the half tones into their background. On this base

Fig. 104 (left). REMBRANDT VAN RIJN: *Man with the Golden Helmet*. Berlin, State Museum. Fig. 105 (right). FRANS HALS: *The Laughing Cavalier*. London, Wallace Collection.

they then put in the lights, the shadows, and whatever local colors were necessary, either with a thin glaze, a semitransparent surface scumble (a blending over-layer), or even a solid area of paint. At the end, they worked in the highlights with a heavy surface impasto (thickness of paint, usually standing out in relief) that caught the light and reflected it back into the eyes of the spectator.

In the main, however, the picture was built up of varying thicknesses of oil paint applied so that the light passed through with more or less depth and speed depending on the effect the artist wished to achieve. If he wanted to make a given area appear dark, he could allow the light to penetrate a thin surface layer of paint to a dark underpainting that would retain the light for a relatively long time. If he wanted the light to be reflected back, he could increase the surface thickness of the paint, and its bright color would reflect rather than transmit light. The value of this flexibility is seen by contrasting two paintings, *Man with the Golden Helmet* (Fig. 104, p. 174) and *The Laughing Cavalier* (Fig. 105, p. 174).

In the first work the painter has created the illusion of a figure emerging slowly from the enveloping darkness, by retaining (absorbing) the light in certain areas as long as possible. Moreover, he has pinpointed tiny flecks of light within the general darkness in order to give a shimmering movement to those portions of the picture. Both effects are "unreal," spiritual rather than material, conceptual rather than perceptual. The Hals painting, in contrast, is open in its fabrication and immediate in its simple physical effect and direct reflection of light. Here the painter wished us to see the path of his brush; he has taken us from one lightly sketched-in area to another and by the directness of his presentation stressed a series of values directly opposite to those found in the Rembrandt work.

The Hals is a physical and surface perception of a somewhat brash and self-satisfied young man, glorified to the extent that everyday portraiture would demand. Rembrandt's picture, on the other hand, has nothing to do with portraiture in the ordinary sense. It would appear to convey some profound spiritual truth, to symbolize a universal tragedy—the old soldier bearing the impress of a world-weariness and sadness that result from his awful responsibility. Where the Hals is a frankly sensuous projection of a young man-about-town, the Rembrandt is a mysterious work that intrigues the spectator.

The interesting thing about such a work as Rembrandt's is that physical appearance itself is not the important element, that the painter may begin with the ordinary face of a Dutch businessman and raise it to the level of a universal symbol of tragedy, world-weariness, or disappointment. The identity of many of Rembrandt's sitters is not known to us today. In the Metropolitan Museum collection we find the *Portrait of a Man,* the *Man with a Steel Gorget, Portrait of a Young Man, Man with a Beard, Portrait of a Young Woman,* and others. Who are these people and would they have any interest for us if Rembrandt had not injected into them the powerful force of his own brooding personality? We do know that the *Man with the Golden Helmet* was the painter's brother Adrian who ran the family mill in Leyden, but who has been raised to the majesty of symbolic meaning by the subtlety of the artist's handling of oil paint.

Later in the history of painting, around the beginning of the nineteenth century and the Industrial Revolution, the workshop relationship and other traditional practices died out; the old studio traditions

Fig. 106. NICOLAS POUSSIN: *St. John on Patmos.* Courtesy of The Art Institute of Chicago, A. A. McKay Fund.

broke down and were replaced by newer methods. Under the stimulus of Romantic individualism the personal approach to painting was encouraged, and oil painting changed radically. The use of successive layers or glazes of paint together with opaque and semiopaque scumbles gave way to direct painting. No longer was there an important preparatory ground—the final color and general effect were indicated in the preliminary sketch.

By the end of the eighteenth century, many artists had already found themselves unable to use the methods of the Venetians with their rich glowing color transparencies. Goya (Fig. 20, p. 33) was perhaps the last master to use successive glazes over a ground color. During the nineteenth century, from Constable to the Impressionists of the 1870's, there was felt a great need to capture the effects of natural light. This led to experiments in using broken tones of color (applying unmixed colors to the canvas, where the eye would presumably blend them), a spontaneous rather than formal method of brushing to achieve the sparkle of light, with little spots of white paint applied with the palette knife to increase the desired spontaneity and luminosity.

We can see the difference in aim and effect by contrasting a traditional landscape painting by Poussin, *St. John on Patmos,* with Constable's *The Hay Wain* (see Figs. 106 and 107, pp. 176, 177) of the early nineteenth century. Poussin was interested in evoking a certain nostalgia for the past, for the time of Early Christianity and the Rome from which it was emerging. Every effort has been directed to establishing serenity and permanence. The man is placed in the foreground plane close to the spectator and on a level with the broken blocks of stone that lie about him as symbols of the pagan past which he and his religion are displacing. Between him and the glories of ancient Rome in the background is a thick and untraversable forest area, signifying the time that has elapsed since that era, a time that can no longer be recovered. Between the poise of the foreground and the stability and permanence of the background, two large trees balance at

Fig. 107. JOHN CONSTABLE: *The Hay Wain.* London, National Gallery.

right and left and anchor the painting in those directions and on that level of space.

Poussin was not interested in the actual appearance of a particular landscape at a particular time but in the creation of a concept through his treatment of nature—a concept of permanence, of solidity, of the past and its relation to his own day. Every form and every color avoids the transient in favor of the permanent. Colors may glow, but they must not sparkle; they may rise in a crescendo of tone, but they must not vibrate.

In the Constable painting, by contrast, we find a commonplace scene, a farmer stopping to water his team in a brook, treated in as everyday a manner as possible. Here is a landscape in which we may picture ourselves walking around the brook, following the path of the little dog, observing the boy pointing to the dog or the ducks swimming in the water. The landscape sweeps in a gentle curve to our feet, inviting us to walk into it and follow the farmer along his path to the stables.

By its inviting quality the picture differs sharply from the Poussin landscape, where a deep open space in the center creates a visual and psychological gap beyond which it is difficult to go. Poussin has established a finite quality in which the view is bounded by the front line of the painting (the stage area where the action takes place), on the sides by the trees, and in the rear by the enclosing mountain. But Constable has done something altogether different. He has carried us along from a heavily loaded left side in a sweeping arc toward the right rear and thus out of the scene. We feel that the view does not end at the picture-frame border but moves along—at least by implication—beyond that point.

Other contrasts derive from actual painting methods: Constable's use of little flecks of white to increase surface mobility, his small flecks of bright red and bright green as complementary, or mutually supporting, colors that reinforce each other and help to create the illusion of clear light. We are struck by the sense of movement in the foliage and the clouds and by the movement inherent in the reflections from object to object. These last are most clearly seen in the water, which consists of a series of bright color areas reflecting light from the sky and the clouds as well as from the house, trees, and wagon. In fact, the water consists of little else but reflections. How different are these moving clouds and swaying trees from the serene blue of Poussin's sky and the quiet of his foliage!

Water color. Among the various media requiring only the paint itself and merely a support or surface (with no intervening ground), the most widely used is water color. Here the pigment is mixed with a medium that can be dissolved in water, which will evaporate after the layer of dissolved paint is applied to the paper surface. Water, then, is not the medium; it is merely a vehicle for carrying the paint and allowing the artist to thicken or thin it as desired.

Water color is one of the oldest media known, having been used in classical times as well as during the long epoch between the Merovingian period (fifth to eighth centuries A.D.) and the end of the medieval era in Europe. Almost all medieval illustration and ornamentation of illuminated manuscripts was done in water color (see Carolingian manuscript, Fig. 50, p. 79). While southern European painters ventured into fresco painting as early as the late thirteenth century (*cf.* Giotto), those in the north continued to use water color almost exclusively. During these same centuries (and later) Chinese and Japanese painters both worked out elaborate esthetics in this medium. Throughout the Far East, water color has been almost the only kind of paint used down to the present day.

With the invention of printing in Europe during the fifteenth century and the consequent decline of manuscript painting, water color became less important, remaining useful chiefly for making sketches and tinting drawings and for painting miniatures. It continued in use for the latter purpose from the sixteenth to the eighteenth century, when there was a revival of water-color painting as a medium important in its own right. In the early nineteenth century, the work of artists like Turner marked the introduction of the water color as we know it today (see Homer, Fig. 108, p. 180).

Before being dissolved in water, the paint is mixed with gum arabic, which comes from the acacia tree. In the medieval era, egg white, whipped enough to make it soluble in water, was usually the medium for carrying the paint, but gums were also used.

In the late medieval era, wood served as the base for panel paintings, and parchment (vellum) for manuscript paintings. Since then, paper, sometimes mounted on card or on linen for additional strength, has become the customary support for water color, at least in the West-

Fig. 108. WINSLOW HOMER: *The Bather* (water color). New York, Metropolitan Museum of Art.

ern world. In the Far East, silk mounted on paper has found favor. Standard water-color paper need have no priming or groundwork applied, since it is treated with some sort of size that prevents it from soaking up color like a blotter. The character of the paper affects the final painting; a heavy, absorbent surface, as used in Homer's *The Bather* (Fig. 108, p. 180), gives a soft, broad, and rich quality. This may be contrasted with a smoothly surfaced, thin, and closely woven or textured surface such as parchment (see Gothic manuscript, Fig. 140, p. 228) which allows delicacy of form and precision of detail.

Water color may be transparent or nearly opaque. Sometimes, as in the Kandinsky *Dreamy Motion* (Fig. 109, p. 181), varying degrees of transparency may appear in the same painting. The less transparent use yields a reflection of light not only from the paint but also from the light as it penetrates the layer of paint and is reflected back from the surface of the paper (see lines, lower right). Where the paper is left blank or where there is merely a thin wash of color across a large area, as in the angles, left, the effect of light is increased many times. Water color of this kind shows one of the most highly charged surfaces in painting. Transparent water color may also allow any preparatory drawing to show through the outer added paint, depending on the thickness of that layer. In many forms of water color the paint is an adjunct to an architectural drawing, scenic view, or manuscript decoration. These we would call water-color drawings rather than water-color paintings.

Since the early nineteenth century, water-color painting has become more complex than in earlier days. Artists have begun to follow the methods of oil painting and to use layers of paint over each other as glazes, the first in monochrome, subsequent ones applied for shadows, form delineation, highlights, and so forth.

Although water color is a free and spontaneous medium, it demands much from the artist in knowledge of the limitations of his medium and of what he wants to do. It does not lend itself to fumbling about, and the serious artist who thinks out his problem for as long as he feels it necessary and only then proceeds to his work will have a better chance of success than the impulsive "hit and run" painter. Many teachers feel it is easier to manipulate oil paints, in spite of the fact that beginners have traditionally been launched with water colors.

Gouache. Opaque water color, or gouache, differs from transparent water color in that the paints are mixed with white. Formerly, white

Fig. 109. WASSILY KANDINSKY: *Dreamy Motion, No. 61.* New York, The Solomon R. Guggenheim Museum.

Fig. 110. CHRISTIAN ROHLFS: *Two Heads* (gouache, 1936). Detroit, Michigan, Detroit Institute of Arts.

lead was used; since the middle of the nineteenth century, zinc white has replaced it. The nontransparency of the gouache medium naturally varies with the amount of white that is mixed with the other pigments, but there is always enough white to perform its basic function, prevention of reflection of light from the background. As a result, gouache does not have the luminosity and brilliance of the transparent water color. It does have a certain light atmospheric quality as well as an almost pastel-like dryness of texture and surface (see Rohlfs, Fig. 110, p. 182). The fact that the white in the paint obstructs the passage of light also means that layers of paint can be gone over and hidden, and therefore in this medium changes and additions become possible which the regular water-color technique does not allow.

Opaque water color, in wide use today, also appeared in manuscript illumination during the later medieval era and in the more ornate works of the Gothic thirteenth and fourteenth centuries (see Fig. 140,

p. 228) as well as in Persian and Indian miniatures. In manuscripts both opaque and transparent forms were sometimes applied to the same work.

Oriental water color. Our final water-color form is that used by the Far Eastern painters, especially the Chinese. In a way, Oriental painting is a marginal form because it is also brush drawing (see Chapter 3). But since there is nothing improvisatory or merely preparatory about this brush technique, and since it often employs carefully adjusted color relationships, we are justified in speaking of it as painting.

Oriental painting is more conceptual than perceptual, that is, it deals more with spiritual ideas or concepts than with material things; in fact, it attempts to project the material world in a summary rather than actual fashion. This does not mean that the Chinese or Japanese painter is unaware of reality in our sense; on the contrary, he spends much time identifying himself with the object to be portrayed so that he can reach its ultimate reality, its essence. This leads to an art relatively nonrepresentational as compared with the light-and-shadow projections of High Renaissance art like Leonardo's and Michelangelo's (see Figs. 43a and 46, pp. 72, 76). Where Western artists like Vermeer or Monet attempt to compete with nature's version of human beings or light effects in landscape, the Chinese take it for granted that imitation by itself is fruitless and that understanding and recapturing the spirit of a flower, animal, or man in movement is more important. As the intermediary between the spectator and the object or scene described, the personality (in the Western sense) of the artist is less significant than is the idea to be conveyed.

The Western painting, as we have seen, is based on the knowledge explicit in the drawings for a given work, as in the *Libyan Sibyl* (Fig. 43, p. 71), or on the actual demonstration of a particular textural quality, as in Vermeer or Pissarro (Figs. 32 and 11, pp. 50, 24). In the East, on the other hand, the painting conveys summarized or ideographic suggestions of form, distance, and movement. The spectator to whom the artist appeals is expected to understand poetic stimuli and suggestions, to be able to fill in, to imagine what is only implied. We can compare Chinese landscape (Fig. 37, p. 60) with a Western landscape like the Constable (Fig. 107, p. 177) to see the difference in approach. The skill in using the brush, in delineating the elegant lines

Fig. 111. KU K'AI-CHIH: *Admonitions of the Imperial Preceptress*, detail. London, British Museum.

that characterize Chinese (and Japanese) painting and its shorthand forms, is far more important in this art than is delineation in the photographic sense.

Two examples of Chinese painting, the landscape by Ma Yüan, and the earlier work by Ku K'ai-chih, *Admonitions of the Imperial Preceptress* (Figs. 37 and 111, pp. 60, 184), show these qualities of line and suggestion. In the landscape, the delicate limpness of the willow trees in the foreground, the lighter suggestions of trees in the middle-ground, and the filmy lines of the mountains in the background imply even more than they state. We should remember that the Chinese painter working in monochromatic ink dissolved in water has a highly developed sense of lights and darks (not the light and shadow of the Western artist) that conveys a feeling of reality as much as does his aerial perspective, which makes nearer objects darker in tone than further ones. However strong his sense of actuality—and we can feel with him the reality of the mist over the hills—the final work exists in terms of a patterned and abstract series of light and dark areas, of filled and empty spaces, of linear trees, hills, bridge, and other forms. The figure painting by Ku K'ai-chih is one of a series of vignettes illustrating the duties of the imperial concubines of the emperor of China. Each figure with its elaborate and involved variations in linear thickness (changes which in themselves define the form) stands in a barely suggested space that adds to the sense of abstraction. In this scroll a small amount of color has been added, but, as elsewhere in Oriental art, the essential factor is the swing of the elegant and graceful line, the line that suggests the calligraphy or handwriting of China.

The Chinese painter sits before a piece of paper mounted on silk and laid flat on the ground. Working from a stick or sticks of ink which, dissolved in water, represent his paint, he holds his brush perpendicular to the paper with three fingers, swinging his arm from the shoulder to create alternatingly delicate and powerful lines. The ink used is a mixture of lampblack and glue molded into a cake and forming a heavy black liquid when mixed with water. When lighter tones are required, some of this black liquid is mixed in a separate vessel with clear water. The lustrous quality of Chinese paintings depends on the character of the ink—its roughness, smoothness, fine or coarse grain, and so on.

The absorptive quality of the material enforces an accurate knowledge of the limitations of the medium. Mistakes are as unallowable here as in Western water color, while the demands on the Oriental artist for delicacy of brush handling are greater than for his Western colleague; the line in its various modulations is ultimately the carrier of the artist's message. With this great emphasis on line, color seems to many Chinese only an adjunct and is seldom, if ever, used in any precise representational sense.

Oriental painting in water color may be said, then, to be an art of suggestion rather than of representation; it achieves the difficult aim of communicating not by what is shown but by what is left empty and inferred. To fill in the details as is done in Western painting seems to the Oriental artist rather tiresome, if not inartistic. When Lord Macartney, ambassador of King George III of Britain, toward the end of the eighteenth century brought to the Chinese court a number of paintings as gifts, the courtiers were shocked by the shadow effects and asked in all seriousness if the people portrayed had in real life one side of their faces darker than the other. To many of these Chinese, the depiction of shadows on the sides of the nose (an accomplishment in Western eyes) was a serious defect—although some of them were willing to believe that it came there by accident.

Pastel. Pastel is sometimes considered a drawing technique, since the colors may be drawn across the surface of the paper with a pastel pencil, a cylinder made up of pigment held together with a little gum and filled out with whiting. It may also be applied by being rubbed in

Fig. 112. EDOUARD MANET: *George Moore* (pastel). New York, Metropolitan Museum of Art.

with the tip of a finger. No matter what the technique, however, the medium represents the simplest of all methods for laying color on a flat surface, thus fulfilling our rudimentary definition of painting.

As its colors consist of almost pure powder pigments without a carrying or light-thickening medium, pastel permits results that are higher in tone than those produced by any other known technique or medium. The colors may be applied to the surface so thinly as to bring into play the effect of the paper itself, somewhat as in water-color painting. The Manet pastel portrait of *George Moore* (Fig. 112, p. 186) illustrates the chalky brilliance and luminosity this medium can achieve. Here the upper left-hand portion shows clearly the effect of the paper beneath, and the rest of the painting shows the effect of the whiting filler. Pastel has its own virtues and need not be used in the fashion of

186

oil painting or some other more ambitious medium. In catching the spirit of the sitter in portraiture—where it has been highly successful—pastel fulfills its possibilities.

The "pastel" quality of the pigments comes from the whiting originally used as a filler, and is one of the unique features of the medium, differentiating it from chalk crayons, which are mixed with oil or wax. Pastel limitations spring from its impermanence—the lack of any real binder for the pigments makes it flaky and susceptible to rapid deterioration. The use of fixatives after the picture is completed is generally not recommended, because this automatically changes the nature of the pastel surface. A covering of glass helps to preserve the work. Degas, among others, worked very hard to devise a fixative that would keep the pastel from deteriorating; one solution was to use pastel in conjunction with a more permanent medium, such as oil or water color.

Another disadvantage of the pastel medium lies in the fact that the white, which all the colors contain, limits the range from dark to light. And yet, in spite of its disadvantages, the pastel allowed many masters of the eighteenth and nineteenth centuries, painters like Maurice Quentin de La Tour, Degas, Manet, Raffaelli, and others, to produce significant works, particularly in portraiture and genre. In Impressionist painting, where the seizing of a moment was of consequence, Manet, Raffaelli, and particularly Degas responded with the brilliant flaky immediacy of the pastel.

7

Prints and People

IN POPULAR PARLANCE a "print" usually refers to a color reproduction of a painting. In the language of the artist, however, a print is a graphic or drawn design reproduced from a wood, metal, or stone plate (that is, slab) or through the mesh of a silk screen.

To make a print, an original design is cut in relief (above the plate surface) or in intaglio (beneath the surface), or is drawn planographically (on the surface of the block or the silk screen). From this design a number of impressions are made or "pulled," either on a special type of printing press or by means of the silk-screen stencil. Each of these impressions has the market status and value of an original, especially if it is pulled by the artist himself, although the designer-artist may turn the plate over to a professional printer for the final operation much as a sculptor-designer might turn over his full-scale model to the stonecutter.

Editions of prints vary in size. If they are prepared for the collector's market rather than for popular distribution, their edition will have as few as fifty copies, a number that insures both adequate return to the artist and a measure of rarity to satisfy the collector. This restrictive practice is relatively new historically and relates to the somewhat esoteric status that art has achieved in modern times. In the past, however, and most recently as well, there has been evidence of attempts to create a really popular art.

188

Qualities of Beauty in the Print

Since most prints are in black and white (although there are also color etchings, lithographs, woodcuts), they have an appeal different from that of paintings, which possess color. In the print, as in the drawing, we are dealing primarily with the abstract quality of a linear art, although some prints, such as woodcuts, serigraphs (silk-screen prints), and mezzotints, also use area as a basic element. The object is represented in a symbolic or shorthand, rather than primarily naturalistic way. Each of the different print techniques has its own linear quality through which we may appreciate its esthetic value and the artist's basic purpose. An artist will deliberately choose a medium, for instance, etching, because he has a particular effect in mind. For other effects, he will choose other types of print making.

We can enjoy the beauty of prints at three stages: the initial beauty of the linear pattern as cut or drawn on the block or plate, the beauty of the line as it emerges from the sheet of paper to which it has been transferred, and finally the beauty of the condition, or "state," of the impression or print. At the first stage, we can visualize the wonderful shininess of an etched copper plate with its web-thin lines, the silvery surface of an engraved plate with somewhat heavier lines, the rough texture of a woodblock, the matte surface of a lithograph stone.

The second attraction is perhaps most characteristic of the medium —the beauty of the line as it appears on a sheet of paper. This involves the entire esthetic of print making. Apart from general considerations of composition and design, line as line has special meaning in a print just as color is the determining factor in most painting. The strength of a contour, the jaggedness of a detail, the continuous movement of a thin supple line from one part of a form to another, the symbolizing of both form and movement through direction—these elements are all peculiar to line.

The third attribute of a print, the beauty of condition in a particular impression, depends partly on the skill of the person pulling the print, the manner in which the ink may be deliberately smeared, and other features, but mostly on the actual state of the plate itself. The first impressions pulled from a drypoint will be richer and deeper than later ones to the degree that the plate wears down and begins to lose some of the ink as it is applied to and wiped from the surface. The first and original edition invariably is artistically more significant than later ones. Certainly when one compares an original impression made from a Rembrandt etching with those pulled from the same plate at a much later date, the difference becomes all too clear: the first is crisp and sharp in definition; the latter blurred, fuzzy, and almost meaningless. On the other hand, original plates, having had a number of impressions pulled, may be electroplated so that they do not wear out. The impressions made from the electroplated surface may look as good as the originals pulled by the seventeenth- or eighteenth-century artist, but they are commercially as valueless as the worn impressions would be. Therefore the mere presence of an important name, such as Rembrandt or Goya, on a print is no guarantee of freshness in state or of original condition.

Although most prints by definition are original designs, some are made to reproduce an artistic work. In this group we find the mezzotint engraving or the steel engraving of portraits and other subjects. During the eighteenth and nineteenth centuries, such prints were frequently made and have always found a ready market among collectors. Just as with many types of original art, when more and more examples are produced, artistic standards come into being, and we are able to distinguish between good, bad, and indifferent prints done "after" a portrait, landscape, or other work.

Changing Uses and Characteristics

For almost the entire period of their existence, prints have been useful as well as artistic. Their use arose during the fourteenth century from playing-card manufacture and from the custom of making hand-colored souvenir devotional pictures to be distributed to pilgrims who visited various European shrines. As the process of printing books was invented or reinvented in Europe in the fifteenth century (it had been known centuries earlier in China) and paper was made available, prints came into use as book illustrations. At that point in history the medieval manuscript, laboriously lettered and painfully hand-illustrated, finally went out of existence and was replaced by the printed illustrated book made from movable types with blocks inserted for the illustrations. These new printed books found a ready market among the growing burgher class of the time, the same people who sponsored or patronized the Flemish and Italian artists of the early Renaissance.

But the print came to be used not merely as an embellishment for a book; it became a vehicle for artistic and religious expression, emerging in the great woodcut and engraving cycles by Albrecht Dürer and other artists of the late fifteenth and sixteenth centuries. So far as we are able to tell, prints in those days were by no means restricted in the size of their edition, as they have been since the late nineteenth century. One finds editions as large as 2,000 copies at the beginning of the history of print making, in connection with such usages as the souvenir colored woodcut prints mentioned earlier.

As late as the eighteenth century, prints were still being mass-produced. Some showed religious subjects (for instance, the 1766 woodcut, *Notre Dame de Bonne Délivrance,* printed in an edition of about half a million), some were political handbills like those produced in quantity before and during the French Revolution, and others were "prints for the people," depicting manners and morals of the time. The last category includes examples of social satire, which reached its first peak in the eighteenth-century works of William Hogarth (see Fig. 19, p. 31) and its second in the nineteenth-century prints of Rowlandson, Cruikshank, Goya, Daumier, and many others. Hogarth engraved reproductions of his own paintings, making them available to the general public as black-and-white prints for a shilling each and thereby earning a great deal of money. Later Englishmen produced original prints in whatever quantity the market would absorb. Sometimes— as with anti-Napoleon prints—this was considerable; even relatively modest editions, however, included many more prints than the "fine etching" editions of modern times.

By the middle of the nineteenth century, prints were being produced in very large editions as newspaper illustrations. These included Daumier's famous lithographic drawings of French manners, morals, and political happenings (*Rue Transnonain,* Fig. 123, p. 206) and Winslow Homer's drawings done behind the lines in the American Civil War and reproduced in *Harper's Magazine* (a professional woodcutter was engaged to transform the drawings into the wood-block medium). During the midcentury, also, the genre artist George Caleb Bingham produced a series of extremely popular lithographs of life in

America, while the colored lithographs of the firm of Currier and Ives remain a permanent monument to the manifold aspects of nineteenth-century life in this country. In the Orient, the colored wood block became popular in Japan at the end of the eighteenth and beginning of the nineteenth century. In that country, painting remained a preoccupation of the wealthy, and the colored wood block, cheap to make for so many more people, became a mass medium. Meanwhile, in the West, the wood block and the lithograph, as used in Daumier's and Homer's newspaper drawings, had become mass media.

In the course of these developments, the metal plate media (etching, engraving, and so forth) took on a somewhat upper-class and restricted quality. In our own times this distinction is expressed by the limited-edition print, already described, in which from 25 to 50 prints are produced for a select market. After this printing the plate may be destroyed or "canceled" (have a series of parallel lines gouged diagonally across it) to guarantee that it can never be used again and that the client therefore has a very limited item. Today's mass print media consist of semi-commercial attempts to popularize "fine prints" by making large-scale editions at comparatively low prices and of the color reproductions or color prints referred to at the beginning of this chapter.

The closest we have come in our day to a mass-produced print like the Japanese wood block or the French Revolutionary throwaway is in the *corridos* of Mexico. These are topical songs with illustrations, printed on flimsy tissue and given away or sold for a few centavos to the public at large; they have a distinctly social function that recalls the time of the French Revolution. Another parallel (at least potentially) is the silk-screen print, for which its advocates predict a mass circulation and application. This very attractive and decorative color print medium has so far had its widest use in advertising, especially poster work.

The silk screen (its technique is described below) is one of the new media of our times, apparently springing from the environment of the business world. Although print media and practice as a whole had gone far downhill by the beginning of the twentieth century, there has since been an important revival of old methods and an introduction of many new ones. The naturalistic movement by Americans of the last decade of the nineteenth and the first decade of the twentieth century, including Sloan, Bellows, and the entire Ashcan School, utilized the

Fig. 113. *A Peddler Robbed by Monkeys* (woodcut, German XVth century). New York, Metropolitan Museum of Art.

traditional etching and the still fairly new lithographic method.

In Paris before World War I a revival in the same techniques showed a more up-to-date stylistic quality, as in the famous illustrated books published by Ambroise Vollard and decorated with etchings, woodcuts, and engravings by Picasso, Chagall, Maillol, and others. Since then various new techniques have come into being, some consisting of mixtures or free applications of older methods, others entirely new in character. These belong for the most part to the period after World War II and are referred to below.

Historically, prints have been divided into three main groups, according to whether they were made from lines standing up in relief, lines beneath the surface of the plate (intaglio), or lines on the surface (lithographic).

Relief Prints

The relief print includes the woodcut, wood engraving, and those metal plates in which lines have been raised in relief by various methods. A rather heavy and viscous ink that will not flow into the hollows of the block is applied to the lines in relief, and a relatively light vertical pressure—even rubbing on the back of the sheet of paper—is sufficient to transfer the ink from the high surface to the paper.

Woodcut. The woodcut has been referred to as "pictorial type"; it prints pictures in the same way that type-faces print letters, by raised lines that catch the ink. In fact the first printed words were actually cut in relief beneath a woodcut picture to explain it. Movable types

Fig. 114 (*left*). LOVIS CORINTH: *Crucifixion* (woodcut). Plate from portfolio, *Biblische Motive*. Fig. 115 (*right*). ERNST LUDWIG KIRCHNER: *Sailboats-Fehmarn* (woodcut, 1912). Formerly New York, Curt Valentin Gallery.

were developed by cutting up this single block of combined picture and letters so that the letters could be saved and re-used. Woodcut pictures are characterized by a flat bold contrast of blacks and whites that is different from the essentially modulated and shadowy effects of an intaglio print.

The raised lines of the woodcut that print black on the paper are merely a portion of the original uncut surface of the wood with which the artist began. Had he done nothing with this block but ink it and apply the paper, he would have had a solid black impression. By working on the block with his gouge or burin and cutting away sections of the ink-taking surface, area after area of white begins to appear. The design is finally a series of lines in relief, the spaces between the lines plowed out by the burin or gouge and therefore prevented from taking the ink, which adheres only to the raised lines.

There are two main methods of cutting the wood: one produces the black-line effect noted above (see Fig. 113, p. 193), and the other yields a white-line effect (see Fig. 114, p. 194). The black-line cut (the woodcut proper) begins with a drawing directly on the block, from which all the whites are cut away. Here the black lines are important;

the white becomes a by-product. In the white-line cut (or engraving), the artist is concerned with the ultimate effect of the white, and the lines are engraved rather than cut out of the surface. The first method envisages the print as starting from white paper and growing gradually toward its black ending; in the second the artist tries to think of the print as emerging from the darkness into the light. The difference lies ultimately in the fact that the black-line woodcutter keeps in mind what he can do with black lines within white spaces, while the white-line master imagines what he can do with white lines within black spaces. Both, however, are artists of line, and both cut into the grain of wood in relief to achieve their purpose.

Because of its execution in relatively laborious and careful cuttings, the black woodcut line is generally powerful rather than graceful, bold rather than delicate, and very effective, as modern woodcut artists have shown (Fig. 115, p. 194) in the expression of emotion. One of the most frequent problems, especially in early black woodcuts, has involved the arrangement of lines in parallel formation, or hatchings, and in sets of parallel formation crossing each other, crosshatchings—both used for indicating shadows; care must be exercised not to break off the thin ridges of wood that result from these cuttings.

Early woodcutting tended to be an art of reproduction—a master would often make a drawing for a journeyman woodcutter to execute. Modern woodcutting, such as that of Paul Gauguin or of German Expressionists like Kirchner, is no longer a simple linear affair, but leans toward the use of tonal areas. It has developed a powerful play of broad dark and light areas flatly applied, often without delicate modulations, and leaping from the print in a way emotionally disturbing because of the strong contrasts.

Wood engraving. The art of wood engraving (see Fig. 114, p. 194), practiced increasingly since the time of Thomas Bewick in England (1753–1828), is characterized by a delicacy and softness foreign to either the earlier or later woodcuts just examined. Through this white-line method Bewick emphasized tonal values by placing his white lines on a black background. The artist was no longer limited to the linear effects of the black woodcut method; he could increase modulations of tone or even abandon the line if it suited his purpose. By the new method he was easily able to execute light and shade effects.

Instead of the laborious cutting of channels on each side of the lines and the even more complex business of crosshatching with its diamond-shaped spaces, the artist merely engraved lines, either parallel or crossing each other, on the wood. These lines appeared on the ultimate print as thin areas of white. In the old days of woodcutting the artist had painstakingly plowed his way across large areas of the block by pushing the burin before him; this new method made it possible for him to engrave lines on the surface, with far less effort and far more grace of manner and result.

During the nineteenth century, before the age of photographic reporting, the technique of the wood engraver came to be used widely in cartoons and illustrations. Charles Keene, Tenniel, and their fellows in Britain, Winslow Homer and his contemporaries in the United States, Doré in France, all contributed to this trend toward dissemination of the printed image. Later, some wood engravers tried to use the medium in ways unsuited to its character, chiefly as a means of reproducing paintings and various works by other artists. Thus, when the camera came along with its far greater reproductive capabilities, line engraving was temporarily finished. Recently, however, this method has been revived.

Metal relief. Relief prints may also be made in metal by protecting with stopping-out varnish those parts of the plate meant to stand in relief, and dipping the plate in an acid bath that eats away the unprotected areas. William Blake used this method, as did the later Mexican printmaker and illustrator José Guadalupe Posada (1851–1913).

Linoleum cut. Very close in spirit and technique to the woodcut proper is the linoleum cut, a relief process in which battleship linoleum is handled much like wood. The greater suppleness of this medium makes it relatively easy to handle. A particular texture often emerges to give a heavy rich tone to the print (see Fig. 116, p. 197).

Chiaroscuro print. The relief methods just described pertain exclusively to black-and-whites. There are also two basic color woodcut processes: the so-called chiaroscuro print and the Japanese wood-block print. The chiaroscuro print, developed during the sixteenth century in Europe, involves two blocks. One prints the usual line drawing outline; the other is a tone block that gives a solid background tone of gray, sepia, pink, or other color, and from which a number of spots are gouged out to render highlights in the final print. The finished print looks very much like a wash drawing and was probably derived from that art form.

Fig. 116. LEOPOLDO MÉNDEZ: *Deportation to Death* (linoleum cut). Mexico City, collection of the artist.

Japanese print. A development of the late eighteenth and early nineteenth century, the Japanese print (see Fig. 117, p. 198) is a multiblock method. A drawing on transparent paper is pasted face down on the block to guide the artist. From this drawing the cutter prepares the key block, which is to print the usual black outline in its entirety. From the key block he next makes a series of impressions on thin paper, one for each color that will be used in the print.

Each impression now stands for a separate color and is marked off into portions for its particular color. Each sheet is pasted face down on a block that is then correspondingly cut in relief. That is to say, the block that is to furnish the blues will show in relief only those portions of the final print which need blue, and so on through the various colors. As each successive block prints its particular color over the primary black outline, a new ink is added.

Although the Japanese wood block is designed to be a popular medium, as distinguished from more aristocratic Japanese painting, it sustains a high quality of delicacy and refinement, far different from the Western notion of the popular print. Gracefully swinging contour lines, limited space projection inward, flat decorative forms, large color

Fig. 117. HARUNOBU: *Lovers under Umbrella in the Snow* (colored woodcut). New York, Metropolitan Museum of Art.

areas applied with a touch of "modern" dissonance rather than blandness of tone, general abstraction of the method rather than naturalism —all these elements give the Japanese print a special character. This form of art had considerable influence on the development of Impressionism, post-Impressionism, Symbolism, and other types of modern Western painting.

Intaglio Prints

The intaglio print, the second category of this medium, draws the ink not from the surface as in the relief method, but rather from furrows gouged out of the plate, into which the ink has been rolled and then dabbed. After the excess or surface ink is removed by wiping muslin across the plate or, often, by rubbing with the palm of the hand, a dampened sheet of paper is applied to the plate, and pressure is applied by passing the plate and paper on a plank between metal rollers. This heavy pressure pushes the paper into the furrows, from which the ink is lifted.

Line engraving. Line engraving, like other intaglio processes, employs a highly polished plate, generally copper, although other metals have also been utilized (see Fig. 118, p. 199). The cutting tool, a graver or burin similar to that used by the woodcutter, is a sharp beveled rod attached to a round handle. In traditional line engraving, the burin acts almost like a plow pushed along in the soil, tending to throw up long mounds at either side. These mounds of metal, known as burr, would ordinarily hold on to whatever ink is spread on the plate and give a fuzzed look to that portion. To avoid this and to achieve the clean hard line which is the engraver's purpose, the burr is removed with a scraper.

Should the artist wish to soften the effect of the engraved line, he may wipe the muslin over the plate so as to draw a bit of the ink out of

Fig. 118. MARTIN SCHONGAUER: *Flight into Egypt* (engraving). New York, Metropolitan Museum of Art.

the lines or furrows and toward the top of the plate. In this way the lines lose some of their preciseness of definition, acquiring a slight fuzz from the peripheral ink. The burr itself could not be left to perform this function since the ridges of metal would shortly be worn down by the great pressure necessary to force the paper into the lines. One of the great virtues of the engraved line, in addition to its strength of out-line, is the fact that in dragging the ink out of the furrows we cause it to stand out against the paper's surface; it is therefore more sharply and crisply defined than wood-block or lithographic ink, both of which merely lie on the surface.

The fact that the line is cut by hand and receives varying force and emphasis as the burin enters and leaves the groove gives the engraved line a pointed end (as opposed to the etched line, which has a square end) . Since the burin is held in a relatively fixed position, fairly formal line results. In order to produce the manifold effects that may be de-sired, engravers have invented a series of complicated devices, produc-ing lines that cross each other at different angles, move in a variety of curves, appear heavy or fine, and so on. It was inevitable that they would adopt conventions for different effects: very short lines for flesh quality, broken wavy lines for visible earth areas, long straight lines for sky, and other usages. Each texture effect soon was suggested by its appropriate kind of line, although the greatest masters, as usual, made their own formulas.

Ultimately, line engraving, like wood engraving, became a repro-ductive device in which inspiration was of far less consequence than technical skill. We may compare, for example, the Schongauer *Flight into Egypt* (Fig. 118, p. 199) , an early engraving of the fifteenth cen-tury, with the reproductive engraving found on a dollar bill. The latter is concerned with reproducing a portrait and architecture (reverse side) , with formalized impressiveness, and with authenticity. None of these things concerned Schongauer, who was interested in the beauty of the individual line (here almost invisible in the flurry of crosshatched tonal passages) and the spiritual aura that emerges from these individ-ual lines. The fact that Schongauer was engraving his own conception probably influenced his approach; the government engraver, after all, is working along well-worn paths.

Between these two extremes—the imaginative and the reproductive —we find illustrative but still significant works produced by the

Fig. 119 (*left*) . MAX BECKMANN: *Man with Bowler Hat* (self-portrait; drypoint, 1921) .
Courtesy Brooklyn Museum, New York. Fig. 120 (*right*) . VINCENT VAN GOGH: *Portrait of Dr. Gachet* (etching, May 1890) . New York, private collection. (Photo courtesy The Museum of Modern Art)

seventeenth-century French and Flemish engravers of portraits, like Nanteuil and Van Dyck; in the same century fine engravings reproduced the paintings of Rubens, and others were executed after the Rococo paintings of the eighteenth century, including works by Watteau, Boucher, and Fragonard. In England this period saw the ascendancy of the mezzotint (see below) , a different type of reproductive method, although William Blake's illustrations for the *Book of Job* are among the finest engravings ever made. In modern times, engraving as an art has been revived in what is today called burin engraving; this is essentially the old process of original line engraving, adapted for contemporary purposes by Picasso and others.

Dry point. Another form of intaglio print is the dry point, in which a long sharp steel needle is used to make scratches on the surface of the polished copper plate (see Fig. 119, p. 201) . Instead of pushing the cutting instrument along the surface, as in engraving, the artist pulls it, as in drawing or writing. As a result, more burr than in engraving is thrown along the *sides* of the line—not in front—but it is not removed, since the desired quality in dry point is a rich velvety line, which the burr, by retaining the ink, readily gives.

Needless to say, this furrow, tiny little curls of the metal, is very delicate, and the pressure of printing soon flattens it. But for the time that the burr picks up that extra bit of ink, the dry point—often used in etchings—succeeds in rendering an effect altogether its own. The print by Beckmann is predominantly dry point, with the small details in the upper portion of the plate etched in the usual way. Picasso, Chagall, and other modern artists have also used this method.

Etching. In etching, instead of pushing the burin or drawing with the dry needle, the artist produces his lines with the aid of acid, which bites into the surface of the metal (see Fig. 120, p. 201). The polished copper plate is first covered with an etching ground, a combination of gummy and resinous substances. A melted form of this mixture is laid evenly on the surface of the plate. The grounded plate is then held over lighted candles, so that a deposit of carbon forms on it.

At this point, having decided what he is going to draw (and etch) on the surface of the plate, the artist takes his etching needle, a short steel instrument set into a wooden pencil handle, and draws his design through the carbon-covered wax, exposing the shiny copper under-surface with each stroke. The plate, protected, except for the exposed lines, by a stopping-out varnish, front and back, is then dipped into a nitric acid bath. The artist removes the plate from the acid bath when the lines he wishes to print lightest are bitten enough; these he stops out with varnish, and then he dips the plate again to reach a second degree of depth for another batch of lines. This process can be repeated as often as the artist feels it necessary.

Should the artist wish to remove the ground in order to pull a proof and see how his work is progressing, the ground must afterward be replaced so that the sufficiently etched lines are covered and those needing more bite are left open to the action of the acid. After further dipping, another proof may be pulled.

The basic difference between the etching and the engraving emerges from the technique itself; it is the difference between the tightly made, slowly cut or pushed line of engraving and the casual, spontaneously drawn line of etching. The line in engraving is more formal than the freer, sketchier line of the etching. The etching line, since it is bitten rather than gouged, has no burr and can be as clear as the engraved line from which the burr has been removed. The etched line is also distinguished by the squareness of its ends, the result of mechanical biting; the tool coming up out of the trough of an engraved line leaves a thinned-out end.

Although etching as a technique has existed for a long time, probably since the days of armor makers, who used to etch designs on the surface of their products, we find no prints before the early sixteenth century. Etching came into its own during the seventeenth century, mostly through Rembrandt, one of its greatest masters. Its delicacy and spontaneity made it suitable also for Rococo forms, as in the works of Tiepolo and Watteau, and for caricature, as in prints by Hogarth, Gillray, Rowlandson, and Cruikshank, who carried its use through the nineteenth century. Also during the nineteenth century, the Barbizon landscapists and, later, the Impressionists employed this method of print making. Today Picasso, Stanley Hayter, Jacques Villon, Paul Klee, Louis Marcoussis, and others have used the etching process.

Tone processes. Among intaglio methods, a number may be described as tone processes; in them the artist seeks to render the effect of areas of tone rather than of a basically linear design. These include mezzotint, stipple engraving and allied processes, and the aquatint. It is true that linear methods of engraving may give the effect of tone through shading, crosshatching, and other devices (see Fig. 119, p. 201); by the use of such devices, however, the inherent quality of line is altered, thus forcing line engraving, dry point, etching, and so on to defeat their own ends as linear media. Tone processes, on the other hand, are designed to produce such effects—often they have no lines whatsoever.

One of the chief tone methods, *mezzotint,* has been described as a negative process, for it works from a dark background to the highlights, reversing the usual procedure of working from a white background to lines and shadows (see Fig. 121, p. 204). The basic technique of the mezzotint is to roughen the metal surface in such a way that, if smeared with ink, it would print a deep black. The roughening is done with a rocker tool, a curved surface covered with teeth of varying heights and thicknesses. Held at right angles to the plate, this tool is rocked across it regularly; an indentation with a small burr is formed at every point of contact between the tool and the plate. These tiny troughs hold the ink, while the burr adds the characteristic quality of the mezzotint.

Where the engraver wishes to achieve a lighter effect, he removes a

Fig. 121. DAVID LUCAS: *Weymouth Bay* (mezzotint after oil by John Constable). New York, Metropolitan Museum of Art.

portion of the burr with a scraper; where he wishes to make a highlight, he polishes down the plate with a burnisher so that no ink at all can be retained. Thus, the mezzotint is actually scraped rather than engraved. Here, as in the dry point, the chief effect of the print comes from the burr; when that has worn down, the mezzotint loses its characteristic. This means, as before, that relatively few good impressions are possible.

As an art form, the mezzotint appeared as recently as the seventeenth century, when it was used primarily for portrait reproduction. It served this purpose during the eighteenth century in Britain (portraits by Reynolds, Gainsborough, and so forth) as well as being used for reproductions of landscape, genre, and other paintings (for example, works by Turner and Morland). Its effectiveness in rendering the softness of a woman's skin, the texture of an animal's coat, or the nuances of light and dark in a landscape or seascape was a very important aspect of the art of the late eighteenth and early nineteenth century. Although the original mezzotint method is still in use today (by Hayter, for example), it has been augmented by the use of a carborundum stone, which is worked over the plate in two or three directions, to produce the roughness necessary to catch the ink and print velvety black.

Another widely used process is the *aquatint,* which gives a more transparent (less deep or rich) quality of tone than the mezzotint and approaches most closely the effect of a wash drawing (see Fig. 122, p. 205). The effect is produced by allowing acid to bite through a loosely laid, porous ground. This ground gives partial protection to the plate. It may be laid by placing powdered resin in a box with the copper plate, blowing it loosely about with a bellows, and allowing it to settle on the plate in the necessary loose granular form. It may also be laid by suspending the resin in an alcoholic solvent, applying the liquid to the surface of the plate, and allowing the alcohol to evaporate, leaving the resin on the surface.

After the ground has been laid, the plate is inserted in an acid bath that bites through the granular openings between the bits of resin and yields a tonal quality, similar to that of a wash drawing, as background for the print. The artist controls this medium, like the etching, by stopping out the white areas, which must not be bitten. The method is

Fig. 122. FRANCISCO GOYA: *Asta su Abuelo* (*Back to His Grandfather;* aquatint). New York, Metropolitan Museum of Art.

Fig. 123. HONORÉ DAUMIER: *Rue Transnonain* (lithograph). New York, Metropolitan Museum of Art.

used in conjunction with etching, dry point, and other techniques for a varied effect such as one finds in the aquatints of Goya (Fig. 122, p. 205).

The aquatint was invented by Jean Baptiste Le Prince (1734–1784), who apparently devised it to reproduce some wash drawings he had made in Russia. During the eighteenth century, aquatints, especially of architectural backgrounds, travel scenes, and other panoramic effects, were sometimes colored by hand to add to their decorative charm. This practice persisted into the twentieth century, when colored aquatints were done by the Hudson River School of landscape artists. But the greatest master of the technique, perhaps its sole excuse for being, was Goya, whose *Caprichos, Disasters of War, Proverbs,* and other magnificent works of personal expression, carried the art to unequaled heights.

Lithographic Prints and Serigraphs

The third large class of prints, the planographic or lithographic, are printed from the surface rather than from above or from below it. Lithography proper is the most important member of this class and may be defined as printing from a drawing made on the surface of a stone. Lithography makes use of the natural antipathy of grease and water and of the fact that some stones, from Bavaria, in Germany, have the quality of absorbing both grease and water.

Lithography. One lithographic method involves drawing directly on the block with a special greasy lithographic crayon. Its grease is retained in the pores of the stone and the surface residue cleaned away with turpentine. The surface of the stone is then treated with a wash of dilute nitric acid that increases the affinity of the drawn lines for greasy substances (the ink which will soon be applied) and increases the resistance to greasy substances of those portions which have not been drawn upon. Water is then applied to the entire surface of the stone, but it adheres to the blank areas only; the greasy drawn-upon areas naturally reject the water. When the ink is applied, it is accepted only by the greasy crayon lines of the design and is rejected by the water-saturated blank areas. Before each sheet is applied to the surface of the block, water is applied anew. The printing itself is relatively simple; the stone and the paper on it pass under a bar of wood on the press and the ink is thus transferred from the block to the paper.

This basic method may be varied in a number of ways, for example, by laying the greasy chalk over the entire surface and then scraping, as in a mezzotint, to bring out the highlights. Or the lithographic crayon can be dissolved and brushed on, giving the effect of a gray wash drawing; this is known as a lithotint. The surface of the stone may also be roughened with sand.

Although stone is the ideal medium for the lithographic technique, chemically prepared metal plates can also be used. Also, instead of executing the direct drawing on stone it is possible to prepare a lithographic crayon drawing on special transfer paper and then to transfer it to the stone by pressure.

The two examples reproduced here (Figs. 123 and 124, pp. 206, 208) reveal the lithograph as a medium with a wide range—much wider than that of the aquatint, for example. Its effects range from the deep rich blacks of the background in Daumier's *Rue Transnonain* to the light grays of the Kokoschka *Portrait,* with its spontaneous sketchy manner of a crayon drawing, and the pearly gray subtlety of tone found in some other lithographs.

Lithographs have also been done in color, for instance, by Toulouse-Lautrec and Kandinsky (Fig. 125, p. 208). As in other multicolor processes, each color demands a separate stone. In its relatively short his-

Fig. 124 (*left*). OSKAR KOKOSCHKA: *Portrait, Ruth I.* (lithograph). New York, Weyhe Gallery. (Photo courtesy The Museum of Modern Art) Fig. 125 (*right*). WASSILY KANDINSKY: Color lithograph from *Little Worlds* portfolio, 1922. New York, private collection.

tory (it was invented by Aloys Senefelder at the very end of the eighteenth century), lithography has been widely used in a rich variety of techniques. Apart from its broad range of possible effects, the lithographic stone, or its zinc plate commercial parallel, also has the advantage of a potentially large number of impressions that may be derived from one stone or plate. The medium is being used imaginatively and creatively in our own times.

Serigraphy. The serigraph, or silk-screen, method of print making, developed at the beginning of this century, is perhaps the latest print technique. It is a color print method, using as many plates (in this case silk screens) as the artist requires colors. These colors are laid on by a stencil method, that is, they are allowed to seep through the silk screen at those points where openings have been left (Fig. 126, p. 209).

In appearance the silk-screen print resembles a gouache (opaque water color) painting, bright and flat in tone, decorative in its broad and relatively unmodulated color areas, immediate in impact. Since each color has to be filtered by hand through a new screen, the print is somewhat more personal than those made by other methods and is more subject to minute variations within the edition. Serigraphy has been employed successfully in the reproduction of paintings, and its practitioners like to think of the process as a kind of multiple-painting method, bringing an original within the reach of the many. As a process, it seems to have grown out of the commercial method for reproducing posters with bold flat color areas and their need for simple striking textures.

The artist works directly on the silk, which has been stretched across an open frame, first making a pencil sketch of the area to be covered by a particular color. He then proceeds to "paint in" that area by stopping up the parts that are not to permit the passage of paint and opening up those through which the paint is about to be squeezed. This stencil preparation is done either by hand or with the aid of a transparent film which is cut out in the desired stencil form and then attached to the screen.

When the different color screens have been prepared, the artist begins to place his successive paper sheets under the first screen for application of the first color. This is accomplished by running the "ink"

Fig. 126. ALVA: *Three Figures* (serigraph). New York, National Serigraph Society.

(a special light oil paint) onto the surface of the silk and by drawing a squeegee over the silk, forcing the paint through the fabric and onto the paper. Each sheet of the edition goes through this process; it is submitted to the successive color screens in the same way until the original planned painting—now available in a fairly large edition— is finished.

The serigraph is fairly cheap to make and is striking in its color and texture possibilities. It is sometimes considered as a way out of the price dilemma of the modern painter, who through this method can gain a larger audience for his work than was ever before possible.

Although paintings are still beyond the economic reach of most people, print media such as the serigraph and the color lithograph and color woodcut offer to the artist a new type of patronage and to the art lover an art object he can aspire to own.

►8

The Minor Arts

IT IS, at best, unsatisfactory to classify some art forms as "minor," distinguishing them from such "major" classifications as painting, sculpture, architecture, prints, and drawings. And yet there are certain distinctions between the major arts and those of ceramics, glass, decorative mosaic and tile, textiles, metalwork, furniture, arms and armor, and even books. The works of these last are not only objects of art; they are also instruments of use. But so is a building—and in this dilemma we may consider architecture as a marginal art, including both functional and purely esthetic elements. The minor arts share with architecture the capacity to remain esthetically important even after the element of utility has disappeared. A ruined and unused temple or home can still appeal to us for artistic reasons; and a sword, vase, or piece of stained glass seen in a museum and far removed from its original sphere of utility can still retain its initial esthetic appeal. The minor arts use the same technical procedures and, often, the same or similar materials as do various major arts. In addition, the objects are planned; their design is usually outlined in a drawing or preparatory sketch, although pottery is sometimes made directly on the potter's wheel.

More than anything else, what impels us to differentiate between major and minor arts is the absence of symbolic purpose in most of the minor arts, their lack of a spiritual significance or deeper meaning. Their aim is either functional or decorative or a combination of the two—purposes which are perhaps less vital in terms of projecting human aims and aspirations than are those of major arts. If it is objected that architecture shares this lack with the minor arts, we may observe that many buildings do have a symbolic meaning and reflect quite clearly the strivings of their eras, as in the cross-shaped Christian basilica (Fig. 178, p. 313) and its Heaven-aspiring extension, the Gothic cathedral (Fig. 22, p. 35).

One category of nonmajor art, industrial art, will be considered in the next chapter. This art deals with a mass-produced object which is as carefully planned as many kinds of major or minor art. It differs substantially from the older categories in that it is designed consciously for a larger public than was ever before imagined and with certain engineering techniques in mind, as well as with an awareness of the new materials developed by modern industry.

Ceramics

One of the most widely applied minor art techniques is that of the ceramist, or potter, whose principal tool is the potter's wheel and whose material is clay. Although at one time pottery was made by hand with the help of round stones or shaped within wicker baskets, the wheel has replaced earlier methods and enabled the potter to achieve greater regularity of form. The soft clay is placed on a horizontally revolving wheel, and the pressure of the potter's hand or of a stick guides it into any one of a number of shapes as the mass whirls about. One of the most interesting processes in the world of art takes place as the clay opens up, flowerlike, into its myriad possibilities. Its initial handling is perhaps the most important part of the process and determines the final result more than do any later modifications. The form can be shaped by hand or with the aid of the jigger, a revolving mold.

After the clay has been shaped, the potter proceeds to fire it, that is, to expose it to heat in a kiln in order to harden it. A second firing process, at a higher temperature than the first, is used for the glaze that is applied to most types of pottery and often vitrifies the object treated. The glaze serves first as a means of making the vessel nonporous (all ordinary plates have a kind of glaze), then as a means of adding color with or without particular designs, and finally as a means of giving to the surface a special smooth texture that is agreeable to both sight and touch.

The pottery object, whether decorated or undecorated, commends itself to us as a sculptural form, as a purveyor of color impulses, as a source of pleasurable touch experiences, and as a container of space and a definer of volume. The wide variety of possible decoration adds to its rich attraction.

Some ceramic objects—many Chinese bowls, for example (Fig. 127, p. 214)—because of the intrinsic beauty of their own shape and the glaze fired on them, seem to the potter to need no further decoration. With other objects, however, the decoration is an essential element of the total result, as in the Greek vase (Fig. 49, p. 79). Here, and in other examples, the figures are so arranged that their forms curve outward to follow the shape of the vase. Minor elements in the decorative scheme, the geometric ornaments above and below, also conform to the shape of the particular portion of the vessel to which they are assigned. Thus if an object has differently shaped parts—for instance, a belly, neck, and stand of a vase, or a lip and well of a plate—each of these parts may be expected to have an appropriate type of ornament applied to it.

Sometimes the ornament is part of the object itself, created by the raising of portions of the surface during the first handling of the clay on the wheel. Sometimes the decorations are incised or are glazed onto the undersurface and remain visible through a transparent outer glaze (see Fig. 128, p. 214). Sometimes the final ornamentation is applied as an overglaze after the previous high-temperature glaze has been applied; this, however, does not give as long-lasting a result as the underglaze.

The motifs or artistic themes applicable to pottery decoration are almost limitless. They range from the plain geometric ornament found on the lip of some tableware through the simple figures used by the ancient Greeks to the elaborate landscape views found in Chinese pottery. It is interesting to observe that the pottery ornament produced in each culture corresponds to the major artistic impulse of the period and to its general esthetic laws. In drawing and proportion, the figures on the Greek vase are typical of their time; the landscape on the Sung bowl shares the characteristics of contemporary Chinese landscape art.

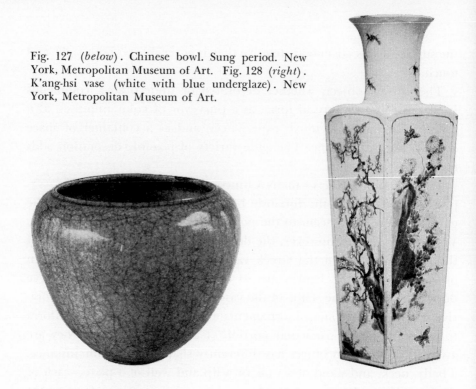

Fig. 127 (below). Chinese bowl. Sung period. New York, Metropolitan Museum of Art. Fig. 128 (right). K'ang-hsi vase (white with blue underglaze). New York, Metropolitan Museum of Art.

Modern ceramics, by the same token, reflect the quality of our industrial art by their elegant but spare and sleek forms, like so many finely planed and tooled parts of a machine, and by their lack of applied ornament.

Glassware

Glass in its molten state is a flowing substance that may be rolled, blown, or molded. The window or plate glass that we have examined above (Chapter 4) as an important determinant of modern architecture is generally made by spreading molten glass on a broad metal table over which a heavy roller is run to achieve the required thickness and flatness. Until fairly recently, such sheet glass was prepared by blowing a large cylinder of glass which, when cut down one side, would be flattened onto the table.

The glass art objects which we shall consider here have traditionally been blown or molded. After a quantity of molten glass has been prepared by heating refined sand with different alkaline chemical compounds, the glass blower dips a long hollow metal rod into the molten

214 THE MINOR ARTS

mass and carries off on its tip as much of the material as he can conveniently blow. He rolls this into a fairly regular shape on a stone slab and then blows through the tube to produce a large bubble. Its form can be controlled by swinging the metal rod, shaping with a wooden paddle, cutting with metal shears, or applying a metal caliper to the outside of the vessel as the rod is spun. Since the glass remains malleable for a reasonably long time, it can be molded and bent into a variety of shapes and degrees of transparency. Glass may be colored by the addition to the original molten mass of such metallic oxides as cobalt oxide for blue, copper oxide for red, and cadmium oxide for yellow.

If pottery making is interesting to watch, a session of glass blowing is actually stimulating, both visually and emotionally. The quick-working craftsmen bring shapes into being against a background of glowing furnaces, sizzling sounds, the snipping of scissors, and the crash of glass fragments abandoned by the cutter. When the glass cools down, it is brittle and breakable, but it can be cut and fashioned further. The traditional process is still used in Murano near Venice, in Mexico City, in parts of the United States, and elsewhere. Today, however, the general practice is to run the molten glass into blowing machinery or into molds from which bottles or other objects can be shaped by mechanical methods. What is known as cast glass is made by pouring molten glass into a mold so that it forms a solid object rather than a vessel. This results in light-admitting glass with visually interesting texture.

Glass objects have been made since the times of the ancient Egyptians, whose ceremonial objects have a unique coloristic beauty. The Romans, first people to use glass for household vessels, developed two new techniques of glass making. They introduced the cutting of glass shapes in cameo fashion, a technique exemplified by the famous Portland Vase with its white relief on a blue background. They also invented millefiori, or "thousand-flower," glass. This is produced by gathering long, thin, noodlelike filaments of different-colored glass into a bundle; while still in a semimelted state, the bundle is cut into slices which are then shaped into bowls. The colors of the original glass strips appear in the finished bowl as little dots, like so many flowers on a contrastingly colored background, from which derives the name (see Fig. 129, p. 216).

Roman techniques of glass making were passed on to the Byzantine

Fig. 129. Roman glass bowl, "mille-fiori" type. New York, Metropolitan Museum of Art.

Empire and, after the conquest of Constantinople in 1453, were embellished with Islamic influences. Glass-making methods were reintroduced into Italy at the shops of Murano in Venice and thence spread to other parts of Europe.

Glass vessels, like ceramics, may be interesting for their shape and texture or chiefly for their surface ornament. One of the simplest examples of the first type is cut glass, in which facets are cut on the surface of the object to catch reflections of light and enhance the appearance of the surface; this kind of glass was particularly popular during the Victorian period. Another, engraved glass, has been in vogue since the eighteenth century and is still in use today. It is made by placing a cast glass vessel against metal wheels that cut lines of varying thickness into its surface in intaglio fashion. Designs may also be etched into the surface of the glass with hydrofluoric acid.

Stained Glass

An altogether different art, that of stained glass, is customarily associated with the cathedrals of northern Europe. It was developed during the early Gothic period (late twelfth century) when large openings in the wall were made possible by the architectural system of vaults supported by flying buttresses instead of heavy walls (see Fig. 130, p. 217).

The stained-glass artist worked from a series of pots, each containing

216 THE MINOR ARTS

Fig. 130. *Crucifixion and Ascension* (stained glass, 26 feet high). Poitiers, France, Cathedral.

a differently tinted glass mixture. From each of these he dipped a mass of molten glass and shaped it to approximately the size and form dictated by a section of his preparatory sketch; he then laid it on a chalk-covered table kept at a constant temperature. When the design was complete, the glassmaker poured hot lead into the spaces between the pieces of glass, permanently joining the various sections as the lead cooled.

Easily removed from the table because of the chalk, the completed panel was reinforced by vertical and horizontal bars that helped bear the great weight of the glass. The glass was prepared panel by panel, with the differently colored bits furnishing the bulk of the design. Folds of drapery, arms, legs, and very fine details such as fingernails, eyebrows, and so forth were put on with a monochrome gray paint, known as grisaille, while the glass was still warm.

So long as the glassmaker was able to work in this mosaiclike fashion, improvising on his sketch as he went along and handling effective masses of color, his art retained its integrity. By the latter part of the thirteenth century, however, the demand for stained glass was so great that workers began to put in mechanical geometric background patterns to save time. By the fourteenth century they painted more than merely small details on the glass, since this was easier. They were already painting pictures on glass instead of cutting glass patterns; by the end of the fifteenth century we can speak of glass painting, an altogether new art. Most modern church windows are in this later technique, which involves drawing an entire design in grisaille on glass of mediocre color quality.

Early medieval glass is lambent and rich in essence; the light passes through it with a spiritualizing effect, exalting some onlookers and surprising all. Because of its very irregularities, medieval stained glass has a twinkling appearance that no modern glass achieves. Many people are attracted also by the decorative splendor of modern painted glass, as in Christ Church at Oxford University, but this is an art entirely different from that of the Middle Ages.

One may question whether any technique which produces an effect so spiritual as that of the stained glass in the great windows of Chartres Cathedral should be termed a minor art. Its purpose is certainly as high as that of any religious easel picture or fresco, but its place as an ad-

Fig. 131. *Emperor Justinian with Archbishop Maximianus and Suite* (mosaic). Ravenna, Italy, San Vitale.

junct to a larger entity (the cathedral) gives it a relatively lesser importance.

Mosaic and Tile

The problem of significance occurs also in relation to mosaic, the art of decorating walls, floors, and ceilings with a permanent design made up of bits of marble and glass. Many instances of its use have been serious in purpose, especially in the medieval era, as at San Vitale in Ravenna (see Fig. 131, p. 219). One might therefore think of mosaic, too, as marginal between the major and minor arts.

Mosaic is made by systematically placing tesserae, irregularly shaped bits of colored glass and marble, into a shallow box of damp cement. Area by area, the space to be decorated is filled out until the pattern has been completed. The cement hardens to hold the tesserae in a permanent design. Mosaic is an ancient technique, much favored by the Romans, the Early Christians, and the Byzantines.

Similar in function to mosaic, tiles are pieces of glazed pottery of regular geometrical shapes—squares, rectangles, lozenges, and the like —arranged in colorful decorative designs and generally used as coverings for walls and floors. This is another old technique, practiced by the early Babylonians and, later, by the Moslems, the peoples of Spain and Latin America, the artisans of Italy. It is still widely used

Fig. 132 *(left)*. The Bayeux Embroidery, scene from Battle of Hastings. Bayeux, France, Public Library. Fig. 133 *(right)*. JAN YOORS: *Leaping Flames* (tapestry, 1955). Courtesy the artist.

in Europe, the Middle East, and the Western Hemisphere. One may distinguish between artistic tile work, like that in the Alhambra at Granada in Spain, and the common commercial type generally used in pools and shower rooms.

Textiles

One of the most important and varied of the minor arts is the creation and decoration of textiles, products with which everyone has had some form of contact: in carpeting, drapes, curtains, furniture coverings, clothing. Textiles exhibit an enormous variety of materials and colors; their possible effects, both commercial and artistic, are many and impressive (see Fig. 132, p. 220).

Like prehistoric basketry, textile weaving began as a craft in the home, and preliminary drawings were neither needed nor used. At some point, perhaps when the designs became extremely complex, as in the Orient, drawn plans came to be prepared; but often, especially when there was a basic repeat motif or decoration, it was possible for the weaver simply to memorize the design. In many cultures, designs became traditional; for example, in southern Mexico today, Indians are selling in the markets of Oaxaca serapes identical in design and color to those displayed in the museums of early folk art; obviously, these weavers need use no drawings. At the other extreme of sophistication and complexity are the narrative tapestries of the fifteenth to sixteenth centuries, made from original designs or from contemporary paintings. Similarly, a drawing is absolutely essential for modern fabrics whether they are commercially printed or are individually woven —like the Yoors (Fig. 133, p. 220) or like tapestries after Matisse, Léger, and Picasso.

Textile materials are both more flexible and much more fragile than those of other arts. They are usually woven into a more or less uniform and continuous material of considerable permanence and great diversity of usage, but they may also be knitted, felted, or made into lace. In textile making, as in painting or sculpture, the basic materials, here those from which the threads derive, largely determine the character of the final product. Textile materials include animal and vegetable substances, such as wool, silk, linen, and cotton, as well as synthetic chemical substances, such as nylon and rayon.

Weaving is done on a loom, an upright frame within which threads are interlaced horizontally (the weft) and vertically (the warp). As the weaver has at his command a considerable number of colors, materials, and thicknesses of material, the possible permutations and combinations of the finished fabric are almost endless. In knitting, needles are used to intertwine lengths of yarn; felting is a process of beating together fibers to form matted cloths, as in the bark cloth of the Pacific islands; lace-making uses an open-work scheme of thread joining to produce a delicate and refined tissue.

Textile decoration may be applied by embroidery, and colors may be added to the fabric by printing, painting, and dyeing as well as by the arrangement of colored threads (Fig. 132, p. 220).

Textile printing is an important branch of textile design, with a long and honorable history stretching back to ancient India and Egypt. In the Western world it became popular at the end of the seventeenth century, possibly as a result of British, French, Dutch, and other contacts with India. There are three chief methods of printing designs on fabrics: block printing, intaglio printing, and stencil printing. The first uses colors applied to wooden blocks and is similar to the woodcut

Fig. 134. *St. George* (Byzantine cloisonné
enamel, XIth century). New York, Metropolitan Museum of Art.

technique (see Chapter 7); the second uses engraved copper cylinders
on a rotating press, a different cylinder being needed for each color;
the third, stencil printing, is analogous to the serigraph process (see
Chapter 7).

Versatile and adaptable as they undoubtedly are, textiles are seldom
created simply for their own sake but almost always with a definite
use in view—as carpet, tapestry, furniture cover, or garment.

Enamel

The art of enamel, too, is an ancient one; its lineage begins in ancient
Egypt and goes on through the entire Middle Ages, including the Byzantine, Romanesque, and Gothic periods. It was also used during the
Renaissance and later. Its two basic types are the *cloisonné* and the
champlevé.

Cloisonné (Fig. 134, p. 222) involves the placing of thin metal
ridges, *cloisons,* on the surface of a metal plate so as to form a pattern
of shallow cells. The vitreous enamel paste is then squeezed into each
cell in accordance with the design. Each cell becomes part of a pattern, the enamel areas separated by the ridges of metal just as the
pieces of glass are separated by the leads in a stained-glass window.

The metal and paste are then baked and fused into a permanent combination.

In the champlevé (lifted field or area) process, sections of metal are removed from a relatively thick plaque to form depressions in the surface. These depressions are filled with enamel paste, the surface smoothed, and the whole baked. The difference in esthetic effect between the two techniques is marked. Cloisonné is delicate and pastel in color and threadlike in its outlines; champlevé shows a generally darker tonality and heavier outlines between the various color areas. Both techniques can be used as part of flat plaques or as part of larger metal forms such as bird shapes, cups, bowls, and so on.

Metalwork

Metal objects have been important throughout history. (Modern metalwork will be discussed in Chapter 9). Such diverse objects as gates, lamps, and grilles of iron as well as items of gold, silver, bronze, brass, and many other metals have been made and used through the ages.

Fig. 135 (left). Wine vessel (bronze; Shang dynasty). Chicago, Illinois, Art Institute of Chicago. Fig. 136 (below). Ardagh chalice (silver communion chalice with gold filigree work, glass studs, and rock crystals). Dublin, Dublin Museum.

Fig. 137. Armor suit (steel; Italian school, *c.* 1480). New York, Metropolitan Museum of Art.

Some are hammered out, chiseled, or filed, like early American silverware; some are cast solid, like Chinese bronze vessels (Fig. 135, p. 223). Jewelry and ceremonial objects, arms and armor, and coins are of particular interest as metal forms that have been created for use and beauty and that often reflect aspects of history.

In the first category, relatively small objects have been made of various precious and semiprecious metals (and, today, nonprecious but decorative metals), sometimes with jewel encrustations, sometimes with enamel inlay. Among the objects made of gold, silver, platinum, and so forth are chalices (Fig. 136, p. 223), crowns, necklaces, pins, rings, and many other articles varying in style from the most primitive to the most sophisticated. Much jewelry has been found in tombs where it was buried with its owners, yielding to modern scholars a valuable body of esthetic and social information.

Armor, weapons and other tools, and metal clothing worn by soldiers in battle, like many minor art objects, have a dual function, in this case to decorate and protect the individual using them. Examples may be found from the Orient and Occident, ranging in time from the Middle Ages through the post-Renaissance era. During the sixteenth century, some Italian, German, and French armor (Fig. 137, p. 224) was embellished by intaglio decorations of great complexity and richness. Weapons, especially where used for ceremonial rather than practical purposes, often sport jewel decorations in addition to engraved motifs. Yet the actual form or design of a piece of armor or a weapon is at least as important as its ornamentation; the balancing of function and beauty then becomes the important consideration.

Coins, among the least familiar as a metal art form, have represented at certain periods a vital branch of relief sculpture. Greek coins, for example (Fig. 138, p. 225), are often as interesting in form as are other Greek arts; and what they tell us about the life, customs, and esthetics of the Greeks is meaningful indeed. Through ancient coinage, we get an idealized portrayal of many famous people, like Cleopatra and Alexander the Great. Also, reproductions on coins have preserved for us the appearance of many masterpieces of sculpture which, famous in their day, have been completely lost. We would have only the most imperfect idea of the Athena figure from the interior of the Parthenon (see Fig. 62, p. 96) were it not for the survival of Athenian coins on which it was portrayed. For an age which left us very few original works of sculpture (most of our knowledge of Greek sculpture comes from Roman copies), the coins remain an important repository of style.

While coins are only occasionally designed by prominent artists, medals are often recognized as significant forms of relief sculpture; in certain eras they have engaged the best available talents. The medals of the fifteenth century in Italy, as exemplified by those of Pisanello,

Fig. 138. Syracusan coin (Greece, late Vth century B.C.). New York, The City College.

Fig. 139. Philadelphia highboy, made in 1770. New York, Metropolitan Museum of Art.

are among the most important works of the time. Medals have been used to commemorate important events and to celebrate distinguished personalities down to the present day.

Furniture

In traditional terms, furniture has involved both the design of a given shape or series of shapes, such as Chippendale, Duncan Phyfe, and other styles, and also the embellishment of these forms with an appropriate type of ornament (see Fig. 139, p. 226). The latter is usually carved directly out of the wood itself and represents a type of dramatic relief carving, or sculpture, in wood. This is especially true of furniture of the Baroque period, in the seventeenth century. Furniture of other periods also corresponds to the leading esthetic attitudes of its age. Thus, Rococo furniture of the Louis XVth era may be equated with the graceful colorful art of painters like Boucher and Fragonard (see Fig. 214a, p. 392), early nineteenth-century furniture with characteristics of neo-Classicism, and so forth.

Since wood and the cloth of upholstery are perishable, we do not have as much furniture surviving from the medieval and classical past as we should like (Egyptian furniture from the dry tombs has endured); and we cannot be sure of its nature at such far removal in time. Nevertheless, judging by analogy, we may assume that classical, medieval, and ancient Near-Eastern furniture would have been similar to the other arts of those periods. Moreover, where we do not have actual examples we can often judge the nature of furniture from its pictured images in works of art, for instance, Greek vase paintings, Assyrian reliefs, or other representations where people are shown sitting, lying down, and otherwise using furniture.

Books

The book as an art form embraces the design of the container or cover, the typography, and the layout of the pages. The book as we know it today (in contrast to the ancient scroll or rotulus) dates from the second century, in its illustrated form from the fourth century. Decorated scroll manuscripts, however, were used in most ancient times. The medieval illuminated manuscript was covered with both decorative and figurative ornament, much of it very serious religious art and therefore to be regarded in the same category as early Renaissance painting (Fig. 140, p. 228).

By the end of the fifteenth century, as we have seen (Chapter 7), the invention of movable types brought the wood-block illustration to replace the painted illumination, and typography developed, necessarily influenced by previous calligraphy or handwriting systems. The hand lettering of the Rhine district, done with a broad quill pen, produced a "Gothic" type face that is reflected in the metal type form of most Germanic countries. Italian printers followed the chastely outlined letters derived by the humanists of the early Renaissance from Roman inscriptions. This so-called Roman type is now used throughout the world.

Today the richly tooled cover is reserved for limited editions as a luxury item. At one time, however, book covers were generally impor-

Fig. 140. French Gospel lectionary (page showing Nativity and Adoration of Shepherds; XIIIth century). London, British Museum.

tant, especially for heightening the significance of religious books. The manuscripts of the early Middle Ages were often placed between ivory or ivory and gold covers, and sometimes even decorated with jeweled ornaments, to underline the sacredness of the text. In our own time the problem of the well-designed book as a whole belongs to industrial art and will be considered in the next chapter.

In any discussion of the minor arts we are struck by the fact that, century after century, craftsmen of all kinds have devoted themselves to the creation and perfection of shapes (and their concomitant ornamentation) designed for useful, even commonplace, purposes. However differentiated from the symbolic purposes of the so-called major arts, these objects of everyday use are important in that they have helped build a better life for the individual, a life revealed to us in their elegant, dignified, graceful, or otherwise cunningly fashioned forms.

▶ 9

Industrial Art

VIRTUALLY EVERYTHING used in our daily lives is related to industrial art. Even the so-called minor art objects discussed in Chapter 8 (pottery—as in Fig. 141, p. 230—glassware, textiles, furniture, jewelry, and the like) now generally respond to the basic requirement for industrial art, namely, that they be designed for mass production and distribution. This is the signature of our democratic age, when we try to make the market as wide as possible, extending it not only to all our fellow citizens but also to people of foreign lands.

Industrial art now includes: consumer goods design; the shaping of commercial equipment and capital goods needed in product manufacture; commercial art that helps sell products—including packaging as well as advertising; and industrial architecture. All these represent the tangible and visible results of our machine civilization, just as the pottery of the ancient Greeks, the jewelry of the Egyptians, the engineering of the Romans were concrete evidences of those cultures.

Certain questions have been raised by the introduction of mass-made objects in our times. One of these questions is whether the machine-made product can be conceded to possess the attributes of esthetic beauty or the qualities of art in an age when traditional arts still hold the field, or when at least the traditional idea of an embellished or decorated surface (as in painting, prints, jewelry) is still dominant. If, on the other hand, the artist in the traditional sense is to be replaced by the creator of machine art, must he become a man without function in our society, existing to gratify the whims—snob-

229

Fig. 141. Black plastic salad bowls. (Photo courtesy Industrial Design magazine)

bish or otherwise—of a dilettante public? Some critics go so far as to suggest, as Sir Herbert Read has done, that the contemporary artist has become "merely a society entertainer."

Another problem related to the emergence of machine art lies in the belief held by some of its practitioners that an object which is functionally successful, that is, which fulfills the idea of "fitness of purpose," is automatically beautiful. Industrial art, as we shall see, must offer more than mere utility if it is to have any artistic significance. Even when the form of an object reflects its function, the object will not necessarily be beautiful. In fact a useful object can be downright ugly or quite ordinary; for instance, a typical suburban garage may be quite effective on a practical level and a bag for golf clubs certainly reflects its function, but they usually have commonplace designs. The element of good design must, then, be applied to the diverse categories of industrial art.

Varieties of Industrial Art

Among *consumer goods* we find household appliances, communications equipment, lighting fixtures, toys, sanitary equipment, and indeed almost every article manufactured for home use, such as razors, radios, mixers, cookers, lamps, washbowls, and so on (see Fig. 142, p. 231). *Commercial equipment* includes items used in connection with business enterprises and their functioning: store refrigerators, measuring and weighing instruments, pumps, beauty machines, office equipment (see Fig. 143, p. 231), and almost any device not used by the consumer himself but rendering him a form of service. *Capital goods* represent such heavy industrial equipment as machine tools used to make other machines, trucks, agricultural machinery, generators, hoists, factory furnaces, and, in general, most of the machinery or instruments of heavy industry.

The next broad category, *commercial art,* deals with the problems and techniques of publicizing what the merchant or service agency has to sell. It includes the designing of posters, signs, advertisements, printed material of various kinds, and a whole new art activity known as package design. This last is a highly developed specialty; its purpose is to offer an attractive container for the product involved. This container may be a simple package such as the cigarette carton or Kleenex box; it may be a container like a lipstick holder, an integral part of the total object that may even outlast its product.

Industrial architecture produces buildings specifically for the accommodation of industrial activities, for example, factories, mills, foundries. These structures entail the special design problems that spring from their use for heavy or light manufacture, their containment of electrical or foundry equipment and the attendant dangers of fire, overloading, or shock, and so on. Industrial architecture also includes buildings erected as adjuncts of various kinds of transportation: railroad

Fig. 142 (*left*). General Electric portable mixer. (Photo courtesy Industrial Design magazine)   Fig. 143 (*right*). Modern typewriter. Olivetti "Lettera 22" model.

terminals, bridges, signal houses, lighthouses, airports, canal locks, and the like. Sometimes a separate category, *machine architecture,* is taken to include the large-scale containers necessary in heavy industry or large farming operations, the turbine enclosures or cases used in power generation, as at the TVA and Hoover Dams, gas tanks, cooling towers, ventilating stations, grain elevators, and silos. Although we may consider some of these structures capital goods, for the most part they have a distinct containing function or offer their own design problems (Fig. 72, p. 113).

Pressures within Industrial Art

Of the many types of objects mentioned above, a number were in existence before the Industrial Revolution of the late eighteenth century; more were not. Such objects as automobiles, telephones, and typewriters have come into existence as necessities of modern life. Furthermore, whatever items did exist before the Industrial Revolution were made and sold on a different basis. The nature of industrial democracy demanded a new fabrication and distribution system. Instruments of everyday utility have been made available to an ever greater number of people. An unfortunate concomitant has been the appearance of destructive competition, a drive to exceed the sales figure of each preceding year, that has inevitably tended toward an economy of planned obsolescence. Thus, objects are manufactured so that they will wear out in a relatively short time, or they will be superseded stylistically by a more fashionable model each season or year; for these reasons more goods are put into circulation than would be warranted by mere necessity.

The constant pressure to sell is stronger now than at other periods of the world's history. In order to maintain our economy in balance, therefore, it appears necessary for manufacturers to plan on product replacement within a fixed period. It is even made worthwhile for the purchaser to dispose of his slightly used car, washing machine, or TV set in favor of a new model, so that business continues to roll onward and the sales figures remain in balance with the production quota. In addition to attractive financial offers, the public is bombarded with a dramatic packaging appeal that makes the newer model of pressing iron, bathroom scale, or radio set more attractive than the previous model. As part of this constant pressure on the customer to buy the newer model, there is an insinuation that not doing so is not keeping up with one's neighbors.

At the same time we must recognize that newer design often results in product improvement.

The Background of Craftsmanship

The idea that an object can be beautiful as well as useful is certainly not new. We have seen that far back in ancient times the Greeks produced vases both for the sake of their beauty and as containers for oil, wine, perfume, and other materials, containers that were functionally designed and lovely in outline and surface decoration. We may even speak of mass production to some extent, since we know of mass shipments of pottery with and without wine, although the objects were undoubtedly produced by hand. Similarly the crafts of the Middle Ages were on a very high level with a long period of development behind them, a historically continuous craftsmanship that produced such masterpieces as the silver work of the Irish and the enamels of the Romanesque and Gothic periods. During the Renaissance, jewelry, ironwork and pottery, to mention only a few of the crafts practiced, still maintained a high standard of designed workmanship.

The basic differences, however, between the pre-Machine Age craftsman and the modern industrial designer are many. Where the former worked with one material or with a limited number of materials such as silver, gold, platinum, or a few kinds of clay, wood, or iron, the industrial designer works with an almost unlimited number of materials. The differences go even deeper because the craftsman worked with his own hands, understanding intimately the nature of the material with which he dealt—a material that, when it left his hands, bore the impress of his artistic personality. The silverware of a Paul Revere, the furniture of a Duncan Phyfe, the jewelry of a Cellini exemplify the warm and personal character of the various minor arts produced in this way.

Today some industrial designers, inspired by the Bauhaus school in Germany (1919–1933) and its American derivatives, also feel that the designer should know his materials at first hand. But often the modern industrial designer, influenced by the very nature of his work, becomes in great part a business entrepreneur. A successful designer's studio today includes many people who pool their respective talents in such skills as drafting, knowledge of media and their limitations, and modeling—all skills which at one time resided in the person of the master craftsman, who might also have been a famous painter or sculptor.

By the time of the Renaissance it had become clear that there was to be an art divorced from the purposefulness, mostly religious, that had previously dominated all the arts. The paganism of that period, its naturalistic interests and secular outlook on life, the growth of an increasingly powerful middle class, all combined to produce an art of display and luxury in which painting and sculpture became symbols of the patron's wealth and decorations for his home. The comparison has been made between "chamber art" of this kind and chamber music which also exists apart from its original religious functions and as a pure intellectual experience. At the same time, as its religious function declined with the Reformation, art became increasingly humanistic, that is, geared to the expression of the everyday and the human.

Whereas many, if not most, artists had formerly been able to turn their hands to almost any design activity (Giotto's architecture, Leonardo's sculpture, architecture, machinery, and so on), the age of the Renaissance saw the beginning of a specialization whereby artists turned more and more to a "fine art" of individual enjoyment, while artisans worked on the practical needs of design: building, crafts, and the like. Hence the distinction arose between what we today call the fine arts and the crafts—a distinction which has always implied, and still does, a question of superiority and inferiority. Nevertheless, although the craftsman during the post-Renaissance period was overshadowed socially by the rising star of the fine artist, important craft productions were created at least up to the time of the Industrial Revolution in the late eighteenth century. The tapestries of seventeenth-century France, the brilliant furniture of the eighteenth century in Britain, the fine silver work of Paul Revere in the colonies, and many more instances attest to the continued flourishing of what we may call craft arts.

Even before industry was mechanized by the Industrial Revolution, however, there was serious deviation from the original intimate relationship between the craftsman and the object he had customarily handled from inception to finish. As manufacturing developed, there came into being a master designer who would delegate various portions of the fabricating process to different workers. We find that in the eighteenth-century shop of Thomas Chippendale, the famous furniture designer, certain men might make one particular chair part all their lives.

Arrival of the Machine

With the end of the eighteenth century and the coming of the Industrial Revolution, an entirely new set of conditions made possible the mass production of articles that had hitherto been produced by hand alone or, like the Chippendale chair or the Wedgwood pottery of that century, by a process of limited repetition. By the early nineteenth century the character of craftsmanship, its intimacy of workmanship and high quality level, had finally given way before the methods of the machine. These methods spread so rapidly that there was simply no time to consider beauty; more and more people wanted the wonderful creature-comfort items the machine was producing.

Although the machine offered the benefits of technological advancement to a far broader public than he could reach, the craftsman found its advent a two-fold disaster. It meant not only the loss of jobs for many thousands of people, but also the loss of standards of beauty. From this point on, the trend was toward very rapid fabrication, which often caused quality deterioration and almost complete ignoring of the decorative factor.

After a lapse of time, British industrialists made conscious efforts to bring back the artistic approach—largely in order to increase the sale of their products. In 1832 the National Gallery in London was founded expressly for the purpose of bringing before manufacturers and their staffs the artistic achievements of the past. Since by then most of the worthwhile talents in art had been absorbed into painting and sculpture—there being no longer any room for the old-style craftsman or designer—the effort to bring some measure of art into manufacture was slow in bearing fruit.

Art and industry continued for the most part to go their separate ways, and further attempts were necessary in order to bring beauty into the realm of the manufactured product. Why should the manufac-

(a)

(b)

(e)

(f)

236

(c)   (d)

Fig. 144. Development of the lantern-slide projector: (a) 1776 type (b) tin kerosene lamp, 1826 (c) kerosene lamp, 1866 (d) kerosene projector, 1876 (e) whale-oil lantern, 1886 (f) oil lantern, 1896 (g) electric projector, 1956. (Photos courtesy Sylvania Electric Products, Inc.)

(g)

237

turers have bothered at all? Certainly a leading reason was that by the middle of the nineteenth century the element of competition had become an overriding factor in world economy and it was felt that something beyond mere technical excellence was needed to make one product outsell another. The middle of the nineteenth century saw the establishment of a number of art schools, museums, and exhibitions dedicated to helping industry and providing the manufacturer with stimulating ideas from the past to apply to the surfaces of his products.

This conscious dipping into the past, into the almost limitless reservoir of historic ornamental styles, often resulted in amusing anachronisms. Thus, we find a factory beam engine, made about 1830, set on a classical podium, with chastely designed Doric columns helping to enclose and beautify the engine. Equally typical is the classicistic stereopticon projector of that era (Fig. 144, pp. 236–237).

Since Romanticism and industrialism grew up together (the former as one means of escaping from the latter), references to the medieval past, a characteristic Romantic refuge, occur in machines and architectural design throughout the nineteenth century. One incongruous instance is London Bridge, a somewhat naïve amalgam of functional ironwork with medieval Scottish architecture in the piers. One of the great advocates of this archaeological point of view was John Ruskin, who said in so many words that the contemporary artist should turn to thirteenth-century Gothic style for inspiration. Out of this attitude came the Gothic railroad tunnels, Tudor railroad stations, and other practical structures decorated with medieval applied ornament or turrets and battlements.

As time passed, other ideas gained favor. Whereas at the beginning of the Industrial Revolution art was at least applied superficially to manufactured products, toward the end of the nineteenth century William Morris declared that art and industry had no meeting place whatsoever, that the machine was the archenemy of civilization. What he proposed was a new society in which the worker, living under decent conditions of housing, clothes, and food, would have the leisure to make useful and beautiful things by hand, as presumably had been done in the past.

Morris's belief in the "hermit craftsman" working by himself to recapture the esthetic delights of a forgotten age was entirely consistent with his refusal to accept the Industrial Revolution. Led by Ruskin and by the period itself to steep himself in the lore of the Gothic era, Morris took the typically escapist and Romantic position that the medieval era had been utopian. Conveniently ignoring their disease, superstition, and widespread misery, he was able to think of these centuries as they had been portrayed by Sir Walter Scott and other revivalist interpreters of the Gothic age—a wonderful and exalted era, its men living in brotherhood and filled with manly ideals.

Morris therefore attempted to revive medieval crafts in what he felt was the brotherly spirit animating their original practice, whereby everyone presumably could enjoy the benefits of the craftsman's creations. Unfortunately the public for the genuinely attractive works of the Morris and Company studios (carvings, stained glass, wallpapers, fabrics, and furniture) was limited to those who could afford them. The mass public was still dependent on machine-made products, which actually benefited to some extent from the designs of the Morris group. Regrettably, however, others attempted unsuccessfully to reproduce those designs by superficial machine techniques.

So long as the craftsman could find no place in modern industry, he naturally gravitated to the various "arts and crafts" groups that took their tone from the antiquarian views of Morris. Even if Morris had been unable to make a permanent impression on industry in the sense of solving its often unfelt, although entirely real, dilemma, he did succeed in reviving the idea of the independent artist-craftsman.

Art Nouveau

During the period from 1890 to 1910, the Art Nouveau movement created a style of ornament that was flowing, organic, and cursive, stemming from natural forms. This was applied, often successfully, to posters, typography, book design, architecture, furniture, and other fields. The buildings of Louis Sullivan in the United States illustrate its impact on architectural decoration, and the flowing contours of many posters by Toulouse-Lautrec exemplify its effects on that medium (Fig. 145, p. 240); Henry van de Velde used it in furniture and design generally.

However interesting from an ornamental point of view the Art Nouveau style may have been, and however influential in the areas mentioned, its applications will always have a somewhat exaggerated

Fig. 145. HENRI DE TOU-LOUSE-LAUTREC: *Troupe de Mlle Eglantine* (poster in color lithography). New York, collection the author.

quality for traditionalists on one hand and more functionally minded persons on the other hand. Essentially it tried to create a new and independent ornamental style for the practical purposes of modern life. But what was apparently overlooked was that while the new style did have undeniable charm and excitement and expressed in many ways the spiritual ferment of the *fin de siècle,* it had little to do with the practical function of buildings, furniture, utensils, and posters as such. That is, it was unrelated to the objects it tried to embellish. The curvilinear growing ornament used by Sullivan to decorate otherwise very functional buildings seems rather inappropriate—although its purpose, to relieve the apparent sternness of straight lines, is quite legitimate.

In a general way Art Nouveau realized its role in the age of the machine, in that it tried to cope with the problem of industrial design from a designer's point of view (Sullivan, van de Velde, and others). But after World War I and the ensuing social and economic upheavals, designers began to think in new terms of a real fusion of art and industry. As the novelty of the Machine Age had worn off long before and as the acceptance of machine-made products had become all-pervasive, people were no longer interested merely in how things worked or how cheaply they could be bought; they wanted something better looking as well.

The Bauhaus and Its Influence

In postwar Germany the famous Bauhaus school was established by Walter Gropius. There, from 1919 until the school's closing by the Nazis in 1933, was fostered the idea of experimental laboratories for new materials and techniques of the Machine Age. There designs and production models for contemporary products were developed.

By teaching in careful and scientific fashion the advantages and limitations of the materials of modern manufacture, the Bauhaus leaders hoped to give the artist-designer a greater understanding of the problems of modern industry, that is, "to liberate the creative artist from his otherworldliness and reintegrate him into the workaday world of realities." They also aimed to "broaden and humanize the rigid, almost exclusively material mind of the business man." Above all, they felt the most vital function of the Bauhaus was to teach the basic nature of design as an integral part of all things used in everyday living, an idea clearly opposed to that of the old "art for art's sake." In the same way they opposed the idea of business as an end in itself, feeling that design should be improved for the sake of as many people as possible, helping them toward the attainment of what is often called the better life.

After 1933, the Bauhaus influence continued to be felt. Its teachers went abroad, many to America (Gropius himself to Harvard) where the original teachings were broadened and altered to meet the circumstances of American life. It is in great measure the direct line of development through schools headed by former Bauhaus people that has enabled industrial design to move forward so rapidly in America.

In addition to the Bauhaus influence, the factor of competition stimulated the spread of industrial design practices. The great wave of business expansion following World War I had come to an end in the late 'twenties, and in order to get more buyers, merchandise had to be made more attractive. During the depression of the 'thirties the need for competitive product styling became greater; as sales dropped, the necessity for designers was clearer than ever. The America of that period was ill prepared to accept this burden in view of the small number of trained people then available. What American designers struggled toward gradually and painfully, European schools such as the Bauhaus were already achieving by organized instruction and experimentation, not only for the purpose of increasing sales but also from the point of view of understanding what was better as design.

The Modern Approach to Industrial Art

Industrial designers today combine in themselves the functions of designer, production supervisor, and sales and advertising manager. For some, the chief incentive is clearly to increase sales; for others, it is the fascination of making something work; for still others, it is the esthetic achievement of a beautiful shape, texture, or color. The most successful design organizations are clearly those which can package the product successfully to make it catch the eye. The fact that many museums have exhibited "useful objects," giving them thereby a certain prestige, does not lessen the basic commercial intention of the manufacturer and his design consultants or design staff. There can be little question that the services of the industrial designer have been most profitable to the manufacturer, facilitating the economic process in a very positive way. Whether or not they have bestowed the benefits of greater beauty is a different problem.

The quality of beauty. If an industrial art product is not always so beautiful as we might wish, this is not the result of the standardization of shape that the industrial process makes mandatory. Nor is a thing necessarily beautiful just because it is the only one of its kind in existence. The machine-produced item can have beauty provided the original design possesses that quality. As to whether the absence of ornament on a mass-produced object precludes beauty in the traditional sense, we have but to turn to the supernally lovely shapes and textures of many ancient Chinese vases without ornament. In fact, Chinese pottery with ornament is often inferior in esthetic effect; so clearly is the emphasis on the shape itself that any decoration seems superfluous.

Modern painting and sculpture have often dealt with purely abstract qualities of form, color, and texture arranged for their own sake, that is, as pure esthetic impulse. On this basis we can also accept the machine-produced metal utensil, chair, appliance, and so forth. The

Fig. 146 *(left)*. Jacobsen stacking side chairs. Courtesy Richards Morgenthau Company. Fig. 147 *(right)*. Side chair. Chippendale mahogany made in Philadelphia, *c.* 1760. Courtesy Brooklyn Museum, New York.

mere fact that it does not have what is often called humanistic content—as traditional painting and sculpture have had—is of no moment, for neither did the traditional arts and crafts for the most part. The latter were humanistic in that they were used by human beings for human ends; their modern equivalents are infinitely more so, in this sense, because they are made for many more people to enjoy.

Although quantity consumption by itself is never a criterion of excellence and although industrial designers sometimes appeal to their audience on the questionable basis of novelty and garish color excitation, by and large industrial designers have something to contribute artistically. They still project the basic elements of sleek form, clean texture, and sparkling exhilarating color in varying proportions to effect a stimulating visual and tactual impact. Nor is the esthetic potential of the industrially made object confined to a superficial physical reaction. One of the ways in which we perceive art of any kind, as demonstrated much earlier in this book, is through the exercise of our intelligence. In the course of this intellectual approach, we see forms, spaces, lines, and so on as consciously related to each other. Another response is the intuitional; although this response is not easily converted into everyday language, it is none the less genuine. Indeed, while some objects may be analyzed in terms of specific mathematical relationships of parts, others must be perceived chiefly by intuition, that is, by a subconscious absorption of their design elements. Thus, even before we are aware of why we react favorably to an art object, we may be pleasurably affected by it.

The object of industrial design, by definition, is a result of organized or planned arrangement. To that extent it can stir our formal imagination as well as can an item designed for individual rather than mass consumption. Is there any basic difference, from this point of view, between the Jacobsen chair (Fig. 146, p. 243) and the American Chippendale chair (Fig. 147, p. 243)? We need not go so far as to claim mystical properties for this kind of geometric, nonrepresentational, or nonobjective art, any more than we would for such an expression in painting—even less, since many abstract paintings do set up tensions and movements that are profoundly disturbing in an emotional and spiritual sense. The product of the machine does not profess to do this; the painter or the sculptor is producing a unique reaction to a formal or emotional situation.

The question of timeliness. What the machine does, in essence, is to give to the object of everyday use, to the machine that makes it, and even to the devices that sell it, an attractiveness of form, color, and texture, a flavor of our times that is in its way as valid as the drinking vessels of the ancient Greeks or the furniture of the eighteenth-century British or Americans. If we can rid our minds for a moment of the Romantic clichés associated with the Grecian urn (in the Keats sense), the medieval object of art (in the Oscar Wilde sense), or any other object for which we have such exalted associations, we can make a new and somewhat simplified approach to the arts and crafts of the past.

Surely the average Greek potter, British furniture maker, medieval jeweler (or the traditional painter, for that matter) did not look upon his work with the notion of divine mission with which we today tend to envelop those creations. What we choose to read into the Grecian urn is perhaps our own conception more than that of the Greeks themselves. It is even possible that future generations will look upon the remains of our civilization, its outworn motorcars, planes, and radio sets, with a somewhat similar nostalgic feeling.

Many of us are willing by now to accept the fact that certain types of architecture and painting are reflections of our dynamic industrial civilization (the Savoye House, the Mondrian *Composition,* and similar parallels). We would probably include in this category certain surviving craft arts. But when we speak of the industrial arts and their admittedly functional and pragmatic background, we are likely to stumble into the centuries-long separation of the artist and craftsman. We often fail to see that the steel tumbler, electric mixer, television cabinet, and automobile show as much of the nature of our time as the older craft-made Italian glass, Greek pottery vessel, Italian credenza cabinet, and Rococo carrying-chair show of theirs.

By the same token, we have a reverse situation—people who accept the industrial article for what it is, namely a useful and possibly beautiful object, may categorically refuse to accept its like in a frame or on a pedestal, traditionally sacred locales reserved for ART. Thus they may admire the functional design of a factory or other useful building or gladly accept the package made by a container company; but paintings like the Mondrian *Composition* or those by Le Corbusier (actually exemplifying the original artistic stimulus of many modern machine products) they will reject as not being ART.

What is ignored here was perceived by Walter Gropius when he called for a "basic unity of all design in its relation to life . . ." We are pleased to read that Leonardo and other Renaissance masters were able to design processions, furniture, banners, costumes, indeed anything that needed to be designed—the Italians even have a word, *disegno,* which means both design and drawing. But too often today's layman, or, for that matter, artist, seems to have developed logic-tight compartments that make it impossible to cross from one area to another, from the sacred fine arts to the not-so-sacred industrial ones.

Whether or not everyone is willing to make the step, either as observer or practitioner, it becomes increasingly clear that in some degree it has already been taken. The influence of modern fine arts on the industrial arts is a matter of record, and indeed men like Le Corbusier illustrate the possibility of engaging an artistic talent in different areas. Many painters have moved successfully into poster and container work, into furniture design and similar occupations, without harm to their work as fine artists. And it is undeniable that they have had an excellent effect on the packages, record albums, and other objects they have designed.

The expression of function. An important factor in modern design

Fig. 148. "Talgo" lightweight train (about half the weight of conventional equipment). ACF Industries, New York. (Photo courtesy Industrial Design magazine)

is the need to produce forms which are in themselves expressive of the function of the object: a car should look like a car and not like a wagon. Furthermore, beauty of form should stem from this functional relationship to purpose, rather than exist as a superficial coating attached to the object in order to make it more salable. For example, a Diesel locomotive (Fig. 148, p. 246) differs sharply in appearance from early railroad engines, which were high and awkward-looking and suggestive merely of an engine with attached wheels. The modern Diesel conveys the feeling of speed in its long streamlined shape —a shape that not only helps to reduce wind resistance (that is, improves function), but also makes the form follow the function.

Much the same line may be followed in airplane design (Fig. 149, p. 247), ship design, and, to a more limited degree, in automobile design. We may agree that the successive car bodies produced since the early 1900's look better, more like moving vehicles. But whether the efficiency of the automobile has been aided by its improved appearance is another matter, since it can easily be argued that many so-called modern automobile designs are actually inefficient in terms of function; certainly poor parking visibility is one result of cars being designed closer and closer to the ground. Also, although streamlining in a car can be justified as suggesting speed, the amount of stream-

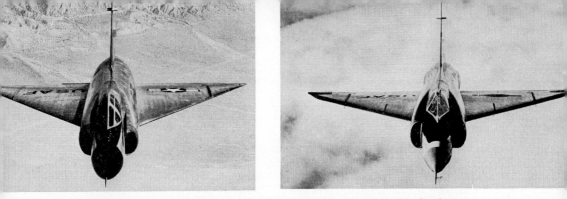

Fig. 149. Convair jet interceptor planes. *Left,* YF-102; *right,* F-102a with fuselage nipped in at the waist to reduce "drag" at supersonic speeds. Produced by General Dynamics Corp. (Photos courtesy Industrial Design magazine)

lining is not directly related to the desirable rate of speed, except in racing cars.

Such lack of relationship between form and function can sometimes be startling, as when we find a child's tricycle, a meat grinder, or a pressing iron streamlined in such a way that the function of the object is unrelated to the superposed sleek new form. On the other hand, although streamlining by itself may not be appropriate for the meat grinder, tricycle, or pressing iron, the process of doing away with the extraneous elements, making the object more compact and simple to operate, gives a new efficiency. The pressing iron is better balanced and may be put down on its end; the tricycle does not fall so easily; and the meat grinder is less likely to stick and is easier to set up.

There can be little question that the place of the industrial artist in our society lies somewhere between the worlds of art and commerce, in different cases coming closer to one or the other. Whatever his influence on our concept of art, however, the industrial designer has contributed enormously toward the achievement of a better life. He has brought into sharp focus the fact that the industrial age need not entail cultural deterioration, that man can profit in many ways from the technological advances of our time.

▶PART III

Form and Content

▶ 10

Planning the Art Object: The Tools, Elements, and Principles of Design

ALTHOUGH SOME EFFECTS in art may be accidental and arise from unforeseen combinations and arrangements, we have observed repeatedly that by and large a work of art is the result of conscious planning. This planning, or designing, is accomplished with the aid of drawings, color sketches, models (for sculpture and architecture), and similar devices. The ensuing plans or designs are the outcome of utilization of the Tools, or Language, of art to form certain Elements, which are then applied according to definite Principles.

The Tools of art consist of *line, light and dark (value), light and shadow (chiaroscuro), color, texture,* and *form;* their manipulation, arrangement, and interrelation give us what we may call the Elements. These Elements are *solids and voids, geometric areas, light and dark areas,* and *space,* all of which are disposed in accordance with design Principles. The Principles include *domination, unity, balance, rhythm,* and *proportion.* Their application toward a preconceived effect may be for intellectual or emotional purposes or both, and constitutes the design and quality of the work.

All works of art employ the Tools, or Language, of design, the resultant plastic Elements or attributes, and the final Principles predominant in their particular category. Even in the most extreme examples of contemporary painting and sculpture, which have recently

249

turned to an emphasis on the creative act itself rather than on the work of art and its structural values, we find at least an effect of unity of expression. Many works show both unity and rhythm, for example, the works of Arshile Gorky or Alva (Fig. 126, p. 209) , and in a number of cases these qualities are combined with balance as well.

What we are speaking of, then, are the form qualities through which the art object is consciously planned, qualities that may be perceived on an intellectual level or on a more subconscious level through the intuition. It is usually possible to reduce the design factor of a given work to intelligible and communicable formulas or descriptive phrases. We must realize, however, that in describing or enumerating the tenets of design employed by an artist to bring about his preconceived effect, we are still far from an explanation of how that effect came into being. For one thing, it is virtually impossible, however articulate we may be, to verbalize the intricate interplay of the various Elements and Principles found in any one work. For another, the artist brings to the work a flair and skill certainly not reducible to formulas. What we do, rather, is to describe the effect of the artist's work, identifying the various features we may observe in it.

Similarly, paintings and sculptures that would illustrate any combination of design Principles might be executed but would not necessarily be successful art. Formulas, apparently, are not always enough. What is needed, by both artist and spectator, apart from innate flair for the subject or the material, is a constant experience with the Principles and their endless possibilities, an experience which ultimately makes application or understanding of these factors an almost subconscious act.

Most accomplished artists apply the Principles without thinking consciously of what they are doing. The patterns of design have become so thoroughly absorbed in the artist's physical and mental being that his hand responds automatically to a kind of subconscious logic. The layout or composition takes shape without his needing to verbalize as we are doing here. Just as the composer will respond to the stimulus of a certain musical idea with a spontaneous chord, the artist will be impelled to create a combination of lines, colors, textures, and so forth. The artist thinks in design terms as the musician thinks in terms of harmony and counterpoint.

For us, the value of dissecting a work of art to discover first its basic

Tools, then its plastic Elements, and finally its Principles is that it increases our understanding of the so-called creative process, conscious or subconscious. A second value is that it provides an accepted language of communication concerning the arts and our feelings about them. As the interested person reads something concrete about a work, knowing the terminology used, he enters into a partial understanding of what the artist was trying to do and is able to advance his comprehension and appreciation from that point on.

Our separate treatment here of the various design factors is only for purposes of identification. We always make the reservation that many simultaneous effects are involved in the design of any work and its impression on the spectator. It should also be understood that we are trying to lay down certain Principles and procedures that will apply to all the arts: the major and the minor, the fine as well as the industrial.

The Basic Tools, or Components

Line. Line is one of the simplest and at the same time one of the most useful Tools in the artist's kit; it is also one of the most subtle, since it may consist of so little and yet do so much. It may be a contour for a given area or form and thus delimit; it may also indicate a direction of movement and thereby an extension of space. Line may be descriptive, as when it helps to create a sense of naturalistic truth (for example, the crosshatching that gives us shadows), or it may be symbolic, as when it generalizes to convey a universal truth rather than a particular fact. The nature of the line is to convey movement directly as we follow it. Its direction may be straight or curved, partial or extensive.

The line can carry the eye diagonally upward to give a feeling of excitement and exaltation, as in Daumier's *The Uprising* (see Fig. 157, p. 278); it may carry the eye downward either diagonally or in a curve to give a feeling of depression or sadness, as in Michelangelo's *Jeremiah* (Fig. 25, p. 38). A horizontal line can express quiet and rest, especially in landscape paintings such as Poussin's *St. John on Patmos* (Fig. 106, p. 176) or in architectural designs like those of the Parthenon (Fig. 62a, p. 97) or an Egyptian temple. Among straight lines we may also notice the effect of the vertical, a forceful indication (or presager) of action when forms strive upward, as in the skyscraper or the Gothic cathedral (Figs. 59 and 22, pp. 92, 35). The vertical line may also be a symbol of dignity when used as in *Le Beau Dieu* of Amiens (Fig. 24, p. 37), moving upward with strength and poise.

In painting, sculpture, and architecture, the line occurs in a limited way; it is really a basic outline of a particular form which has many other qualities as well. In its strictest sense the line functions only in a drawing or a print (see Figs. 41, 118, and 124, pp. 70, 199, 208). Here the almost magical function of the line in creating something out of nothing becomes clear; the draftsman ventures out over the barren terrain of the white paper and sets down a series of marks that become symbols of form, hints of space, limitations of area, creators of solids and voids.

In painting, sculpture, and architecture, the line is accompanied by other design factors. The basic diagonal movement of *The Uprising*, for example, may be described as a line of movement, but the actual effect of movement results from the manipulation of light and dark areas, forms, and colors as well as from the diagonal motion. Sometimes the effect of texture and geometric area, of color, form, and so on may be added to that of line.

Curved lines are almost always lines of movement, in landscapes, like Constable's *The Hay Wain* or *A Sage under a Pine Tree* (Figs. 107 and 37, pp. 177, 60), or in figure paintings, like Botticelli's *Primavera* (Fig. 36, p. 59), where the curved line carries the eye gently but inevitably from one side of the picture to the other. A more violent example of the movement of a curved line may be seen in Michelangelo's *Creation of Adam* (Fig. 35, p. 57), where each area, each muscle and movement is described within the framework of the curved line. When such lines turn more rapidly, the result is an exaggeration of the basic effect of the curve. Thus we may contrast the long and slow-moving curves in the Botticelli with the more rapid and dynamic emotional curves in Rubens' *Descent from the Cross* (Fig. 17, p. 29). While Botticelli was trying to indicate a dream world with its languor, Rubens was concerned with the suffering of Christ and the need for expressing this suffering in immediate and dynamic terms. Yet neither artist relied solely on line; each brought into play his own type of value, color, rhythmic effects, forms, and geometric areas. These may be contributed to by line, or they may be entirely independent of it, as are color and texture.

The way in which a line, particularly a curved line, is actually drawn carries a certain emotional effect. Apart from the general effect of the long "S"-curve formed at the top of the Botticelli picture or the flaring "X"-form of the Rubens, the drawn line in the Botticelli painting has a tightness and hardness that contribute to the unreality of the scene. For another example, the line bounding the relief sculpture from Assyria (see Fig. 180, p. 318) is of such a tense nature as to give a sensation of harshness and even cruelty. Often a swelling curved line can convey the feeling of abundance or sensuality, as in the Rubens (Fig. 17, p. 29) —or even elegance, as in *Odalisque* by Ingres (see Fig. 219, p. 398).

Most of our examples of line and its application have been drawn from the graphic arts or from painting, and yet sculptures can have a basic line or outline either in the absolute sense of a contour or in the sense of a directional thrust. The Parthenon frieze (Fig. 89, p. 136), for example, like the Assyrian *Winged Deity*, shows the importance of line in determining the final esthetic result; the Greeks used a curved but firm line to impart a dignified strength. In the *Discobolus* (Fig. 86, p. 132), a three-dimensional work, the dominant direction of movement implies a line through which the arm continues in the shoulder and into the other arm and the leg below. This profile of the sculpture creates the wonderful continuity that symbolizes motion itself.

Buildings also have a linear emphasis from the time they exist in the architect's mind, through their existence in the sketch, and into their final shape. The line may be the sweeping curve of the base of the Philadelphia Savings Fund Society Building (Fig. 73, p. 114), the continuous upward movement of the masonry in the Woolworth Building (Fig. 59, p. 92), or the impressive spherical sweep of Hagia Sophia (Fig. 68, p. 109).

Light and dark (value). Most works of art show relative degrees of light and dark. These are known as values, and they range from white to black, encompassing thousands of "light," "medium," and "dark" intermediate values. To the artist these values may have esthetic, emotional, and psychological importance.

One of the first things one notices in a painting (after one has "read" the work for content and, by implication, its intent) is its distribution of lights and darks. Some paintings necessarily use greater light and dark contrasts; others use very little, and some stand midway between these two extremes and give an over-all grayish effect. Rembrandt's *Man with the Golden Helmet* (Fig. 104, p. 174) exemplifies the first usage; Dürer's *Adoration of the Magi* and the Minoan *Cup-bearer* (Figs. 195 and 29, pp. 340, 43) illustrate the second, and Watteau's *Embarkation for the Isle of Cythera* (Fig. 168, p. 297) shows the third. Where the artist diffuses his light, as in the Watteau, he achieves a tranquil effect; where he uses very violent contrast, as in the Rembrandt, the effect is emotive. There are many more ways of achieving emotional expression than these few value indications demonstrate, but generally speaking we have to consider this factor as contributing to the emotional effect of the painting.

Value also plays a part in sculpture and architecture, where it is necessarily less fixed. In painting, relative light and dark quality does not change from season to season, whereas in the other arts, including the minor ones, the values change with the outside light that shines on them. In a building or sculpture, the projections, bumps, bosses, and so on, catch the light one way in the morning and another way in the afternoon, this way in summer and that way in winter, depending on the position of the sun or other illuminating agency. This is dramatically illustrated by the different aspects of buildings photographed by day and by night. Even more effective in contrast quality is the heightened appearance of such a building as Notre Dame in Paris or the *Madeleine* (Fig. 150, p. 255) under the floodlights which are thrown on it at night with such stunning results (Fig. 151, p. 255). It is almost as though we were looking at a building we have never seen before, and we are overwhelmed by the startling intensities of light and dark.

Another illustration of the possible changes in value occurs in sculpture which, seen from the front, makes a familiar impression. But when a camera is moved around the object, with its lens manipulated and fixed for the most interesting shots, the results may be quite startling. Whether these tricks of lighting are esthetically legitimate may be questionable, but they are certainly exciting. Although it is true that paintings too can be so exhibited that they become more effective through isolation from other works, special lights, and the like, the fact remains that the relationships of light and dark within them do not change so readily.

A more natural value change in architecture and sculpture is brought about by the shadows that normally occur during the day and affect the

Fig. 150 (*left*) Church of La Madeleine, Paris. Fig. 151 (*right*). Church of La Madeleine. Seen at night under artificial lighting. Paris.

appearance of a building. These may be taken into account in the planning and may be tested from a model of the structure subjected to changing light. In sculpture, particularly relief sculpture, there is a strict correlation between the visibility of the figure and the shadows it casts, a high relief casting a deeper shadow and a low relief a lesser shadow. The Parthenon frieze (Fig. 89, p. 136), a low relief on the wall behind the columns, casts faint shadows that make the forms stand out clearly in the relative obscurity of that spot. Where forms are in high relief, as on the outside of the Parthenon in the metopes showing the conflict between Centaurs and Lapiths, they have to be arranged far enough apart so as to avoid having deep shadows fall on each other and hence obscure the forms. Every metope bears two figures, each clearly separated from the other; but in the procession on the frieze the faint shadows enable the figures to be run together without doing violence to the outlines. The sculptor must remember, therefore, the ultimate place for which his sculpture is designed.

Light and shadow (chiaroscuro). This is another basic descriptive Tool for the painter, graphic artist, and draftsman. It may readily be exemplified in typical early Renaissance paintings, for example, Masaccio's *Expulsion from the Garden* (Fig. 193, p. 338), where the light appears to come from the right, striking the side of each form and moving gradually into the shadow. Light-and-shadow is an artistic convention approximating actuality and therefore entirely suited to any artistic system interested in the depiction of actuality. It is generally known as chiaroscuro (from the Italian *chiaro,* light, and *oscuro,* dark or shadowy) .

Color. Another basic design Tool is color, customarily described in terms of hue, value, and intensity. Hue simply refers to the name of the color, red, blue, orange, and so forth. Value, as we have seen, refers to the degree of light and dark; this is a property possessed by color. We speak of light reds, light blues, light oranges, dark reds, dark blues, or medium reds, medium blues, and so forth. Intensity, also called chroma or saturation, refers to the brightness of color. For example, we may take two greens, one as dark in value as the other, but the first may be a bright or brilliant green, the other a dull green. A good illustration is powder blue which is a dulled version of ordinary blue just as old rose is a dull form of red. Thus, to speak accurately of any color we must refer to its hue (red, blue, orange) , its value (light or dark or somewhere between) , and its intensity (bright or dull) .

Colors may be classified as to whether they are cool or warm; the blues and greens are cool (as in grass, trees, and sky) , and red, yellow, and orange are warm (as in fire and sun) . The warm colors, when applied to a canvas or other surface, give the impression of being nearer and are known as "advancing colors." Contrariwise, the cool colors give the impression of being farther away and are known as "retreating colors." A simple experiment in which identical areas of red, green, and blue are placed side by side will show how the red seems closest to the spectator, the green seems farther away, and the blue appears farthest. The importance of these characteristics can be illustrated in such paintings as van Gogh's *Night Café* (Fig. 39, p. 63) in which space relationships are partly governed by the fact that some areas are in red and advancing, some in green and receding.

Color is important to the artist from many other points of view. First, we may be struck by its emotive quality, as in the same van Gogh, in which the sense of futility is emphasized by the bleak combinations of clashing reds and greens. The El Greco *View of Toledo* (Fig. 38, p. 62) in its use of dull grays and greens gives us a feeling of foreboding and nervousness. In the same way, some colors, such as

256 PLANNING THE ART OBJECT

yellow, are stimulating and cheerful; others, such as blue, are restful, and still others, notably red, are quite exciting. In choosing certain dominant colors for his works, the painter will be setting an emotional level for them.

Color may have the symbolic value seen earlier in Beckmann's *Departure* (Fig. 40, p. 64), where the light blue in the background of the middle panel acts as a relief from the darkness of the side panels and moves away (as a cool color) into the distance, that is, into the future. Blue has been used as a symbol of infinity, as in the background of van Gogh's paintings. Time and again Gauguin spoke of symbolic effects and meanings he intended, just as van Gogh did. We should keep in mind, however, that although the examples we have chosen are intelligible to almost everyone, often the symbolic value of a color will have a more personal flavor and will demand from us more analysis and sensitivity.

Color may function, too, in the creation of space effects. The receding and advancing properties of various colors enable the painter to give certain parts of his canvas a forward movement and other parts a retreating movement. In the actual creation of shape and form, we see painters like Cézanne model a cylindrical or other mass by taking advantage, for example, of the fact that yellow comes forward and blue retreats.

Color can exist simply on the level of decorative value—although this attribute also operates in connection with as many other qualities as the artist requires to bring about the desired result. In *The Young Sailor* by Matisse (see Fig. 225, p. 407) the charm of the various hues is quite clear, but the final result is achieved with the aid of linear elements and other factors.

The most important thing about color or any other Tool of design is the way it is handled, the arrangement of colors and the relationships that are effectuated between them, as in the Matisse, Giorgione (Fig. 175, p. 308), and van Gogh examples. In the Matisse, the relationship brings decorative and visual excitement; in the Giorgione, a sensuous warmth; in the van Gogh, a disconsolate world-weariness. A painting may be predominantly one color, like *The Blue Boy* by Gainsborough, or it may be a combination of different hues.

A word should be said about the use of color in fields other than painting. In architecture and sculpture, intrinsic color quality exists in the material itself—red brick, green glass, white marble, and red, black, or brown wood. Color quality may also be added to the surface of the building or the sculpture—terra-cotta sculpture, which has its color added before baking, like the Della Robbia (Fig. 92, p. 141). Color may be added to buildings in the form of exterior stripping, as at Lever House in New York (Fig. 78, p. 120) and the Lake Shore Apartments in Chicago. These color effects in sculpture and architecture have their own significance, just as does color in jewelry, textiles, or any of the minor arts.

Texture. Texture, or surface effect, is another quality shared by all the arts. It results from the individual structural essence of every substance. We may actually feel this quality through our fingers in sculpture, buildings, and many forms of industrial and minor art. We may also receive its stimuli through the eyes; paintings, prints, and drawings each have a visibly different surface quality based on the roughness of canvas, the smoothness of parchment, and so on.

But while the painting may only look smooth (Vermeer, Fig. 32, p. 50) or rough (van Gogh, Fig. 39, p. 63), other types of art, such as architecture, sculpture, or fabrics, not only look smooth or rough but actually are smooth or rough. In addition to the tactile or touch stimulus in terms of direct physical contact, the surface is provided with an interest that supplements its color, line, and other characteristics. In fact, certain kinds of texture will affect color just as they will affect light and dark quality. A smooth texture avoids shadows; a rough texture will cause shadows to appear.

Texture should agree with the basic form or composition of the object it serves, as in the modern typewriter (Fig. 143, p. 231) or any other industrially designed object where serviceability dictates the use of smooth texture and simple flat color. Again, as with the other Tools of design, most importantly, textures should be arranged compositionally as part of a unified effect.

Paintings with high textural interest include Holbein's *Portrait of George Gisze* (see Fig. 197, p. 342), Vermeer's *Young Woman with a Water Jug* (Fig. 32, p. 50), and Ingres's *Odalisque* (Fig. 219, p. 398), all predominantly smooth, almost enamel-like in texture. Nearly as different as possible in effect are Pissarro's *Peasants Resting* (Fig. 11, p. 24) and van Gogh's *Night Café* (Fig. 39, p. 63), which are rough in texture; the former imparts a sparkling impression, the latter a nervous tension. In the first group of paintings, especially in the Holbein and the Vermeer, the purpose of the texture is to give the actual physical sensation of the materials encountered: the glossy smoothness of wood, enamel, or glass; in the Ingres the smooth texture idealizes the quality of the woman's skin. Pissarro and van Gogh use texture in different ways, the first to give a sense of movement and the other to give a sense of strain.

Form. Although we often speak of form as one of the basic Tools or components of design, it will be seen that all forms, whether two-dimensional or three-dimensional, representational or nonrepresentational, are actually the result of an interaction of the Tools previously considered: line, light and dark, light and shadow, color, and texture. We may therefore consider form in the simple descriptive sense, as a shape belonging to a given figure; we may also consider it as the more complex arrangement which constitutes the design as a whole, that is, the "form" of the painting, sculpture, or building.

We have arrived now at the point where we may examine the second-level factors, what we called earlier the component Elements of the work of art. These were listed somewhat arbitrarily as the solids and voids, the geometric areas, the light and dark areas, and the spaces. To these we may now add the Element of form, or volume.

The Elements

Volume. Volume, or form, is that property of any art which enables the spectator to apprehend length, breadth, and thickness as applied to an object. It is most easily felt in those objects which are inherently solid, such as buildings and sculpture, or in the many types of industrial art in which the very attribute of occupying a certain segment of atmosphere and having a certain mass gives the quality of volume. We may walk around the sculpture, go inside the building, run our hands over the object of industrial design; and in each we have a direct perception of its solidity and tangibility—its volume. In painting and other two-dimensional arts we must invent or simulate this sense of volume through an arrangement of lines moving in a given direction, textures significantly arranged, colors moving backward and forward, or lights and shadows.

Volumes may be perceived visually through contour lines that lend each object its shape, as in a Chinese pottery vessel (Fig. 127, p. 214) or a Greek vase (Fig. 49, p. 79). They may also be perceived through the chiaroscuro qualities of the object, that is, by the shadows cast; this factor also conveys a sense of solidity. A third, although minor, aid in perception is the possible effect of seeing the reactions of other people when they touch, lift, or strike a solid object.

The relationship of solid forms to other solid forms represents one of the vital components of design. The R.C.A. Building (Fig. 58, p. 92) is a calculated arrangement of stepped-back volumes of stone moving upward to their climax; the Parthenon (Fig. 62a, p. 97) is a rhythmically related series of cylindrical, rectangular, and pyramidal volumes (the columns and so forth). In sculpture, *Le Beau Dieu* with its rectangular volume is designed to fit the volume of the pier on which it is set (Fig. 24, p. 37); the elongated figures on the façade of Chartres Cathedral (Fig. 22, p. 35) fulfill their artistic destiny as their volume is altered to suit the columns to which they are attached.

Solids and voids. In their uses of solids and voids, the various arts deal not only with combination of volumes as in the R.C.A. Building but also with volumes that alternate with empty areas. This combination may be found in the Philadelphia Savings Fund Society Building (Fig. 73, p. 114), where the volume of the rectangular upper part of the building relates to the attached elevator portion; such a shape attached to a building necessarily leaves an empty area with proportions calculated and considered in the final design. We may look on the whole design of Rockefeller Center in New York as an asymmetrical and visually exciting alternation of rectangular volumes and the space intervals between them. Lever House (Fig. 78, p. 120), which consists of a large slab structure perched on an open courtyard, offers a daring interval between the two portions of the building.

In sculpture, especially modern sculpture, the deliberate omission of a portion of the volume for the sake of emphasis, simplicity, primitive feeling, and many other possible ends, creates an altogether new quality. In the work of Henry Moore, Jacques Lipchitz, and Theodore Roszak (Fig. 82, p. 127) the eye is carried from one volume of the work to another over what the artist tries to make a visually effective pause or void in form. The interrelationship between these fullnesses and emptinesses may be just as effective as between fullnesses alone.

The two-dimensional arts offer their own version of this phenomenon. In them, it depends less than in sculpture on the omission of volumes or parts of volumes at given places, although such omission may occur, especially in the free-form, or biomorphic, volumes of some modern artists like Miró and Klee. Basically, however, these arts are concerned merely with the disposition of representational or nonrepresentational forms in a design intended to give a purposeful alternation of filled and empty spaces. The decoration on the Greek vase (Fig. 49, p. 79) will illustrate this point, as will the Oriental painting considered earlier (Fig. 37, p. 60).

Geometric areas. Geometric areas or arrangements in painting represent an important component of design on this second level of organization and experience. These areas are generally two-dimensional and are often square, rectangular, circular, triangular, elliptical, or free-form. What is important here, as elsewhere on this level of apprehension, is that the areas are compounded of line, color, and light and dark effects. Further, the areas (or arrangements), of whatever shape they may be, will serve as the basis of the composition, involving a variety of geometric shapes in an interplay that is one of the chief means of creating design quality. The possibility of grasping the artist's basic layout or plan, in terms of a relatively simple combination of geometric areas or in terms of one geometric area, is of inestimable help in understanding the whole idea of planning.

Keeping in mind the fact that these areas are purely arbitrary, we may consider such arrangements as the triangle, the parallelogram, the radiating shape, the circle, the "S" shape, and the "L" shape as bases for directing the eye of the spectator from one part of a composition to another and laying the groundwork for further understanding. These arbitrary layouts are, as noted, only two-dimensional and in that sense are distortions of the nature of the plastic arts, which are three-dimensional by definition. Yet we can speak of the triangular arrangement of Leonardo's *Madonna of the Rocks* (see Fig. 154, p. 273), the parallelogram described by Raphael's *Alba Madonna* (Fig. 16, p. 28), the "X" shape of Rubens' *Descent from the Cross* (Fig. 17, p. 29), the radial shape of Vermeer's *Young Woman with a Water Jug* (Fig. 32, p. 50), the scale arrangement of the van Eycks' Ghent altarpiece (Fig. 103, p. 172). What we mean when we use these simple geometric descriptions of the works is that in a vertical plane their plan tends to follow a system of line, light and dark, or color which causes such a pattern to emerge.

Naturally each of these works suggests, through the use of other attributes such as space (including perspective), solids and voids, and volumes, a third dimension as well. The *Descent from the Cross,* for example, presents its X-shaped area in terms of strong light and dark contrasts and the actual disposal of the limbs and bodies of the figures. But each form or volume in this picture also exists on its own merits and contributes to the three-dimensionality of the work, as does the light and dark element. Although the "X" movement here remains mostly in one plane, other geometric shapes may be found to move quite easily from one plane to another. Thus the *Madonna of the Rocks* by Leonardo, a basic triangle, becomes on further examination a pyramid of form, that is, a three-dimensional geometric volume.

The radial nature of the *Young Woman with a Water Jug* strikes us as primarily two-dimensional, but when we see the overlapping of forms, the movement of lights and darks throughout, that is, from front to rear as well as from side to side, a three-dimensional effect emerges. The *Alba Madonna* of Raphael shows this phenomenon of change from two- to three-dimensional visualization within itself, for the parallelogram described by the enclosure of the Madonna's outstretched leg, the shoulder line, and the right arm, moves from a forward plane in the picture to a plane further back. Here it is as though the area arrangement were set cater-cornered into the picture space. A similar phenomenon often occurs in the representation of an oncoming ship in a painting.

In those arts which are of themselves three-dimensional we do not have to make this distinction between the initial impression and any later one, and yet in those arts also it is possible for us to perceive geometrical arrangements. A very simple instance is the circular movement of Myron's *Discobolus* (Fig. 86, p. 132), in which a swinging arch is carried from the discus through the right arm, shoulder, left arm, and into the leg. In architecture, similarly, the disposition of the parts of a building may well suggest basic geometric arrangements such as the arch (Arch of Titus, Fig. 164, p. 289) or the rectangle (Palazzo Farnese, Fig. 155, p. 275), but the three-dimensionality and space-enclosing quality of most buildings is so strong as to make this

Fig. 151a. CARAVAGGIO: *Death of the Virgin.*
Paris, Louvre.

approach in architecture relatively unimportant except for the purpose of analyzing façade composition, as in the earlier consideration
of the Pazzi Chapel (Fig. 30, p. 45).

Light and dark areas. Also on the level of the plastic Elements as
attributes of design we may consider the effect of light and dark, not
in terms of value as discussed earlier, but rather for its compositional
use in the entire work. Thus in Poussin's *St. John on Patmos* (Fig.
106, p. 176) the basic effect is gained through the movement of masses
of alternating light and dark areas from one plane to another. We find
our eyes carried from the foreground to the middleground to the background, slowly but powerfully and inevitably, the effect giving the
composition a certain strength. Caravaggio's *Death of the Virgin* (Fig.
151a, p. 263) exists for us in terms of the movement of actual light

areas from one figure to the next, jumping, as it were, over the intervening dark areas, to make us move visually with the artist's intention.

In sculpture we have such examples as the *Ecstasy of St. Theresa* (Fig. 98, p. 153) wherein the entire surface is given a feeling of movement and unity through the manipulation of alternating light and dark areas created by the artist's drill working its way under the drapery folds from one end of the work to the other. A somewhat similar effect is found in late Gothic sculpture in Europe, with its wooden or stone drapery folds.

Architecture may also show the operation of this attribute, again as in many Gothic or Baroque examples. Cathedrals such as those of Paris, Chartres (Fig. 22, p. 35), Reims, and Amiens with their openwork surfaces naturally catch a great deal of shadow, which flickers across the entire building and augments the sensation of endless movement. A Baroque structure like San Carlo alle Quattro Fontane (see Fig. 214, p. 388) shows a more involved but equally effective surface movement of lights and darks that gives the building its strange sense of restlessness and its emotional quality.

Space. Space as an attribute of design may be regarded as perhaps the most important single Element, in that it appears to be the prime function of the arts to create, simulate, or enclose space (in sculpture, painting, and architecture respectively). Each of the arts deals with space as a property of itself.

In painting, space creates a kind of artistic reality or logic as well as a reality reflected from the world of fact. It also exists as a means of unifying the picture and establishing its tensions. Whatever its purpose at a given moment, it may be suggested in a variety of ways. One simple method is through the overlapping of forms, as in Byzantine mosaic (Ravenna, Fig. 131, p. 219) or in abstract geometrical painting such as the Mondrian *Composition* (Fig. 33, p. 50). In both examples, the space indications or hints infer the existence of a tight space by compressing the inner and outer forms. The effect of space may also be induced through the interpenetration and transparency of forms. Thus a Picasso work (Fig. 224, p. 406) in the Cubist style presents a series of forms that not only overlap one another but which show a certain amount of light going through from one surface to another one underneath. (This technique is used in a much more dramatic way in the Pevsner sculpture, Fig. 84, p. 129, wherein planes actually interpenetrate one another.)

One of the most effective space builders in painting (and relief sculpture) is perspective, both linear and aerial. Linear perspective, as seen in Chapter 6, is based on the fact that parallel lines moving away from us appear to converge; when we draw an object with converging lines, we reproduce the phenomenon and create a sense of distance. It is also based on the fact that objects farther away appear to be smaller. This is true because the eye functions through images derived from rays of light coming from the object. The rays from the top and bottom of that object pass through the lens of the eye, where they are reversed and projected on to the retina in a size proportionate to the distance they have traveled. We have only to diagram this process with its crossed diagonals for the rays of light to see that a foot-high object at a long distance will make a smaller image on the retina, whereas the same object a short distance away will give a larger image. A classic instance of the working of linear perspective may be seen in Leonardo's *Last Supper* (Fig. 99, p. 159).

Aerial perspective uses value changes in the colors of the picture. By moving from darker values in the foreground to lighter ones in the middleground and very light ones in the background, the painter reproduces in some measure the phenomenon in actual experience by which objects farther away appear lighter, that is, harder to see and out-of-focus. For an instance of the working of aerial perspective we may turn to Constable's *The Hay Wain* (Fig. 107, p. 177).

Distance (or space) may also be indicated, as seen earlier, through the use of advancing and retreating colors, which allow some portions of the picture to come forward (or appear to) and others to recede. Warm and cool colors will appear, for example, in the foreground and background respectively of a Cézanne landscape or still life (see Fig. 223, p. 405) or of a Renaissance work such as Giorgione's *Concert Champêtre* (see Fig. 175, p. 308).

Relief sculpture may share some of these effects, for instance, the Paradise Gates of Ghiberti (Fig. 90a, p. 139), wherein linear convergences are much used and aerial distance is simulated by the fuzzing of forms that are supposed to be further back. In sculpture in the round, spatial relationships, as in the *Laokoön* group (see Fig.

187, p. 325), are created when some forms are placed before others.

As already implied in connection with the Byzantine mosaic and the Mondrian painting, space is not necessarily naturalistic; the artist's purpose may be conceptual rather than perceptual, that is, concerned more with the projection of ideas and states of being (for example, tensions) than with actual physical appearances. Thus the Chinese painting of the *Admonitions of the Imperial Preceptress* (Fig. 111, p. 184) shows figures existing in an ideal rather than an actual space. Much the same kind of impression is made by the space effects in the Parthenon frieze (Fig. 89, p. 136) where, again, it is difficult to specify the place in which the people move about. Needless to say, the omissions of naturalistic representation are not the result of lack of observation but of an artistic and moral purpose, to reduce the forms and the world in which they move to a series of calculated and idealized symbols. We cannot, therefore, say that the space in the Byzantine mosaic, or the modern painting, represents an absence of space; rather, a different kind of space is involved, a space differently motivated from that of the Renaissance and post-Renaissance tradition. Each in his own way, the Byzantine mosaicist, the modern geometric painter, the Oriental calligrapher sets up a different space tension that, viewed through the senses, makes a work of art esthetically meaningful.

Space may be created through suggestions of the flow of light and dark from one area to another (see Poussin, Fig. 106, p. 176) as well as by the change in size from one object to another, by the fitting of one form into the next, by the projection forward of certain objects and the corresponding rearward projection of others.

The relationship of architecture to the problem of space is somewhat different from that of painting, since the builder-designer creates space by surrounding it, as it were, rather than by the magic of perspective, light and dark manipulations, and similar devices. For some architects the problem is more of space limitation than of space creation, but for the true designer there will be the constant problem of relating the interior spaces to the mass and volume of the building, to the exterior or façade of the building, to the purpose of the structure, and perhaps even to the environment in which it finds itself.

Both the architect and the painter must keep in mind the existence of (a) continuous space, (b) limited space, and (c) infinite space. In architecture the first may be illustrated by the interior of the Tugendhat House by Miës van der Rohe (Fig. 64a, p. 102) in which one room space flows into the next without permanently fixed walls. Similarly in painting, we may speak of a continuation from one area into the next, as when Vermeer (Fig. 32, p. 50) or Terborch takes us from one room into the next or from the house into the street.

Limited space is derived from walls that are meant to cut off the inhabitant from the outside or the spectator on the street from the inside, as in the cold and forbiddingly closed Romanesque cathedral (see Fig. 190, p. 333) or the Roman home with its expressed desire for extreme privacy in the blind façade it turns to the street. In painting a whole series of works have spatial intentions which are finite and closed in quality. The *Death of St. Francis* by Giotto (see Fig. 176, p. 310) begins at a given point in space, the picture line, moves back to the wall and sideways to the porches, stopping at all three places and not trying to go any further. The Poussin landscape, *St. John on Patmos* (Fig. 106, p. 176), begins downstage with the saint, moves into the middle area, and ends with the mountains in the rear and the trees at either side. Its effect is one of strict containment within its frame. The Byzantine mosaic and the Mondrian painting are limited even more severely in their deliberately shallow and tension-creating movement.

Infinite space appears in the architecture of the Gothic with its annihilated walls and inferential endlessness of movement, its constant light passing between inside and outside. In painting infinite space is implied in Expressionist-type works such as El Greco's *St. Martin and the Beggar* or Baroque works such as Rembrandt's *Man with the Golden Helmet* (Figs. 151b and 104, pp. 268, 174). In the first, horse and rider project forward toward the spectator and backward through the violently contrasted low-lying landscape into a dominant sky that swallows the entire work. Both the forms and the space are dematerialized and cannot be thought of as having limits. In the Rembrandt work, with its symbolic intent to project a universal and eternal symbol of tragedy, it becomes impossible to identify the place or the time in which the man is set. The form disappears into shadow, the space flows out of the picture frame into an unidentifiable endlessness.

Fig. 151b. EL GRECO: *St. Martin and the Beggar.*
Washington, D. C., National Gallery of Art, Mellon
Collection.

Open or closed, the importance of space in pictorial design cannot
be exaggerated. It is the living fabric of the painting, the source of its
tensions, the source of its illusions of reality or its presentation of
the world of the artist, in which forms move under the motive power
of the pictorial imagination alone.

The Principles of Design

The third level of design involves such Principles as domination,
unity, balance, rhythm, and proportion as they are applied to the
Elements. Here also we merely attempt to describe the visual thinking
of the artist and the potential observer. We do not say, be it noted,
that because certain works follow these Principles of design, they
are therefore great art.

It is an interesting experience to go back only a few years to books which demonstrate the so-called Principles by works that were undoubtedly popular at the time but today seem quite meaningless as examples of good art. Part of this apparent paradox stems from the change of taste away from the sentimental illustrationism of the early part of the twentieth century. And yet it is somewhat baffling to see how a modern writer will use a famous painting from the past, for example, a Rubens, Rembrandt, or Titian, to exemplify a certain Principle and then point to an artist such as Meissonier (Fig. 220, p. 401) as a further instance of the same idea. Although such more recent artists also demonstrate the workings of rhythm, balance, and so forth, they are more interested in story-telling for its own sake than in form or design in the Old Master sense. Where such an artist uses form, it is in terms gleaned from the textbook rather than from a living and virile tradition of his own.

Although we discuss here the Principles of design separately in their application to specific works, we shall soon find that one work may illustrate many different Principles. It is this interrelation of Principles that gives a work its particular effectiveness. An object may

Fig. 151c. RAPHAEL: *School of Athens*. Rome, Vatican, The Papal Apartments.

primarily illustrate unity or rhythm, but it will scarcely ever exist without the working of one of the other Principles as well.

As with other aspects of design, we note that although we may use certain arbitrary geometric shapes to suggest the nature of the artist's thinking, for example, a curve, a square, or a circle, an artist almost never thinks out a picture in outline any more than he would a sculpture or building. Although people often regard the work as suggesting simple two-dimensional forms, further examination always shows that the artist has thought in tones, or values of light and dark accents.

Domination. One of the simplest Principles to demonstrate, domination, or climax, illustrates three-dimensionality quite clearly. In *Descent from the Cross* by Rubens (Fig. 17, p. 29) we see the apparent domination (and therefore to a degree the unifying effect) of a swinging curve from the upper right to the lower left. A second look shows that this curve exists in terms of light and dark values, that is, as a contrast between the illuminated body of the Christ and the relative darkness around it. The curve shape, moreover, tends to tilt from one plane forward into the next to create a sense of depth. But domination alone cannot account for the effect of this work; it also shows balance in the arrangement of figures at right and left, rhythm in the constant movement and repetition of the swelling contours, and other Principles as well.

Rembrandt's so-called *The Night Watch* (*Sortie of Captain Banning Cocq's Company of the Civic Guard,* Fig. 152, p. 271), though without an obvious dominant figure, does project toward the spectator a similarly illuminated light area against contrasting darks. This creates a center of interest dominant in terms of light, from which we move out into the relatively uncharted depths of the opposing darkness. When such a contrast is absolute, we may think of it as achieving domination; when it is relative, as it is here, we have climax. Climax also occurs in pictures like the *Death of the Virgin* by Caravaggio (Fig. 151a, p. 263), where the artist directs his light in such a way as to carry the eye of the spectator from one end of the picture to the other until it reaches the climactic point, the face of the dying Virgin.

The middle panel of the van Eycks' Ghent altarpiece (Fig. 103, p. 172) shows the physical and spiritual dominance of the central area with its altar toward which all the other groups of figures move in from the sides. This centralization gives both dominance and unity

Fig. 152. REMBRANDT VAN RIJN: *"The Night Watch,"* *Sortie of Captain Banning Cocq's Company of the Civic Guard.* Amsterdam, Netherlands, Rijksmuseum. (Photo courtesy Netherlands Information Service)

to a great extent, as well as balance from the relatively equal distribution of masses of form about the central point.

Domination may also be accomplished through the use of a single color or group of colors in a work, for example, the varied blues in Gainsborough's *Blue Boy* or in Vermeer's *Young Woman with a Water Jug.* The blues in the latter move from the glass of the window at the left through the deep blue gown of the woman and the light blue shadow on her face, then to the blue cushion on the table, the blues in the fabric on the table, and the blue rod holding down the map on the wall. This repetition gives not only color dominance but also a high degree of unity.

Dominance (as well as climax) is often achieved by strong movement upward, as in the Gothic cathedral (Fig. 22, p. 35), both inside and out, with its emphasis on the verticality of the pointed arches. Similarly we may say that buildings with domes, like Hagia Sophia

Fig. 153. ANDREA DEL POZZO: *St. Ignatius Carried to Heaven*. Rome, Sant' Ignazio.

(Fig. 68, p. 109), are dominated by that feature, which looms over the entire structure and gives it its special quality. This looming may be more or less effective to the degree that the dome really dominates and does not merely roof the building. In painting, this vertical, upthrusting, and climactic movement may also be found, as in *St. Ignatius Carried to Paradise* by Andrea del Pozzo (see Fig. 153, p. 272) where wave on wave of upward movement culminates with the saint finally disappearing heavenward into the clouds. In the domed church, the proportion of the dome to the base is an important factor in the ultimate effect; in the del Pozzo painting, the proportion between the figures and the space in which they operate helps to achieve the climactic leap upward.

Unity. Both dominance and its related phenomenon, climax, contribute to the unity of a given work. This second Principle of design is in some ways even more significant for the success of a work of art because from it springs the all-important cohesiveness of the various parts, the sense of planned relationship of the parts to the whole and to each other.

Unity may appear in the object of art as the quality of self-sufficiency, or all-inclusiveness, demonstrable in works designed in a continuous and more or less self-enclosing plan. *Creation of Adam* by Michelangelo (Fig. 35, p. 57), a painting arranged in an oval, attains a high degree of unity, first, through the amazingly effective approach of hands of the two chief figures. Second, unity is enhanced through the continuous movement along their arms from God to Adam, then back through Adam's leg, over again to God, and strongly left once more. Paintings centered around an oval pond, or buildings laid out with a patio as the central area, may also attain this all-inclusiveness and unity.

Another type of self-sufficiency may be demonstrated in such compositions of the High Renaissance as Leonardo's *Madonna of the Rocks* (see Fig. 154, p. 273), and Raphael's *Alba Madonna* (Fig. 16, p. 28). In these works a basic three-dimensional geometric unity—a pyramid

Fig. 154. LEONARDO DA VINCI: *Madonna of the Rocks*. Paris, Louvre.

in the first and a parallelepiped in the second—constitutes the framework within which the artist operates. He tries—and this is one of the
measures of his success as a designer—to work out his drama and its
formal elements of lights and darks, solids and voids, spaces, and so
on, within that severely limiting area. Such an arrangement results in
what is called a "closed composition," a particular form of all-
inclusiveness and self-sufficiency.

But unity exists also on another level, the level on which we speak
of the overriding emotion, idea, or form of the particular work. We
may look at the R.C.A. Building (Fig. 58, p. 92) and ask, "What is
the basic form idea the architect is trying to express in this building?"
Here the answer would appear to be that the building must, initially,
be related to the other structures in the Rockefeller Center complex,
first in general slab form and second in proportion, that is, agreeably
larger and dominant in the Center composition. Finally, it must have
within itself a certain basic shape to which all the contributing parts
will be subordinated. Since the vertical slab is the basic shape here
and since the designer was compelled by city ordinance to "set back"
his building at various levels to avoid monopolizing light and air, the
indentations on both front and side of the building were composed to
conform to that general pattern.

On the front of the building a symmetrically balanced trio of
vertical slabs is set on each prescribed setback level, the center one
higher than those at the sides. This arrangement is related to that on
the sides of the building where the setbacks are laid out in clear
correspondence with those on the front, going slightly farther back
on each level. Thus we may say that the building has been designed
with the idea of unity clearly in the forefront of the architect's mind.
It also possesses rhythmic value in the periodic repetition of the
setbacks, balance in their arrangement around a central axis in the
front, proportion in the relationship between the size of the window
openings and that of the masonry slabs which form the shell of the
building.

What is important here is that we have witnessed the emergence
of a planned effect in which one factor, rectangular verticality, unifies
the structure. To this factor everything else is subordinate: the vertical
piers separating the windows, the shape of the setbacks, the shape of
the windows. Furthermore, each of the buildings in Rockefeller Center

Fig. 155. SANGALLO, MICHELANGELO, AND DELLA PORTA: Palazzo Farnese. Rome.

to some extent shares this rectangular verticality, although it is differently worked out in each—different heights, different proportions, different orientation of the buildings themselves—so that we finally get a unified but varied effect, supplying what is often referred to as variety within unity.

The Palazzo Farnese in Rome (Fig. 155, p. 275), referred to earlier in many other connections, illustrates as do many Renaissance buildings this concept of a single driving idea in form and the varied means through which it is expressed and embellished. Here the underlying form is the simple two-dimensional rectangle of the façade with its four dominant horizontals beginning at the heavy cornice and ending at the ground line, with two stringcourses dividing the horizontal rows of windows from each other. To counteract this basically horizontal movement, the designer gives us elegantly plain vertical windows. Within the unity of these windows that are so tightly related to the long and short axes of the building, he offers variety by changing the ornamental detail at the top of each row of windows. The bottom row shows a simple horizontal projection; the second, alternating tri-

Fig. 156. Air view of the Palace of Versailles. Versailles, France. (Photo courtesy French Embassy Press and Information Division)

angular and curved pediments; the third, open triangular pediments. Similarly the base of each row of windows is varied so that although we have the pleasant repetitive rhythm on each level, a change ensues as we move from one level to the next.

To avoid the possibility of a monotonous straight line effect throughout, the designer has injected some curves as well: the curving and projecting (therefore important) entrance doorway, the curving coat of arms above the balcony, and finally the curves in the second-story pediments. These three curved elements form a kind of cross-shape within the main design and echo the sideways and up-and-down quality of the straight line arrangements. Everything, then, is subordinated to the basic horizontal rectangle of the design.

If we turn for a moment to another horizontally arranged rectangle, the Palace of Versailles (Figs. 156 and 156a, pp. 276, 277), we find a somewhat different and apparently less unified building. Although this structure presents an undoubtedly impressive and even monumental appearance in its totality of architecture and formal gardens, it cannot by its very grandiose nature have the tightness and all-inclusiveness of the Palazzo Farnese. Its plan is as symmetrical as that of the earlier building; it also shows a high degree of balance in the relationship of parts within the building to each other and to the embracing palace-plus-gardens layout. But basically the arrangement here, with the various sections offering a constantly moving and shifting interrelationship, is far more dynamic than in the Farnese. Part of the building moves forward, while the balancing wings at either side move backward—when seen from the garden side. On the entrance front, however, this movement is reversed. Moreover, the actual visual and physical sensation of roads on one side and gardens on the other, radiating from and to the palace, provide a physical as well as symbolic center of royal France. Perhaps this, in the final analysis, is the unifying element of the palace complex—fully apparent, however, only when we see Versailles from the air or in an aerial photograph.

Unity of form prevails in sculpture and painting as well as in architecture. In Bernini's *Apollo and Daphne* (Fig. 177, p. 311), the unifying quality is the consistently curved upward movement of the two figures as they constantly approach each other but never quite meet. Legs parallel legs, arms move in the same curved direction,

Fig. 156a. Hall of Mirrors, Palace of Versailles. Versailles, France. (Photo courtesy French Embassy Press and Information Division)

Fig. 157. HONORÉ DAUMIER: *The Uprising*. Washington, D. C., Phillips Memorial
Gallery.

broken surfaces on one figure are continued in similar broken surfaces
on the other.

Daumier's *The Uprising* (Fig. 157, p. 278), which exemplifies
the element of climax, also embodies one overriding idea, the forward movement of the mass of people charging through the streets
in their symbolic attempt to overthrow oppression. Out of this inchoate
mass of dimly seen figures, a group in the right foreground emerges,
with its white-shirted and isolated foremost figure moving violently out
of the picture as its symbolic summation.

Balance. The principle of balance may seem, at first, a rather
obvious component of design. But it is obvious only in those compositions which are governed by the most elementary arrangement of
equally weighted figures placed at either side of a larger central figure.
The *School of Athens* by Raphael (Fig. 151c, p. 269) represents a
rather overt balance, since the figures of Plato and Aristotle at the
head of the stairs act as a center point around which identically long
bars swing at either side. The *Arnolfini Marriage* by Jan van Eyck

(Fig. 8, p. 21) presents a somewhat similar balance with two equally large figures at either side of the room.

But neither of these two works, it should be kept in mind, derives its entire sense of balance from the almost naïve formulation we have deliberately given. In the Raphael, balance is established just as much, if not more, by the midway position of the same major figures between the background and foreground and the manner in which the arches above diminish toward them and the groups below merge in the same direction. What Raphael has done is to create an interesting spatial world on a flat wall surface by placing or "spotting" forms at various depths in the composition. In the van Eyck, the two figures are related to each other through the arcuated arrangement of their arms, to the mirror and candelabra above that repeat this rhythm, and finally to the light that streams in from the left.

A variant example of balance established through symmetry and spatial alignments may be found in *St. John on Patmos* by Poussin (Fig. 106, p. 176). Here the saint in the foreground is balanced against ruins at the left, while the middleground trees balance each other. A row of trees slightly beyond the middleground runs along from right to left; in the rear, architecture and a large mountain complete the procession of inward-moving elements. The balance in this picture is much more important in its operation from foreground to background than from left to right. With his untraversable forest in the middle, the artist balances the saint who represents the present (Christianity) against the architecture which represents the past (paganism). This is Poussin's way of using material objects for symbolic purposes.

Poussin's arrangement on each plane or level of inward projection is not so symmetrical as was that of the previous two pictures; actually, symmetry is by no means a necessity for balance. For instance, many works are balanced by the juxtaposition of quite different elements, but these elements are placed in significant positions that make up for the apparent difference. A simple illustration of asymmetrical balance is found in Ruisdael's *The Mill* (Fig. 158, p. 280). Here a large object, the mill, is set at the right of the canvas in the middleground, apparently in a fashion that might create a one-sided or overweighted area. Yet immediately the painter causes the eye to move left through the band of trees beginning under the mill, and through

Fig. 158. JACOB VAN RUISDAEL: *The Mill*. Amsterdam, Netherlands, Rijksmuseum.

the rustic dike which begins at the lower right and swings up toward the left. More important as a left-pulling and hence counterweighting device is the small boat a considerable distance from the mill, and the succession of land lines that carry the eye into some indefinite part of the left side and out of sight. The fact that in imagination we can go as far as we like to the left enables the artist to place a heavy object at the right, for the entire open world on the other side counterbalances the great weight. We may compare this sort of arrangement to a see-saw on which a lightweight child sits at one end and the older person playing with him sits on the other side close to the center so as to achieve balance. Many Dutch landscapes of the seventeenth century and British landscapes of the eighteenth to nineteenth centuries follow this formula (see Constable, Fig. 107, p. 177).

Other aspects of asymmetrical balance may be seen in the Savoye House by Le Corbusier (Fig. 31, p. 48). This building shows a regular, even symmetrical, arrangement of the main floor and its parts, but on the upper floor, or play deck, the light-blue, curved wind break is placed far to one side of the roof and would cause serious visual overbalancing were it not for the ground floor garage and workroom. This area is much larger and is dark green in color, although related to the upper story in its curved side and to the main part of the building in its straight lines. In this building the architect anchors the structure to the ground with the work section, raises it to mid-air in its main portion, and relates it to the heavens in its upper story.

Another type of asymmetrical balance is seen in Myron's *Discobolus* (Fig. 86, p. 132), which bends far out from the perpendicular and moves the center of gravity a considerable distance from its usual position in such figures as the ultrasymmetrical *Khafre* (Fig. 88, p. 133). But there is little question of the Greek figure's essential balance; the line from the discus through the shoulders and the left arm and then back through the left foot and out left prevents any sensation of falling to the right that the bent-over pose might engender. Myron has also created a movement to the left through the arched back of the athlete, a curve that cuts across the curve moving to the right.

Daumier's *The Uprising* (Fig. 157, p. 278), a convincingly climactic work, also conveys a curious sensation of balance. In the act of going somewhere, the chief figure heralds its own arrival at that spot and therefore helps balance the work in that direction. Yet it does not fall out of the picture, for as we move strongly to the left, the painter slips in a flat plane of space in the rear, the line of houses that indicates the street, thus carrying the eye back in the opposite direction. This is a favorite device of Daumier (see his *Washerwoman,* Fig. 9, p. 22), who invariably gives us a strongly dynamic sense of balance in his works.

Rhythm. Rhythm is found in all aspects of life as a product of nature's activity: the recurrent wavy lines in a leaf, the concentric rings within a tree, the beating of the waves on a shore—all constitute examples of rhythm in nature. In the tempo-based arts of music and literature, the function of rhythm is clear and necessary to the impact and ultimate success of the individual composition, poem, or other work.

In the spatial arts of architecture, sculpture, painting, and the minor and industrial arts, rhythm is an ever-present factor consciously used by the designer. Through the repetition of a given architectural element, as in the Palazzo Farnese (Fig. 155, p. 275), a certain regularity of emphasis is achieved; in this case, it gives additional dignity to the building—small but elegant. In the Palace of Versailles (Fig. 156, p. 276) the repeated columns, monumental in size, produce another feeling altogether, one of grandeur and slow pomp.

Rhythm may be restful and idealized, as in the sweetly spaced and

Fig. 159. ROGIER VAN DER WEYDEN: *Descent from the Cross*. Madrid, Prado.

proportioned columns of the Parthenon (Fig. 62a, p. 97). It may be lyrical, as in the gently swinging curved movement above the heads of the figures in Botticelli's *Primavera* (Fig. 36, p. 59). In Rogier van der Weyden's *Descent from the Cross* (Fig. 159, p. 282) the rhythms are staccato, and the eye moves abruptly from side to side— from the bent back of the young John at the left to that of the weeping Magdalene at the right, from the angularly carved figure of the Christ to the paralleled form of the fainting Virgin, from the man holding the legs of Christ to the woman supporting the body of the Virgin.

Where van der Weyden attempts in his rhythms to express a certain angular strain, an almost wood-carved impression of emotional out-pouring, the artists of the *Altarpiece of the Lamb* (Fig. 103, p. 172) have adopted a broad flowing series of curves as the basis for their rhythmic effects. The two groups at the lower corners curve upward and then down to the Fountain of Life at the bottom. Here the lower side of the fountain becomes the narrow part of an ellipselike movement made up of the inner edges of the large bottom masses, which repeat in the two arcs formed by the angels about the altar and once again in a pair of sideward movements into the upper corners. Thus there is a continuous gentle, sweeping rhythm of curves running through the painting in a symmetrical and dignified way, in keeping with the worshipful mood that is established.

In the paintings of El Greco (see Fig. 151b, p. 268), the religious quality assumes a mystic aura of ecstasy in which the lights and darks alternate in a staccato rhythm expressive of the state of exaltation in which the artist finds himself. As our eyes move across the surface of *St. Martin and the Beggar,* we find the regular alternation of a pulsating light area and a vivid expressive area of shadow—these latter areas are not black but colored, filled with the characteristically expressive and unreal, and yet very effective, stridencies that give El Greco's work its strange emotional impact. The rhythm of these back-and-forth, light-to-dark changes creates a visual and hence emotional anxiety. Nevertheless, as in any well-organized work, the rhythms are continuous, with one part flowing into another. This continuity exists not only in the patterns of lights and darks and the geometric areas indicated by the lighted forms, but also in the relationship between the color in one portion of the work and that found elsewhere. As the eye roams over this surface and into the interior planes or spaces of the picture, it encounters repeated touches of red, greenish gray, or other colors which aid the rhythmic unity of the work.

A repeated motif, color, or form may well offer certain elements of boredom if not carefully handled, that is, spaced, proportioned, or otherwise altered. In the Palazzo Farnese (Fig. 155, p. 275), for example, we saw a clear instance of a repeated motif in the continuous series of windows on each level. There the artist avoided the danger of monotony by making changes on each level up to the cornice. A somewhat similar circumstance occurs in the arrangement of the arcades on the façade of the *Cathedral and Leaning Tower of Pisa* (Figs. 160 and 161, p. 284). On the cathedral a row of long narrow arches is arranged horizontally. Directly above, on the next level, the shape of the row and the nature of the rhythm are altered by a shift to a truncated pediment form that cuts down the heights of the vertical colonnettes. The third row repeats the proportions and shapes of the first, although the row itself has been shortened. Finally at the top a

Fig. 160 (*left*). Cathedral of Pisa. Pisa, Italy. Fig. 161 (*right*). The Leaning Tower. Pisa, Italy, Cathedral of Pisa.

pedimented arrangement gives us a new variant of the arches, which move from normal central units to short ones at the ends. Here the architect has deliberately altered his rhythms as he moved upward from one level to another. Moreover, he has also shifted the position of the columns so that they do not appear directly above each other—all in the interests of variety within repetition.

On the Leaning Tower itself (Fig. 161, p. 284), although the colonnettes are placed directly over each other, the planner achieves variety by providing a different base and a different top element. As for the six circular rows of colonnettes in between, these are subtly narrowed in circumference as we move up from one level to the next, so that there can be no absolute repetition. Where sameness has thus been changed by enlargement or making smaller, we may speak of progression rather than of repetition.

Proportion. Proportion, the last of the Principles to be discussed in this brief survey, involves a relationship between the size or dimensions of one part of a work of art and that of the other parts or of the whole. This idea of proportional relationship may also be applied to colors, light and dark areas, textures, and any other measurable element or factor in design. The idea of proportion may be simply expressed in the everyday sense of the size of a man's head being out of proportion to the length of his body. Just as there exists in everyday life a so-called norm of proportion, there are such norms in art as well. As we shall see later (Chapter 14), these norms vary from one age to another, depending on the existing ideals of physical beauty. But proportion can be esthetically effective and important, as we have already seen in the Cathedral of Pisa or its Leaning Tower, in which alterations of proportional relationships lend an added quality of variety and interest.

An alteration of the proportions of the human body in a painting or sculpture may be made for reasons of emotional expressiveness, for reasons of idealization, or for the purposes of elegance. Thus in Romanesque sculpture (see *Isaiah* of Souillac, Fig. 189, p. 331), in El Greco's works (Fig. 151b, p. 268), and in other types of emotionalized projection, the length of the body will be exaggerated and its thickness decreased to accentuate the spiritual rather than the material. In classical art, on the other hand, the artist (see Fig. 185, p. 324) attempts to achieve a proportion that expresses a human and emotional ideal, a calm rather than a crisis, poise rather than passion. A sculptor like Bernini in his *Apollo and Daphne* or Praxiteles in his *Hermes* (see Fig. 136, p. 223) will lengthen the proportions of the hands and feet, elongate the head, and so on, to achieve a certain aristocratic quality and reserve. The same is true of the figures of Gainsborough, Van Dyck, Sargent, and many other portraitists catering to the upper classes (see *The Hon. Mrs. Graham,* Fig. 170, p. 300).

Besides these emotional uses, proportion is even more valuable in establishing the form-validity of any work where the adjustment of a ratio of lengths, widths, thicknesses, and so forth underlies other elements—balance, rhythm, or unity. In Vermeer's *Young Woman with a Water Jug* (Fig. 32, p. 50) the artistic problem is the balancing of the various elements within the picture space so that they do not crowd the space or each other as the painter ties them together. The woman is made to dominate the picture through her relative size or proportion to the other objects as well as through the relative intensity of her blue gown against the light blue of the window and the other blues in the picture. Vermeer could very well have altered the dimensional proportions of the elements involved to give us more or less map, window, or table—and in some pictures such as his *Lady with a Lute* (in the Metropolitan Museum of Art) he has done just that. But in the latter work, it should be noted, the lady herself is

Fig. 162. JAN VERMEER: *Lady with a Lute*. New York, Metropolitan Museum of Art.

much smaller than the lady with the pitcher (Fig. 162, p. 286).

Although there is no absolute proportion in spite of the many efforts that are made from century to century to find a "canon" (Polyclitus), "golden section" (the modern Cubists), and the like, a just proportion can be and often is very useful in determining the quality of a work of art. It is certainly true that bad proportion is immediately perceptible in its effects. In the *Laokoön* of the Hellenistic period in Greece (Fig. 187, p. 325) we are disturbed by the relative proportions of the father and his two sons, for although the latter are shown in much smaller scale than the father (as though they were young children), they are actually full-grown men and should be shown in the same relative scale.

Contrariwise, we find that the proportions of the smaller elements in the Palazzo Farnese (Fig. 155, p. 275) are well adjusted in that the vertical and horizontal accents of the windows have an effect opposite to those of the main outline of the building, thus tending to set up a balance of contrasts. This subtlety of arrangement does not always pertain to the many adaptations that have been made of this building. In the *Banqueting House* at Whitehall (Fig. 163, p. 287) designed by Inigo Jones, where the building itself is closer to square, the proportions of the windows with their reminiscent rhythmic arrangement are too large for the façade space into which they are set. In this way the proportions of the Farnese windows to their façade are more restful; the same elements in the Banqueting House give a feeling of tightness augmented by the obtrusive character of the pilasters attached to the middle of the façade.

We shall return to this question of proportion in our final discussion (Chapter 19) attempting to establish qualitative values. What we have tried to do here in our survey of the Tools of design, its plastic Elements, and its Principles is to lead the reader more or less along the path often followed by the artist in designing the work, and to see, so far as such brief observation makes possible, the vital importance of planning. For the artist it is almost indispensable; for the spectator this systematic approach should enhance understanding as he moves from the elementary aspect of the Tool, or Component, to the more complex meaning of the Element, arriving finally at the reasoned and calculated significance of the Principle (or Principles) of design.

Fig. 163. INIGO JONES: Banqueting House, Whitehall. London.

▶ 11

The Arts and the Story of Man

AT THE VERY BEGINNING of this book we recognized that one of the advantages of studying the art of the past lies in its telling us how the nations and races of mankind have lived. More specifically, through such study we can discover something of the other man's viewpoint about manners and customs, famous personalities, religion, social ideas, political attitudes, and so forth. In the history of civilization, the differences in approach from one era to another are revealing and valuable; and they are equally significant in the history of art. In addition, our delving into the art of the past (or of the far-away present) reveals that ideals of physical beauty and, more important, ideals of artistic beauty change with time and place.

Just as taste in regard to physical types changes from period to period (one age preferring women robust, another liking them thin), so opinion as to what is artistically desirable also shows differences from epoch to epoch. By artistically desirable we mean the standards that determine the arrangement of color, line, form, composition, space, proportion, and other esthetic factors. Unfortunately, while we readily understand that our grandfathers preferred a type of feminine beauty that is a little strange for us, we are not always quite so ready to accept the fact that taste in art can change just as easily.

In the mass of information gleaned from the art of the past, we find that our material comes from a careful consideration of both the

Fig. 164. Arch of Titus. Rome. (Photo courtesy Trans World Airlines, Inc.)

style (that is, the manner of expression) and the content, or subject matter, of the work of art. Each has its story to tell. Furthermore, as we have seen previously (Chapter 2), our examination of art as visual history is often a confirmation of what we know from such other sources as written records. In many cases, new relationships emerge from this study.

Manners and Customs

In the area of manners and customs, we may take as a simple illustration the Arch of Titus (first century A.D., Fig. 164, p. 289), commemorating the destruction of the Hebrew Temple in Jerusalem by Emperor Vespasian and his son Titus. The monument typifies the militaristic aspect of Roman life, according to which victorious generals were granted a "triumph" for a successful campaign, here the devastation of the tiny kingdom of Palestine. A triumph was an elaborate procession; Roman legionaries in dress uniform, special groups bearing the booty of the campaign, and captives chained to the victors' chariots, all passed under the symbolic yoke-shaped arch of Rome.

On the inside walls of the Arch of Titus are sculptured panels portraying the looting of sacred vessels from the Temple (Fig. 164a, p. 290)

Fig. 164a. *Spoils from the Temple of Jerusalem,* detail from the Arch of Titus. Rome.

and the triumphant passage of the Emperor, an allegorical Victory figure holding a crown over his head. For the Romans, such arches were part of their history, more plentiful and important in some periods than others; for the conquered, they became bitter symbols of defeat. For centuries it was considered a grave religious offense for any orthodox Jew to walk beneath this monument to the cruel humiliation of his people.

Another example of manners and customs recorded by a work of art is the beautiful illuminated book known as the *Très riches heures du Duc de Berri.* Its pages (Fig. 21, p. 34) are painted with scenes from the lives of people of early fifteenth-century Flanders. This is a book of the Hours of the Virgin, recording the appropriate times or hours for particular prayers, and made for the Duke of Berri, an important art patron of that day. On its handsomely colored pages are portrayed the castles and other properties of the Duke (generally in the background) , as well as scenes showing banquets, processions, hunting parties, and other events associated with particular times of the year and with the kind of people the artist was working for. In addition, there are scenes from the everyday life of the peasants who worked the estates of the noble lord. These men and women are shown sowing grain, shearing sheep, gathering firewood, and so forth, again in accordance with different times or seasons. In their several ways these pages picture the life of early fifteenth-century Flanders as seen by a manuscript painter.

Personalities

In regard to famous personalities and what is revealed of them through works of art, we find a rich, although sometimes perplexing, field of interest. Houdon's portrait of *Voltaire* (Fig. 165, p. 291), like most studies of famous people of the past, brings to life the physical quality—and perhaps some of the character as well—of a person known to us otherwise through his accomplishments. In this case, the plays, novels, pamphlets, and essays of the great eighteenth-century satirist and antimonarchist have left in some minds the picture of a cynical, bitter, and even violent personality. The sculpture, however, does not bear this conception out; it depicts rather the worldly-wise and even tolerant expression of a man who has lived through much, and here at the end of his life appears as a hero garbed in the robes of ancient Roman republicanism. Whatever our impression of Voltaire from his writings, whether of the violent dissident or of the clever skillful satirist, the portrait makes us ponder his personality, makes us wonder if the artist's (or writer's) personality necessarily agrees with the nature of his work.

In another example, Baron Gros's *Napoleon among the Plague-stricken at Jaffa* (Fig. 166, p. 292), we have an interesting side light on the character and accomplishments of the Emperor. However much we may have read about Napoleon, the function of Baron Gros

Fig. 165. JEAN ANTOINE HOUDON: *Voltaire.* Paris, Théâtre français. (Photo courtesy French Goverment Tourist Office)

Fig. 166. ANTOINE JEAN GROS: *Napoleon among the Plague-stricken at Jaffa*. Paris, Louvre.

as official painter and propagandist adds to our knowledge of the cult of Emperor-worship and how it was fostered. Gros's job was to show Napoleon in as favorable a view as possible; in his descriptions of the great man's battles and campaigns (some of which Gros witnessed from a discreet distance and others not at all), his chief aim was to make a good report for the people at home.

Napoleon is shown here in a converted mosque that served as a hospital during the Near-Eastern phase of his wars. Accompanied by members of his staff, he stands in the center of the painting, touching the horrible sores of a plague sufferer. Gros makes the Emperor look like an Early Christian saint or martyr, silently suffering and willing to risk even this horrible death for the love he bears mankind. To some, the picture of the leader rolling his eyes heavenward in an access of religious feeling may appear very impressive: to others, as they ask themselves who caused all this trouble, it will seem the essence of hypocrisy. Obviously Gros's glorification of Napoleon is as far from the truth as are the Napoleonic caricatures by the

Englishman Gillray during the same period. It is clear that with Napoleon, as with many other dictators past and present, the cult was encouraged by planned action and organized propaganda. Thus portraits like the *Voltaire* are far more likely to be honest estimates (however personal) than those of political figures like Napoleon who can control the result.

Religious Outlook

What can we learn from art about religious attitudes as they have changed from century to century and from country to country? Upon examining a typical fifteenth-century Flemish religious painting like Rogier van der Weyden's *Descent from the Cross* (Fig. 159, p. 282) and comparing it with an equally typical early sixteenth-century Italian painting like Raphael's *Alba Madonna* (Fig. 16, p. 28), we are brought to realize that the very essence of religiousness is different in the two periods—and therefore in the two paintings.

The Flemish master gives us a work filled with high compassion, a tensely tragic and symbolic version of this awful moment. What is shown here is no everyday sorrow of grieving mother and dead son, nor are the attitudes of the various participants anything but formal and ritualistic. Observing their faces, we see immediately that few of the characters are psychologically concerned with each other. Each of them seems to be concerned with himself alone, looking inward rather than at his companions. It is quite probable that the late medieval artist intended the figures to stand by themselves as generally recognizable symbols: Joseph of Arimathea, Mary Magdalene, St. John, Mary, and the others, as they might have been shown on the façade of some earlier cathedral. Indeed, the background of this picture reflects the architecture of a Gothic cathedral and the figures are arranged two-dimensionally, yet sculpturally, across the surface of a narrow ledge.

What really interests the painter, however, is the symbolic and mystic identification of the Virgin and her suffering with that of her Son. This is accomplished by a parallelism in the forms, including the downward-drooping right arms of both, their upraised and supported left arms, and the curvature of both bodies. Each is part of a moving group arranged as though the two tragedies were part of a ritual in which balanced groupings move in parallel, yet separate, fugal rhythms. They are clearly related, though separate, and not even His mother looks at the suffering Christ, for Her pain echoes His.

Although early Flemish painting in general has a concentrated, symbolic, and mood-charged quality, a mystic sense of absorption in the facts of revealed religion that identifies it with medievalism, this is hardly true of the contemporary and slightly later Italian painting. Raphael's *Alba Madonna* can stand as typical of the essential worldliness of the Italian school, of its warmly human and even everyday quality. To be sure, this is no tragic scene, but its warmth and secularity are as characteristic of Raphael's time and culture as the mysticism and profound religiosity of the earlier work by Rogier van der Weyden were of his. Where van der Weyden shows a world of symbolic and nonidealized personages, Raphael—the Renaissance master—while idealizing his characters in the physical and mental sense, increases their attractiveness as human beings. Mary and the two children (young St. John the Baptist and the Christ Child) are all very attractive people whose psychological relationships are warm and close. John gazes adoringly at the Christ, who returns his look in a sweet childish way, while Mary in turn gazes at them both in her charming womanly and motherly manner. Even the pose of the Virgin is such that her body surrounds the children symbolically in an enclosure shaped like a parallelogram.

Different religious attitudes are expressed by these two works: the earlier one is more directly concerned with deep spiritual truths, the later one with the expression of a worldly and even elegant ideal. An early chronicler tells of a pious Italian woman who left to her parish church a Flemish painting which she considered her most precious possession because, as she put in her will, "it is so religious."

The distinction between these two religious attitudes, the medieval and the humanistic, can also be seen on a more exaggerated level in the contrast between a Gothic and a seventeenth-century work. Let us compare the *Virgin Portal* of the Cathedral of Notre Dame in Paris (Fig. 167, p. 295), which bears a series of sculptures dating from the early thirteenth century, with Caravaggio's *Death of the Virgin* (Fig. 151a, p. 263), painted around 1600. Here we recognize a religious subject treated four hundred years apart in different countries, the general theme of the death and coronation of the Virgin.

On the Gothic cathedral the sculptor has chosen to represent a deeply

Fig. 167. Virgin Portal. Paris, Notre Dame.

spiritual and symbolic scene in which the lowest register shows three prophets and three kings, relating to those who prophesied Christ's coming and those who were His ancestors. The middle section deals with the Resurrection of the Virgin—or better, the translation of her soul to heaven at the moment of her death. There in the presence of the apostles who have been brought from the far corners of the earth for this event, Christ appears to conduct His mother's soul to Her place of honor at His right hand (upper section) where She is crowned Queen of Heaven. Here, even more than in the *Descent from the Cross,* is a suspended emotional quality, a restraint related to the essentially symbolic rather than active or realistic nature of the scene depicted.

There is a sameness about many of the apostles, prophets, and kings, who do not have to be distinguished from each other in any detail, since they are formal symbols readily recognized by anyone of that period. They stand about the sacred bier as the angels lift the Virgin's soul out of the coffin, with only the Christ (who has a crossed halo) turning away from the plane parallel to the main line of the relief. Although the apostles are supposed to be contemplating the great miracle, no facial or physical attitude shows this (compare to the van der Weyden above). The important point is that this is a symbolic scene designed for a particular public; it is the product of a particular spiritual need for which this formal solemnity was desirable. Everyone was "religious" in a way that we cannot begin to understand today, and therefore was immediately affected by the stimulus of the common-place symbols set before him.

A century later, when Giotto painted his *Death of St. Francis* (see Fig. 176, p. 310) it was already necessary for the artist to inject a humanistic appeal, like the surprise of the monk at the left of the couch and the overt but controlled sorrow of the others. When we arrive at the seventeenth-century painting by Caravaggio, we see an emotional attitude more exaggerated than in the Giotto work and certainly far more open and expressive than in the medieval work at Notre Dame. Not only this painter but many others of the period seem to display a violent emotive quality, as though they felt a strong necessity to stimulate people.

This work removes the death scene from the remote and symbolic height of both the Notre Dame sculptor and Giotto, and places it on a clear everyday level that makes it more appealing to the average man. Here the Virgin is no celestial being but rather an ordinarily dressed, simple woman who has died. Her friends and relatives—as ordinary and naturalistic as She—have gathered to pay their respects and to grieve rather than to contemplate any miracle. Moreover, the artist is much concerned with stirring up his audience. For this pur-pose he has dramatized the scene by focusing the light in an arbitrary but effective way; it is made to fall upon the tops of the spectators' heads and illuminates fully the form of the Virgin on the bed below.

If it is true that Western man in the Gothic era was filled with a faith that did not have to be reiterated and constantly supported, it is equally true that by the seventeenth century, during the period of the Counter Reformation, the Church felt it vital to strengthen the failing spirits weakened by the doubts and revolts of the preceding Reformation. That is what makes a Baroque work like this necessary and typical for its time. In the Gothic era the more generalized the figures and their faces, the more symbolic was their effect and mean-ing; in the Baroque age the more naturalistic in detail the people and their emotions, the closer was their identification with the observer.

Social Attitudes

Just as works of art can and do reveal the religious outlook of their time, they also tell us much about the social and political attitudes of the artists and their clients or patrons. Conclusions about social levels

Fig. 168. JEAN ANTOINE WATTEAU: *Embarkation for the Isle of Cythera*. Paris, Louvre.

(the classes from which the individuals came) can be drawn from comparing and contrasting two French paintings of the eighteenth century, Watteau's *Embarkation for the Isle of Cythera* (Fig. 168, p. 297) and Greuze's *The Father's Curse: The Punished Son* (Fig. 169, p. 298). In the first, painted in the early part of the century, we see elegant men and women walking about in shiny satiny costumes. Their high heels and tight trousers cause the men to move mincingly in what seems to us an affected manner; the broad billowing skirts of the ladies make them appear to float gracefully above the ground. The entire work breathes an air of artificiality, of make-believe, as though the people were going through the steps of an aristocratic minuet or the paces of a play.

Much of this we can see without knowing anything about Watteau the painter or the specific circumstances under which he worked. But these very impressions tell us that Watteau painted for clients who demanded this charm and elegance, that one of the ideals of their lives was the mannered love-making and courting which we observe in the painting. When we learn more about the painter, we discover that he was a product of the gay Regency period in early eighteenth-century France. In the theater (to which Watteau, as a former scenic

Fig. 169. JEAN BAPTISTE GREUZE: *The Father's Curse: The Punished Son.* Paris, Louvre.

painter, was devoted) and in the period generally, the ideal of a charming gallantry, an elaborate code of love-making, was indeed held by aristocrats.

At the extreme right, the painting itself shows a pair of elegant lovers, the gentleman whispering sweet nothings into the lady's ear. Next to them, another couple represents the second step in *galant* courtship, as the gentleman raises the lady to her feet. A third pair shows a young lady being led away by her lover down the grassy bank to join other couples, who are gathered about an elaborately and delicately carved ship that will carry them off to mythical Cythera, the isle of love.

The ideals of the upper classes as revealed in works of this kind stand in strong contrast to those revealed by such paintings as Greuze's *The Father's Curse: The Punished Son,* a work of the latter part of the eighteenth century. Conditions had changed considerably, if we can judge from pictures of this newer type. These pictures also suggest the theater, but not the theater of artificial love-making. Even a cursory glance reveals a new seriousness, even melodrama, the fact that the painter is trying to point up a moral lesson by his depiction of the repentant broken sinner at the right who has returned to find his parent dying and noisy weeping relatives clustered about the deathbed. Although its exaggerated emotional expression is not congenial to present tastes, this sort of work in both painting and literature was very popular in the late eighteenth century, even with the different social group that had patronized Watteau earlier.

We can see without too much difficulty that the figures in the Greuze are not aristocrats but rather ordinary middle-class folk going through the kind of emotional purge that the motion pictures and radio and television melodramas offer to the many today who still find it attractive. The change from Watteau's elegance and artificiality to Greuze's exaggerated naturalness of feeling is a measure of the shift of power from the upper to the middle classes, the latter becoming increasingly important in the life of the country as the century advanced.

The contrast in social viewpoint emerging from these two paintings can also be noticed in works of art from other countries or periods. We may take as another pair of differentiated works two eighteenth-century English pictures: Hogarth's *Marriage à la Mode* and Gainsborough's portrait of *The Hon. Mrs. Graham* (Figs. 19 and 170, pp. 31, 300). We can tell from the costumes and from the titles that in both pictures members of the aristocracy are involved either partly or completely. Hogarth, however, injects a note of British humor and caricature into his treatment, while Gainsborough would seem to lean in the opposite direction, toward dignity and seriousness. This difference may be a symptom of the origins of the painter or of his sympathies—but whatever its cause, the work of art embodies a social viewpoint.

The fact that both artists were financially successful would indicate that there was room for both the pro- and the anti-aristocratic viewpoints in the England, as in the France, of that period. But where the gaiety and charm of the Watteau are accurate expressions of the courtly class for whom the artist worked, the elegance of Mrs. Graham is the result of a somewhat unreal exaggeration of the proportions of the figure—everything moves upward in a slim and elongated manner, the column at the right adding to the impression of length. In-

Fig. 170. THOMAS GAINSBOROUGH: *The Honourable Mrs. Graham*. Edinburgh, National Gallery of Scotland.

deed it was Gainsborough's business to make his clients look well-bred, slender, and elegant, and people apparently came to his studio because he did so. We may say, then, that Gainsborough reflects the fashionable and noble ideal toward which the upper middle class and the rural aristocracy of his time aspired.

Hogarth discloses a rather critical attitude—the title of *Marriage à la Mode* indicating an aversion to that kind of empty social ambition. The picture itself, one of a series by this illustrious critic of the manners and morals of his age, shows a young couple seated at the left; the youth is a typical attitudinizing fop of the period, the maiden is a sulky, pouting, spoiled daughter of a wealthy father. These two are about to be affianced without love on either side, the young man bringing his aristocratic name to the match, the young woman her father's fortune. They are not exactly engrossed in each other, a fact underlined by the suave young fellow hovering over the bride—the notary's assistant with his eye on the future. At the right, a fussy little notary is acting as intermediary between the pompous aristocrat with the gouty leg and long family tree and the wizened near-sighted rich man offering his heap of coins.

Although in such works as the *Marriage à la Mode* series it is relatively easy to read a story and its social intention, this intention can also be read from less obvious works such as the Gainsborough portrait, or even in subjectless material such as buildings. Since buildings, made by people for people, are formed with specific practical needs in view, these needs quite readily reveal themselves to the spectator. The more we know about the particular epoch in which a building was constructed, the more valuable and richer our realization of its social purpose.

Even without knowing anything about seventeenth-century France or eighteenth-century America, we can see that the social importance of the builder of the Louvre (Fig. 171, p. 301) was relatively greater than that of the owner of the Royall House (Fig. 172, p. 302). Obviously, the former building is larger, richer, and more elaborate in every way. Just as clearly it must have taken much more time, money, and power to erect. The same rule of thumb might be applied in contemporary architecture if we were to compare a simple one-family suburban home and a mansion in a large city.

But size alone is far from the only criterion of social importance, for great size might indicate sponsorship by a powerful king, a democracy, or even a dictatorship. By the same token, a relatively small building like the Tugendhat House by Miës van der Rohe or the Cali-

Fig. 171. CLAUDE PERRAULT: East façade of the Louvre. Paris.

Fig. 172. Royall House. Medford, Massachusetts.

fornia house (Figs. 64 and 56, pp. 101, 66) is typical of the private residence increasingly built for the modern well-to-do. Far more important than size in the social evaluation of a building is its function or functions.

The Louvre on examination proves to have an enormous number of rooms in its fabulously extensive layout: service quarters for the innumerable attendants necessary in the operation of a huge court; numerous apartments for the courtiers and their retinues; space for executive, religious, storage, stable, and every other conceivable function. Such an extensive arrangement was made necessary by the fact that this building was one of two major official residences of King Louis XIV—the other being the Palace of Versailles outside of Paris. That the Louvre must also be regarded as a symbol of the power and importance of the king is attested further by the fact that although his real headquarters were at Versailles, his ministers felt it important for him to have an official residence in Paris, however little used it might be.

The modest dimensions of the Royall House (in Medford, Massachusetts), which is less than fifty feet long, thirty-eight feet wide, and about thirty-six feet high, cannot begin to compare with even a single section of the Louvre shown here, which by itself is about 600 feet long. Obviously the owner of the house is of far more modest means and power than Louis XIV, yet in colonial New England the Royall

House was considered an important and impressive home. This is true in spite of the fact that functionally it was made for one family with its modest contingent of servants—the family of a prosperous business-man who represented as high a class as democratic America had.

In America, as in France, there were other types of residences by which we may judge our examples. The French varieties ranged all the way down from the king's palace to peasants' hovels—with aris-tocratic châteaux and merchants' homes in between. In the American colonies one could find, in addition to our rich merchant's dwelling, the plantation manor of the South, the farm home of New England, the log cabin of the western territories, and many other types, each indicating the social position of the builder.

Palaces are not always so elaborate as that of Louis XIV, nor resi-dences of businessmen so modest as that of Isaac Royall. Degree of splendor depends on the circumstances, and these are revealed to us by the buildings themselves. The circumstances of colonial America with its New England Puritan background made inadvisable a more elaborate merchant dwelling, such as those of the late Middle Ages in Europe, exemplified in the House of Jacques Coeur at Bourges, or those of early twentieth-century America, like the old Rhinelander mansion in New York City.

The Louvre is not necessarily typical of palaces, although it was imitated by many monarchs of eighteenth-century Europe when they had the necessary financial and political facilities. We may compare a monarchical center like the Louvre with an earlier palace; the Pa-lazzo Farnese in Rome (Fig. 155, p. 275) is a residence building which, although far more impressive than the Royall House, is very small compared to the French structure. The rulers of Italy in the six-teenth century when this palace was constructed were small princelings, some of them viceroys of Spain or France ruling a small portion of Italy in the name of their foreign masters. Their residences had to be a symbol of viceregal authority, but for the function that they performed such relatively modest structures were quite adequate.

All the buildings thus far considered in this section have been in-dividual residences, no matter how elaborate their arrangement and important their ultimate function. In recent times, with the new con-centration of population, many of these old buildings in Rome, Paris, Madrid, and other cities, originally homes for the aristocracy, have become multiple dwellings for workers. At present, with the rejection of this unsatisfactory rabbit-warren residence and its blood brother, the genuine tenement, we find ourselves moving toward the most socially useful solutions of the problem of housing large numbers of people. These are the low-cost individual housing project and the large-scale apartment dwelling.

We may take the Gratiot-Orleans Redevelopment Project of Detroit during the 1950's (Fig. 79, p. 122) as an example of a recent housing project. It represents an attempt to utilize the means of mass production—perhaps the most characteristic development of our society—to take care of the many people drawn to the city to carry on its multifarious activities. Because these apartments are mass-produced, they are relatively cheaper than the individual home built in the suburbs or, often, than the ordinary city apartment. They give the consumer more for his money, as does the mass-produced radio or automobile.

Political Meanings

Political attitudes are implicit in the content and form of many works of art. This we have already seen in Michelangelo's Tomb of Lorenzo de' Medici (Fig. 34, p. 54), with its indirect critical attitude toward a ruling family, and in Gros's *Napoleon among the Plague-stricken at Jaffa* (Fig. 166, p. 292), with its overt praise of the dictator. Praise of a ruler presents few problems; condemnation, on the other hand, is much riskier, and where authority has been absolute, the political atmosphere has not been conducive to such expression. Social institutions were attacked as early as during the sixteenth-century Reformation and Counter Reformation, when Catholics and Protestants issued a great spate of caricatures against each other. But political commentary long remained allegorical or symbolic like the Medici tomb or the paintings of Pieter Brueghel which were directed against the sixteenth-century Spanish invaders of the Netherlands.

David's *Oath of the Horatii* (Fig. 173, p. 305), painted in 1784, shows the oblique method of political commentary that prevailed on the eve of the French Revolution. Like many other liberals of his day, the painter felt strongly about political life, the most important aspect of which was the rising revolutionary sentiment against the monarchy. But he did not—and indeed could not—come out directly with his

Fig. 173. JACQUES LOUIS DA-VID: *Oath of the Horatii.* Paris, Louvre.

sympathy. Rather, he has allegorized the feeling that love of country must transcend in importance even those dearest to us.

Deriving his theme from a seventeenth-century play, David presents three young Roman warriors, the Horatii, who pledge themselves to fight to the death against a neighboring city with which Rome is at war, although their three sisters (seen weeping at the right) are married to men from the enemy city. Earlier in the century, it would have been inconceivable that anyone should place country above family; now, in the new atmosphere of political morality, patriotism or love of country had become a substitute for worship of any monarch. This is the era when, for the first time, a modern national army replaced the still typical mercenary armies of the eighteenth century. While Greuze's father of the family (Fig. 169, p. 298) preached family unity, David's preaches patriotism.

More overt political paintings also existed during this period, such as the 1804 Gros painting already examined, but that is favorable to the ruler. Opposed to it, violent denunciation of Napoleon is offered in Goya's famous *Execution of the Citizens of Madrid* (1808, Fig. 20, p. 33), which gives us an altogether different impression of the Emperor and his armies. This incident occurred during the Peninsular War in which the French invaded Spain and the English helped the Spaniards. On May 2, 1808, the inhabitants of Madrid revolted against the brutal occupation of their city by the French and their North-African mercenaries. In reprisal for this civilian attack on the troops, the invaders gathered in as many people as they could find, lined them up, and executed them out of hand, as shown in this work. Goya was incensed at what was being done to his country; in his eyes, the French grenadiers were monsters and his own people were both pathetic and brave—all this is told in a violent political statement. What made such a picture possible was the fact that, unlike David's work, it was not and could not be shown until much later.

Some ten years afterward, Géricault exhibited in Paris his *Raft of the Medusa* (1818–19, Fig. 2, p. 8), in protest against the inefficiency of the French navy and the abandonment of a group of enlisted men by their officers during a shipwreck. The painting was banned by the authorities. Nevertheless, during the course of the nineteenth century, political protest became increasingly possible, especially in newspaper caricatures where it had the greatest role to play. This may be illustrated by one of Daumier's lithographs, the famous *Rue Transnonain* of 1834 (Fig. 123, p. 206), a bitter indictment of the new French government and its ruthless suppression of a strike. During this period such criticisms became a part of the French political scene as they had been somewhat earlier in Britain—but primarily on a journalistic or graphic arts level. In painting it was not until the first quarter of the twentieth century that politically minded and politically critical works became general. The revolutions that followed World War I were actively supported by painters, poets, and musicians, whether of the Left or of the Right.

Although often the art produced under revolutionary governments was bombastic and superficially illustrative, the painting of Mexico in the years after 1920 is an exceptionally exciting political art. The Mexicans Orozco, Rivera, and Siqueiros display specifically political painting and graphic work, designed to inculcate certain ideals in the minds of the people. Pictures like *The Proletarian Victim* by Siqueiros (Fig. 174, p. 307) manifest powerful sympathy for the oppressed, as did Goya's work. But this modern subject differs in that it does not refer to a specific incident; instead, it symbolizes oppression, as do the works of Orozco. A more explicitly didactic political note is struck in the mural paintings of Diego Rivera.

Fig. 174. DAVID SIQUEIROS: *Proletarian Victim*. New York, The Museum of Modern Art.

Concepts of Beauty

Our exploration of the art objects of the past also discloses the kind of physical beauty that different periods considered desirable. This may seem less important than some of the other data gleaned above; but often our first hint of the existence of different tastes in various epochs comes from the fact that one period prefers heavily built women, another slimmer types, and still another emaciated types. We have already noticed these taste differences in physical beauty; now we may examine works from varying eras that express this fact and its implications.

The Flemish *Arnolfini Marriage* (Fig. 8, p. 21) shows, first, that a portraitist is not always concerned with beautifying the male personage, no matter how rich or important he may be. Further, in view of the social position of this resident Italian financier who surely had his choice, the young lady must have been considered personable. But we find her appearing thin-chested, as a result of the popular tight bodice, and with an enlarged stomach, as a result of a fashionably swaying posture and the folds of cloth held before her. Most people today will

Fig. 175. IL GIORGIONE: *Concert Champêtre.* Paris, Louvre.

not consider either the man or woman attractive, and yet there is every reason to suppose that the artist was portraying them with all the dignity he could muster and as much chic or style as was called for by a commemorative picture of this sort. We do not, however, have to make a choice between the taste of the fifteenth-century Flemings and our own—there is no question of their women being more beautiful than ours or the reverse. We leave them their taste and keep our own, making an effort to understand what they are trying to do and accepting it within those limitations.

Although we are all brought up to revere Italian art of the Renaissance, the nude forms in a famous example, like the *Concert Champêtre* by Giorgione (Fig. 175, p. 308), may seem to us too full. This work, however, is a poetic and sensitive one, showing two young men completely absorbed in each other and in their memories of the past, ignoring the attractions of the nymphs in this pastoral environment. We are asked to consider the contrast between the pleasures of the moment as represented by the women and the suspension of time as represented by the gestures of the men.

Even in modern times we find that preceding generations had tastes in human beauty that we no longer share. The Lillian Russell ideal with its hourglass figure is surely a thing of the past, but variants of it still crop up. And not too long ago there was a vogue among college girls in the United States for a slouching stomach-protruding posture not unlike that of Mrs. Arnolfini. Surely Giorgione would not have approved such a conception of femininity.

Although we have confined our discussion of Concepts of Beauty to people, it might also be extended to include landscape, furniture, clothing and a multitude of other taste areas in which differences occur from epoch to epoch.

Artistic Styles

The art of the past demonstrates not only that there are different conceptions of physical beauty, but also that there are different standards of esthetic or artistic beauty in various ages and cultures. This implies first that fifteenth-century Flanders or sixteenth-century Italy consider men and women attractive for divergent (and sometimes even opposite) reasons. It also means that the works of art which reveal these variations of physical taste are beautiful to their epochs for different esthetic reasons.

It must surely have occurred to the reader by now that different types of art have different virtues, and as indicated earlier, that these virtues may not always be apparent to a generation trained in its own system, in another way of looking at things—another artistic language. All of us, from ancient man to contemporary man, are conditioned (generally without realizing it) to some viewpoint, that is, to what is considered the "proper" way for a painting or other art object to look. Each age, as the result of inherited tradition and the changes it has introduced itself, formulates for its own use certain standards for space, composition, proportion, and other artistic components. Within the intellectual climate of that age, these elements together constitute the artistic or esthetic standards of the time, its standards of beauty, its style or manner of expression.

When we speak, then, of the "style" or "styles" of Romanesque sculpture or Renaissance painting, we mean the manner of expression developed during those periods and considered as standards of artistic beauty in those times. We know that artists have often been rejected— or at best considered very daring—when they departed from the stand-

Fig. 176. GIOTTO: *Death of St. Francis*. Florence, Santa Croce, Bardi Chapel. (Photo courtesy Italian Tourist Information Office)

ards or styles. What we are concerned with here, however, is the fact that it is entirely natural for each culture to have its own style or styles, each as logical an expression of its period as ours are of today's life, and therefore as worthy of respect.

Giotto's *Death of St. Francis* (Fig. 176, p. 310) represents one stylistic viewpoint, that of early fourteenth-century Italy. This viewpoint may be contrasted with the stylistic quality of another epoch in Italian history, the early seventeenth century, as exemplified by Bernini's *Apollo and Daphne* (Fig. 177, p. 311) or Caravaggio's *Death of the Virgin* (Fig. 151a, p. 263). In general, the early work shows an imposing dignity of mood, whereas the other two are much more overtly dramatic. This is not only a trait of stylistic expression; it is also a distinguishing mark of the cultural climate of the two eras and their respective emotional needs, as discussed previously.

In actual form, the Giotto has a rigid arrangement in which the group at the right is balanced by one at the left, both swinging about a central element, the dying saint. The entire grouping is arranged within a space box that begins at the front line of the picture and ends at the back wall. This gives a definite form and limitation to the composition, front and back; the groups of mourners at left and right afford the same completeness in those directions. Finally, everything here moves from the outside in toward the center. This tight and complete arrangement is typical of the period. Individual forms are massive and blocklike, the result of a forcefully drawn outline that tenses and loosens as the artist wills, draping the cloth loosely about a hip or tightly about a shoulder to give the impression of a body beneath the drapery.

This kind of form and arrangement differs from that of seventeenth-century works such as the Bernini sculpture and the Caravaggio painting. In the Bernini, a wild tumultuous feeling is revealed by the face of the wood nymph Daphne who, about to be seized by Apollo the sun-god, turns into a tree; bark begins to cover her form, and branches and leaves to project from her arms and fingers. But above the basic emotional distinction, we also note that the work arranges itself into a curved diagonal from the lower left to the upper right. It is diagonal and dynamic in arrangement rather than horizontal and static like the Giotto. It has no specific beginning and end, but moves from a point outside the "frame" to another equally far removed from it at the upper right. The proportions of the figures are clearly very different from those of Giotto's block forms.

We may similarly contrast the Giotto painting with the Caravaggio

Fig. 177. GIOVANNI LORENZO BERNINI: *Apollo and Daphne*. Rome, Borghese Gallery.

work, where both medium and purpose are more directly comparable. Caravaggio's painting presents real and even startling differences from the Giotto mural work with its square finality, balance, block forms, and, above all, great calm and dignified control. Like the contemporary Bernini sculpture, the Caravaggio painting is diagonal in its movement (from upper left to lower right) as the figures all move toward the dead Virgin, the areas of light paralleling this motion. Moreover, there is nothing final about the work, as there was in the earlier painting; here the figures at the left crowd out of the picture, while the room at the right seems to extend beyond the picture space. Balance, another point of contrast, is not the result of a simple A-B-A arrangement of blocks of form horizontal to the main line of the picture. It is derived from a related pair of diagonals—the light accents bouncing along toward the face of the Virgin, and the diagonal coming from the opposite corner and formed mainly by her body.

The individual shapes are not clear and relatively unaccented statements of form as in Giotto, nor are they indicated by the special functioning of a contour line. Caravaggio's figures exist as light-accented forms created by the changes from areas of shadow to areas of light, more or less as in nature. (This is the light-and-shadow method of painting or drawing described earlier as chiaroscuro.) Nor are the people handled like so many geometric forms; the accent is on naturalism throughout.

It is in the emotional content, however, that Caravaggio offers the greatest contrast to Giotto. The artists embody the respective spiritual climates of two periods: the earlier Age of Faith versus the later period of doubts—doubts that have to be overcome. The Giotto painting is the product of a time when worship and belief were very much taken for granted; the Caravaggio work is produced by the Counter Reformation, by the need of the Church to strengthen belief. These few points, however summary and general, testify that there is a different manner of expression or style characteristic of each of the two periods—certainly of each of the two artists. These styles have features that are shared by other artists in each era.

Another and somewhat different pair of examples that underline style differences and their cultural motivations are the Early Christian church of Sant' Apollinare in Classe at Ravenna and the Hōryū-ji Temple at Nara in Japan (Figs. 178 and 23, pp. 313, 36). Both these

Fig. 178. Sant' Apollinare in Classe. Exterior view. Ravenna, Italy.

structures are religious, and they are fairly close to each other in date, the sixth century and early seventh century A.D., respectively. Although we may compare a monastic center such as Nara with one of Western Europe—and there are noteworthy resemblances in purpose and function—the Occidental and Oriental ways of looking at such a building are quite different. Our very first glance at these two buildings shows the austerity of the Christian example and the charm and elegance of the Buddhist. Moreover, the former has a simple block form, while the latter shows a gracefully curved silhouette formed by the upward-curving and important roofs. Where the color of the Christian building is reserved for the inside (see Fig. 131, p. 219) with its marble columns and floors, its gold ornaments and highly decorative colored mosaics, the Buddhist building reveals on the exterior its colorful wood, plaster, and tile construction.

Above all, however, the European building is a clear and powerful enclosure of space areas in which elaborate ceremonies take place. In the Japanese (and other Oriental buildings), the emphasis is not on the enclosure of space volumes but on the articulation of graceful external walls, often highly decorated with sculpture, stucco, plaster, woodcarvings, and so on; the interior is not necessarily so functionally

ARTISTIC STYLES 313

spatial as that of Christian buildings. The Western tradition echoes that of Rome with its great bare enclosures dominated by vaults and domes and built of stone, concrete, and other strong and lasting materials. Japanese, Chinese, and other Eastern and Near-Eastern architecture gives an impression of a light thin screen of wood and plaster or stucco, of a kind of impermanence that stems from the delicacy and decorative charm of its basic purpose.

There are, then, different styles appropriate to different periods. We know that there is a history of style or styles, not only in the visual arts but also in the literary, auditory, and other arts. The information derived from a study of the culture (including art) of the past is extensive and valuable, not only for the general reasons already given, but also because even a sketchy knowledge of these past styles will provide, as we shall see, a vital critical tool. We shall be able to observe the relationship (superficial or profound) between the work of a later and of an earlier artist, for whatever this teaches us of the pervasiveness of cultural traditions; and we shall also derive a useful means of identifying what we encounter.

The historical approach here is designed not to manufacture art historians or experts but to aid in setting up a critical vocabulary or common terms of reference through which we can more readily communicate with one another about art. For example, we may speak of a Classical, Romantic, or Baroque style of expression in referring to a Picasso of the 1920's, a Berman of the 1930's, or some other contemporary work that may suggest any of the traditional modes, but just what is it that we mean? Further, what are the limitations and perhaps the contradictions of these terms? Just how far can they be useful to us in communicating our reactions and opinions?

We propose, then, to sketch in some of the chief standards of beauty (or styles) from ancient to modern art, with enough comparative examples of each successive style to make meaningful as many aspects as possible. Our brief historical view of the visual arts will necessarily be centered on the significance they bear for us today.

►PART IV

The Development of Traditions

▶12

Styles in Art: From the Ancient World through the Renaissance

X THE COMMONEST WAYS of tracing the styles of the past are through historical epochs or through national characteristics. The first involves styles that are associated with a broad chronological period, embracing many different nations that contribute to the general quality. As an example of historical categorizing we may take International Architecture of the twentieth century, which cuts across national boundaries to include almost every country in the Western World and some in the Near and Far East. Such a style does not exclude the possibility of local variations within its scope, for example, Argentine or Brazilian modern, Italian or United States modern.

The second or national way of tracing styles in art deals with styles that refer to one country alone. Examples of the national category are American primitive painting of the past three centuries and the Dixieland jazz of our own century. Both are peculiar to the American cultural climate, and both are very different from the styles of folk art and folk music in other areas.

Our survey of styles in art will deal with both the historical and the national categories.

316

Ancient Art

The first known international art style is that of late Paleolithic or Old Stone Age man (c. 25,000–8000 B.C.), extending from Western Europe to South Afrjca (Fig. 28, p. 42). After the Middle and the New Stone Ages (c. 8000–3000 B.C.) a later and better known style arose that we call Ancient Art, associated with the ancient Mediterranean world and lasting from c. 3000 to c. 500 B.C.

Geographically, this Ancient Art category stretches north to south from Crete to Egypt and west to east from Crete to Cyprus, Phoenicia, Asia Minor (the Hittites), Mesopotamia (Assyrians, Babylonians), and the Iranian Plateau (Persians). Although many diverse national cultures are included in this list—as well as a long period of time—the artistic expressions of each of them share enough basic qualities to identify them all as parts of an international and long-enduring historical movement.

These nations produced an art of abstract—that is, nonnaturalistic —form with certain fairly well-defined characteristics that can be related. The differences between their various formulations (and it would be surprising if there were no differences) lie more in the realm of emotional projection than that of physical shapes. As the fortunes of war or commerce shifted from one part of the Ancient World to the other, there was a diffusion of cultural forms and ideas. The cultural dominance of the Egyptians, the commercial impact of the Cretans and Phoenicians, the imperial dominance of the Assyrians —all resulted in the spread of language, craftsmanship, business practices, and many other features of cultural development.

Although it is not our task here to trace the various national relationships in detail, we can compare an Egyptian sculpture, such as the wooden *Panel of Hesire* (Fig. 179, p. 318), c. twenty-ninth century B.C., with the Assyrian stone relief known as *A Winged Deity* (Fig. 180, p. 318), c. ninth century B.C. These works, separated by 2000 years in time and the expanse of the Arabian Desert in space, nevertheless share certain form qualities that make their styles similar.

In the Egyptian sculpture, we find a tall, broad-shouldered figure rigidly placed so that every portion of the form is parallel to the flatness of the panel itself. This unnatural, formal impression is heightened by the arbitrary proportions of the man's body as well as by the

Fig. 179 (*left*). Panel of Hesire. Cairo, Cairo Museum. Fig. 180 (*right*). *Winged Deity* from the Palace of Ashurnasirpal, Nimroud Calah. New York, Metropolitan Museum of Art.

impossible stance of the feet, one directly in front of the other, the shoulders square to the front, and the head to the side, although the eye is full face. Such a "frontalized" method is conceptual rather than representational—that is, things are arranged according to a prepared or set conception in the mind of the artist rather than according to what he perceives with his eyes. The conceptual method, however, is as valid as the representational and suitable for the rigid, unchanging psychological and social needs of this priest-king culture with its desire to make aristocratically idealized images that imply eternal life.

Turning to the Assyrian sculpture, we notice first a similar shallow kind of relief that also places the various parts of the body on the same plane of projection outward. This is the first element of comparable arbitrariness. The second is the tight, springy outline of the form, which takes on therefrom a tension and artificiality that have certain emotional qualities. Finally, there is the important and comparable "frontalizing" of each part of the body: hips, shoulders, eyes, and so forth, and the showing of the inside of one leg and arm and the outside of the other. It is this linear expressiveness and decorative quality—and, above all, this frontality—that characterize so much of ancient Mediterranean art and make up the common denominator.

The variations between the two cultures are equally apparent. The respective proportions are quite different, the Assyrian showing squatness rather than height and slimness. Other changes appear in the later work's emphasis on musculature, such as the incised lines for biceps and calves. The final, and perhaps most important, difference comes in the sense of elegance implicit in the Egyptian work and the sense of power—even brutality—emerging from the Assyrian.

Although we could use statues from the same two nations to demonstrate sculpture in the round, we can broaden the scope of the term *Ancient Art* by including works from Crete and Mesopotamia. What we say here of the four nations chosen for this discussion applies also to the other national groups of the ancient Mediterranean, such as the Hittites, Cypriotes, and those of less importance to our immediate story.

The three-dimensional, hard-stone statue of *Gudea* (Fig. 181, p. 320), *c.* twenty-fourth century B.C., from the Sumerian city of Tello in southern Mesopotamia, could readily be equated with nearly contemporary Egyptian works, for example, *Khafre* (Fig. 88, p. 133) of the twenty-sixth century B.C. We would find the same formal rigidity, set (though differing) proportions, parallelism of parts, and emphasis on line. For comparative purposes, however, we shall turn to a free-standing Cretan figure, that of the so-called *Snake Goddess* (Fig. 182, p. 320), *c.* 1500 B.C. The chief similarity we note in these two sculptures is the principle of frontality that causes the sculptors to make the figures confront the spectator as directly as possible, with all parts presented in parallel lines: eyes, shoulders, arms, legs, and feet. Ancient Mediterranean sculpture in the round generally can be cut into two equal portions, an important enough point of similarity. As for differences, we may observe the greater rigidity of the *Gudea* and the incision of facial features and muscles. Moreover, the large, life-size power of the Mesopotamian figure contrasts vividly with the diminutive

Fig. 181 (*left*). *Gudea*. Paris, Louvre. Fig. 182 (*right*). *Snake Goddess* (ivory and gold). Boston Museum of Fine Arts.

delicacy of the tiny Cretan figure. The *Snake Goddess* is softer, not merely because it is a woman's form; the expression also is softer. Cretan culture by the sixteenth century B.C. had reached a point of sophistication and suavity that made its art more flexible within the strict formulations of pose and proportion characteristic of Ancient Art.

We recognize, finally, that most of these nations were ruled by priest-kings, such as Gudea, and that, within the framework of a rigid hierarchy, their art was dominated by prescribed and unchanging sets of rules, the most restrictive of which were frontalization and denaturalization. This is perhaps most evident in Egypt, but Assyrian bas-reliefs or works from the other nations give the same sense of deindividualized art. Nevertheless, a personality may emerge in spite of the formula, often through a degree of emotional content as in the *Gudea*. Many such examples exist in other formalized art systems, such as the later Byzantine or the Indian, where artists also work according to rigid rules or even handbooks. Here and there certain works are executed with greater flair, visual excitement, and virtuosity than usual.

Classical Art

Around 500 B.C., which marks the approximate end of the nonnatural-istic Ancient Art trend, we come to what is known as the Classical style. This is ordinarily taken to refer to the art of the Greek nation alone, although a related subdivision of this national style is the Roman Classical that follows directly from it—with the necessary variations. The very word *classical* carries certain connotations. For many it means something old and accepted, as in "classical music" or the "classics" in literature. What does *classical* mean in art?

For the purpose of this discussion we may consider three examples: the *Athena Lemnia* (Fig. 183, p. 322), a copy of an original presumably done by the great Phidias to fill a strategic spot overlooking the Acropolis hill in Athens; the *Theseus* marble (Fig. 184, p. 322)—also known as *Mount Olympus*—from one of the Parthenon pediments; and the *Doryphorus* (or *Spear Bearer*) by Polyclitus (another copy, see Fig. 185, p. 324). Here are three works from the Greece of the fifth century B.C. Do they have anything in common that would enable us to think of them as related within the boundaries of one style?

Initially we observe in them a kind of dignity and poise, a sense of restraint that is characteristic of the Classical style. The warrior-goddess, patron of Athens, is shown not in her militant guise with the customary helmet but looking downward and far removed from action. This reserve is also seen in the reclining godlike *Theseus* and in the magnificent form of the spear-bearing athlete. Though all three figures are obviously very powerful in physical appearance and potentialities (the goddess is not only big; she is masculine in quality), none of them is inclined to make this physicality overt, to move violently. Excitement would be inconsistent with the predominantly controlled nature of the art of this period. The control is not only physical but also psychological, for it would be difficult to describe the expression of any of the three. What are they thinking about? What are they feeling? In fact, are they feeling anything? We cannot know, since in accordance with the self-prescribed limitations of the Classical style, dignity (both physical and mental) dictates this reserve.

Fig. 183 (*left*). *Athena Lemnia*. Dresden, Germany, Albertina Museum. Fig. 184 (*right*). *Theseus* (from the East pediment of the Parthenon). London, British Museum.

Proceeding further, we become aware of the kind of beings envisaged in the sculptures. Two of them, Athena and Theseus, are deified; the spear-thrower is human. Yet the uniformity of the qualities just examined makes the divine and the human not at all different, as conceived by the sculptors of Classical Greece. The Greeks thought of their gods as glorified humans, just as they thought of their heroes as godlike beings. This close relationship between the human and the divine in Greek life is attested to by the constant references in their literature to the role of the gods in the lives of the people.

For this reason, and because early Greek society was founded on an aristocratic social base, the nature of Greek artistic expression turns away from the everyday and toward the ideal. Did the Greeks actually look the way Polyclitus has shown his *Doryphorus?* A little thought and comparison with other artistic circumstances elsewhere will indicate that the Greeks no more resembled these fifth-century forms than did their everyday speech resemble the expression of the abstract ideas of Plato. Both art and philosophic abstractions represent an idealized conception toward which artist and writer strove. We do not suppose that Michelangelo's *Adam* looks like a sixteenth-century Italian.

In the course of his striving, the Greek artist tried to project the most noble and impressive human being, animal, or whatever he was representing. Furthermore, he tried to remove the accidental factors that distinguish one man or woman from another and thus to produce a general type rather than a specific form—a man who expresses the idea of manhood rather than the image of John Smith, an athlete who sums up the whole idea of athleticism in its nobler and more reserved context. The *Doryphorus* is Greek youth as a whole, going out toward the stadium, spear on shoulder, to practice this sport. We may also observe that whatever the action performed by this athlete or by any other figure engaged in strong movement (see the *Discobolus*, Fig. 86, p. 132), the sculptured facial expression retains its character-istic calm and detachment. In one famous instance, a pediment sculp-ture from the Temple of Zeus at Olympia, a young maiden is being carried off by a centaur, and although she struggles with great vigor to escape this fate, she maintains an impassive facial calm throughout.

The search for an ideal state of existence led the Greeks to work out what they felt were ideal proportions for their sculptured or painted human beings, their architecture, pottery, and other arts. The *Doryphorus,* as it happens, was considered in its time to be the *canon* or rule by which all other male bodies were to be constructed; in other words, for the Greeks it possessed the most desirable proportions. This actually meant a specific and measurable relationship between, for instance, the length of the head and the length of the body, the width of the shoulders and that of the hips, the length of the foot and that of the leg. This arithmetical relationship of parts lends a certain consistency to the visual art of the Greeks during the Classical period. When, later, the ideal proportions were changed, a new con-sistency was sought and found within each era and in terms of a new ideal of proportion.

Most works of the Classical period show an expected sense of balance, ensuing in great measure from their physical restraint as well as from a gentle, swelling rhythm of parts. Finally, much of Classical sculpture is monumental both in form and in purpose. There is a certain largeness of conception (which has nothing to do with size) that may derive from the physical relationship between the figure and

Fig. 185. POLYCLITUS: *The Doryphorus*. Naples, Italy, National Museum

its environment. In the *Theseus* and the *Athena Lemnia,* monumentality is associated with purpose, since both were planned for architectural use, the first as an integral part of an actual temple, the second as a free-standing figure designed to dominate an architectural complex.

The majority of Greek sculptures in this Classical fifth century B.C. were made as part of temple buildings, which may contribute to their largeness of conception and the simplicity of form that enables them to be seen clearly from a considerable distance. Yet, in spite of this position that entailed an approach usually from the front alone (the *Theseus,* for example, was set into the gable or pediment of the Parthenon), the Greek figure as a rule is dominantly silhouetted in form, unlike the blocklike outline of the Egyptian figure. This silhouetting makes it possible for the spectator to approach most Greek figures from almost any point of view—from the front, side, or rear; whereas the Egyptian, Sumerian, and other ancient Mediterranean sculptures, because of their intentional frontality, can only be seen successfully from the front.

This interesting silhouette also exists in later periods of Greek art, when the other fifth-century qualities are gone. If we would use the term *Classical* in its purity, then we should apply it only to this limited period; the closer that later styles in any other culture approach this reserve, unemotional quality, idealism, balance, and so on, the closer they conform to the Classical idea. We shall meet the term, used with more or less accuracy, in connection with many later styles. If we realize the standard or norm, we are in a better position to understand the later versions and to evaluate the artists' efforts. Whether or not the modern Classicist consciously imitates the Greeks of the fifth century B.C., we now have a measurement to utilize.

In later Greek art the genuine Classical qualities apply much less. *Hermes and the Infant Dionysus* (Fig. 186, p. 325), a fourth-century B.C. work by Praxiteles, differs first in its more attenuated and grace-

Fig. 186 *(left)*. PRAXITELES: *Hermes and the Infant Dionysus*. Olympia, Greece, Olympia Museum. Fig. 187 *(right)*. *Laokoön*. Rome, Vatican Museum.

ful proportions and then in its feminine rather than masculine quality. It has soft instead of powerful flesh; it is sinuous in shape (a kind of reverse "S") instead of architectonic; and, most important, it shows an emotional quality. By contrast with the negative and impersonal character of fifth-century Classical feeling, the *Hermes* reveals a thoughtful and introspective, an almost dreamy, emotional character and a languorous charm that remove it considerably from the works of the earlier period. To the degree that it is less reserved in emotion and physical quality than the earlier examples, we can think of it as less Classical.

That these qualities are matters of degree can readily be seen in the famous *Laokoön* (Fig. 187, p. 325) produced during the first century B.C. Here reserve has been thrown to the winds in an orgy of emotional outpouring. The Trojan priest Laokoön (who had warned against the wooden horse) is punished by the gods through serpents sent to destroy him and his family. Although we have not tried to indicate historical reasons for the change in taste from the fifth to the fourth century B.C. and here to the first century B.C., it must be apparent that the general viewpoint of artists certainly had altered since that earlier time. The agonized expression on the face of the father, who in the midst of his own death must witness that of his sons, is as naturalistic as are the straining muscles throughout the work. Very particularized, rather than generalized like the *Doryphorus,* this is a concrete story involving definite individuals (the tale comes from Vergil's *Aeneid*), a special emotional, even individualistic problem, and finally an exaggerated rather than idealized anatomy.

When we talk of Classical art, therefore, we must be specific and indicate whether we are thinking of one phase or another. By the same token, it is important for us to say *Greek* or *Roman Classical,* since the Romans took over and varied many cultural ideas from the Greek world. Such works as the *Laokoön,* for example, are part of what is known as Greco-Roman art; this art belongs to the end of the late Greek or Hellenistic period and the beginnings of Roman leadership in the Mediterranean world. The *Laokoön's* outspoken naturalism and emotional power are qualities shared by the later Greeks and the Romans, passed on from one to the other and varied by the latter in accordance with their own needs.

The Romans (like the men of the Renaissance and many mid-

Fig. 188. *Augustus* from Prima Porta. Rome, Vatican Museum. (Photo courtesy Italian Tourist Information Office)

nineteenth-century intellectuals) felt the tremendous prestige of Greek culture and its unquestionable superiority in many areas. To speak Greek, to own Greek works of art, to have their children educated by Greek tutors—for Romans these were signs of social accomplishment. When the Romans looted the ancient Greek cities in the course of their conquest, they brought back from Greece numerous works of art, including sculptures, and—since there were not enough works of art to go around to satisfy this growing taste for the Greek—an art industry in copy-making arose to fill the need.

The pre-eminence of Greek culture in Rome was especially noteworthy during the first century A.D.; it may be represented by the free-standing figure of *Augustus* from Prima Porta (Fig. 188, p. 327), traditionally believed to show the emperor haranguing his troops. Although the pose and movement of this figure suggest those of the *Doryphorus,* as well as the latter's reserved manner, many significant distinctions may be found between this work and Greek sculpture in general. Here we have a specific individual. His emotional attitude, instead of the complete withdrawal of the *Spear Bearer,* is more on a level with the *Hermes* (Fig. 186, p. 325)—that is, a gentle but perceptible psychological reaction: the typical Roman gravity. Although this period in Roman culture called for idealism, the prevalent naturalism of the Roman artist made the final result a compromise between the Classical point of view and a more detailed and material attitude.

Augustus is recognizably himself in hair, cheekbones, pointed chin, and so forth. Moreover, he is doing something specific and is dressed in a specific costume, a suit of armor bearing figures emblematic of the period of the Augustan Peace. The little cupid on a dolphin at his side is an allusion to the divine origin of his family: descent from Aeneas through Venus and Cupid.

Even within so-called "Roman Classicism" there are varieties—the stark naturalism of the period before Augustus, the modified idealism of the type just seen, and the again increasingly naturalistic styles of the centuries following. Each of these in its way shares the monumentality and dignity of the Classical style as defined earlier.

The respective architectures of Greece and Rome are closely connected in some ways but profoundly different in others. If we take as typical the famous Parthenon in Athens (Fig. 62a, p. 97) of the fifth century B.C., dedicated to the local goddess Athena, and the equally famous Pantheon in Rome (Fig. 67, p. 109), a national temple of the second century A.D.—both houses of worship—we may see almost at a glance the basic similarities and distinctions. The Greek Parthenon is a carefully and delicately proportioned marble building, meant to be viewed primarily from the outside where the bulk of its sculpture is concentrated. As we observed earlier, it is not noted for extensive interior space, because worship was conducted out of doors. Like the *Doryphorus* and other examples of Classical art in that century, the Parthenon follows certain logical and deliberate rules of proportion that contribute enormously to the sense of balance and calm, the great dignity of such a structure, and its linear perfection.

Although the Parthenon is by no means a small building (*c.* 104 by *c.* 228 feet), it does not overwhelm us by its mass as does the Roman Pantheon, with its inside diameter of 142 feet and its portico 101 feet wide and 59 feet high. The latter is a compact bulky structure, consisting of a massive cylinder into which a concrete hemispherical dome has been inserted, the whole preceded by a giant portico. Yet massive as it is, the Pantheon represents a type of building that, unlike the Parthenon, is dedicated to the expression of interior space

(140 feet high). This space was needed because, in the typical Roman public-service building, large crowds of people had to be accommodated. For purposes of impressiveness as well as function, the Romans therefore were obliged to develop the one-piece concrete dome used here (and the vault), which could be flung across large spaces; whereas the simple post-and-lintel Greek system was limiting in its dimensions, serving more modest local needs.

The relationship between the Roman and the Greek is seen in the portico affixed to the front of the Pantheon, an enlarged and somewhat vulgarized form of the front of the Greek Parthenon. In its new and adapted form, the portico is utilized for prestige as a carry-over from the past that would give dignity to the present—much as we use Classical forms in public buildings today. Architecturally speaking, however, the Roman portico as shown here is an afterthought, blending into the design of the building more because we are accustomed to seeing it there than because it really belongs. It is attached to—rather than integrated into—the design. Moreover, it is a grandiose and desensitized version of the Greek model, reproducing the outer form of the original without the latter's sensitivity of proportion and relationship of individual section to the entire structure. The Roman building, no matter how much it may ape the elements of the Greek, is gigantesque where the earlier form was majestic. This is true to the extent that its needs are in the direction of the overwhelmingly powerful, while those of the Greek were based on the expression of a certain dignified logic.

The Greeks therefore must be credited with the invention and development of this Classical vocabulary, which would be applied by subsequent centuries in various ways—in the Renaissance and in the seventeenth, eighteenth, and nineteenth centuries—and labeled accordingly.

Medieval or Christian Art

Following on the heels of the Classical period comes another historical and international style, lasting roughly from the fifth to the fifteenth century A.D. Developed in the Western European world as well as in the Eastern (Eastern Europe, Near East, and North Africa), the many phases of this long-lasting style, with its many changes and varieties, are related to each other by the unifying elements of Christian belief and subject matter.

In its Western version or tradition, medieval art stemmed from the late Roman viewpoint; in the Eastern version it was related as much to the Semitic and Oriental point of view. The Western heritage may be traced through the art of the Roman catacombs, barbarian art, Carolingian (Fig. 50, p. 79) and Ottonian forms, thus carrying us down to the year 1000. In the Eastern line are Egyptian Coptic, Syrian, Armenian, and the various Byzantine formulations (Fig. 131, p. 219) of the Imperial court at Constantinople and its many dependencies, bringing us down to modern times. We cannot therefore speak of Christian or medieval style without specifying which phase is referred to: the era, the country, and the specific stage of development.

Although we could choose from a far greater number of examples in the medieval area than was available in either the Ancient or the Classical category, we emphasize here a climactic period of Christian development, the Romanesque and Gothic ages. These cover the four centuries between approximately A.D. 1000 and 1400 and include most of the countries of Western Europe: France, Spain, Germany, Britain, and Italy. During these four centuries, the Christian tradition in the West reached a peak in the power of the monastic church (the Romanesque period of *c.* 1000–1150). At the same time, the growth of towns and town life promoted an individualism that marked the end of purely medieval life and the beginning of the Commercial Era (the Gothic period of *c.* 1150–1400).

The vital differences in expression between these two phases of medieval art may be understood by comparing the *Isaiah* from the Church of Souillac, a French Romanesque work of the early twelfth century (Fig. 189, p. 331), with the so-called *Le Beau Dieu* of the Cathedral of Amiens, a well-known example of thirteenth-century Gothic sculpture (Fig. 24, p. 37). The Romanesque work impresses us immediately with its tense, nervous quality, its strained posture and violent movements, as the prophet crosses one leg over the other, swinging his left hand toward the scroll held in the right—the scroll of his prophecy. Looking closer, we notice the elongated character of the body, its flattened form, the carefully pressed-down folds of cloth, and the curiously arranged ropelike strands of the beard that enframes the wide-eyed staring face. These are all elements of exaggeration and

Fig. 189. *Isaiah*. Souillac, France, Church of Notre Dame.

distortion, worked in for the purpose of projecting an emotional quality, to impart the ecstatic and visionary feeling that the sculptor tries to express.

In *Le Beau Dieu* (Christ), a three-dimensional figure comes to rest in a niche especially prepared for it. Unlike the *Isaiah*, who appears to be hemmed in by the area in which he is shown, *Le Beau Dieu* stands comfortably on a symbolic adder and basilisk representing the forces of evil which He overcomes in a quiet but positive way. Nor does His figure seem to be attached to the building and straining away from it; it conveys instead the feeling of a work carved for a specific spot in a carefully planned structure. Moreover, the Christ is carved so as to stress the vertical movements of the building itself and not to be in conflict with the basic architectural shape. The slot including the overhead canopy and the pedestal was left for the sculptor to fill. Working on the ground near by, he designed a solid, sculpturesque, and "real" figure to fit the three-dimensional rectangular area.

The naturalistically draped Christ is calm and self-confident, a gentle teacher rather than an ecstatic prophet. Where Gothic art possesses this sweet, kindly, naturalistic, and human quality, the Romanesque favors violent movement, a strong feeling that sometimes verges on the frightening, and a sense of physical distortion rather than an imitation of nature. The Gothic sculptor tends more and more to render the world of man and his surroundings, while the Romanesque craftsman projects his vision of another world. In the former case, we may speak of a *perceptual art* that records the artist's perceptions of the world; in the latter, we may speak just as readily of a *conceptual art,* in which the artist projects his conception of the universe without necessarily utilizing the material of the everyday world except in the most detached way.

The Romanesque period marks the height of militancy of the monastic church in the Middle Ages with its definitely reformist tendencies, its attempts to control the minds and hearts of men. Thus *Isaiah,* the Old Testament prophet of doom, becomes an instrument in the hands of the twelfth-century preacher—in this case foretelling the advent of a Messiah or, perhaps better, a Judge who will call the world to account. Such works represent actual efforts toward reform within the monastic movement, practiced by such orders as the Cistercians.

By contrast, the Gothic figure seems to express a distinctly new feeling. The prophet of doom or punishment has become a mild teacher raising his hand in a gesture of blessing rather than spasmodic movement. Through it we may sense the more human qualities of the Gothic period. Under the influence of the relatively free towns, under the impact of a growing secular rather than an exclusively monastic control, religion becomes a matter of great faith rather than of compulsion or fear-evoking preachments. Thus the very gesture of teaching, of imparting truth, takes on importance, since the purpose is to buttress faith rather than to instill fear. Christ convinces the spectator not because He disturbs but because He is an actual being, tangible and solid, His form emerging from beneath the drapery. We have only to take a final look at the *Isaiah* to see how great is the change in the method of visualizing the human form, from the earlier, highly complex, and linear conception to the later simple blocklike shape.

thedrals where dogma was tempered with faith and faith buttressed by logic.

The Southern and the Northern Renaissance

The growth of city life begun in the Gothic period moved at a rapid rate during the fourteenth century, especially in Southern Europe—that is, in Italy. It was accompanied by an increasing secularization (or interest in the everyday world) as opposed to an earlier emphasis on the world of the spirit. With this came a quality described as *humanism,* in which everything relating to human beings took on added importance. The various aspects of the world in which man moved also became important—hence the growth of science. In contrast to the preceding medieval period, man during this new period was encouraged to be an individual, to compete with others, to be an entity in himself rather than part of a vast inchoate mass of unidentified ciphers. As part of this development, the identity of artists was now cherished and also the difference between one artist and another. By the fifteenth century, these circumstances were common in the north of Europe as well as in Italy.

Because of the differences in background between the two sections of the continent, there were bound to be deviations in the way Northern and Southern Europe expressed themselves during this so-called

Fig. 192. Cathedral of St. Pierre. View of façade. Angoulême, France.

Fig. 193 (*left*). MASACCIO: *Expulsion from the Garden.* Florence, Santa Maria del Carmine. (Photo courtesy Metropolitan Museum of Art) Fig. 194 (*right*). HUBERT AND JAN VAN EYCK: *Adam and Eve,* detail of altarpiece *Adoration of the Lamb.* Ghent, Belgium. Cathedral of St. Bavo. (Photo courtesy Metropolitan Museum of Art)

"Renaissance." If we look at two typical paintings of the early fifteenth century—*The Expulsion from the Garden* by Masaccio in Italy (Fig. 193, p. 338) and the Adam and Eve sections of the *Adoration of the Lamb,* the altarpiece by the van Eyck brothers in Flanders (Fig. 194, p. 338) —we can begin to evaluate the similarities as well as the differences. Both artists show a clear interest in large-scale or monumental figures as well as in the real and tangible existence of the people portrayed. But owing to the Roman (that is, Classical) background of Italy, such artists as Masaccio tend to represent their forms in a general rather than in a detailed way. They emphasize the broader aspects of form instead of the tiny details of naturalism seen in the van Eyck figures, where every wrinkle and hair is visible. The Italian artist involves the spectator to the extent of making him imagine those aspects of the form that are not actually shown, whereas the Flemish painter sets down a number of small details from which his totality is built.

Equally important are the emotional differences between the two portrayals, the Italian concentrating on human values of the moment and the Flemish on symbolic values. This would mean that the secular and psychological value is more significant in the classically derived Italian scene: as the ancestors of the human race are driven from the Garden, the man evinces his shame and the woman her discomfiture. In the Flemish work the figures are more stereotyped emotionally and are presented to the audience as reminders of the original sin of mankind. They stand in their niches like figures from the façade of a medieval cathedral—again consistent with that background. The Flemish artist has inscribed the names *Adam* and *Eva* above the two figures in a didactic medieval fashion, and two little compositions above them complete the allegory or lesson: the Sacrifice of Cain and Abel (above Adam) and Cain Slaying Abel (above Eve).

Thus, in spite of the everyday and secular interests of most fifteenth-century painters in Europe, the north because of its enduring medieval tradition maintains a strong naturalism and didactic quality. The south, because of the long Classical history of that area, moves toward powerful generalities of form and the universal emotions portrayed by Masaccio's people, who are used as pretext for the expression of some larger truth in the new human terms.

In the High Renaissance at the end of the fifteenth and the beginning of the sixteenth century, we may compare Leonardo's *Madonna of the Rocks* (c. 1482, Fig. 154, p. 273) with Dürer's *Adoration of the Magi* (1504, Fig. 195, p. 340). Once again we find the Italian and the German works sharing an interest in largeness of effect and in the humanity of their subjects. Even more, we see a definite leaning toward carefully controlled geometric compositions in each case. The pyramid shape of Leonardo's work is repeated in a similar arrangement by the German painter, who was influenced by the Italian point of view in many ways. In Leonardo's picture, from the Madonna's head (the apex of the pyramid) the eye is carried diagonally downward to the plants at the left and the angel's drapery at the right. Similarly in the Dürer work, the arched ruins in the upper center of the picture mark a starting point from which our eyes move downward, left toward the Virgin and right toward the waiting figure on that side.

These two works afford an interesting comparison, because, by the early sixteenth century, Italian ideas had begun to penetrate many

parts of Europe and to influence artists, particularly those, like Dürer, who visited Italy and were very much in touch with what was going on there. Dürer's *Adoration* not only has a pyramidal composition but also a more specific awareness of the work of such artists as Leonardo (whose portrait he seems to have painted here as the standing wise man at the left). In the background of his picture, Dürer repeats the idea of rearing horsemen from Leonardo's *Adoration of the Magi* (Uffizi Gallery, Florence); in the gracefully dreamy posture of the dark-skinned wise man at the right he repeats a typical Italian pose from other sources (compare *David* by Michelangelo, Fig. 211, p. 377).

Yet the differences between the Italian and the German artist are as great as the similarities. First is the usual Italian tendency toward generalization; although details are plentiful, they are distinctly subordinate to the broad and majestic effect that the artist wishes to achieve. In the German work, on the other hand, Dürer wants us to see the minute fact (he is one of the greatest engravers in history) as much as the general statement. A tiny plant form emerges from the stones at the lower left, a little goat is seen at the extreme upper right, and so forth. Dürer's painting, like a line engraving or woodcut, is to be "scanned," while in Leonardo's work we are initially impressed by the sculpturesque forms, the elegance of draperies, and the way the various figures are drawn together into a pyramidal unity through their crossed glances, hand gestures, and the like, and then set off against the romantic background of the picture. As in most Italian works, the consciously achieved unity and impact are in no way affected by the artist's attention to the little plant and rock forms that are taken from nature as directly as are Dürer's.

The German painting, like the van Eyck Adam and Eve details or the van der Weyden *Descent from the Cross* (Fig. 159, p. 282), leaves us with a series of individuals seen in great and painstaking detail but not brought together with the same concentration as in the Italian work. We feel that the Italian painter had prepared in advance a pyramid outline within which the various forms were to be fitted. In the Dürer, on the other hand, a number of people look off into the distance as though unconcerned with the act of Adoration, standing immersed in their own thoughts and feelings. Detached from the world of reality, even though they themselves are real enough, like figures in the niches of the earlier cathedrals, they appear once more to symbolize some kind of religious truth. Yet an intensity of feeling in the oldest king approaching the Child with his gifts is typical of the earlier Northern and emotive viewpoint as contrasted to the simple warmth and sentimentalism of Leonardo's Mother and Child relationship.

In spite of specific attempts by the German artist to be what might be called "in vogue" at this moment of history, Dürer's inbred naturalism, his withdrawn intensity of feeling, and his tendency to irregularize his composition make him part of the Northern trend—as do the facial features of his characters. We may point, finally, to the inherent nobility of the Leonardo personages, seen in the restrained elegance of the Madonna, the aristocratic charm of the angel or the Child. This quality is usually lacking in the more bourgeois art of the Germans and the Flemish, as witness Dürer's plump Madonna. The difference was rooted in an Italian awareness of the nobility of the function of art, perhaps in the Classical sense, and their attempt to attain prestige through art, a desire that may exist in any society which has been commercially successful for long enough to want something more. This was less possible in Germany, to the extent that it lacked this Classical

Fig. 196 (*left*). TITIAN: *Portrait of a Young Englishman*. Florence, Palazzo Pitti. Fig. 197 (*right*). HANS HOLBEIN THE YOUNGER: *The Merchant George Gisze*. Berlin, State Museums.

background or, indeed, the whole tradition and continuity presupposed in the Italian style.

A final pair of works will serve to underline some of the distinctions we have established. Titian's *Portrait of a Young Englishman* (*c*. 1540, Fig. 196, p. 342) and Holbein the Younger's *The Merchant George Gisze* (1532, Fig. 197, p. 342) carry us to a slightly later date than the Leonardo and Dürer. The Titian painting represents the height of this artist's work as a portraitist in which he is able to impart nobility, serenity, and self-confidence to the sitter. His feeling of complete assurance is achieved partly through the warm restraint of the dark garment relieved by the whiteness of the ruff and cuffs and the simple gold of the chain, but more through the dignity of pose and the absolute mastery implied in the glance. The subject is not interested in us or in impressing us. He takes himself and his importance very much for granted, and yet he is withdrawn in a poetic fashion characteristic of the Venetian school to which Titian belongs.

If we contrast this work with the Holbein portrait, we appreciate that a different type of humanity is represented by *The Merchant George Gisze*. Although carefully and elaborately dressed for the painting (you have a feeling, unlike that from the Titian, that this is a special occasion), this man has an uneasiness that is almost distressing to the spectator. Does he look this way because he is a harried businessman? Surely not, for he is apparently financially successful, well dressed, and important enough to have his picture painted by one of the leading artists of the time. The unease lies in the glance of the eyes, in his refusal to face us, in his looking away as though expecting someone, as though he had something to worry about. He is far from detached in the serene self-assured sense of the Titian personage.

Technically, there are many divergencies between the two works; the German gives us the usual concentration on detail and the Italian the typical generality of form. Holbein's painting is very linear in quality as well as detailed; the line forms clear indications of the boundaries of his figures and helps to create a design pattern in which the human form participates in such a way as to become an artistic entity. This line has a tightness and tenseness of its own; it may be compared in a general way to the hardness of Dürer's line, the line of the engraver and woodcutter in the German tradition. In keeping with this quality, the colors are often hard, bright, and close to the surface—enamellike in character. Tension is conveyed by the cluttered quality of the picture and by the way that certain objects, for example, the bottle of flowers and the book on the shelf, appear about to fall.

In the Titian, the form is presented not merely in the broadest possible (that is, nondetailed) terms, but is built up in a series of layers of transparent color that give it a different kind of existence from the relatively hard surface colors of Holbein. There is no line as such in this kind of painting but rather the manipulation of a brush that paints and draws at the same time. Titian's handling of color belongs to a tradition that he did a great deal to establish, later used by Rembrandt, Rubens, Fragonard, Renoir, and other masters of the layer-built form.

Holbein, on the other hand, betokens a survival of the art of the late medieval period through the resemblance to manuscripts, woodcuts, and so on. At this point of history that tradition is swept up into the turbulence of the mid-sixteenth century with its financial difficulties, religious revolts, counterrevolts, and other problems that marked the end of one era and the beginning of another. Titian is still filled with the sensation of personal assurance and manifest destiny seen in Leonardo's *Madonna of the Rocks*—that is, the characteristic Italian High Renaissance look. Holbein, who had lived through the Reformation in Switzerland and in Germany and who was now working in England, expresses in his nervously restless and uneasy attitude some of the tension of the first post-Renaissance period, the age of Mannerism (see Michelangelo, Ch. 15). In some ways, perhaps, modern times were already beginning.

Before completing this historical development and bringing it down to the present, we shall turn to a number of general questions concerning style and its determinants.

▶13
Individual Style

IN THE PRECEDING CHAPTER we compared the work of one artist with that of another as representatives of their particular cultures—that is, we compared two parts of general historical periods of art. Because the Renaissance laid such stress on personalities, we turn now to a different comparative outlook: the individual esthetic character of two artists working in the same locality at the same time, of two artists working in the same locality but at different times, and of one artist as a young man and at a later stage in his career.

We are concerned, first, with the special elements that cause one artist to express himself differently from another. Second, we wish to identify the specific qualitative aspects that enable us to distinguish between the work of one man and another. The problem of individual style exists in all the arts and in other walks of life. The way an athlete handles himself on the field, the "attack" of certain musicians, the little tricks of an actor—these are style elements in the area of performance. In the area of creativity, there is also an individual quality that distinguishes a Leonardo drawing from one by Michelangelo (see Figs. 45 and 43, pp. 75, 71), an Ingres from a Delacroix, and so on.

We can readily see that there are significant differences between works of various periods, between an Egyptian and a Greek sculpture, between a Renaissance and a Cubist painting. When we come to art-

Fig. 198. FRANS HALS: *Officers of St. George's Company*. Haarlem, Netherlands, Hals Museum.

ists who are part of the same culture, the distinction is not quite so obvious, but it is the more important for us to apprehend, if we are to arrive at or even to approach a qualitative differentiation and understanding.

Artists in the Same Locality and Time

Rembrandt and Hals. Two artists who worked in the same locality at the same time were Rembrandt and Frans Hals. We may compare *Sortie of Captain Banning Cocq's Company of the Civic Guard (The Night Watch,* Fig. 152, p. 271) and the *Officers of St. George's Company* (Fig. 198, p. 346). Both are group portraits of seventeenth-century Holland, depicting the semimilitary groups that still existed in that country in the wake of the long-drawn-out war with Spain. Both painters were faced with the problem of giving their respective groups of clients an attractive and interesting rendition.

For Hals, this study became a multiple version of his own *The Laughing Cavalier* (Fig. 105, p. 174). In place of one objectively shown and flashily painted form, we now have a number of well-dressed and well-fed gentlemen waiting to have their pictures painted in a fashion reminiscent of the modern banquet. Each of these men is equally important in the picture, and it is evident that the artist is

346　INDIVIDUAL STYLE

not too concerned with dramatic or symbolic values, however competently the work may be painted. This is entirely consistent with Hals's previous painting, and we may therefore consider this work typical of his style (or of one of his styles).

In Rembrandt's so-called *Night Watch,* the social purpose is similar; but, as noted in our general discussion of painting, this is an artist who thinks differently from Hals. His outlook is more subjective, more dramatic, more specifically Baroque in quality (see Chapter 15). He therefore feels that the problem cannot be stated so simply as in Hals's more typically bourgeois picture. Instead, Rembrandt chooses an interesting moment in which to involve his group, the visit to Amsterdam of the exiled queen of France, Marie de' Medici, and the turning out of the guard to receive her. The work becomes a form of ceremonial excitement, a dramatic scene in which light-and-dark effects are much in evidence, in which individual figures are singled out for attention, all looking toward some imaginary point where perhaps the guest may be arriving.

Not only does Rembrandt give us a concentrated and dramatically lighted scene in contrast to Hals's diffuse and regularly lighted group-

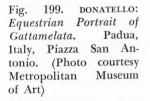

Fig. 199. DONATELLO: *Equestrian Portrait of Gattamelata.* Padua, Italy, Piazza San Antonio. (Photo courtesy Metropolitan Museum of Art)

ing, but the actual handling of paint is quite different. Hals's paint is flaky and light, thin and sparkling, showing at all times the path of the artist's brush, the actual way he painted. Rembrandt's method is rich and controlled primarily from beneath (the Titian method). Light is sucked into certain areas and held there for a time, thus creating shadows; in other areas a brilliant surface red, violet, or yellow is flashed back into the eye of the spectator for a vivid contrast. But the total effect is of a highly finished and polished work, although far less detailed than the Hals, more realistic than naturalistic. This method is consistent with what we have observed so far of Rembrandt's style (see Fig. 104, p. 174); we shall see later that it is consistent with his entire development.

Donatello and Verrocchio. A second pair of comparable works may be chosen from Renaissance Italy: two famous equestrian bronzes, Donatello's *Equestrian Portrait of Gattamelata* and Verrocchio's *Monument to Bartolommeo Colleoni* (Figs. 199 and 200, pp. 347, 349). Both artists are fifteenth-century Italians, both are Florentines —making the differences between them even more striking than between the two seventeenth-century Dutchmen, who originated from different cities in Holland. If the great stylistic variance here is not owed to the time, to national or local tradition, to medium or subject matter (both bronzes represent mercenary captains of the time), we must attribute it to actual differences in style between the two artists themselves. Even without previous experience with these artists, we see at once that their respective approaches are quite divergent and, in fairness to our problem, that their subjects must have been men of quite dissimilar temperaments.

Leaving out the captains themselves for the time being, we may contrast the generalized handling of the horse's body in Donatello's work and the much more specific—that is, detailed—handling in Verrocchio's. Also, the former animal is bare of ornament, while the latter is dressed in an elaborate harness; the former is quiet and controlled (as is Donatello's habit in all things), while the latter moves forward impatiently and energetically. This movement of the two animals is consistent with the character of the two works.

The types of individual portrayed in the riders' heads are just as different as the other elements. Donatello's *Gattamelata* ("Honeyed Cat") is a bleak and stern personality, who suggests Rembrandt's tragic

Fig. 200. ANDREA DEL VER-
ROCCHIO: *Monument to
Bartolommeo Colleoni.*
Venice, Italy. (Photo
courtesy Italian Tourist
Information Office)

Man with the Golden Helmet (Fig. 104, p. 174) but is far more dangerous, far more wound up and tense and, although quiet and controlled, not a man to trifle with. Verrocchio's *Colleoni* sits in his saddle with his body turned sideways, very much the man on horseback, the leader, showing harsh, outspoken, but slack features, a noisy type but not one to fear. Each artist in his way has created a great work on the interpretive level, Donatello of the ruthless and able commander and Verrocchio of the braggart and ladies' man.

Other works by these sculptors would disclose the same and additional differences. Basically, the distinction is owed to emotional orientation and to the way Donatello *suggests* certain effects, while Verrocchio feels constrained to be explicit. In the *Gattamelata's* face, for example, the inner structure of the head has been rendered by the device of tightening the skin about the chin, cheekbones, and forehead, as though the skeletal framework were wrapped in the skin and flesh.

With *Colleoni,* the artist takes us into every nook and cranny of that wrecked countenance, showing us quite specifically what kind of man this is.

It is not too difficult to answer the question of why such diversities exist between two contemporary Italians of the same city (or between two Dutchmen of the same time), even considering the fact that, by and large, they were subject to similar social and esthetic interests. First, they may have come from dissimilar family backgrounds; certainly they came from different parents and to that extent from separate environments. Second, they had individual nervous systems and physical make-ups—hence distinct artistic handwritings—that is, differing ways of handling a brush or chisel, differing reactions to color stimuli, and so forth. Finally, they were trained in separate workshops by different masters who, within the Florentine school, represent two of the many variations that run side by side through any local or national tradition. It is apparent, therefore, that emergence from the same city and epoch is not enough to ensure identical performance or its approximation.

Artists in the Same Locality at Different Times

Niccolò Pisano and Giovanni Pisano. It has been said that if a teacher were to take a half-dozen students and set them to drawing the same tree, the result would be six different trees, even though all the students had been trained by him. This is plain from the wide divergence often found among pupils of the same teacher, especially in modern times when the apprenticeship period is relatively short, and the tendency is to allow the student to develop his own personality. In the past it was otherwise, since the relationship between master and apprentice was long and intensive, beginning in childhood and ending in early manhood, so that it is possible for the expert to identify pictures or sculptures from the workshop of a master—works that are so close to the style of the master as to be clearly associated with him. Yet even in circumstances of this kind, it is possible to distinguish, for instance, between the works of Rubens and those of his pupils.

An interesting example of such a connection, refining further our process of comparison, demonstrates precisely this workshop relationship. The case is particularly interesting because it involves a master

Fig. 201. NICCOLÒ PISANO: *Annunciation and Nativity,* from preaching pulpit. Pisa, Italy, Baptistery of the Cathedral of Pisa.

and pupil who are father and son, Niccolò and Giovanni Pisano, with their respective characteristics and stylistic personalities. These artists illustrate, too, a distinction between men working in the same locality at different times, since they represent two generations of central Italian art at the end of the thirteenth and the beginning of the fourteenth century and show how a local tradition may vary from decade to decade.

Niccolò taught his son the art of sculpture, which they both practiced in the decoration of preaching pulpits with marble reliefs. For a while, the son worked as his father's assistant and then branched off on his own. The sharp disparity between them may be illustrated by Niccolò's detail from the *Annunciation and Nativity* on the pulpit of the Baptistery at Pisa (Fig. 201, p. 351) and Giovanni's detail from the *Nativity and Annunciation to the Shepherds,* a similar pulpit at Sant'Andrea in Pistoia (Fig. 202, p. 352).

The basic contrast between the two works stems from Niccolò's attempt to generalize in a classical fashion and Giovanni's interest in the

Fig. 202. GIOVANNI PISANO: *Nativity and Annunciation to the Shepherds,* from preaching pulpit (from a cast). Pistoia, Italy, Sant'Andrea Pistoia.

chatty and charming naturalism of the later Gothic sculpture of France. The son turned toward this style as soon as he was free of parental supervision, possibly because it was fashionable but more likely because he was an individualist and a somewhat unpredictable character, according to surviving documents. As a result, Niccolò's composition centers on an impressive and outsize Madonna reclining in a Greek or Roman fashion and draped in the antique style. She looks straight out at the audience without a glance for the Child lying in His crib. Giovanni's Madonna, on the other hand, is proportioned closer to the others in her panel, and represents graceful and charming womanhood rather than some powerful goddess. She is a woman very much concerned with her Child, whom she looks at quite tenderly in the Gothic manner.

In the women shown washing the Child (in a scene below and slightly to the left in each case), we distinguish again between heavy, powerful, antique forms and gracefully elongated figures. Moreover,

Niccolò's women have not the remotest idea of how to bathe the baby (an enormous infant for a newborn child), whom they have plumped into the open classical Krater and on whose innocent form they are pouring water. The more knowledgeable or natural women in Giovanni's relief test the water before putting the child in—one pouring, the other testing with one hand while she holds the Child quite capably in the crook of her other arm.

Joseph sits rather stolidly in the earlier relief, since Niccolò's classical formula does not make much allowance for the expression of overt emotions. In Giovanni's sculpture, Joseph is a psychological study, gazing in tortured puzzlement at what is going on.

It is not a question of who has done his job more competently but of two men who, for reasons of personal inclination and viewpoint, have chosen to interpret Scripture each in his own way, in spite of the close relationship between them. Neither this relationship nor their common tradition can make them react identically.

As we have observed, there is such a thing as the French tradition or the Italian, which may pass on from generation to generation certain qualities, for example, monumentality that appears during the course of three centuries in Giotto, Masaccio, and Michelangelo or the charm that appears over a period of almost two hundred years in Watteau, Fragonard, and Renoir. But these artists, despite whatever common tradition they follow, have identifiable differences that are just as important, if not more important.

The stimuli that create these differences in individual style are, first, the personal factors. These, in turn, may lead the artist to give preference to, or to borrow, a particular style element from another source, either contemporary or traditional. This special element will cause a serious and even crucial change, as in the case of the Pisano family. Naturally, at a longer distance in time, the possibility of stylistic dilution is much greater.

The Same Artist at Different Times

Rembrandt. Having traced stylistic differences between comparable works by artists of the same country (or city) and time, and those of comparable works by artists of the same country (and indeed the same family) at different times, we turn to different phases of one

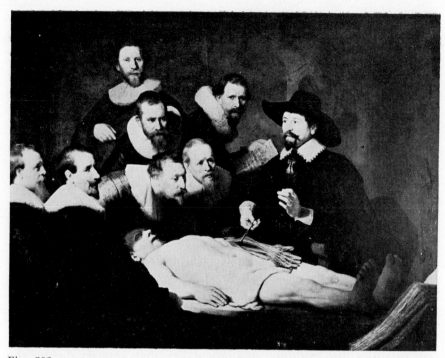

Fig. 203. REMBRANDT VAN RIJN: *Anatomy Lesson of Dr. Tulp*. The Hague, Mauritshuis. (Photo courtesy Netherlands Information Service)

artist. When we examine the production of an artist at various stages, for example, Michelangelo or Rembrandt as a young man, middle-aged man, and old man, we find that there is such a thing as personal development and we perceive different style levels. Between his early and his late works there may well be—and often is—a significant and clearly perceptible variation.

We have already experienced this sort of change in the work of Rembrandt. His *Anatomy Lesson of Dr. Tulp* of 1632 (Fig. 203, p. 354) is a relatively mundane group portrait. Although composed in a Baroque manner, it gives each member of the group his due in almost a commercial fashion. In the previously examined *Night Watch* (Fig. 152, p. 271), dated 1642, we saw Rembrandt pulling together his group in a new, dramatic, and exciting way, painting more warmly and giving new force to light penetration and light-and-dark quality. About 1650, he painted the *Man with the Golden Helmet* (Fig. 104, p. 174), more subdued in color and mood, more expressive of deep inner compulsion, that brings forth some universal and important ideas.

These few indications of personal style changes point to the kind of qualification that must be kept in mind when we speak of the work of Michelangelo, Rembrandt, Cézanne, or anyone else. We may prefer to think that there is an "average" Rembrandt or Cézanne and that once we learn the specific identifying trick involved, we are prepared to speak intelligently about him. The norm may be important as a rough rule of thumb; more meaningful is the fact that an artist began somewhere, probably with a teacher from whom he derived certain ideas. Then he went on to something original—or he did not. In the first case, his stylistic or personal contribution is significant; in the second, he is one of the workshop or "school" and little else. The final step comes when the artist fuses these two elements (the teacher's and his own) into something transcendent in the creative sense. This is his ultimate contribution to art. Such a transformation does not happen at a particular and easily identifiable point; it is a gradual process that we follow in the course of unraveling the strands of development in an artist's style.

Our understanding of the problem of style, therefore, involves an awareness of the fact that periods—for example, the Ancient—have a style, that nations—for example, Greece—have a style, and, of course, that individuals have a style. In each case a developmental pattern is quite clear, even as briefly outlined here. Moreover, various aspects of a style—that is, the factors that comprise it: proportion, space, and composition among others—have their own histories. Indeed, those factors change from period to period as part of the general style changes that identify specific eras.

The Historical Uses of Proportion, Space, and Composition

WE HAVE ESTABLISHED by now that art, like literature, music, and other cultural expressions, has its own history; that the use of various techniques, such as oil paint and engraving, may also be traced through the centuries; and that style, too, has a history which may be approached by period, nation, or individual. In all this evolutionary material we have been careful to avoid the implication that any one era, nation, or individual master is superior to another.

We will have noted that in order to understand the style of a particular period or individual it has been necessary for us to consider such factors as proportion, space, and composition and the different manner in which they have been handled by different eras and individual artists. These methods of articulation also have a history and in discussing the handling of such component elements of style we must again be careful to avoid distinctions of quality and not to imply that the space, proportion, or composition of any one period is superior to that of any other.

We shall try to indicate in this series of developments how each level in the evolution of the elements of delineation differs from the pre-

356

ceding (as well as from the following) ones. Each of these levels has its environmental or historical reasons, and each level is as valid esthetically as every other. From this should emerge the sometimes unfamiliar truth that what we may regard in other cultures as deficiencies, to the degree that they differ from our levels of today, are not necessarily bad or incompetent. The earlier aspects of proportion, space, or anything else are perfectly valid for their time, and even essential. They are not the product of ignorance or astigmatism, but the product of a real social, religious, or other need.

Why should it be necessary for us to understand that the proportion system or space indication of an earlier culture is as "right" as our own? Simply because the problem is often raised in those very terms: that the proportion of, say, Romanesque art is "off," or that the perspective effects in Egyptian painting are sadly lacking. What the layman means by this sort of statement is that the proportion or perspective of that alien culture is strange to him and therefore it must be wrong. Our concern here is to demonstrate that these differences should not be looked upon with the provincialism of the person who rejects any strange idea merely because it is strange (or any religion, race, tradition, or custom, for that matter). We should, rather, regard this strangeness as symptomatic of the fact that we ourselves lack certain ingredients of understanding.

Fortunately, the kind of person who turns up his nose at a strange cultural phenomenon is becoming increasingly rare. Once it is pointed out, most people today accept the principle, for example, that Oriental or Egyptian space is necessarily different from Renaissance space. But these same persons too often adopt a more stubborn attitude toward modern space techniques or other elements that they do not like or do not understand. This difference in approach probably arises from the fact that these persons are more closely involved personally with contemporary judgment than with any earlier or exotic culture.

In general, our attitudes today toward such things as proportion and space are mostly conditioned by the Renaissance tradition under whose influence we still live. According to this viewpoint, the naturalistic representation of proportion or space, as rendered by the photograph or magazine illustration, is the most desirable. Our brief survey of the history of these representational tools will show, however, that the naturalistic or photographic method applies only to a relatively short period of human history. This means that for several thousand years artists have distorted proportion and space (as well as other elements) in the interests of the kind of expressiveness they wished to achieve.

Our final conclusion is that, if the proportion, space, composition, and so on of each age is as valid as that of another, we do not have the right to criticize a specific period for not trying to accomplish the aims of today. We cannot compare the proportions of Greek sculpture with those of Romanesque sculpture or the space in Renaissance painting with that in Byzantine mosaics. To be fair or accurate, like style must be compared with like in whatever element we are discussing, and like artist with like. One may very well have a favorite artist or even a favorite period of art—and many people do—but one may not say that Impressionist painting is the most worth while or that Baroque sculpture is the least interesting, except to the individual and for personal reasons. Even with understanding of a style there may be an emotional dislike, which is therefore difficult to overcome.

In many cases, nevertheless, greater understanding of the purposes of the artist (or the period) will draw us deeper into the artistic experience. As we follow the genesis of a given expression and its flowering, that very process of following and comprehending will often give us a form of pleasure beyond mere understanding. At the least, our willingness to have a strange art form state its case is a phase of democratic practice that might well carry over from other walks of life into the cultural sphere. Even slight experience with a German Expressionist painting, a Japanese Kabuki dance, or an early American folk song is partial introduction to the aims and ideals of the people who produced those art forms.

Varieties of Proportion

A typical Egyptian sculptured relief, the *Palette of Narmer* (Fig. 204, p. 359), which was employed as a receptacle for the ceremonial face paint used by the pharaoh, shows the ruler of Egypt grasping a foe by the hair, while in the space below them are two fallen enemy soldiers. Confronting the pharaoh in the upper right-hand corner is the hawk symbol of the god Horus. The ruler is seen as the largest figure in this relief; his proportion is specially designed to indicate his social

Fig. 204. Palette of Narmer. Cairo, Egyptian Museum.

importance, a consistent device in Egyptian art. This means that the technique of the Egyptian artist is not a result of any whim or incompetence but of the demand made by custom in that society, where the proportion of an important personage, however unreal it may appear to us, is tied to his position in the social hierarchy. (We call this *hierarchic proportion*—that is, proportion based on the social or religious importance of a particular figure.)

Not only is the Egyptian pharaoh different in proportion from his enemies and even from the symbols of the gods (see the Hathor cowheads above), but his body itself offers a number of deviations from the so-called "norm" or truth. Egyptian figures like this one are always shown with broad shoulders, narrow hips, long legs—and long feet, too. If we ask ourselves how this conforms to the physical truth, the explanation is that the proportions of the male figures have nothing to do with visual truth or the way the Egyptians looked. They represent, instead, an ideal of a strong, majestic figure appropriate for the ceremonial use to which it was being put, in the king's tomb.

Perhaps we feel uncomfortable with this deviation from the norm and are more at ease with such a classical Greek figure as the *Doryphorus* of Polyclitus (Fig. 185, p. 324). "Ah, yes," we murmur, "this is more like it." To be sure, this sort of figure is far more familiar to the average person. But upon closer examination, and with the recollection of what has already been said of Classical sculpture, we find that the *Doryphorus* represents an attempt on the part of the Greeks to find an ideal male form. Its proportions, as we previously noted, are as carefully calculated in relation to each other as are the proportions of the Parthenon temple; a certain consistent ratio exists between the length of the head and the length of the body, the length of the hand and that of the arm, the length of the foot and that of the leg, and so forth.

Surely there is nothing wrong with this; but it infers that even the more acceptable or at least more familiar type of figure is also a result of some artificial and aristocratic attempt to find the most beautiful human body. Here again, we may note, this ideal form has little to do with that of the average Greek of the fifth century B.C. Furthermore, the Greeks, too, used hierarchical proportion, as had the non-realistic Egyptians. In the pediments or gables of a Greek temple (see the Parthenon, Fig. 62a, p. 97), the central figures of Athena on one side and Poseidon on the other are much larger than those of the people they judge or help. This is partly due to their importance as deities and partly to the exigencies of the shape of the pediment itself, which offers a large space in the center.

However acceptable to our eyes today (since it conforms to an ideal familiar to us), the Greek figure is a convention, an artificial concoction dictated by the social and philosophical ideals of the time. This is as it should be, and it is one of the reasons that Greek art has its particular kind of appeal. We might merely point out that for many peoples living in ancient times, especially those outside the direct influence of Greek civilization, this well-tempered formality, this beautiful restraint, may have appeared somewhat mawkish—an intolerant attitude, perhaps, but a very human one.

When we come to the Romanesque tympanum relief of *Christ Enthroned among the Four and Twenty Elders* of the Church of St. Pierre at Moissac (Fig. 205, p. 361), we find again the varied proportions seen in Egyptian art. Christ is seated in the center as the chief figure and is much larger than either the four Evangelist symbols around Him (the Man of Matthew, Lion of Mark, Bull of Luke, and Eagle of John) or the two lean angels arranged parenthetically

Fig. 205. *Christ Enthroned among the Four-and-twenty Elders,* tympanum of West door. Moissac, France, Church of St. Pierre. (Photo courtesy French Press and Information Service)

on each side of Him. In addition to these three levels of proportion, there is the additional group of four-and-twenty elders of the Apocalypse, who represent another step in the religious hierarchy that apparently dictated the varieties of proportion. As in the Egyptian relief, individual forms, such as those of the angels or the Christ, are distorted from the normal or everyday appearance. They are long, lean, thin figures with their own consistent system of representation, which is different from the broad-shouldered, majestic Egyptian figure or from the ideally proportioned Greek form. As we saw before, however, Romanesque is by no means the only kind of medieval art; we may recall that more naturalistic proportions prevail in Gothic art (*Le Beau Dieu,* Fig. 24, p. 37).

In the art of the Italian Renaissance, as represented by Raphael's *The Alba Madonna* (Fig. 16, p. 28) or Leonardo's *Madonna of the Rocks* (Fig. 154, p. 273), we arrive at a new version of the idealism seen in ancient Greek art. Raphael, like most of his contemporaries,

Fig. 206. EL GRECO: *Nativity*. New York. Metropolitan Museum of Art.

evolved for his own art what is called a "normative" type of figure. Not only is it always recognizable as his, but it is also in line with the production of an exalted form of humanity, almost divine in quality, as the great Greek heroes had been. Again we should notice the deviation from the everyday, however much has been written about Raphael using peasant types as his models. At least it is fair to say that Raphael's Madonnas, like the athletes of Polyclitus, represent the highest form of human being the artist could create. The actual proportions utilized by the Italian artist display the same idealized naturalism as those in the Classical world.

At the end of the sixteenth and the beginning of the seventeenth century, such an artist as El Greco reverts to a proportion distorted for purposes of greater emotional expressiveness. In his *Nativity* (Fig. 206, p. 362), as in the Romanesque tympanum at Moissac, the figures are elongated and thinned out, dematerialized in form and substance to make them more spiritual in quality. The figures are drawn out proportionally until they are almost flamelike in shape. Their very solidity is affected; their color is arbitrarily heightened; and their space is exceedingly unreal. Since El Greco does this regularly (see *St. Martin and the Beggar,* Fig. 151b, p. 268), we must again assume a certain system in his approach rather than irrationality, incompetence, eye-illness, or other deficiency.

Alteration of the proportions of a figure to evoke greater emotional power may apply in any period—including our own—where a similar necessity arises. In the section *Christ Destroying His Cross* (Fig. 207, p. 363) from Orozco's Dartmouth College frescoes, the modern Mexican painter willfully elongates the body of the avenging Christ in order to convey His anger and power. Christ has come back to earth to find His name used by warring nations, and this He cannot permit; He cannot leave them His Cross to defile any further. The actual proportions of the figure provide a tall form with wide shoul-

Fig. 207. JOSÉ CLEMENTE OROZCO: *Christ Destroying His Cross,* panel from the Dartmouth College frescoes. Hanover, New Hampshire. (Photo courtesy Dartmouth College)

ders and a small head, reminiscent in one way of medieval and in another of Egyptian proportion. Like many other artists, Orozco changed his system of proportion with his own growth and with the needs of the particular project on which he was engaged.

Perspective and Space

In the area of perspective and space, our sensory reactions are more complicated than in our response to proportion, which emphasizes sight and touch. In order to apprehend space, we must involve, in addition to sight and touch, the sense of balance and the sense of direction, whether as spectators or as creators. Conveying the feeling of space is a complex process; and understanding the motivations that impel the use of one form of spatial delineation instead of another (especially in painting) is even more difficult—yet it is an important part of understanding the relationship of the artist to his own time. The motivations that are briefly sketched here are as revealing as the changes in proportion from one era to another.

Let us return to the *Palette of Narmer* (Fig. 204, p. 359) as a starting point, since in formalized art of this kind our own type of visible distance is not present. Here again the artist adopts a convention— this time for showing space—a convention in which objects that are supposed to be behind each other are placed in registers, or rows, one over the other. On one side of the palette the beheaded enemies are piled one on another in this way, and on the other side the two dead soldiers in the "foreground" are shown beneath the pharaoh in the "middleground." Just as with the delineation of a figure (see *Ancient Art,* pp. 317–321) , certain traditions were established to show as much as possible of the figure (hence frontality) and to represent the scene in its final and permanent form. The Egyptian artist is not interested in how the thing might appear at any one moment; he is much more concerned with the eternal fact: that so many enemies were beheaded on this occasion. Once we accept this convention (or any other) , our enjoyment and understanding can be increased tremendously. If, for example, we accept the idea that in a modern Fauve painting one eye may be red and another green—and that art in general is not a color photograph or colored model—we are in a better position to let the work of art perform as it was meant to.

Fig. 208. *Theseus Conquering the Minotaur* (fresco). Naples, Italy, Naples Museum.

A second type of spatial depiction in relief occurs in the *Horsemen* from the Parthenon frieze (Fig. 89, p. 136). Instead of the magical space formulated by the Egyptian, in which objects are held unchangeable forever, the Greek artist devises a kind of ideal space. The figures are moving along *on* something and even *in* something, but it is impossible to be specific about the nature of the atmosphere (and the space) in which they move. It is as though the already-idealized creatures are given an altogether new environment in which to exist; but, although it is not quite so naturalistic as some others, it is still real. These same comments also apply to Greek painting (see Fig. 49, p. 79).

The differences between the Greek and the Roman points of view may be seen in the fresco of *Theseus Conquering the Minotaur* (Fig. 208, p. 365) found at Pompeii, in which the spectator feels not the neutrality and idealism of Greek space but a tangible light and air in keeping with the increased materialism of Roman society. (The Roman also gives us a highly developed art of portraiture and genre— that is, everyday—painting and sculpture.) The light here is descriptive in that it rounds out the individual figure, just as it helps to delineate the background.

Here, for perhaps the first time, a geometrically conceived perspective appears in which parallel lines, as they move away from us, are made to converge so as to simulate the sense of distance. This distance extends to the left toward the exit from the labyrinth where Theseus slew the Minotaur and toward the right with its group of spectators. The Greco-Romans devised and developed this linear spatial method; and they formulated in their painting the feeling of atmosphere that, coming between the spectator and a distant object, causes the object to look out of focus and blurred. By reproducing this visual process in their painting (we call it aerial perspective), the Alexandrians and later the Romans were perhaps the first to develop the art of landscape painting in the modern sense. In both the geometrical projection of the *Theseus* and the aerial distance of the landscapes, the Romans anticipated many later ideas.

This sense of spatial actuality, so typical of the late Greeks and the Romans, did not last beyond the Roman Empire itself. By the Early Christian period the depth of Greco-Roman space was beginning to disappear, and with such works as the mosaics from the Church of San Vitale at Ravenna (see Fig. 131, p. 219) during the sixth century a new spatial system appeared. Clearly the space here, although it exists since some individuals are shown in front of others, is much shallower than the Roman. It will not do for us to say, as do the uninformed, that the Byzantine craftsmen working in this Italian outpost of their Empire did not know any better. They represented the East Roman Empire with its high cultural level, and they were still bound in many ways to the Roman tradition; therefore we must assume that this difference in artistic and religious viewpoint was a result of deliberate choice and not of incompetence. In Constantinople, the center of this great Empire, one of the most significant cultures in the medieval world was developed.

The chief concern of Byzantine art was religious and imperial, the two aims closely identified with each other in a highly centralized, despotic outlook and a harsh, unyielding, highly spiritualized, even mystical religion. Byzantine artists were far less concerned with the everydayness of art than had been the Romans; rather they moved toward a series of formalized and permanent symbols in which substance—that is, three-dimensional form—and atmosphere or space were almost completely removed. Instead of showing the actual forms and spaces, they symbolized them (compare Egypt, p. 359), so that the figures overlap two-dimensionally and the atmosphere in which the figures move is extremely limited by the neutral gold background and the sideways-moving lines. In this way the figures tend to come toward instead of going away from the spectator, for example, the fountain. As in modern painting (see Cézanne's *Card Players*, Fig. 210a, p. 371), a kind of space tension is established that has its own validity as much as any other spatial system—and they are all systems, let it be remembered, even those we may happen to favor as the most real, such as the methods of the Renaissance and post-Renaissance periods.

Let us consider the so-called "reality" of *The Last Supper* by Leonardo (Fig. 99, p. 159). The artist has set his figures around the table so as to achieve what he feels will be the maximum dramatic effect. Hence they face us rather than spread about the table as they might normally. The table itself is placed lengthwise toward the spectator and exactly parallel with the picture plane—that is, the bottom line of the painting—again arbitrarily rather than naturalistically. The protagonists are arranged in groups of three about the central figure of Christ, toward whom they move and from whom they recede like so many waves.

To aid in the concentrated effect for which he aims, Leonardo has utilized a sharp and abrupt type of linear perspective to bring all the lines in the walls and on the ceiling directly back to the head of the Savior, which is framed by the vertical window at the rear. In the presumable space between the table and the back wall, we do not feel any real distance, and yet so sharp is the convergence of the lines on the wall and ceiling that we get the illusion of a strong movement backward. We certainly cannot think that Leonardo did not know what he was doing. What, then, was his purpose in creating this paradox of space? One answer could be tension, as we have seen it before in cases where the artist controls his space arbitrarily. Leonardo literally sweeps the entire space into the lap of the Christ; instead of conventional recession—even on a naturalistic level—the artist deliberately swings his group back toward the spectator and the picture plane. He handles this (seemingly descriptive) medium of projective geometry in an entirely arbitrary and unnaturalistic—but very effective—fashion.

Let us keep in mind, first, that linear perspective of this type is predicated on the single vanishing point at the horizon line (here the head of Christ) ; second, that it is an arbitrary method like any other and the product of the scientific interests of its time; and last, that the purposes of linear perspective are not necessarily always purely descriptive. They may be, as here, a combination of the descriptive and the symbolic or emotional. In modern painting there are many such instances, as in works of the Surrealists (for example, Dali) with their endless perspectives to indicate the dream world and the passage of time.

An interesting variant of the linear perspective method occurs in Northern painting of the fifteenth century as exemplified by the *Adoration of the Lamb* (Fig. 103, p. 172) by the van Eyck brothers. In this central portion of that great altar it is evident that the painters were very much aware of the idea of recession in space, effected both by means of converging lines and by the diminishing strength of color as we move back in the picture. Yet when we test the linear indications, looking for a single point of convergence as in *The Last Supper* (Fig. 99, p. 159), we find they do not work quite so well. Most of the lines seem to be moving in the direction of the Lamb, but further testing shows that there are pairs of lines coming from the fountain at the base of the picture, from the sides of the altar itself, and from other objects in this panel, converging not at any one point but rather at a series of points, one above the other, on an imaginary vertical line. This line passes through the post of the fountain, the Lamb, and up through the rays emanating from the dove of the Holy Ghost to the dove itself.

Paintings of this kind are apparently controlled by a vertical line toward which everything seems to move, which results in tilting the contents of the picture toward the spectator. Here we have a different type of spatial delineation from the conventional geometric projection of Leonardo. Instead of things moving back into the picture, they seem to be moving upward and to be kept from going too far inward. This is another system, perfectly suitable in the transition from the medieval period with its flatness of space to the modern—that is, Renaissance—era with its depth of recession into space.

In the sixteenth century the single-point perspective of the Italian Renaissance (see Leonardo, Fig. 99, p. 159) gives way to a new method of using geometry. This is illustrated in *The Last Supper* by Tintoretto (Fig. 209, p. 369), a work that is filled with dramatic linear conver-

Fig. 209. TINTORETTO: *The Last Supper*. Venice, Italy, San Giorgio Maggiore.

gences but has no *one* point of focus. The table lines move back toward the rear wall and far beyond the haloed Christ in the upper center; the floor lines move off to the right somewhere outside the picture; the bench at the left points to another spot; the lines in the ceiling go toward still another. In this breakdown of the unified spatial focusing of the High Renaissance, there is a tendency for some of the lines to indicate that they meet outside the picture space. In this sense, as well as in its melodramatic religious intensity, the work of Tintoretto is a transition to the Baroque of the seventeenth century.

For the seventeenth century, we choose a well-known painting by the Spanish artist Velásquez, *Las Meniñas* (*The Maids of Honor;* Fig. 210, p. 370). By this time, the self-contained Renaissance space of Leonardo's *The Last Supper* has disappeared almost completely. The earlier emphasis was on the "closed" statement where everything was set forth explicitly, the composition complete in the form of a full geometric shape, and the space controlled by the one-point perspective. Now the Baroque painter presents a space that is part of a continuous

Fig. 210. DIEGO VELÁSQUEZ: *Las Meniñas*. Madrid, Prado.

area, beginning outside the picture, coming into it, and then going on again to some other place outside.

In *Las Meniñas* we are tied to the outside space at the left by the large canvas on which the artist is working, whose lines converge away from us in that direction. By the same token, the lines on the right-hand wall move toward the servant standing on the stairs in the rear of the picture and outside the main space. Finally, the light comes in from the window at the right, spreading across the little Infanta and her maids of honor and giving us another dimension—that is, to the right. The entire group looks toward the spectator and toward the King and the Queen who are having their portraits painted and whose images are reflected in the small mirror at the rear. Although the Infanta may be the ideological center of this work, linear movement and light movements radiate out from the mirror toward infinity.

Besides the earlier variety of traditional space mechanisms (and meanings), another approach has been in force in modern painting since the end of the nineteenth century. This is found in all countries where the modern movement has taken hold, so that "modern" painters even in Japan and India use this approach in place of their own traditional methods. The new kind of space was introduced by the post-Impressionists of the 1880's and 1890's, chiefly by Cézanne, although Gauguin and others also participated. As seen in Cézanne's *Card Players* (Fig. 210a, p. 371) or in his many landscapes and still-life pictures, the procedure is to project very plastic forms within a very limited spatial area—here the solid and monumental peasants against the shallow room. The table legs come forward to the picture line, while the man in the rear with his back to the wall is seemingly placed tightly between that wall and the man at the left. In this way the artist creates a spatial tension that is magnified in an interesting and novel manner.

Many constituent parts of the composition are made to relate to the frame of the picture by actual visual contact. The man at the right is contiguous to the frame on two of its sides and is also connected with the top of the frame through the curtain. Much the same thing

Fig. 210a. PAUL CÉZANNE: *Card Players*. New York, Stephen Clark Collection.

happens to the man at the left through his chair and the individual behind him, who touches the wall and the top of the frame. This series of contacts now brings the various figures into the same plane, which is very close to the picture or front plane (and hence that much closer to the spectator) instead of being pushed back into the picture space in the older conventional manner. The table in this scene remains a focal point toward which all the men are carried and through which they are brought forward toward the spectator. This table, also touching the picture frame, moves toward the spectator instead of away, in a reverse perspective that recalls the Byzantine mosaic (Fig. 131, p. 219).

Such a tense, limited space not only occurs in the works of Cézanne and the other post-Impressionists (Gauguin, Seurat, van Gogh, Hodler, and so forth) but also it has an important influence on the entire modern movement: the Cubists, Fauves, Futurists, *de Stijl,* and many other groups.

Varieties of Composition

In the period since the Middle Ages, when there emerged the panel painting and the fresco as we know them, composition has gone through a number of interesting changes corresponding to the needs of succeeding periods. Renaissance composition has already been discussed in several instances. Here we need only remind ourselves of the balanced and concentrated composition of Giotto's *Death of St. Francis* (Fig. 176, p. 310), where an equal number of figures were placed on either side of the dead saint and where everything in this pre-Renaissance picture moved toward the center or focal point.

The same thing happened with Leonardo's *The Last Supper* (Fig. 99, p. 159), and in both cases there was the additional factor of completeness. In both pictures (as well as in the further example of Leonardo's *Madonna of the Rocks,* Fig. 154, p. 273), a closed and final statement was made. Nothing was left to the imagination in the form of an incomplete building, chair, or arm. In the course of arranging this "closed composition," the painter or sculptor (see Michelangelo's *Moses,* Fig. 87, p. 133) utilized a recognizable geometrical shape as the limiting device. For *The Last Supper* it was a rectangular box, as in the *Death of St. Francis* and the *Moses;* for the

Madonna of the Rocks, a pyramid; for Raphael's *The Alba Madonna* (Fig. 16, p. 28) a parallelepiped; for other works it might be an ovoid, a sphere, or another shape. The Renaissance artist appears to have been dealing with a finite and measurable world.

During the Baroque period we have already remarked that psychological and philosophical needs opened up the composition, changing it from a finite and closed form to an infinite and open form. Thus Andrea del Pozzo's *St. Ignatius Carried to Heaven* (Fig. 153, p. 272) moves heavenward like a star surrounded by planets; Rubens' *Descent from the Cross* (Fig. 17, p. 29) flares out into the four corners and out of the picture; Velásquez's *Las Meniñas* (Fig. 210, p. 370) definitely aspires to project its figures into another sphere; Rembrandt carries us out of his works through diagonals, limitless and space-defying darkness, and a deliberate cutting-off of edges and parts of forms—as in so many Baroque works. Where Renaissance composition was controlled and stable, Baroque composition tends, for its own purposes, to be unlimited and unstable, emotional rather than calm. These tendencies hold true in the field of architecture and sculpture as well as in painting, as seen in the church of San Carlo alle Quattro Fontane (Fig. 214, p. 388) and the Bernini sculpture of *St. Theresa in Ecstasy* (Fig. 98, p. 153), where the artists carry us jubilantly and excitably into the beyond, where the forms melt into each other in a tumult of light-and-dark expression, where the elements are in constant movement and do not stop after a given point.

During the eighteenth century and even throughout most of the nineteenth century, basic compositional schemes did not change; artists seemed to re-use Baroque and other design systems, along with new methods of drawing, coloring, and so on. Toward the end of the nineteenth century, the Impressionists projected a new compositional device in such pictures as Pissarro's *Peasants Resting* (Fig. 11, p. 24). In such a work the artist takes his position before the subject, but not in the traditional manner of standing directly in front of it. In the interest of creating an unusual and temporary effect, he prefers to stand to the side and even slightly above the scene (compare van Gogh, *Night Café,* Fig. 39, p. 63), taking the same vantage point as does the Japanese printmaker. The various parts of such pictures as *Peasants Resting* are tied together by nothing more than the colored atmosphere with which the painter has filled the scene. This conveys us from any one point to any other in the work. Although such post-Impressionists as Cézanne felt that this sort of composition lacked solidity and strength, those qualities were exactly what the Impressionists did not want, and to that extent Cézanne's criticism was not valid.

We must, whether we like it or not, evaluate a given form of expression only in terms of its expressed aims and not tax it with what it never pretended to do in the first place. It would be possible, for instance, for a Renaissance artist to criticize the *Palette of Narmer* (Fig. 204, p. 359) for its lack of balance and symmetry; but if the Egyptian artist is trying to make a utilitarian statement for eternity rather than a piece of architectural or other decoration, that statement is more important for his purposes than are what we would call esthetic values.

With post-Impressionism, traditional stability was restored to composition. The works of Cézanne and Gauguin show, in addition to their surface tension, a clearly visible symmetry. Sometimes this compositional method is fairly conventional; at other times it may deviate from notions we have met earlier. During the period since World War II, there has been a tendency to emphasize the creative act itself rather than the work of art, as in the contemporary school popularly known as Abstract Expressionism. Here (see the silk-screen print by Alva, Fig. 126, p. 209) there is a pouring forth of a presumably spontaneous emotional reaction, during the course of which we are permitted—even asked—to ignore conventional compositional and other values. Whether this viewpoint will survive remains to be seen.

▶ 15

The Work of a Major Traditional Artist: Michelangelo

IT IS IMPORTANT on many grounds to consider the development of the individual artist. Without development, no artist attains major stature; without understanding his development, we are left with meaningless stylistic and critical clichés that overlook the various changes he has undergone. Such artists as Rembrandt, Michelangelo, and Cézanne, we have already realized, began somewhere with someone. They added a personal touch or quality—which they were fortunate enough to possess—and from the mixture produced what finally seems significant in the light of history.

It is possible to distinguish developmental patterns in artists of the past because of their definite antecedents, their equally apparent growth, and their evident relationship to the social, intellectual, and other streams of their times. To exemplify this process of evolution, we turn here to a great master of the Renaissance, the painter-sculptor-architect Michelangelo.

With almost any artist of the past, we are able to make these three important points: he is related to a national tradition as well as to the period in which he functions; he is related to previous as well as to subsequent art; and he has his own chronological development. Because of his functioning role in society—that is, because he is more or less accepted as an artist and employed as such—his work naturally responds readily (and recognizably) to the spiritual, political, social, and other climates of his time, in a way that is not always so possible or clear with a modern artist.

Background and Early Work

Michelangelo developed out of the general Italian tradition of monumental realism which we have seen in many examples: Niccolò Pisano in the thirteenth century, Giotto in the fourteenth, Masaccio, Donatello, and others in the fifteenth, and finally Michelangelo's contemporaries in the early sixteenth century (Leonardo, for example). In his own time this artist embodied the then-typical search for an ideal normative figure, the perfection of a Michelangelesque, Raphaelesque, or Leonardesque type. These personages are monumental, dignified, beautiful, and strong—figures that represent the highest ideal of mankind. Theirs is a secularized serenity, characteristic of what is known as the High Renaissance.

Michelangelo's specific relationship to the past (to his own national tradition) is easily traced in such examples as the detail from the Sistine Ceiling in the Vatican, showing the "Expulsion from Eden." Here it is clear that he has seen the works of Jacopo della Quercia in Bologna (an early fifteenth-century sculptor) or Masaccio in Florence. Other details bearing this kind of relationship indicate his knowledge of and perhaps borrowing from such sources as Donatello and even Niccolò Pisano. Michelangelo's influence on subsequent art is evident in the sixteenth-century Tintoretto's *The Last Supper* (Fig. 209), the seventeenth-century Rubens' *Descent from the Cross* (Fig. 17, p. 29), the nineteenth-century Delacroix's *Massacre at Scio* (Fig. 217, p. 395), and many other works of his own time and later. The sense of controlled and then unleashed physical power, the swelling musculature of the forms, the feeling that abstract spiritual as well as emotional ideas can be projected through movements of the human body—these follow from Michelangelo.

For our brief analysis here, we shall observe only the general evolution of the various facets in this artist's style, not presuming to detail

Fig. 211 (*left*). MICHELANGELO: *David*. Florence, Italy, Academy. Fig. 211a (*right*). MICHELANGELO: *Pietà*. Rome, St. Peter's. (Photo courtesy Metropolitan Museum of Art)

every turn in the road or to deal too much with this great sculptor's painting. Michelangelo Buonarroti (1475–1564) was a product of the late fifteenth century, where we must seek the facts of his background.

Apart from his general relationship to the Italian school, Michelangelo made certain contacts as a student that were to influence his development. His art was to bring a new climax to the generalized realism that the masters of the fifteenth century had carried a step beyond the expression of Giotto—the monumental school stemming from Masaccio in painting and Donatello in sculpture. In Michelangelo their magnificent realism would turn to more universal forms and ideas, as with most other artists of the High Renaissance.

Early works, like the famous *David* of 1504 (Fig. 211, p. 377), illustrate the transition from the fifteenth to the sixteenth century. As in his other works of approximately this time (for example, the *Pietà* in the Crucifixion Chapel of St. Peter's in Rome, Fig. 211a, p. 377), the artist moves from the naturalistic or detailed to the realistic or generalized. There is great awareness of the underlying structure of the human body, of its skeletal elements in the Donatello sense, a feeling that appears in the boniness of the hands and feet and the revealing of the rib cage. (The influence of Donatello was still felt in Michelangelo's day; in fact, Michelangelo had studied for a while with Bertoldo, a pupil of Donatello.) We may also compare in a general way the fierceness of glance in the face of the *David* with the controlled menace in that of the *Gattamelata* (Fig. 199, p. 347). Even the hooked position of the right hand of the young giant (the figure is actually eighteen feet tall) is a borrowed detail from the earlier sculptor.

Yet, by and large, Michelangelo at this point already presents a more idealized form and a more generalized effect than did Donatello, and these characterize him as a man of the High Renaissance. In addition, there is a new kind of tension here, arising from two different directions of movement that are clearly indicated. The body sways toward the right with the weight concentrated on the right leg, while the other leg moves lightly in the opposite direction; the glance and the abrupt upward movement of the arm with the sling-shot also move to the left. We are pulled back and forth visually with a resultant alertness of pose, as though the figure were about to spring in the direction from which the danger presumably comes. Tension is further increased by the tightening of the throat muscles as the head turns and by the different heights of the shoulders as the body moves on its axis.

Another important point is Michelangelo's plainly expressed interest in the original block from which the form was carved and his refusal to allow the finished figure to protrude beyond those limits. This interest in the original block gives to all his work (and that of most other High Renaissance artists) the sense of self-containment that is characteristic of the era. A comparison with almost any fifteenth-century single figure in sculpture will reveal the difference between that period's comparatively diffuse attitude toward form and the tightness of organization in the typical Michelangelo figure. A

Fig. 212. MICHELANGELO: *Bound Slave,* for the Tomb of Julius II. Paris, Louvre. (Photo courtesy French Government Tourist Office)

sculpture, he is reputed to have said, should be able to roll down a hill without any part breaking off.

The Beginnings of Maturity

A second step in this artist's development is seen in the *Bound Slave* (Fig. 212, p. 379), one of a pair of sculptures designed originally to be part of the Tomb of Pope Julius II that was never carried out; all that remains of Michelangelo's great conception are these slaves and the famous *Moses* (Fig. 87, p. 133). The slaves are believed to have been done around 1514–1516, about a decade after the *David.* Where the latter is still a specifically oriented work in that it is bound up with a particular moment (the instant before David kills Goliath), the *Bound Slave* is a general statement of mood and allegory. It is sometimes taken to be a symbol of the liberal arts that were freed by Julius II, the great patron of the arts, and then enslaved again after his death.

Besides this basic difference in approach, there are other differences that are equally significant. First, the *Bound Slave* is more abstract in form—that is, less detailed—as well as more generalized in the face. Second, it projects emotions and ideas through the attitude of the body. The *David* gave us a vivid sense of power held in check through the balancing of thrusts, as part of fifteenth-century restraint, made more effective here through the violent forthrightness of the glance. Michelangelo used the nude form of the *David* as a means of expressing in esthetic terms the idea of tension, much as Myron might have done in the *Discobolus* (Fig. 86, p. 132).

In the *Bound Slave,* however, we approach a new concept for which Michelangelo is justly famous. He uses the poses of the nude human body to express not merely esthetic ideas but emotional and symbolic ones as well. Here, the body is posed in violent *contrapposto,* with the upper part moving in one direction and the lower in another, as it turns and twists within the arbitrarily stated limits of the original block of marble, thus symbolizing the restrictions placed on human expression and thought.

It must be kept in mind that the two slave figures were not meant to be seen as isolated museum pieces but as formal and symbolic accents on the base of the gigantic tomb that Michelangelo had planned for the interior of St. Peter's, which was then being rebuilt (see pp. 6–7). In that capacity they undoubtedly would have had greater meaning for the spectator than they do in their museum setting. The restraint of which we constantly speak in connection with Renaissance art is expressed in a more vivid way than before in the contrast between the obvious physical power of the figures and the languor of the *Bound Slave* or the inability of the other, the so-called *Rebellious Slave,* to move. We may note also that during this period when Michelangelo was detached from the Tomb project, he did the paintings on the Sistine ceiling (see Figs. 25, 35, and 43a, pp. 38, 57, 72) in which similar formal and symbolic ideas are promulgated.

Climax of Michelangelo's Development

A decade or so later (*c.* 1525–1535) appears a group of works that represent a high point in the artist's sculptural achievement, the Medici Tombs in the new Sacristy of San Lorenzo in Florence (see

Fig. 34, p. 54). This is another of the many unfinished Michelangelo projects, but it offers far more than the Tomb of Pope Julius in the way of completed plastic formulations. The artist has finally reached the fulfillment of his aims of using the human body as the sole means of expressing abstract concepts.

As we observed in our earlier discussion of the symbolic meaning of these monuments (see Art as Symbolic Experience, pp. 54–56), the various figures of Night and Day, Dawn and Twilight, express the passage of time and also certain concrete reactions to life. This is accomplished through the actual physical properties of the body in each case: the idea of Day is symbolized by the half-completed head turning toward us over the shoulder of the figure, that of Night through the figure asleep (with symbolic attributes of the poppy blossoms under her left foot and the owl under her left knee). But the figure of Night possesses the further element of contrast between the great power of the woman and her worn-out body with its sagging breasts and loose abdominal muscles. It goes a step beyond the type of contrast shown in the *Bound Slave* or the *Creation of Adam* (Fig. 35, p. 57) with their opposition of power and the inability to move. This much used and worn-out body, that has perhaps borne many children, represents another and more involved version of Michelangelo's constant theme—the futility of human effort. This idea is conveyed now through languor and despairing poses rather than through bonds.

The symbolism in the Medici tombs is more complicated and sensitive in execution than in the earlier works; there is also greater complexity of form for the individual figure and the pattern it makes. This is apparent in two factors: in the more involved *contrapposto* now utilized by the artist, and in a new and disturbing relationship between the figure and its block. On the first point, the left leg of Night is not only raised but also forced back to meet the forward-moving right elbow that proceeds from the powerful curve around the shoulders—a thoroughly impossible pose, but one that is made plausible by the naturalistic details of breasts and stomach muscles.

The relationship of the figure and the block is no longer so concrete and controlled as before, when the figure was made to move in spiral fashion from bottom to top and thence outward (see *Moses*, Fig. 87, p. 133). Here each figure presents its own form problem to convey part of the restlessness and despair that affected Michelangelo. The sense of nervous tension imparted by the forms is accentuated by the uneasy poses they hold and by the fact that they do not seem closely associated with the tombs on which they presumably rest, but, rather, dissociated from them, even sliding off. Thus the most positive factors in these tombs, the symbols of Day and Night, have no set niches like the portrait figures above, although they are actually more important and expressive. Whereas in an earlier style, such as the Gothic or even the early Renaissance of the fourteenth to fifteenth centuries, there is a reasonably close relationship between architecture and sculpture, Michelangelo has approached or initiated some of the feeling of Baroque architecture-sculpture relationships of the following century when, as here, there is conflict between the two (see the church San Carlo alle Quattro Fontane, Fig. 214, p. 388).

By the 1530's, when the Medici tombs project was terminated, Italy had already fallen under the heel of the invader and had become a principality of the Spanish-Hapsburg monarchy. Michelangelo experienced a personal frustration in this connection—again an important project was not to be completed, since only two tombs were executed instead of four as originally planned. This had a good deal to do with the sensation of the futility of human endeavor that hangs over the work.

The Medici tombs are a symbol of protest in the powerful and poetic rhythms of that phase of the artist's life, but his later *Pietà* (Fig. 213, p. 383), in the Cathedral of Florence, becomes a hymn of resignation and a turning to God in a powerfully mystical fashion. Unlike his earlier works, this *Pietà* has a new elongation and thinning of the forms that may be compared in a general fashion to those of El Greco at the end of this century; El Greco was undoubtedly influenced to some extent by this later work of Michelangelo. As in the case of the Spanish artist, the Italian sculptor also dematerializes his forms in the interests of greater spiritualization.

The figure loses its solidity as the artist evolves from an earlier, distinctly sculptural quality to a more pictorial, even linear, quality, while the relationship of the various figures is far more involved than ever before. There is the outline made by the arms of the Savior and the left arm of the supporting figure at His right, and that made by the arm and head of the Virgin at the right as they move toward the

Fig. 213. MICHELANGELO: *Pietà*. Florence, Italy, Cathedral.

left arm of the Christ, sliding under it, and continuing into the cloth band on His chest. Finally, there is the twisting movement in a spiral direction through the body of Christ into that of Joseph of Arimathea in the background. The latter figure represents Michelangelo himself, for whose tomb this group was originally designed. Here we find less emphasis on mass, for the composition is dominated by the flow of one area into another, of light areas into dark, of lines that move restlessly up and down and across the surfaces. This approach is consistent with the general artistic feeling of the period between *c*.1530 and *c*.1560, of the style known as Mannerism, to which this straining mystical work belongs.

In the sculptor's identification with his subject, he places himself in a haunting, brooding, and pitying pose over the tragedy of the Deposition. It is part of the great turning toward religion of this Mannerist style in art with its tensely nervous, linear, two-dimensional approach. In religious history, this is the beginning of the Counter Reformation. Among Michelangelo's paintings, this work may be paralleled in a general way by the great *Last Judgment* fresco on the far wall of the Sistine Chapel; in his poetry, by the later sonnets devoted to religious and mystical themes.

Although these few examples of the work of Michelangelo by no means exhaust the style changes in his career, they fulfill our purposes of making clear the organic relationship of this artist to his past, to his own time, and to the future—in other words, his history as an artist. But not only does this artist (and all others) have a history; individual works themselves, if they are sufficiently important, may also have a history. Projects, such as the Tomb of Pope Julius II, have a long and tortuous story to tell from the point of view of patronage and economic problems; others, such as the Sistine Chapel ceiling, show actual changes in style as the artist moved from one phase to another.

Michelangelo worked on the mighty Sistine ceiling intermittently from 1508 to 1512. First, there were two preceding plans for the ceiling as a whole before the present plan was adopted. From circles and squares like those on the ceilings of the papal apartments, he moved to alternating rectangles and octagons and, finally, to alternating large and small rectangles for the central area as the basic design of this project.

More important is the stylistic evolution of Michelangelo as a painter while this work was in progress. From documents, we know that he began to paint at the entrance of the chapel, so as to leave the opposite, altar side free for services as long as possible. Thus the *end* of the story of the Creation of Man and his subsequent sin that would demand the advent of a Savior or Messiah came *first* in actual time of execution. The *Drunkenness of Noah,* which would normally be the end of this particular cycle following upon the *Deluge* or Flood scene, was done first, since it is near the door, while the Creation scenes, beginning with *God Dividing the Light from the Darkness* came at the far end of the ceiling. It is therefore no surprise to find that Michelangelo's style develops from the relatively complex and involved early narratives, such as the *Deluge,* to the increasingly monumental and simplified scenes, such as *Creation of Adam* (Fig. 35, p. 57) , and finally to the end scene, the solitary and mystical figure of God hovering over the world He is about to set into motion as He separates light from darkness.

The Sistine Chapel ceiling had its first public viewing on August 14, 1511, after which the painter went back to add the triangular areas that show the ancestors of Christ. It was finally opened to the public in its present form on October 31, 1512.

Other points are to be noted in connection with the history of the Sistine Chapel frescoes. First, they were undertaken after Michelangelo had been forced to abandon his earlier and to him much more important project, the Tomb for Pope Julius II. Second, Michelangelo had virtually no previous experience as a muralist, let alone as a painter of ceilings. Finally, his art not only developed in the manner indicated above but also was necessarily responsive to what other men were doing and had been doing only shortly before this work was undertaken. The *Deluge* seems to have been influenced by an engraving done by Baccio Baldini; and the *Sacrifice of Noah* by Botticelli's *Cleansing of the Lepers*. The use of the symbolic decorative nudes on the corners of each large rectangle seems to derive from the late Greek *Laokoön* (Fig. 187, p. 325), which had been discovered in 1506, only two years before the ceiling was begun. In the *Laokoön,* Michelangelo apparently found support for his already-existing need to use the human figure in an expressive and emotionally significant manner.

Since he lived in an age when the artist was a useful member of society and consistently and gainfully employed, Michelangelo was bound to reflect the nature of his times and to develop with the times. These reflections appear in the relationship between the Medici tombs and the expulsion of the Medici from Florence and the sack of that great city; and they appear in the mysticism of the later *Pietà* and the tensions of the beginning Counter Reformation.

Not only was the traditional artist a useful member of society but when he was judged outstanding by his contemporaries (as in Michelangelo's case), he was sought after and commissions were thrust upon him. Apart from such profitable and socially useful employment, the artist of the past expressed in many ways the glory of the patron, whether individual, state, or Church. As late as the seventeenth and eighteenth centuries this functional relationship still prevailed, but by the nineteenth it began to change.

Before considering the special characteristics of the modern period that determine the stylistic development of the typical modern artist, we may trace briefly the various styles from the late sixteenth to the twentieth century.

▶PART V
From Traditional to Modern Developments

▶ 16

Styles in Art: Post-Renaissance to Modern

WHILE THE PROTESTANT REFORMATION of the early six-teenth century was having its tremendous effect on religious loyalties, the changes from feudalism resulted in both a new commercial, moneyed economy and the growth of sovereign states. In one way or another these radical social and historical changes were operative in the world of art. Holbein's *The Merchant George Gisze* (Fig. 197, p. 342) reflects, as we have seen, some of the spiritual unease of the post-Renaissance period as well as the growing although still in-secure role of the merchant class in that changing era (see Chapter 12). Michelangelo's Mannerist *Pietà* (Fig. 213, p. 383), on the other hand, stems from the Counter-Reformation desire to maintain the power and influence of the Church through a strong spiritual expression dif-fering markedly from the more worldly art of the previous Renais-sance period. By the end of the sixteenth century this religious cam-paign reached its full flower; by the same period also the merchant class and the monarchies had arrived at their new and enlarged sta-tions. These changes appear in the art of that epoch.

Baroque and Rococo Periods

In the Roman Catholic countries of Italy, Spain, and Flanders, the Counter Reformation engendered a seventeenth-century art devoted to the exaltation of religion and the glorification of the new mon-archies. This so-called "Baroque" art with its splendorous architec-

Fig. 214. FRANCESCO BORROMINI: San Carlo alle Quattro Fontane, Rome.

ture, sculpture, and painting moved into a more spacious, more emotive sphere than had been known before. Stimulated by the needs of the Church for an art of inspiration and impressiveness, artists produced works to bolster the faith of waverers and to bring new people into the fold to compensate for the losses suffered during the Reformation. Buildings such as San Carlo alle Quattro Fontane in Rome (Fig. 214, p. 388) and paintings such as Andrea del Pozzo's *St. Ignatius Carried to Heaven* (Fig. 153, p. 272) fulfilled a new function.

These two Italian works sum up the attempts of the Roman Catholic Church to create an art of surging movement and emotional stimulation. Within San Carlo, we enter a broad and spacious interior minus the clearly marked divisions into nave and aisles that were typical of buildings of earlier periods. Now the problem is to get as many people as possible into the building in order to preach to them. Externally, the façade is far different from the simplicity of Renaissance buildings. There is constant movement in all directions; spaces are deeply indented to receive large-scale sculptures that seem to move out of their niches and to create a dramatic light-and-dark quality. Flaring corners and in-and-out curving surfaces seem not to have terminations but to shoot out into space. The result is not only a feeling of restlessness and excitement—an almost operatic character—but also a sensation of endlessness that is one of the prime qualities of Baroque art.

The Renaissance artist (Leonardo, Michelangelo, and the like) with his closed form always makes us aware of a beginning and an end; the Baroque master achieves an openness of composition where there is more than meets the eye, where we are literally carried out of the composition into some far-off, infinitely distant realm. This new quality may be explained in terms of a new relationship between man and the universe that grew up in the course of the sixteenth and seventeenth centuries. With it came a broadening of horizons from discoveries in the New World and, more important, a change from a man-centered to a sun-centered world. After the extreme humanism of the Renaissance, with its emphasis on man as the center of the universe, we are now conscious of an endless system wherein the earth is but one small unit and not the center of that system.

In the del Pozzo painting of *St. Ignatius Carried to Heaven*, we are reminded of this new attitude by the way the artist has opened up the ceiling. The picture merely begins in this area and literally ascends heavenward. St. Ignatius, founder of the teaching and preaching order of Jesuits, himself responded to the needs of the Church during this period; the painting supplies a missionary message to exalt man and to inspire him to turn to religion more directly. Compositionally, paintings of this type are an interesting corroboration of the new outlook on the world. Not only do they oppose an infinite to a finite arrangement, but in centralizing St. Ignatius and causing the other figures to swirl about him, the main character becomes a kind of sun with planets following in circular or elliptical orbits. In any case, we may regard arrangements of this kind as *radiating from* a central point rather than *coming to* a central point as formerly done in a Giotto or a Michelangelo.

During the Baroque seventeenth century, similar expressions of upper-class emotionality appear in Spain, France, and Flanders. Rubens in Flanders produces such works as *Descent from the Cross* (Fig. 17, p. 29), offering a typically heightened Baroque expression of suffering that appeals to our sympathies. The powerfully muscled body of the Christ is lowered diagonally from the Cross, His helplessness in dramatic contrast to His recent great strength, just as the gentleness of the men lowering Him contrasts with their obvious physical power. Like many other works of the period, this picture projects its message through a forceful light-and-dark arrangement (here running diagonally from upper right to lower left) focusing on the main character and singling Him out for special attention in the theatrical manner of this art. The composition is an "X" arrangement with the corners flaring out into space through the women kneeling at the lower left, the ladder at the lower right, and so on. Again we are reminded that the Baroque artist seeks escape from his picture space rather than confinement within it.

This characteristically Baroque picture diverges from the art of the Renaissance, first, through the violent free motion of the individual form and the grouping of forms in a new open manner; then through exaggeration of the physical power of each figure; and finally in the use of a dramatic lighting system. Other works of the period—San Carlo alle Quattro Fontane, the ceiling painting of St. Ignatius, and other Italian or Italian-derived works of the time (see Bernini's *Apollo and Daphne,* Fig. 177, p. 311)—are bound by monarchistic strictures and emotional requirements similar to those of the sorrowing, well-dressed figures in Rubens' painting.

But what happens when we turn to such a middle-class and non-Catholic country as seventeenth-century Holland? Rembrandt's *Anatomy Lesson of Dr. Tulp* (Fig. 203, p. 354) offers a different type of individual and situation from those in the Rubens painting. Owing to Protestant dislike of religious art, most of the creative energy of Dutch artists is diverted into other channels, primarily into glorifying the Dutch way of life or portraying the Dutch land and its contents. Here is a group portrait memorializing a public demonstration that the licensed medical practitioner in Holland was obligated to make periodically and which as a formal event was depicted in a dressed-up fashion. As Dr. Tulp, at the right, elegantly demonstrates the anatomy of the cadaver's forearm, the eager audience groups about him in a series of concentric arcs from the upper left through the cadaver with the dramatic light on it and to the lower right where an anatomy textbook carries us out of the picture.

We have the same diagonality that we noted before, a similar highlighting of the "martyred" figure (in this case the corpse of an executed criminal), and the same thrust out of the picture space. This is effected through compositional movement into the corners, cutting off the book, and through the partially seen man at the lower left, so that again we are forced to go out of the picture with the artist. The mysterious shadows also carry us out toward infinity. All these factors bear strong comparison to similar ones in the Rubens painting and indicate that a work may be Baroque in spirit and in style without being either Catholic or royalist in background. We may say, then, that there is a Baroque style applying to most, if not to all, the art of the seventeenth century in Western Europe. This style is to be differentiated from that which came before (the Renaissance) and from that which follows (the Rococo).

The chief European style of the eighteenth century, although by no means the only one, is the Rococo. It may be exemplified by such French works as Fragonard's *The Lover Crowned* (Fig. 214a, p. 392), one of a series of panels made for Madame du Barry. Although at first glance the arrangement, or composition, seems similar to that in Baroque paintings, the feeling and style are very different. The central figures, the two lovers, are highlighted much as before and are placed between a figure at the lower right and a group of statuary at the upper left, thus effecting a diagonal movement as in Baroque art. Also, the lovers and the light in which they are seen create a movement from lower left to upper right, forming an irregular cross shape. As for emotional quality, there is certainly an appeal to the spectator's sympathies here, too.

On further examination, however, we find that the chief figures are encircled by the dark areas so that they do not project into infinity as in a Baroque painting. Their emotions, moreover, are tender, soft, and sentimental and, to that extent, far different from the passionate expressiveness of Rubens or the dignified seriousness of Rembrandt. This is an inevitable result of the artist's purpose of extolling the tender emotions, the kind of boy-and-girl love represented here. As to the forms and the way they are drawn, these offer a softness of texture and a delicacy of color differing greatly from the Michelangelesque strength of Rubens' figures or the deep, penetrative overlays of color in a Rembrandt. These distinctions extend even to the fluffy and transparent foliage, which has the artificiality of a stage set rather than the power of a scene in nature. The entire painting, like many works of this period, has a quality of make believe, of the

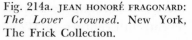
Fig. 214a. JEAN HONORÉ FRAGONARD: *The Lover Crowned*. New York, The Frick Collection.

pastoral theater of the eighteenth century rather than of the powerful operatic works of the seventeenth century that Rubens recalled (see also Watteau, *Embarkation for the Isle of Cythera*, Fig. 168, p. 297).

Delicacy and charm of style and expression pervade most Rococo creations: paintings, sculpture, furniture, interior decoration, or anything else. Thus the interior of the *Hôtel de Soubise* (Fig. 215, p. 393) has an intimate quality and grace far removed from the relatively heavy and formal seventeenth-century interiors of the same country (see the Hall of Mirrors at Versailles, Fig. 156a, p. 277). It is as though this room were designed for the tender tête-à-tête of the Fragonard painting rather than for the elaborate and impressive functions held at Versailles under Louis XIV.

Rococo rooms have elaborately carved panels in ivory framed with gilt stucco. Mirrors add to the grace of the area, as do irregularly shaped decorative wall and ceiling paintings in the favorite pastel blues, pinks, and yellows of the period. The subjects of these paintings run to fanciful scenes of love with cupids and Venuses, scenes of entertainment and charm with imaginary Oriental types and equally fantastic animals representing the foibles of human nature. Basically, Rococo is an art of pleasure, painted or carved accordingly, while Baroque is an art of seriousness and strength executed in various appropriate ways. Both styles are international in scope, the Baroque because of the widespread influence of the Counter Reformation and the Rococo because of the increasingly important role of France in European culture. This latter mode developed in France and spread to most other European nations, as did many later styles that were evolved in that country.

Classicism versus Romanticism

By the latter part of the eighteenth and the early part of the nineteenth century, two new art categories appear: the neo-Classical and the Romantic. The first is a reaction to the casualness and charm of

Fig. 215. Hôtel de Soubise. Interior view. Paris. (Photo courtesy French Embassy Press and Information Division)

Fig. 216. ANTONIO CANOVA: *Perseus*. Rome, Vatican Museum.

the Rococo, and the second, at least in part, is a reaction to the formality of the new Classicism. But styles are not only reactions against earlier styles—this would make the history of art independent of history in general—they are also reactions to the times themselves. The softness and love-play of the Rococo style had reflected the interests of the decorative and unfunctional upper classes of the eighteenth century, while the new (*neo-*) Classicism was a response to the more severe and moral attitudes of the rising middle classes in the later eighteenth century.

When, during the 1760's, excavations at Pompeii and Herculaneum in Italy uncovered impressive remains of ancient Roman civilization, it seemed appropriate that the neo-Classical style with its reminiscences of Roman political virtue and classicistic humanism—that is, individualism—should be associated with the aims and aspirations of the militantly virtuous middle class. The formal and Classical *Oath of the Horatii* (Fig. 173, p. 305), by David, in 1784 was an appeal to sterner patriotism and was understood as such. In the United States of the late eighteenth and early nineteenth century, the new Classicism attracted the public for the same reasons. Later, as the style most closely associated with the success of the French Revolution, it became firmly imbedded in the French national consciousness and lost its original quality of protest, continuing merely as an official or governmental style.

Thereafter in early-nineteenth-century examples, such as Canova's *Perseus* (Fig. 216, p. 394), we find a fashionable Classicism, using the ancient material for its elegance and prestige. At that juncture of history, and in reaction against the conservatism that caused this usage, a new style arose, as exemplified in Delacroix's *Massacre at Scio* (Fig. 217, p. 395). The two works differ in both style and mood. While

Fig. 217. EUGÈNE DELA-CROIX: *Massacre at Scio*. Paris, Louvre.

the sculpture recalls, in general form, the qualities of ancient Greek art (compare *Hermes and the Infant Dionysus,* Fig. 186, p. 325), it carries little if any of the elusive poetry inherent in the older work, and exists primarily on an artificial basis to embellish the society of which it is a part. The Delacroix painting, on the other hand, inspired by the war of independence of the Greeks against the Turks, derives esthetically from the style of the seventeenth century in that it also tries to arouse our sympathy for those contemporary martyrs.

In actual execution, a neo-Classical work is cold in color, hard and precise in form, emphasizing the outline in the approved Classical fashion; the Romantic is warm in color, diffuse in form, and de-emphasizes the linear wherever possible. Whereas the neo-Classical is stately and reserved in its deliberate lack of movement, the Romantic is filled with physical excitement. In our example of the first, the *Perseus,* the eye moves slowly and easily along the prescribed track laid down by the artist; in the second, the eye is impelled to move erratically back and forth, stimulated by color change as well as dynamic light-and-dark quality. The lack of movement and its reverse are symptoms of the chief attributes of these two works, of the absence of defined or intense emotion in the one, and of the presence of a well-defined and very intense emotion in the other.

Romantic emotion differs from the turbulence of Baroque emotion that was designed to arouse a generalized sympathy for a martyr or to draw a man to God. Romantic emotion is an extremely personal thing, the reaction of a man at odds with his environment. His revolt is symbolized by sympathy for the underdog (as in this case), by refusal to accept some convention with which he disagrees (like the official Classical style), or by escaping from his uncongenial environment to an exotic or otherwise different background. Thus the *Massacre at Scio* is doubly significant for the Romantic. First, it symbolizes an injustice that arouses his outrage at the oppression of the individual. Second, it takes place in a far-off and "interesting" location—this time the isles of Greece, on another occasion Algiers or North America.

Another important thing to note about the Romantic attitude is that it is no more confined to the early nineteenth century than is the Classical attitude (we have already seen a number of variants of the latter; see Chapter 12). If we define Romantic emotion as an individual response in emotional terms—often involving the artist's de-

Fig. 218. *Dying Gaul*. Rome, Capitoline Museum. (Photo courtesy Metropolitan Museum of Art)

sire to arouse sympathy for the suffering and the oppressed (including himself) —we then can discover this kind of reaction in almost any period of the world's history. We have, for instance, a piece of ancient sculpture dating from the third century B.C., *Dying Gaul* (Fig. 218, p. 397) , that was set up as part of a memorial by the Greek rulers of the Asia Minor city of Pergamum in honor of their victory over the invading Gauls. If we contrast this marble (copy of a bronze original) with the modern *Perseus* by Canova, the latter paradoxically appears more genuinely Classical than the ancient work.

Dying Gaul, because of its very apparent emotional content, differs quite sharply from the *Perseus;* its specific details of hair, mustache, and twisted circlet about the throat are also deviations from the Classical generality. Where *Perseus* has the long, swinging line already mentioned, the *Gaul* moves the upper part of his body in one direction, the lower part in another—a pose expressing the slow but final collapse of this dying man. Here is a real human being whom the ancient sculptor tried to identify by his racial characteristics and by his actual emotional reactions, which are as pitiful as anything in the *Massacre at Scio.* An enemy soldier many miles from home is mortally wounded

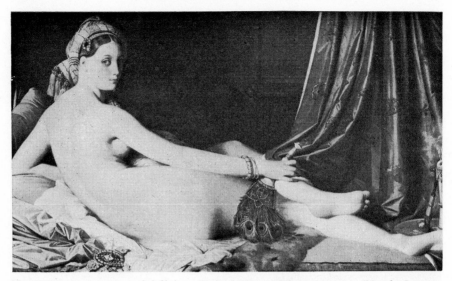

Fig. 219. J. A. D. INGRES: *Odalisque*. Paris, Louvre. (Photo courtesy French Government Tourist Office)

and is slowly expiring before our eyes as the blood oozes from his side. The figure is as Romantic in his individualistic misery and appeal as the medieval hero of the *Song of Roland,* Charlemagne's knight who died in the Pyrenees far from home after a Moorish ambush.

Turning to a nineteenth-century neo-Classical painting, the *Odalisque* by Ingres (Fig. 219, p. 398) , we may contrast it with the ancient sculpture just examined. Apparently Ingres is interested in an elegant swing of line comparable to that of Canova's *Perseus.* In this case, the line moves with infinite grace from the back of the neck through the artificially but beautifully arched back and then to the curved portion of the curtain in shadow. Parallel in movement, another line swings from the front of the neck along the elongated arm and directly into the curtain again. Just as in other neo-Classical works, the color is cold, the form precise, the emotion restrained to the point of disappearance, the entire effect gracefully static—all qualities in direct opposition to those of *Dying Gaul* with its warm dark-and-light surface, its passionate appeal to our sympathies.

Ingres's *Odalisque,* like the *Massacre at Scio* and other exotic paintings by Delacroix, exists in a strange, colorful environment, here the Near-Eastern harem. Yet, in spite of the potential exotic interest of such themes, it is possible—and, indeed, for a man like Ingres it is mandatory—to paint them in his typical cold, linear, and precise way. What this ultimately means is that subject matter itself is not the chief determinant of the Romantic or Classical quality of a given work; it is the mood in which this material is transmitted to us and, even more vital, the technique or style with which it is handled. Romanticism may be found in ancient Greece in such works as the *Dying Gaul* or the *Laokoön* (Fig. 187, p. 325); and Classicism may be found not only in Renaissance, seventeenth-century, or nineteenth-century examples but during our own times as well—as in so many of Picasso's paintings of the 1920's, in his illustrations for an edition of the *Metamorphoses* by the Roman poet Ovid, or his *Woman in White* (Fig. 231, p. 435).

We have tried here to establish Romanticism and Classicism as tools, as means of description and understanding that will enable us to communicate on these matters concerning the art of any period or country. Picasso's Classicism, then, becomes part of a way of expression that may exist in every period, just as the Romanticism of some twentieth-century artist taking refuge from his time in a new form of escapism may be akin to Delacroix.

Naturalism versus Realism

The conflict between the neo-Classicists and the Romantics, a serious struggle in the early nineteenth century, gave way to a new phase of the artist's effort to find his place in the sun. By the mid-century, conservative followers of both camps were now the accepted artists, purveying a photographically detailed but dry and uninspiring mass of exotic and historical subjects. To new artists who reacted strongly to the growing materialism of that day, such repetitions were unacceptable; instead, they offered a type of still emotive expression, concerned not so much with the fate of the individual in the older sense as with the character of the life of their time. These Realists, as they were known, included writers as well as artists.

Their approach is represented by Daumier's *The Uprising* (Fig. 157, p. 278). This painting may be differentiated from Romantic works because its mass action encompasses a large group of people as the collective hero, whereas in the *Massacre at Scio* our attention is called to a series of individual scenes of pathos in which we become involved.

The intent of Daumier's work lies along the path of a general truth —in this case social, in other cases referring to the nature of the world in general. Although this painter is also interested in violence of movement in the diagonal Baroque way used by Delacroix, he does not show the specific factors that attract the Romantic artist who feels that the more data offered, the more convincing will be his picture. Daumier convinces us of the existence of these various forms as generalities, somewhat in the Renaissance sense (see Masaccio, *Expulsion from the Garden,* Fig. 193, p. 338), making them real but without recourse to the photographic detail typical of some other methods of delineation.

What we have described as Realism differs from Naturalism—that is, from the constant reference to facts as seen in nature—illustrated in paintings like Chardin's *Child with a Top* (Fig. 18, p. 30) or Vermeer's *Young Woman with a Water Jug* (Fig. 32, p. 50). In Naturalism the artist relates as many factual details as possible, building up his picture carefully and meticulously with constant recourse to the actual photographic appearance of things, their shape and texture, the reflections of color from one object to another, and so on. Chardin, for example, describes the gloss on the edge of the bottle, the tiny details on the top of the quill, the table edging, the glow of the top itself.

Obviously, these are two different ways of doing things, each equally valid for its time, circumstance, and practitioner, each possible in different ages. Chardin's Naturalism has its counterpart in various types of later as well as earlier art—for example, Vermeer. Similarly, Daumier's generalized method, which seems real in spite of the lack of so-called "fact," can be found earlier (Masaccio) and in our time, too. Here again our purpose is to create a term, a descriptive tool that will enable us to know what an artist or critic is talking about.

Finally, in connection with both Naturalism and Realism, neither takes the position of a color camera. No matter how detailed the works of a Vermeer or a Chardin, there is still more than enough room for the creative artist in composition, texture, emotional expression, articulation of form, and so forth. Even though we have used the photographic analogy for Naturalism, if the painter merely heaps up details without arranging this material, he is not being an artist. With Realism, of course, the same problem does not arise.

Fig. 220. J. L. E. MEISSONIER: *The Sergeant's Portrait* (engraving after the original in the Louvre).

However different the method followed by Daumier on the one hand and Vermeer and Chardin on the other, both types of art strive for monumentality of form and seriousness of purpose, or inner meaning. It is quite possible, however, for any method—particularly the more literal ones that engage the imagination less—to be used in a shallow and ineffective way. Let us compare the dignity of Chardin and Vermeer (the one influenced by the other) with the relative triviality of Naturalistic work in the nineteenth century, as exemplified by Meissonier's *The Sergeant's Portrait* (Fig. 220, p. 401).

In making the comparison, we notice that Meissonier, like Chardin, went back to the Dutch style of the seventeenth century for inspiration, since both artists were interested in a good Naturalistic prototype. But the purposes of Chardin (and Vermeer) were more serious to the extent that he wished to poeticize simple things and sentiments, while Meissonier was interested primarily in narrative value. The results, therefore, were bound to differ in significance. Chardin's Naturalism is filled with mood and dignity, while Meissonier's is filled with "interesting" and "catchy" illustrative material of the sort found on today's magazine covers.

Chardin elevates the simple childish act of spinning a top; Meissonier narrows down his interests to the obvious story-book elements that anyone will recognize, the way people look when their picture is taken. This difference in esthetic purpose is even more serious than our present comparison would indicate, for it deals with the degree to which the artist feels he can make the spectator contribute to the artistic experience—that is, the amount of understanding and effort the spectator would be willing to exercise. In going beyond the immediately and obviously understandable, the artist makes his own contribution.

Impressionism and Expressionism

Two major stylistic developments of the later nineteenth century are Impressionism and Expressionism, terms often confused by the layman. Essentially, Impressionism, as exemplified in such a picture as *Isle on the Seine near Giverny* (Fig. 221, p. 403) by Claude Monet, is an extension of the Naturalism of the nineteenth and earlier centuries. Since Monet's work concerns itself with certain minutiae of visual experience—in this case the effect of natural light (sunlight) on a given object at a given time—it may be compared in a general way with Chardin's concern with the effects of light on the drawer knob or Vermeer's interest in light reflections coming through the blue glass of the window and coloring the white hood of the young girl. The earlier Naturalists, however, were concerned with an effect of permanence and even timelessness, whereas the Impressionist, product of an increasingly hurried environment and momentary experiences, tends to receive and to translate to the spectator momentary and impermanent "impressions." This painter no longer probes carefully into the form of his objects or into their emotional value.

Looking at the various shapes represented in this picture, we find that the artist is far more occupied with the light that falls on the trees than on whatever solidity those forms themselves have. Not only does the object represented so impermanently lose solidity—it never stands still long enough to take form in our eyes—but it also tends to lose

Fig. 221. CLAUDE MONET: *Isle on the Seine near Giverny*. Columbia, South Carolina, collection Mrs. B. D. Chambers. (Photo courtesy Frick Art Reference Library)

emotional value as well. Just what does the *Isle on the Seine* represent in terms of feeling? Is the artist happy or sad about his visual experience, or is it, as we stated at the outset, fundamentally a visual experience? Some may consider this a rather limited aim, but as we shall see, the history of modern art from that point on is often a story of similar esthetic experiments, of concern with the "how" of painting rather than with content or subject matter.

The outdoor Impressionist style is based on the use of clean spots of unmixed color applied separately in specified relationships that augment or intensify each other's brightness (complement each other). The outcome of this method is to set up a series of vibrating effects in the eye, that give the picture a twinkling quality to help the notion of impermanence that the artist wishes to convey. Outdoor Impressionist paintings are also far brighter in appearance than any traditional art has been, and indeed the introduction of this new clean color sys-

Fig. 222. VINCENT VAN GOGH: *Cornfield with Cypress*. London, Tate Gallery.

tem (traditional paints had been mixed on the palette before application) made it a permanent feature of modern painting.

This typical Impressionist painting of the 1870's might be compared with a post-Impressionist picture of the 1880's, van Gogh's *Cornfield with Cypress* (Fig. 222, p. 404). Post-Impressionism is usually divided into two aspects: the emotional (pre-Expressionist), represented by van Gogh and Gauguin; and the structural, represented by Cézanne (Figs. 223 and 210a, pp. 405, 371) and Seurat. From the first aspect come most of the emotive and symbolic movements of the late nineteenth and twentieth centuries; from the second (especially from Cézanne) come the form-seeking developments of modern times. The bright Impressionist palette or color system was carried over by all the post-Impressionists but used in a markedly different fashion by each.

Van Gogh introduced a new, exciting, expressionistic quality. In *Cornfield with Cypress,* instead of little, spontaneously applied, roundish spots of color, there are elongated strokes in wriggling shapes. Where Monet's painting produced an effect of twinkling as the eye brought the various spots into coloristic relationship with each other, van Gogh's painting causes the eye to move jerkily along the constantly repeating crooked paths that the artist's nervous brushstroke has followed, thus arousing a feeling of disturbance rather than simple visual pleasure. This sensation of disturbance is enhanced by the frequently lumpy paint that may be put on the canvas with the palette knife, the thumbnail, or the wooden tip of the brush. Finally, a tension is aroused through the color relationships themselves that are often much less bland or complementary than the Impressionist's combinations; here there is a sense of color conflict rather than color complementation, which again raises the emotional tempo.

We have already indicated that there is an emotional character to these pre-Expressionistic works; this, of course, becomes the most obvious difference between the descriptive and external purposes of Impressionism and the emotional and internal purposes of Expression-

Fig. 223. PAUL CÉZANNE: *The Basket of Apples*. Chicago, Illinois. Courtesy The Art Institute of Chicago.

Fig. 224. PABLO PICASSO: *Violin*. Otterlo,
Netherlands, Rijksmuseum Kröller-Mül-
ler. (Photo courtesy The Museum of
Modern Art)

ism. Through the latter, the painter is trying to express a given feeling,
usually an unhappy one. It is impossible to look at pictures of this type
without sensing something of the inner conflict that agitated the soul
of the painter (see *Night Café* by van Gogh, Fig. 39, p. 63).

Van Gogh carried forward a style of painting that reminds us, in a
general way, of the form and color distortions of El Greco (see Fig.
151b, p. 268). It was destined to have strong impact on the actual Expressionist movement of the twentieth century, particularly that of
Germany and Austria (see Beckmann's *Departure*, Fig. 40, p. 64, and
also Kirchner's *Sailboat* and Rohlfs's *Two Heads*, Figs. 115 and 110,
pp. 194, 182).

Cubism and Fauvism

Both Cubism and Fauvism arose during the first decade of the twentieth
century as consequences of the artist's increasing concern with methods
of expression rather than content (influenced greatly by Cézanne) and

also as a part of the pre-World-War-I period's need for expression of subconscious fears and tensions. Far more deliberately experimental than earlier styles, Cubism as represented by Picasso's *Violin* (Fig. 224, p. 406) is an attempt to look at the object simultaneously from as many viewpoints as possible, each view represented by a "perspective box." The entire composition is designed to analyze the form into its component parts as well as to achieve a dynamic effect of movement. The form is taken apart and then put together again in a new and visually more exciting way.

From this interest in form analysis and motion for their own sakes derived a number of later significant experimental movements that also negated the traditional importance of subject matter. Futurism is an even more dynamic type of Cubist form-analysis; Synchromism is a more colorful version of Cubism. Dutch *de Stijl* (see Mondrian, Fig. 33, p. 50), Russian Constructivism, and many other variants of this method bring us down to the present day with its newer interpretations of artistic geometricity.

Fig. 225. HENRI MATISSE: *The Young Sailor*. Chicago, Illinois, collection Mr. and Mrs. Leigh Block. (Photo courtesy The Museum of Modern Art)

Fauvism, contemporary with Cubism, is a more immediately color-ful type of composition-building through which the canvas is set in motion by vivid color contrasts and dissonances suggesting van Gogh, by sinuously curving contour patterns, and (as in Cubism and modern painting generally) by a flattened space whereby the artist retains con-trol of the world in which he works. This flattening of the space as seen in Matisse's *The Young Sailor* (Fig. 225, p. 407) gives an added ten-sion to the canvas, pushing the figure toward the spectator instead of away from him in the traditional Renaissance and post-Renaissance method. Although it is less influential historically than Cubism, Fauve painting has been consequential in applied design—for example, in the theater, in commercial art, and in similar areas.

We have now brought our story to the threshold of modern times, always following the idea of international forms of expression and na-tional modes. Within each category we have seen a breakdown into smaller units, where we had to distinguish, for example, between Ital-ian and German Renaissance, Italian and Flemish Baroque. And all these forms of creativity are comprised of a host of smaller units—the individual artists who amongst them in different periods and in differ-ent localities make up the various historic or national styles.

▶ 17

Special Problems in Modern Times

WHEN WE APPROACH modern—or contemporary—art, we immediately become aware of obvious differences in the appearance of art objects when compared with the traditional examples we have viewed previously. To account for these differences, these strange-appearing variations, we must take into account a number of new ideas and problems that belong to the contemporary world. The latter include the question of understanding and accepting modern art, new techniques, new subject matter, the problem of nonobjective art, the effects of technology on modern art, interrelationships of the arts in modern times, and the political and social functions of the modern artist.

Problems of Understanding and Acceptance

Even today, inflexible teaching methods in various parts of the world, especially on the primary and secondary levels, make it possible for persons to grow up without any real or conscious contact with modern art. This is dramatically illustrated by the confused behavior of the large crowds who visit modern exhibitions in the United States. Drawn by the novelty and freshness of what is being shown (but, in surprisingly numerous cases, unaware of the significance of the material), these people illustrate the still-existing gap between the modern artist and the public. Although much progress has been made in public understanding of modern (and other) types of art, this understanding is relative to a specific nation, the size of a city, and other factors. While

409

in some places conditions may be better, entire areas on this and other continents reject "modern" art completely. Sometimes the reason is nationalism (Mexico), sometimes political motives (the Soviet Union), and sometimes the region involved simply has not come abreast of the modern movement (Australia).

Whatever the reason for this state of affairs, we must realize that the "modern movement" is now more than a half-century old. Moreover, a great number of its esthetic ideas have been absorbed into the fabric of our daily lives in free-form furniture designs, modern typography, and packaging. Yet we still show remarkable reluctance to accept these same ideas within the sacrosanct boundaries of a picture frame. Because of retarded artistic education also, many people still prefer the illustrative, storytelling type of picture or sculpture rather than the kind of work that presents elements of powerful design and decorative color or emotional distortion of form, color, and space or rigid but meaningful mechanistic forms. These persons still proceed on the assumption that the closer to photographic naturalism the specific work comes, the better or more desirable it is. If, however, the function of the painter was merely to tell a story in a pleasant and sentimental fashion, there would be no need for such artists as El Greco, the Egyptians, Rembrandt, Titian, the decorators of the Byzantine churches and the Romanesque cathedrals, the painters of ancient China, and many others.

We have seen that the aims of the modern artist in terms of space, proportion, composition, form, and color distortion are not incompatible with those of some earlier periods. Why, then, is there still antagonism at this late date? Let us examine some of the motivations that work against the full acceptance of modern art.

The educational indoctrination, even in democratic countries, is a reflection of the status of art in each area. For a long time, conservative doctrine has been paramount in higher art schools, academies, honorary societies, and so forth. Since the development of modern democracy in the late eighteenth century under the auspices of neo-Classicism (see pp. 393–399), the representational ideal has remained the most powerful. In the century and a half that has elapsed, artists have tried to develop new methods and styles consonant with the more dynamic character of modern life. But to those in authority who awarded commissions for public buildings and their decoration, who admitted artists to the various salons and other exhibiting agencies, the innovations were not acceptable to the degree that they varied from the familiar and to the degree that they exalted the individual above society at large.

This struggle (in various forms) has gone on throughout the development of Romanticism, Realism, Impressionism, post-Impressionism, and the manifold twentieth-century movements. The artist in each successive style has been excluded from the direct benefits conferrable by modern democracy and has taken refuge in a series of increasingly "esthetic" rather than directly communicative techniques—since there was little public left to him. Becoming thus more concerned with the methods of painting and sculpture than with their content (as the traditionalist still had to be), the artist in the modern trend has moved in the direction of the abstract. Reacting to the multiplying complexities and traumatic experiences of modern living, he has inevitably produced an art that mirrors the confusions and tensions within modern man. For this purpose he has found himself creating a new artistic language.

At special intervals, the artist has been subjected to political persecution, when it suited opponents with a particular ax to grind. It is true that certain artists in modern times have been politically-minded —just as have writers, musicians, and people of all kinds—but not in such numbers as would justify marking them out especially. Unfortunately, the nature of our news media is such that artists are always "good copy," even if for the wrong reasons. Ironically enough, these artists, the great individualists of our times, who are often considered "radical" in democratic society, represent everything that is distasteful to such totalitarian governments as those of Soviet Russia and Nazi Germany.

Abstract painting, sculpture, graphics, and so on exist as a genuine expression of our era, created by talented people who have given their lifetimes to this activity with very little hope for the kind of remuneration they might have received in a comparable profession. If our pretensions to democracy amount to more than pious gestures, we have the obligation of trying to understand their viewpoint. If after examination of the evidence, we decide that we still do not like the material, this remains our privilege.

It is apparent that the form differences that shock many spectators are based on concepts quite divergent from those animating the Renaissance, Baroque, or other art periods (see Chapter 16). This must be kept in mind, because it helps to establish the fact that an art such as Cubism is a considered doctrine followed by a good many artists since the early twentieth century and not merely the aberration of one or two. Such doctrines have been formulated into concrete expressions that exist as manifestoes, catalogues for exhibitions, articles, and even books on the subject. Whether we like it or not, these ideas have currency among leading artists and art lovers—and have had for some time.

Modern artists are more self-conscious about what they are doing than were the men of the Renaissance, but this is perfectly natural in the circumstances. From the early 1800's on, men sat about little café tables in Paris (and later elsewhere) debating the successive new methods of painting and how to get into the so-necessary exhibitions. Always they were aware that what they were doing was not the acceptable thing. By the early twentieth century, the modern idea caught on with a number of dealers and a small number of appreciators who have since formed the core of the patronage of the modern movement. These individuals have produced or sponsored or helped in different ways the production of articles, books, monographs, and other works on modern art. Although they are a limited group even today when compared to the potential audience, these people remain a constant but, unfortunately, economically inadequate public for the ever-growing mass of artists. Through spreading education, more and more artists are produced, just as more and more members of the public become educated. But the latter are bound to lag behind in the selective and informed experience that is needed as well as in the funds necessary for the purchase of art works.

This lack of understanding stems not only from insufficient art education in schools but also from the involuntary "education" deriving from commercial sources. The advertising industry, on one level, has made extensive use of contemporary art forms but, on another level, uses the lowest common denominator of illustrative material to sell its products—and keeps hammering away at the public mind with it. The movies, television, and popular magazines, in addition, do an enormous amount to accustom us to the naturalistic image. In earlier periods, neither advertising nor these communications media existed. Art, it is true, was certainly illustrative (as, for example, Michelangelo), but it contained symbolic and compositional value as well as fulfilling doctrinal requirement. The artist was transmitting spiritual, intellectual, or other important ideas rather than compulsive buying stimuli.

New Techniques

The modern work of art is a summing up of a form sensation that the artist has experienced and that he tries to transmit to the spectator by underlining certain elements of that form and its colors. If the form sensation comes to a geometrically-minded individual, such as Mondrian, it may take the shape of the *Composition* (Fig. 33, p. 50). This, it should be noted, does not arbitrarily bring together lines and hues for their own sake but to re-create a form feeling—from a man, animal, landscape, or other objects previously viewed or from a situation witnessed. In a freer, more flowing type of nonobjective painting, for example, Kandinsky or Alva (Figs. 125 and 109, pp. 208, 181), the artist's aim is to transmit to the spectator a state of being or feeling by persuading him to move along with the painter in the rhythmic, pulsating, sometimes disturbing, sometimes lyrical direction the lines and colors may take.

Both these types of modern pictorial thinking are extensions of slightly earlier ones we have already seen. Mondrian's reduction of a given form or forms to a series of elementary horizontals, verticals, and primary colors recalls the beginning of the breaking up—or analysis—of form that we encountered in Picasso's Cubist period (p. 406). Kandinsky's or Alva's Abstract Expressionism displays a more spontaneous and lyrical emotionalism than the rugged and powerful expression of van Gogh or Rohlfs (Fig. 110, p. 182), but they are both based on the same attitude of getting inside the subject in order to capture the essential meaning thereof; by destroying its form or purposefully twisting it out of shape, the artist goes beyond the surface aspect. These Expressionists (van Gogh, Rohlfs, Beckmann, Kandinsky) may be said, then, to be striving to "express" the true meaning of a given object or situation with which they try to identify themselves, or in which they try to submerge themselves by exaggerating color quality, elongating or otherwise distorting form. It is also possible to combine the two approaches, one form-analytical, the other form-destructive, in such paintings as Picasso's *Guernica* (see Fig. 234, p. 438).

We now become aware that there are certain entirely new techniques used by the modern painter, such as Cubism (Picasso), Neoplasticism (Mondrian), Abstract Expressionism (Kandinsky, Alva), and many others, as well as equally new sculptural and architectural techniques (see Savoye House by Le Corbusier, Fig. 31, p. 48). In order to understand these things fully or even partially, we must make a special effort to see as many of the works as possible, to read about them, and, above all, to take it for granted that what is being shown usually is neither a hoax nor an attempt to subvert the spectator.

New Subject Matter

Modern art has its quota of new subject matter as well as new techniques. Traditional Western art up through the Renaissance had confined itself for the most part to religious subjects, battle scenes, portraits, and an occasional interval of genre and landscape interest, such as were found in the Hellenistic, Roman, and Medieval periods. During the post-Renaissance era, landscape—including seascape, cityscape, and so forth—became important in its own right (Poussin, Constable, and others). Genre painting also grew increasingly important (Chardin), as did the painting of manners and morals (Hogarth) and the political anecdotal painting or sculpture (Gros). These types of subject matter gained in response to the new needs of the period from the seventeenth to the nineteenth century and are clearly related to the life of their times.

From post-Impressionism—that is, from the 1880's to the present —when the artist's isolation from the body social became crucial, his art tended to divorce itself from direct social meaning. Even before this, the idea of "art for art's sake" had become prominent in the literature of the early nineteenth century. By the middle of that century, painters—especially Realists—were saying that any subject the artist painted was legitimate; by the last quarter of the century it was clear that *what* the artist painted was far less important than *how* he painted. Thus a still-life painting by a modern artist—Cézanne (Fig. 223, p. 405), for example—is an assemblage of objects combined artis-

Fig. 226. J. B. S. CHARDIN: *Supplies for Lunch*. New York, Metropolitan Museum of Art.

tically in an effective way because of form and color properties—that is, combined for "art's sake" rather than for symbolic, genre, or other reasons.

Such modern pictures may be contrasted with a traditional Dutch or French still life (Fig. 226, p. 415), in which an artist has seen a subject in a kitchen or elsewhere and has rearranged it in order to express a certain hominess, sadness, joy, or other emotional quality. The important thing is that the Dutch or French still life is related to a real life situation. The Cézanne is an arbitrarily composed group in which the artist has joined apples, a wine bottle, a napkin, biscuits, and other objects that really would not necessarily be found together in the working relationship that a traditional still-life picture presupposes.

A modern painter has described how he once watched Picasso sitting at table after lunch in a Paris restaurant. The great man absentmindedly put together a bit of bread, a matchstick, a fragment of

Fig. 226a. French School, XVIIth century: *The Card Players*. Cambridge, Massachusetts, The Fogg Museum of Art.

paper from his cigarette package, a tiny piece of meat—and what emerged was a Picasso composition!

In the same way, we may compare Cézanne's *Card Players* (Fig. 210a, p. 371) with any earlier card-playing subject, such as those found in the seventeenth century, in this instance, the Caravaggio-influenced *Card Players* (Fig. 226a, p. 416) of the French school. Once again Cézanne's emphasis is on monumentality of form and composition, which are the main interests of the modern painter; conversely, in the earlier work it is the activity or symbolic meaning of card playing itself that is important.

The subject matter of the modern artist—the painter and the sculptor—is subordinated to technical and esthetic considerations. Because he has been dissociated from the needs of the community, he is not constrained to go outside the studio for his subjects, to the homes of clients, to the church or palace. Although there are still many artists who show us the life of the streets, the athletic field, and so forth, there is a growing number of studio artists who do not have to leave the studio for their themes. The model comes (if the artist happens to be using a model) and is posed one day with a guitar, another day with a different object or costume—in other words, in some artistic disposition of forms, lines, and colors whose combined sensation the artist then tries to set down. If no model is used, the painter or sculptor may put together a conveniently shaped bowl, portrait bust, bottle, and something else that happens to be in the studio and that can be used in the manner indicated.

Nonobjective Art

In addition to studio subject matter (the ubiquitous guitar is found in so many studios and is a favorite of the Cubist painters), modern art has also developed a nonobjective approach—in other words, an art without objects. The Mondrian *Composition* (Fig. 33, p. 50) and the Kandinsky *Dreamy Motion* (Fig. 109, p. 181) can be taken to represent these nonspecific but nevertheless form-searching types of construction or feeling. To be sure, there have been earlier periods in the history of the world where subject matter has been rather thin, as with the art of the Moors in Spain. But in that kind of expression the aim of the artist was purely decorative, as in the arabesques of the mosques at Cordova; the same, however, cannot be said of the Mondrian and Kandinsky works.

It is interesting that most of us are quite willing to accept a work of art such as a carpet or a piece of pottery with purely decorative ornament rather than subject decoration, but we may be unwilling to accept the same kind of material within a picture frame. Something about the easel painting can bring out the most conservative reactions in spectators, as though there were a sacred and traditional quality about frames. We seldom realize that painting in its present form is only a few hundred years old and perhaps not entitled to such superstitious reverence. In any case, an entire area of art without subject matter—at least as applied to painting and sculpture—is something quite new and is bound to upset the more conventionally minded folk who look for anecdote or symbol.

Nonobjective art also includes other categories in addition to the geometric (Mondrian) or Abstract Expressionist (Alva, Kandinsky). There is the Abstract Surrealist (Arp, Fig. 91, p. 140; Masson, Miró, Matta, Gorky, and many others), whose purpose is to create the atmosphere or feeling of the dream world but without the use of the concrete forms retained by such Surrealists as Salvador Dali. The object (or subject matter) disappeared from the most "advanced" painting in the 1940's and 1950's, and it also removed itself from sculpture and the graphic arts, as in the sculpture of David Smith, Ibram Lassaw, Herbert Ferber, Nahum Gabo, and Antoine Pevsner and in the graphics of men like S. W. Hayter.

On the other hand, it would be extremely foolhardy for us to say that modern art concerns itself only with nonobjective formulations. We must distinguish between "modern" and "contemporary." The first applies to the various types of abstraction and nonrepresentationalism deriving from the post-Impressionists (Cézanne, Gauguin, van Gogh, Seurat) and the men of the pre-World War I generation (Cubists, Fauves, Expressionists, Futurists, and so on). "Contemporary" may apply to anything being created today, including the "modern" but also taking in the representational, more objective or concrete, forms that move in a realistic or naturalistic direction, for example, the Classical works of Picasso (see Fig. 231, p. 435), the socially oriented works of the Mexican school (Orozco, Siqueiros, Figs. 207 and 174, pp. 363, 307), and the regional works of contemporary Americans, such as Grant Wood and Thomas Hart Benton. All three of these figurative groups belong to the period since 1920, and yet they are far from "modern" in the sense of the Mondrian or the Kandinsky.

Between these two extremes we may place a whole group of works that are also considered "modern" but that are far more figurative than the Mondrian-Kandinsky type of production. These would include, among the works we have already seen, van Gogh, Matisse, Beckmann, and many others. They differ from the Benton-Wood style because they are partially and expressively distorted for emotional reasons and because they are distinctly part of a tradition stretching from the post-Impressionist period to our own times.

Just as we have appealed to the sense of tolerance in the consideration of avant-garde art, we must now ask for a certain amount of consideration in connection with representational forms of contemporary painting and sculpture. Recently, at least in the 1950's, these older modern techniques have been very much on the defensive against what has been called the intolerance of the most advanced—that is, nonrepresentational—artists. But there is no single way to express the spirit of a given period, especially in such an age as ours when there is a premium on individualism in art and when so many methods of expression are open to an artist. At a distance of some hundreds of years, the spirit of the High Renaissance, let us say, appears to express itself thoroughly and grandly in the typical Raphael-Michelangelo-del Sarto-Leonardo kind of work. But there were artists even in that epoch who cannot be pigeonholed quite so easily.

Above all, it was easy and even necessary then for art to be more or less directly related to the needs of the time. In our own age, we have the contrary situation where novelty is almost required, where the artist is far more self-taught than the earlier product of a workshop tradition; where, moreover, he has the wealth of the ages to draw upon —and we are bound to find more variety of expression. It may also be surmised that we are probably passing through a transitional period in art as in many other things.

The Effects of Technology

While a certain portion of the art world is now concerned with the newer ideas (the modern museums in the United States, France, Germany, Italy, Brazil, and other countries) there are many areas, as we have remarked, in which modern theories of art either are not known or are unwelcome. This condition is similar to that which exists in technology; it is possible for a four-engine passenger plane to land a stone's throw from the most primitive pueblo or village. Ultimately, one may expect that the varying parts of the world will be raised to higher technological—and artistic—levels. In today's world, ideological isolation becomes increasingly difficult, except within certain types of governments that delay the process of intellectual growth.

Technology has been an important factor in the dissemination of artistic thought ever since the invention of printing and the spread of art ideas from Renaissance Italy to the rest of Europe through the mechanism of the steel engraving. Later the etching, the mezzotint, aquatint, and lithograph enabled an artist in one country to know what was going on elsewhere. Today through newspapers, magazines, and books, many more people than before are in touch with new points of view.

A well-known artist living in the southwestern United States once remarked that the greatest influence on his art had been van Gogh. Asked where he had encountered examples of van Gogh, the answer very simply was: "In a magazine." Many art ideas have been transmitted in this way. The famous book written by Kandinsky in 1912, *Concerning the Spiritual in Art* (*Über das Geistige in der Kunst*), was translated into several European languages and into Japanese, resulting in the spread of his exceedingly advanced nonobjective concepts to different parts of the world. Similarly, increased ease of communication, travel, and other contacts makes it possible for Europeans and North Americans to participate fully in the important biennial exhibitions in Brazil, or for Australian and Canadian students to learn to use ethyl silicate, vinylite, and other new paint mediums from a Mexican painter.

Technological progress is also responsible for specific alterations in the form and content of modern art. In painting, techniques in the main have not altered appreciably since the Renaissance. An exception has been the mural movement of Mexico where impermeable plastic paints have been evolved (as above), which will not spoil under exposure to rain and sun.

The two areas in which technological progress has been most effective are sculpture and architecture. In the first, the development of various new media—aluminum, steel, wrought iron, and other materials, such as plastics—has meant a virtual revolution in the possibilities of sculpture. The relatively limited traditional conception of this art, depending on a process of either taking away or adding (as in marble-cutting or clay-modeling), has now given way to a new open concept of form. This has been made possible by the attenuations achievable in wrought iron and similar materials, or by a transparency that was never before conceivable but is now a reality through the use of plastic materials. These new forms are as valid as those produced by painting, although in the latter art the great changes have hardly anything to do with the medium—for even the ethyl-silicate murals are not radically new in esthetic form. With sculpture, however, the turn to the new materials has given us an art as nonobjective as that of Kandinsky or Mondrian in painting—imaginative or geometric as the case may dictate. But the new materials do not necessarily mean that the artist has to produce nonobjective sculpture; he may employ the materials for more objective and representational purposes—although, significantly enough, he has not for the most part done this.

In architecture, as we have seen, new materials and new technology have actually made the modern form possible. The esthetics of this architecture are naturally influenced by the materials, because these materials make possible certain shapes not otherwise feasible, as, for example, the cantilever seen in Frank Lloyd Wright's Johnson Wax Company Laboratory Tower (Figs. 75 and 75a, p. 116). Again, there are certain transparent effects owed to the use of glass brick, neon tubing, and so forth, as in the Johnson Wax Company Administration and Research Center (Figs. 61 and 66, pp. 95, 106). Some shapes of modern architecture are related esthetically to certain forms in painting, as we have seen in the comparison between the Mondrian *Composition* and the Le Corbusier house (Figs. 33 and 31, pp. 50, 48). This resemblance is not so much the result of functional considerations as the result of a general artistic climate during the 1930's.

The pervasiveness of the new materials has affected architecture particularly in the use of certain kinds of trim for the façades or even for the interiors, for example, the neon tubing utilized by Wright in the Johnson Wax Company Administration and Research Center, the shiny metal columns used by Miës van der Rohe in the interior of the Tugendhat House (Fig. 64, p. 101), and the striking color effects created through various new substances applied externally by the latter architect in more recent structures, especially for industry. Here again we may note the receptivity of the general public to the functional character of all these buildings, which, when transformed into sculpture or painting—let us say, in the kind of work represented by such Constructivists as Gabo and Pevsner—would cause (and has caused) considerable uneasiness on the part of the uninitiated spectator.

The benefits of technological progress are not necessarily all on the "plus" side. Just as advanced mass-production techniques generally make possible certain simplifications as well as vulgarizations in the industrial field, they can and have affected the artistic field as well. The most obvious instance is in sculpture, where for some time it has been possible to reproduce mechanically the clay or plaster model prepared by a master sculptor. In large-scale sculpture jobs—for example, in public buildings that demand a great deal of decorative relief work —we find the master sculptor preparing a series of working models from which his assistants, using a pointing machine, can transfer the proportions of the model to the finished stone. Artistically, such a process is about on the same level as a mezzotint by John Raphael Smith made after a portrait in oils by Reynolds. Unfortunately, the use of the pointing-machine method is fairly widespread and to that extent damaging. Yet, with the modern tempo (the desire for a quick and cheap job), this is often inevitable.

By the same token, the unwillingness and inability of young people to subject themselves to a long period of apprenticeship has meant the gradual disappearance of the skilled bronze-caster. Whether the decreasing demand for bronze has helped this or whether it was the other way around, large-scale bronze-casting appears to be dying out. Conversely it is possible for many artists who never could have afforded to work in bronze to turn to wrought iron and other welded sculpture, which can be managed with a small investment and where the popularity of free-form and spontaneous work has added to the interest.

Relationships of the Arts

The invention of new media and the development of new styles have only aggravated one crucial problem of the modern artist: how to establish a relationship between the basic art of architecture and those of sculpture and painting. The severe forms into which modern buildings have developed often have led their designers to believe that it would detract from their functional quality if they were embellished with sculptures and paintings. This is a serious departure from the practice up through the nineteenth century, when something was generally added to the building in the way of sculptural or pictorial ornament inside and out. Today this kind of ornamentation has become the exception rather than the rule, and it is only in the more traditionally designed building that there seems to be room for the other arts. But the modern painter or sculptor is not especially interested in decorating a conservative edifice, nor is he usually employed for such a task. In the more modern type of architectural design, it has been necessary to propagandize the designers into utilizing some small amount of the other arts.

The role of the industrial and applied arts in our time reflects, as does the role of architecture, the present character of the fine arts in general. This is not unusual, for history shows that this was also true in the time of the ancient Greeks or in the Renaissance; Greek pottery and Italian furniture reveal how closely they mirror the age in which they were made. The significant difference between those times and our own lies not in the relationship between applied arts and fine arts but rather in the introduction of methods of mass production, which necessarily change to a certain degree the quality of the original design. This happens partly because the product is machined rather than produced by hand and partly because the manufacturer may be unwilling or unable to use high-priced designing talent.

Industrial art can utilize and has utilized designers of very great ability in a variety of fields, and giant corporations are in a position financially to do so. But the requirements for a popularly designed automobile that will appeal to many people of limited taste are not quite the same as those demanded of a specialized item, such as fine textiles, furniture, or ceramics. By their very nature, the latter articles are not customarily aimed at the largest possible audience and can therefore expect more of their purchasers in the way of taste. We are constantly surprised (and not always pleasantly) by what Detroit turns out in the way of car designs; and conversely, we can look with far more artistic pleasure at a piece of well-designed glass or fabric. The regular exhibitions of useful objects prepared by such institutions as The Museum of Modern Art in New York give some idea of what can be done in this general area. Although we are using the term *designer* to indicate the planner of such forms, these are (or at least can be) craft arts on the same level as Renaissance iron work, majolica, or furniture.

The identical cars, home furnishings, furniture patterns, clothing styles for both men and women, and many other items that we continually see are the result of mass production and of the merchandising of these articles through mass publications with circulations in the millions. In contrast to this too-often uniform mediocrity of taste (which extends into entertainment and many other cultural areas), such a thing as the individually produced house is frequently quite superior in quality. Moreover, the independent design may differ quite markedly from one part of the country to the other.

For better or worse, and as a result of the difficult conditions of today's market for the fine artist, more and more so-called "fine artists" are turning to industrial and applied art. Where they are given an opportunity, this has been beneficial for both artist and client: it relates the artist to some tangible social need; and it may improve the quality of the client's product.

Political and Social Involvements

In times past, up to the nineteenth century, the overt social role of the artist, as we judge from the material seen earlier (see Chapter 11), was relatively limited. Although the artist often directly reflected the time in which he lived, his own participation in its events was necessarily restricted. Such men as Jan van Eyck and Peter Paul Rubens functioned as ambassadors for their respective kings; Michelangelo was military engineer for the city of Florence during a seige of the Republic; but this is about as close as artists in the past came to exercising any direct influence on the course of events.

In modern times, however—at least since the French Revolution of 1789—there do appear in increasing number artists who are more directly involved in the events of their time. Jacques-Louis David (1748–1825) was a member of the French Revolutionary Convention as well as official artist of the Revolution; Gustave Courbet (1819–1877) led a group of Parisians during the Commune that in 1871 pulled down that symbol of Napoleonic tyranny, the Vendôme Column. During the 1870's it became fashionable for the first time to accuse artists of subversion, particularly the then-advanced Impressionists. Of these, actually Degas was a confirmed Royalist, Cézanne was a practicing Roman Catholic, and the others were in varying degrees concerned with nothing but painting and getting their works into exhibitions. Among the entire group only Pissarro was in any way politically minded—a fairly common average for a group in any field. During the following decade or two, those opposed to advanced art (next it was post-Impressionism) used the designation *anarchists*.

At the end of World War I, in Germany, Mexico, and the new Soviet Russia, the artist emerged for the first time as a real social factor. In Germany, the Workers Council for Art, a product of the German Revolution of 1918, functioned for a brief time, as did the active modernists in Russia who proclaimed in vivid declamatory accents that the "new world" had arrived.

Mexico, whose Revolution against oppression had lasted from 1910 to 1920, produced a crop of artists who played a direct role not only in the intellectual side of that upheaval but also in the military events themselves. Orozco was military artist for a Carranza regiment, while Siqueiros at the tender age of fifteen was already a member of the so-called *Batallón Mama*. The revolt of Mexican students at the Academy of San Carlos against the old-fashioned academic European teaching of that day was among the sparks that ignited the Revolution. When the struggle was over in 1920, many artists were employed by the government to do murals on the walls of public buildings to celebrate both the accomplishments and the ideals of the Revolution.

Although traditional European artists' guilds had begun to disappear by the sixteenth century, to be replaced gradually by the academies of the seventeenth and eighteenth centuries (which set the new standards), the nineteenth century saw the formation of artists' groups or societies. Some were purely artistic, such as the Impressionists and the later exhibiting organs: the *Section d'Or* (Cubists), Fauves, *Brücke,* and Blue Rider. Others were more specifically social, such as the already-mentioned German Workers Council for Art (a group to bring together art and society) or the Mexican Syndicate of Technical Workers, Painters, and Sculptors. The latter was a kind of trade union that dealt with the government and protected the interests of the artists.

The degree to which the modern artist has been separated from society and placed more or less at the mercy of business has not only forced him into isolation with his various abstract styles but has also forced him in some cases to organize into self-protecting and self-helping groups. Although the general public seldom hears of some of these organizations, they are extremely important in bringing their members together for social, exhibition, and other purposes. Some have functioned as part of the political situation of our times; but whether socially oriented or entirely esthetic in purpose, the increasing number of such organizations underlines the economic and esthetic plight of the modern artist—his curious, sometimes increasing, sometimes decreasing isolation in the past century and a half.

▶ 18

The Evolution of a Major Modern Artist

IN THE EVOLUTION of a traditional artist, such as Michelangelo, we were able to see a comparatively close relationship between the artist and his time. We observed, for example, how the Medici tombs were the sculptor's partial response to the unsettled political situation of that time and his own helplessness before it. Later, the *Last Judgment* on the far wall of the Sistine Chapel represented Michelangelo's reaction to the disorientation of the Counter-Reformation period in Italy. It is possible to say, then, that such an artistic development is integrally a part of the sixteenth century, because the artist was working directly for a leading religious body and for important merchant princes and political figures.

In the evolution of the typical modern artist, such as Picasso, we can also see certain clear reflections of his time. However, to the degree that he is not working for governments and institutions but for museum and gallery exhibitions, for the ultimate private, upper-middle-class art lover who uses the object of art as a higher form of entertainment or social prestige, his art is less directly based on our times. Thus the style of the modern artist generally will develop in a less logical and organic way than that of the traditional artist like Michelangelo, Rubens, Giotto, Rembrandt, and those whose work had to be directly answerable to public demand, standards of the era, and similar circumstances. Where the traditional artist was a responsible citizen creating an art often on view before the world, the modern artist is an outsider. What he creates is either for himself or for the special and limited art world.

426

Traditional versus Modern Artistic Development

In the development of a traditional artist we can very often detect the change from an early and tentative manner—during which the young practitioner was absorbing the influences of the past and those of his immediate environment—to a more assured and original level that characterized his major contribution. He might continue on the second level or might go on to a philosophical, contemplative, mystic, or some other manifestation in later years of greater mental maturity and ripeness. Socially, he had emerged from the shelter of the workshop of the master who trained him into the stream of competition between workshops or masters whose ranks he had now joined. The existence of a guild of artists had restricted the numbers who could become masters, at the same time that it had set certain standards to which the artist was forced to conform—both by custom and by actual contract. Furthermore, his relationship with the client had been direct (at least until the end of the seventeenth and the beginning of the eighteenth century), without the intermediary efforts of an art dealer.

Finally, since everything needed for the well-to-do home had been designed by one of these master craftsmen and manufactured by hand, the relationship between the artist and the everyday world of furniture, pottery, jewelry, and many other "useful" things was a real one. The applied arts and the so-called "fine arts" having much in common, the artist could think without any embarrassment of planning some utilitarian object needed for a wedding, festival, birth present, hope chest, and so on, because such things had always been part of the craftsman's job. For these many and differing reasons, the traditional artist was a part of his time in a sense difficult for us to comprehend today.

The development of a contemporary master, as we have noted, is not so integrated into the fabric of modern society. It becomes rather difficult for us to mark out various artistic stages as part of a logical form evolution, unless we are familiar with the twists and turns in the modernist's style. Compared with the changes in Michelangelo (see Chapter 15), the complicated evolution of Picasso—to choose the best known modern master—is difficult to follow. This fact is important largely as an indication that the artist is not working for society in general but for a small segment thereof. Although it is true that the traditional artist also worked for the educated classes, far more of his work was exhibited to the general public for one reason or another than is the case in our own times. For the most part, the work of modern artists since the latter part of the nineteenth century has been produced for the very small public that reads the art magazines and goes to the galleries. Instead of having to speak a more-or-less public language, the modern artist speaks an increasingly esoteric tongue not geared to or meant for the average person.

The development of even such an outstanding master as Kokoschka shows the importance of publicity, of getting a dealer to handle his work, of a changing vogue, and of other factors that have little or nothing to do with art as such. A modernist will necessarily start with a given style derived from his teacher, from some interesting (to him) style in the museum, or from an existing trend with which he may be in sympathy. After a while he may reverse himself and start off on a new tack, either through boredom or the power of some new fashion or the example of an overwhelming artistic personality (like Cézanne or Kandinsky) or the circumstance that improved means of communication have made so many styles available. For the average art student, the choice of style may be a genuine problem; often it is confusing and discouraging, and only the wisest teacher can guide him in this question.

A period such as ours, seen at close range, with its multiplicity of styles and substyles, is bewildering to the outsider—that is, the non-art-loving public. To some extent this confusion was also true in the past, although from this distance a number of leading tendencies seem to have crystallized rather neatly for each epoch. Today we have what appears to be a far richer diversity of stylistic approaches, not only between artist and artist but also between the early work of an artist and his own subsequent about-faces and back-and-forth movements.

The case of Kandinsky is characteristic of the lack of direct relationship to the world at large and the substitution of a loyalty to the art world, a world unto itself where the critics establish what standards there are and where tradition as such plays a minor role. Here we must distinguish between the desperately lonely role of the artist in the middle and late nineteenth century, in the face of antagonistic critics and public, and the position of the artist in our own time. Such a contemporary modernist as Beckmann in the twentieth century still has no general public in the sense that Giotto or Michelangelo did, and many aspects of his work are unknown to the public at large. But he does have an intelligent minority on his side, a group with both taste and money; these people are drawn to him by the equally intelligent efforts of a dealer who, in his role of intermediary, makes them aware of a new talent. Even those who cannot afford to buy can afford to read about this talent, go to see his work, buy a color print, and otherwise partake on their own economic and intellectual level.

The painting or sculpture becomes a form of art merchandise to be used for enjoyment and prestige purposes, fashioning an individualistic role for the modern artist. He may now be expected to produce a typical Henry Moore, Derain, or Rouault, so that the client gets his money's worth. But because the artist rather than society is the determinant of what goes into the art, he can and often does create a norm or vogue after which both other artists and the art public run in droves.

Pablo Picasso

In considering the various ramifications of Picasso's style changes, we must keep in mind the fact that no one else in modern times has made so many shifts as he or had so many successes either; but his case will dramatize our principle. Pablo Picasso (1881–   ) is the son of a Spanish drawing master. He became interested in art as a child of ten and put up his first exhibition at the age of sixteen in Barcelona. In 1900, he paid his first visit to Paris but soon after returned home. Picasso's style at this point was related to nineteenth-century Realism, for example, Steinlen. The following year he visited Paris again and became interested in the modern movement, first through the Impressionists (see Monet, Fig. 221, p. 403) and then through the works of Gauguin, van Gogh, Toulouse-Lautrec, Vuillard, Denis, and so forth. The latter group combined in their work the emotional side of the post-Impressionist movement and the tortuousness of the Symbolism of the late nineteenth and early twentieth century.

From 1901 to 1904 Picasso went through what is known as his Blue Period. In these works, the melancholy of the Symbolist painters (particularly Toulouse-Lautrec) and the elongations of El Greco's mystical figures play a considerable role (see *Absinthe Drinker*, Fig. 227,

Fig. 227. PABLO PICASSO: *Absinthe Drinker*. New York, formerly Gershwin Collection.

p. 430). Where Toulouse-Lautrec used a harsh green to achieve some of his mournfulness, Picasso adopts a kind of bluish green whose saddening quality is quite in keeping with the nature of his subject matter: prostitutes, drinkers, poor mothers, blind beggars, and the like. During this early period of his life in Paris he was desperately poor. He got to know such writers as Max Jacob with whom he shared a room—at night Jacob slept while Picasso painted; during the day the painter slept in turn.

The circus pictures that followed were a similar combination of mannered elongations and mysticism, but tinged with pink—the Rose Period. During the next two years or so, Picasso turned to a more serene, less strained style in which the breadth of expression of nineteenth-century Classicism (for example, Puvis de Chavannes) is mingled with the more lyrical aspects of the art of Paul Gauguin. Occasionally, the references to Classicism are quite strong (1906), almost Greek in quality. Life at this time was still very difficult, and even though he sold an occasional picture to the dealer Vollard, things were by no means easy, however interesting and exciting the milieu of Bohemian Paris.

According to Picasso, his change to a more sculpturesque form was

430   THE EVOLUTION OF A MAJOR MODERN ARTIST

Fig. 228. PABLO PICASSO: *Grande Danseuse*. New York, Collection Walter P. Chrysler, Jr.

influenced by ancient Iberian (pre-Roman Spanish peninsular) sculpture and resulted in works that were very archaistic, for example, the famous *Gertrude Stein* portrait of 1906. A number of paintings done during that year would confirm this Iberian influence in their heavy, stiff quality. At the same time, a great sensation was caused by the Fauve exhibition of 1905 in which Matisse, Vlaminck, Derain, Friesz, and others participated. Their disavowal of nature and their interest in primitive and exotic cultures next led Picasso (and many others) toward African sculpture. In addition, at the *salon* where the Fauves caused their sensation, there was a place reserved for ten paintings by Cézanne. The year following this event, ten more Cézannes were shown, and in 1907, the year after the great artist's death, at a giant memorial show fifty-six of his pictures were exhibited.

Grande Danseuse (1907, Fig. 228, p. 431) indicates Picasso's growing interest in artistic problems for their own sake rather than in the expression of a literary and anecdotal pathos, as in the earlier *Absinthe Drinker* (Fig. 227, p. 430). Where in the immediately preceding pictures Picasso emphasized a squat heaviness of the figures, he now turned to an angular, almost weightless type of form that (like the bathers in the later paintings of Cézanne) is closely related to the background of the picture with little evident space intervening. The face is no longer a face; it is a mask, as in African sculpture, with violently carved-out planes. Both the African and the Cézannesque elements are here useful to Picasso. The former gives him a simplicity of form and angular planes that, in crossing each other, create a new dynamic and yet tense, restricted space quality; the latter injects a new limited—that is, background into foreground—space relationship. In *Grande Danseuse* a curtain at the right, the figure itself, and the background become inextricably mixed from the spatial point of view, carrying one step further the process begun by Cézanne in the 1880's and 1890's (see Figs. 210a and 223, pp. 371, 405).

After a short interval of artistic hesitation, Picasso evolved during 1909–1912 what is known as Analytical Cubism (see *Violin*, Fig. 224, p. 406). Just as the Impressionists of the 1870's had attempted to analyze the effect of light as it twinkled across a given surface, the Cubists led by Picasso (and Braque) tried to approximate the appearance of form movement. The idea of *simultaneity*—that is, of seeing various aspects of an object at the same time—has been referred to earlier in connection with Cubism (see above, p. 407). Such Cubist pictures as *Violin* give the effect of a kaleidoscope of visualization in which the artist has stepped into the picture space through the frame and walked around the object. Thus he has picked for his composition various aspects of the violin that met his eye—the strings, the scroll, the sides of the instrument—and has rearranged them into this oval composition.

The next phase of Picasso's art, Synthetic Cubism, lasted, with interruptions and variations as indicated below, until about 1923. This new type of simultaneous vision involves a much more arbitrary visualization of the object in which, instead of simulating the process of walking around the object, the painter merely chooses in a purely compositional manner a number of aspects that seem interesting from the point of view of their form or color, as in the *Mardi Gras* (or *The Three Musicians*) of 1921 (Fig. 229, p. 433). Here the emphasis is on

Fig. 229. PABLO PICASSO: *Mardi Gras* (*The Three Musicians*), 1921. New York, The Museum of Modern Art.

decorative quality rather than on space penetration, although the element of form suggestion is quite clear. Color is far stronger than before, while two-dimensional movement within the limited space between the background and the front plane has increased greatly.

The various interruptions during this development include a series of "realistic" portraits during 1914–1915 and the Russian ballet costumes, curtains, and similar work of the 1917 period in Rome. These two phases enclose the war years, whose effect on Picasso (as on many other artists, but not all) does not seem too important—perhaps because he was a Spaniard and therefore not directly involved. Picasso continued to work with the sophisticated theater group in 1919–1921 also.

During the 1920's, Europe in general was affected by a revulsion against the excesses of the earlier modern styles. Together with the lassitude of the immediate postwar years, this brought about a Classical revival in several countries. Picasso's neo-Classicism was now much more specific than his earlier tentative efforts in this direction around 1905. A good many of his "Classical" works of the 1920's have a ponderousness of form and static quietness of mood. *The Race* (Fig. 230, p. 434), with its stunning blue background, sets the giantesses in motion running across the sands in a strange, almost Surrealist-tinged ec-

Fig. 230. PABLO PICASSO: *The Race.* Owned by the artist. (Photo courtesy The Museum of Modern Art)

stasy of fear. Used in enlarged form as a curtain for the Diaghilev ballet *Le train bleu,* its heaviness afforded an effective contrast to the charmingly light spectacle of seaside athletic activities. Between this work and such monumentally reserved and Classicistic pictures as *Woman in White* (Fig. 231, p. 435) of the following year, Picasso continued to do Synthetic Cubist works, including the already-noted *Three Musicians.* The serene and ultimately genuinely Classical *Woman in White* is only another facet of Picasso's neo-Classicism in one of his richest and most productive periods, which included, besides others, such widely differing creations as this one, *The Race,* and the beautifully linear and chaste drawings for Ovid's *Metamorphoses.*

In the next phase of his development from 1923 on (and for many years to come), we find Picasso taking the angular Synthetic Cubism of the *Three Musicians* and giving it a decorative but now curvilinear form, as in the well-known *Red Tablecloth* and other such paintings. This did not prevent him, however, from returning occasionally to the earlier angular Cubism. Running parallel with the Curvilinear Cubism is a new and increasingly emotive kind of "disquieting" or "convulsive" Cubism—here we employ words frequently used by the already-existing Surrealist group of the 1920's whose Manifesto had appeared shortly before such pictures as the well-known *Three Dancers* (Fig. 232, p. 436). With their accent on the fear-evoking and the abnormal, the nightmarish and the frightening, these inaugurate a very important period in the artist's life.

Picasso's own metamorphoses (*c.*1927–1930) may be related to the work of the younger and more abstract Surrealists of that day, for instance, Miró and Tanguy, but they are also an important source of inspiration for the sculpture of many artists in the quarter-century that followed, such as Moore, Lipchitz, and others. Their basic idea is the emergence of one form from another, unreality heaped on unreality, figures that suggest some primordial state of existence, creatures from a strange and unknown planet.

Around 1931, Picasso varied his Curvilinear Cubist method to include a series of strong black outlines and produced what is known as his Stained Glass Cubism, exemplified by the famous painting in The Museum of Modern Art, New York, *Girl Before a Mirror*. While continuing this style, he also turned out a number of interesting sculptures, many influenced by the earlier metamorphic forms and others like the widely known *Le Grand Coq* (Fig. 233, p. 437), a rich, pulsating, and slightly disquieting combination of heavy curving forms. A new series of neo-Classical etchings, 1930–1936, mark a high point in poetic sensuality.

By 1934, he had begun to work with bullfight subjects after a visit

Fig. 231. PABLO PICASSO: *Woman in White,* 1923. New York, Metropolitan Museum of Art.

to his home city of Barcelona. These add a note hitherto visible only
in the background of his thoughts, an Expressionistic violence of mood,
a horror-struck quality that prefigures quite clearly the accents of
Guernica (of 1937, Fig. 234, p. 438). This latter work is a monochromatic combination of Expressionism, Surrealism, and Cubism. It
resulted from the painter's angry reaction to the bombing of the de-
fenseless Basque city of Guernica by the German air force operating
for General Franco. Here Picasso brings together the fear-evoking
qualities of the Surrealist nightmare, the violent emotivity of the Expressionist search for inner meaning, and the highly appropriate frag-
mentation of form of his own Cubism. Perhaps no painting of our time
has summed up so forcefully the sadism and brutality of that period,
which seemed so inhuman and insane to the Spaniard Picasso.

What especially distinguishes some of the forms in this and Picasso's
works during the next few years is the deliberate twisting of a head
so that its two eyes and two sides can be seen at once. This differs essentially from the early Cubist procedure in which the artist more or

less arbitrarily selected different perspective views of one object. The new twisting of form toward the spectator gives an unusual quality of violence to the painter's potential expressiveness. It is, however, applied later to works whose meaning seems decorative rather than violent, although it is hard to look at some of the pictures of the late 1930's without a slight emotional tremor, especially when these distortions are accompanied by a van Goghlike atonality of color.

From 1940 to the end of the war period—that is, to 1945–1946, Picasso's painting returns to a relatively flat type of expression, brilliantly colorful and curvilinear in outline and purpose, twisted in perspective like the earlier "two-faced" figures. A high point of his sculpture is arrived at with the monumentally expressive and moody *Man with a Lamb* (1944, Fig. 235, p. 439). Here again it is difficult to find any clear association between the artist and the greatest war in history, difficult to see where it touches his art. His life in Paris under the Nazis was, of course, far from pleasant, and the outstanding proponent of modernism suffered from incredible annoyances, more from collaborationists trying to curry favor with the occupying power than from the Germans themselves. Beyond this, however, his presence in Paris during those bitter years was a constant inspiration to intellectuals who saw in him a symbol of free expression. For his firmness against the Nazis, Picasso was the featured artist at the *Salon de la Libération* in 1944, but this event brought an anti-Picasso demonstration, in part be-

Fig. 233. PABLO PICASSO: *Le grand coq* (bronze; 1932). New York. Collection Peter Watson.

Fig. 234. PABLO PICASSO: *Guernica*. Owned by the artist. (Photo courtesy The Museum of Modern Art)

cause the artist had just declared his membership in the Communist Party.

Since the end of World War II other discernible stylistic changes have appeared in the various media practiced by Picasso. He has been especially active in the graphic arts and in the field of ceramics. *Red and White Owl* (1953, Fig. 236, p. 439) demonstrates his feeling for the latter medium with its colorful and textural possibilities. In the graphic area he has gone off into many different types of expression, one of the most interesting being a style of lithography very close in two-dimensional form and spirit to the Paleolithic cave paintings of eastern Spain.

His paintings during the immediate postwar period represent continuations and relatively mild variations of the style just before that period—that is, strongly contoured but spiky forms with double faces and van Gogh color dissonances. By the end of the 1940's, he turned to a more lyrical, imaginative, and poetically colorful version of this style with the emphasis on elaborate allegory in large, violet-tinted compositions. A major exhibition of Picasso's painting held in Rome during the summer of 1953 revealed not merely another style but a wealth of styles that had not been seen before, except by those who were fortunate enough to know his studio. One of the most unusual notes in this magnificent sequence of works was a series of Romantic-

Fig. 235 (left). PABLO PI-CASSO: *Man with a Lamb*, 1944. Philadelphia, Pennsylvania, Collection R. Sturgis Ingersoll. Fig. 236 (right). PABLO PICASSO: *Red and White Owl* (ceramic; 1953). Paris, Galerie Louise Leiris.

Expressionist landscapes dating from this postwar period, pictures of a bitter poetry and twisted, heart-rending form. The great 1957 show at The Museum of Modern Art in New York marked the climax of his fame in the United States.

For something like sixty years, Picasso has gone from one style to another, absorbing and taking for his own whatever he needed for his artistic purposes. He has been influenced by contemporary movements but has raised them all to a newer and fresher level than before.

Although Picasso's problem of making a living was solved in great measure at an early point in his career (1907–1908) by a dealer, Kahn-weiler, who had enough confidence in the artist to back him by making regular purchases of his work and promoting them, his relationship to the public at large was not solved. For some time, his chief customers were rich foreigners, such as the Russian Tschoukine who began to buy Picasso around 1907; publisher-dealers, such as Vollard who used him for book illustration; or the Ballet Russe de Monte Carlo with its scenic and costume problems. With the birth of the Weimar republic in 1919, various German museums bought his pictures and those of other modern artists, until the advent of the Nazis in 1933.

Compared to most modern artists, Picasso, in spite of his appeal to a relatively small group of art lovers, has had phenomenal success financially. But this must be contrasted with the lack of financial success of so many others until relatively late in their careers—particularly in the countries where dealers will not take chances on artists in the same way that Kahnweiler took the risk he did with Picasso.

All this apart, however, the thesis we set out to illustrate—the relatively abrupt, personal, and inorganic development of the modern painter after a certain point—would seem to be clear. That it is part of his indirect rather than close relationship to the times also seems evident. Two world wars do not appear as such in Picasso's work, either in style or subject matter. The only overt contemporary reference is the *Guernica* of 1937 which is the reaction of a patriotic Spaniard. In 1945, Picasso was working on a mural project called *Charnel House,* to show the inhumanities of the Nazis against the Jews in concentration camps, but apparently never got beyond the sketch stage.

An elaborate pair of allegorical canvases entitled *Peace* and *War* (1949–1950) arise from the painter's new-found interest in left-wing politics. They reflect the pressures upon him of his recent associations rather than those stemming from his own development as an artist. Painted a number of years after World War II, with neither the immediacy of the earlier *Guernica* nor its personal appropriateness, these works remain almost his sole latter-day excursion into social contemporaneity.

The modern artist by his special position vis-à-vis society, by what has been called his dislocation, and by the limited and artificial nature of his patronage is necessarily concerned with his own soul and with artistic rather than mundane problems; this is the way he must behave. Our account of Picasso's style changes is not to be taken as criticism. It is, rather, evidence of the modern artist's flexible approach and the measure of the difference between him and the artist of the past.

▶PART VI
Evaluating the Art Object

▶19

The Approach to
Standards of Judgment

HOW DO WE judge a work of art qualitatively, even in general terms —or is everyone his own judge? Can the criticism of art be considered a skill in itself (surely it is not a science), or is the untrained layman just as qualified to pass judgment?

The professional activity of experts who at least can judge the genuineness or falsity of a given work of art argues the existence of some sort of standard by means of which the expert determines the provenance of the work—that is, its origin and source, its period and authorship. For this discernment the layman pays the art expert a more or less standard fee, just as he pays for medical, legal, or other professional advice. The art expert attains his ability to identify a painting, print, or other object from years of professional contact with such works. To some extent he can verbalize his judgment, tell us in so many words about the background of the work and why he feels it is genuine or not—just as the physician can state his diagnosis. The art expert will say, for example, that the features of a Madonna are too coarse to have been done by Raphael or that the proportion of the legs to the rest of the body does not conform to a certain norm. This is akin to the physician's enumeration of the symptoms that contribute to his diagnosis.

Beyond such details lies the total experience of the expert or the physician in which a similar or identical combination of factors has presented itself many times and which, therefore, leads each man, respectively, to say that the picture is false or that the patient is suffering from a certain illness. Although these judgments often appear to be intuitive, they are only remotely so; they are the product of experience as well as of the operation of a subconscious logic that results from training. When the physician orders a patient to bed, the ill man follows his advice; when an art expert tells the prospective purchaser of a painting that the work is questionable, the would-be buyer customarily does not purchase it. (Both patient and buyer, of course, may look for a second opinion.)

When, however, the art critic (not the gallery or auction expert) makes the statement that an artist is important (or insignificant), scores of would-be critics among laymen are perfectly willing to contradict him on the basis that their opinions are as good as his. Where no one (or hardly anyone) would dispute the judgment of authenticity made by the recognized expert on Old Masters, countless people will dispute the quality judgments of the critic of contemporary art. Such disputes are clearly not the same as varying opinions among critical colleagues, whose judgments stem from a thorough knowledge of contemporary art and artists acquired from daily contact over a long period of time. The fact that critics may disagree, however, does not necessarily permit the layman to assume that this reduces the entire problem of judgment to a matter of opinion—any more than it would in some other field. Unless there is direct evidence to the contrary, the layman may assume that the critic through his long experience knows more and is therefore in a better position to make a judgment.

Building a Value Judgment

In the course of this book, we have seen that each culture sets up its own standards by which its works may conceivably be rated successful or unsuccessful. Disregarding the accidents of social connections, wealth, and influence that may bring a man to the fore in a given period, we know that a particular era does have a standard (or series of standards) that will affect the status of an artist. Past standards, as we have tried to show, are not ours today; contrariwise, our preferences or prejudices cannot be applied to the works of an earlier age. Here is a two-way street with barricades at both ends: we cannot judge Raphael in terms of Picasso or the RCA Building in terms of the Parthenon.

The critics as well as the experts may deduce the standards of a period by careful study of the chief works of that time or critical statements made by contemporaries of the artists involved—where such statements exist. In this way, we can discover certain positive criteria for each age, even though our taste today may be considerably different. For example, eighth-century T'ang painting, with its poetic meaning, with its own set of canons, and without the kind of spatial content to which we are accustomed, must be judged by its own rules, which it clearly has according to Chinese literature of the past, and not by our current standards. To do otherwise would be comparable to criticizing a Chinese for speaking his own language instead of English.

Within these separate areas of taste—that is, areas of period taste—we find that the ideals of artistic excellence or quality are not always achieved. There are variations between Watteau and Lancret in eighteenth-century France or between Rembrandt and his followers in seventeenth-century Holland. Just as it is possible for us to perceive that there are more or less successful painters in those eras, we can ascertain that there are more or less successful works by one artist.

At the same time, however, a specific period may—and often does—produce several different trends. This is illustrated by the fact that, while we may make general comparisons between such painters as Vermeer and Terborch during the Dutch seventeenth century (see Figs. 32 or 162, 13 or 237, pp. 50, 286, 25, 446), the paintings of Rembrandt fall entirely outside the Vermeer-Terborch category and must be judged on a different basis.

But such an artist as Rembrandt may also be evaluated comparatively—in terms of the imitators of the master (where they exist, as in Rembrandt's case) or in terms of the man's own unique accomplishments. Fortunately for the possibilities of arriving at an estimate, no artist springs full-grown from the head of Jove (except possibly for the untaught primitives). He is part of a tradition, and, since his craft has been learned somewhere, it becomes possible to gauge the young Rembrandt in relation to his sources or the early El Greco, van Gogh, or Picasso in relation to theirs. The later or mature Rembrandt will have to be weighed by the standard that he has created for himself and that is his distinctive contribution to the arts. Because we know that an artist often sets himself special problems in a specific kind of experimental work, we are aware that all Rembrandt or El

Greco paintings are not equally successful—or equally genuine, for that matter. Only long and constant acquaintance with the particular master's work will bring out these relative values.

In such critical assessment, it is only reasonable to assume that the average layman, however sensitive he may be or claim to be, is at a certain disadvantage without the knowledge, background, and sheer familiarity that the professionally trained and experienced person brings to critical analysis. This lack of knowledge surely does not exclude the layman from enjoyment of the work of art on his own personal level, and no one questions that he can be helped toward a broader and deeper enjoyment and understanding.

The Artist Related to a Standard of His Period

If, for example, we were to attempt to appraise Terborch's *The Concert* (Fig. 237, p. 446), a Dutch work of the seventeenth century, we would first have to determine to some extent the painter's relationship to that period as a whole. If we compare him with the great Vermeer, as in the latter's *Young Woman with a Water Jug* and in his *Lady with a Lute* (see Figs. 32 and 162, pp. 50, 286), Vermeer seems generally concerned with establishing a series of parallel planes within the picture space. These planes are parallel to the main horizontal line of the picture frame itself. Terborch, if we may judge from *The Concert* and similar works, seems concerned with creating a more extensive and diagonal space conception in which certain elements are so placed as to lead the eye out of the picture at an angle. Here the spinet, the cello, the chair on which the woman sits, the angle of her body, and the draping of her dress across the chair—all move in that direction. If we were to sum up Terborch's procedures, we would perhaps say he emphasized angularity of perspective and textural quality of fabrics, wood, glass, and so on.

Vermeer also is interested in textural qualities, as in the *Young Woman with a Water Jug*, but these are less an end in themselves and far less obtrusive than in the Terborch work. In Vermeer, texture is subordinate to the effect of the work as a whole. As for space and perspective effects, here also there are basic differences in viewpoint and organization. Vermeer's treatment of space may be more fully understood when compared with that of Mondrian, his twentieth-cen-

Fig. 237. GERARD TERBORCH: *The Concert*. Berlin, State Museums.

tury countryman (see Fig. 33, p. 50), in whom we also find a rigid geometry of square or rectangle overlapping other squares or rectangles, the latter shifted slightly and altered in proportion, as with the earlier artist. Both Vermeer and Mondrian work inside the self-prescribed limits of a relatively narrow space within which the entire action takes place. This tight relationship between the forms and their surrounding space helps to set up the tensions that are often the chief effect or essence of the picture.

To this degree, and in this sense, we may perhaps say that the aims of Vermeer are essentially somewhat more subtle and concentrated than those of Terborch with his interests in (1) surface effects of tactile or touch values, and (2) the more obvious and spectacular diagonal reaching for infinite space. Moreover, Vermeer's women are the hub or meeting point of all the movement in their pictures; Terborch's people help to create the outward drive.

We may say, then, that although this branch of Dutch painting is generally interested in geometrical space definition, textural effects, and open rather than closed compositions (also illumination that causes objects to cast reflections on each other), the fact remains that within this general style complex the two artists show certain clearly defined differences. To that extent, it becomes somewhat difficult to compare one with the other, except in the general way we have seen.

The Artist Related to His Own Aims

We turn, therefore, to another Terborch to compare it with *The Concert*, the *Girl Reading* (Fig. 238, p. 447). In both works, in addition to the very strong touch quality of objects, we can see clear evidences of the painter's interests in a diagonally moving space, in lines carrying us out of the picture at an angle. Neither work shows concentration on the main figure as a receiving point for movements

Fig. 238. GERARD TERBORCH: *Girl Reading.* Von Pannwitz Collection. (Photo courtesy Rosenberg and Stiebel, New York)

inward as the Vermeer does. Both of Terborch's pictures use the people as vehicles for movement outward. In *The Concert,* the white satin dress fills the left-hand corner and takes us out in two directions, as do the arm and the head of the cello. The spinet lid and the painting on the wall to which it is attached visually perform the same function in that direction, while the strong color accent of the picture on the left carries the eye to the left.

Having established the relationship of the two Terborchs to each other and their differences from Vermeers, we may try to compare the Terborchs qualitatively. One of the most important distinctions between them lies in the proportion of the human beings to the space. In the *Girl Reading,* the trim little figure plays a very effective role. Not only does it act as a starting point for the typical diffusion of movement (to its chair, the table, and to the wall map), but it fits quite comfortably into the space within the work. In *The Concert,* however, there is a certain ambiguity in the way the cellist dominates the clearly limited space within the painting, her arm coming somehow under the spinet and her head apparently reaching to the same plane as the front corner of that instrument. Thus she is not presented in true or effective proportion to the spinet or to the accompanist behind that instrument.

The other woman, in a violet-colored bodice that is designed to take her away from us, does not appear to fit comfortably into the space assigned to her. Indeed, the upper part of her body gives the feeling of having been cut off or of representing some sort of sculptured bust sitting on top of the spinet. The portrayed distance between the two women does not justify the sharp alteration in scale between them. The lines of the floor tiles, which add to the feeling of space in Vermeer's *Young Woman with a Water Jug* (Fig. 32, p. 50) or in the works of any other artist of the period including Terborch, do not seem to have come off too well in this instance.

In the light of these simple points of difference between the two Terborch pictures, it is possible for us to say that the artist fulfilled his aims of space and proportion in *Girl Reading* but not in *The Concert.* Concerning the general impression made on the spectator by these two works, here again we can say that there is a simplicity and concentration of effect in the former, while the latter tends to mix up its constituent parts and bring about a certain visual confusion.

The Artist Absorbing the Influence of a Great Master

Obviously it is possible for an artist to have a bad day or even a bad year. It is also true in periods like our own, when serious changes are taking place in the art world or when certain personalities (Picasso, for example) dominate style, that it takes many other artists a long time to grow into their own skins. This difficulty is illustrated by the Italian Renaissance painter Raphael, some of whose works have already been discussed. Here was a man endowed with a wonderfully serene temperament, who would eventually be able to bestow on his figures a nobility of manner and strength of form characteristic of the Renaissance period in general. His greatest strength as an artist was apparently to be achieved on the basis of gentle, even sentimental expression. The storm and strife of Michelangelo was essentially not Raphael's kind of thing; his chief effectiveness as an artist would lie in the realm of gentle dignity and quiet emotional projection within the framework of a deep-extending space, as in the *School of Athens* (Fig. 151c, p. 269) or the *Alba Madonna* (Fig. 16, p. 28).

When, however, in 1507, he set out to paint the *Entombment* (Fig. 239, p. 450), Raphael was still under the strong influence of Michelangelo, and the latter's emotional power simply overwhelmed him in this work. We observe a straining for effect in the way the two men carry or pretend to carry the body of the Christ, an unnecessary degree of muscularity that underlines the "overacting" of the work in general. In the interest of setting the human body in motion, Raphael shows the woman at the extreme right kneeling, her knees toward the spectator, the upper part of the form turned away to enable her to receive the fainting body of the Virgin in her arms, an entirely unnecessary and unconvincing piece of physical melodrama.

But we must keep in mind that Michelangelo's influence was at work. What the twenty-four-year-old Raphael had done was to borrow the slight figure of the Christ from the great sculptor's *Pietà* (Fig. 211a, p. 377), but Raphael's form certainly does not need the amount of tugging and hauling that appears here. In the same way, Raphael had taken the idea of a kneeling woman with twisted body from Michelangelo's *Holy Family*, or *Doni Madonna* (Florence, Uffizi Gallery) painted *c.*1504. However, where the earlier work shows the Madonna taking over her shoulder the form of the little Jesus, Raphael

Fig. 239. RAPHAEL: *Entombment*. Rome, Borghese Gallery.

presents a thoroughly improbable act in which a woman in this position supposedly holds the heavy, fainting body of an adult.

These adaptations by the younger artist may have seemed like good ideas at the time, but they result in a confusing welter of legs and a melodramatic effect, suitable perhaps to the provincial atmosphere of Perugia where the work was to be set over the tomb of the murdered tyrant Astorre Baglioni. Although Raphael did not cease borrowing form ideas from Michelangelo because of this one "mistake," his later influenced works are more mature in composition. We may compare the later murals in the Vatican, such as the typically spacious *School of Athens* (Fig. 151c, p. 269) with the cramped spatial quality of the *Entombment* where the landscape overwhelms the figures.

Today a great many artists are as students superficially influenced by Picasso, Beckmann, and other great figures of our time. Should they not go beyond this point—and many do not—they remain mere followers. Some, on the other hand, do emerge on a higher and more profound level of influence and become part of a movement that may owe a great deal to any one of the leaders of modern art but is not necessarily submerged by him.

The case of Raphael, for our purposes, is that of an artist who may be compared with himself in terms of space, balance, and so forth and at certain points also with his sources. To the extent that Raphael or any other artist absorbs and makes into his own spiritual expression the ideas and forms taken from others, to that extent does he become an individual master in his own right. This certainly the later Raphael succeeded in doing, as the *Alba Madonna* and the *School of Athens* amply testify.

Imitation and Loss of Quality

In some cases, as we have said, followers remain followers, never managing to rise above the level of a badly digested series of borrowings. This we may ascertain from our contrast of works by different men of reasonably close artistic aims, such as Rembrandt and many of his followers or Watteau and the group that imitated him, including Pater and Lancret. Both these latter men imitated the compositions, color arrangements, and certainly the *galant* subject matter of Watteau. And yet when we compare a typical Watteau, *Players of the French Comedy* (Fig. 240, p. 452), with a typical Lancret, *La Camargo Dancing* (Fig. 241, p. 453), there are significant qualitative differences.

The typical Watteau composition (see also *Embarkation for the Isle of Cythera*, Fig. 168, p. 297) has continuity of movement from one side to the other. *Players of the French Comedy* starts out from the shadows at the left with the musicians, moves to the central lighted area, and then proceeds in a series of broad light-and-dark waves or curves through the young man with his back to us and out with the couple at the right. Moreover, the glances exchanged by the young man and the dancing lady are warm enough to carry from the center to the side of the picture. Lancret, on the other hand, ties his figures together with the somewhat primitive device of having the dancer stretch her arms to the right and left.

The second important difference lies in the nature of the forms themselves, the imitator often failing to give them convincing substance or sense of movement. La Camargo looks formless, like a doll and not a woman. This can hardly be said of the charming and even

Fig. 240. JEAN ANTOINE WATTEAU: *Players of the French Comedy*. Berlin, State Museums.

tantalizing little women of Watteau who really express the idea for which they are there.

A final significant difference may be noted—and in this lies the whole meaning of the respective paintings. Watteau gives us a sensitive work of the imagination in whose suspended and poetic mood an actual scene from contemporary theatrical life becomes a stimulating and exciting allegory of love in general. Such is almost always the case with Watteau's art. Lancret, on the contrary, is more specific and down to earth. His picture portrays one of the times when the famous dancer appeared either alone or with her lover of the moment. The picture becomes a playful tribute to a specific woman and not to love.

Pitfalls and Aspirations

Should the reader be interested in carrying this kind of comparison further, he may set the works of Rembrandt's pupils Nicolas Maes and Gerard Dou against those of their teacher. Such comparisons, however, must be qualified by the fact that often the pupil may be trying to do something different from what Rembrandt did, and this can be determined only by examination of many works by both men and not a single example of each.

Furthermore, the temptation to compare a man's youthful work with his later production may lead to somewhat invalid conclusions, because when the artist was younger, he was surely not trying to do what he did when older. For example, we say that the early work of Rembrandt is less profound than his later work and that it is thus-and-such by contrast; but we do not thereby throw the earlier works into the discard. We merely take them for what they are, for what the young man was trying to do at that moment in time.

In the terms of reference we have employed throughout, the study and enjoyment of art, like other forms of cultural experience, would appear to be more complex than some laymen would like to believe. This is not surprising in view of the fact that technically trained people have been producing various kinds of art over thousands of years, each period engendering a sprinkling of different categories. Some of us may well be content with the simple and indeed elementary joy of recognizing or identifying a work of art or music. Although often

Fig. 241. NICOLAS LANCRET: *La Camargo Dancing*. Washington, D. C., National Gallery of Art, Mellon Collection.

gratifying to the ego, such activity is essentially not very significant on the level of understanding.

Others of us may wish to go forward to another level of appreciation. Such a path can be followed only through constant contact with art of all varieties and especially with originals, where they are available. When we approach these works, as we have here, in the spirit of trying to find out what the artist was attempting to achieve and then endeavoring to judge on a comparative basis the relative success of his achievement, we have taken the first significant step toward understanding the arts.

Bibliography

Architecture

Built in U.S.A. Post War Architecture, Henry-Russell Hitchcock and Arthur Drexler, eds., New York, Museum of Modern Art, 1953.

Fitch, James Marston: *American Building,* Boston, Houghton, 1948.

Hamlin, Talbot: *Architecture through the Ages,* New York, Putnam, 1940.

Richardson, A. E., and Corfiato, H. O.: *The Art of Architecture,* London, English Universities Press, 1938.

Zevi, Bruno: *Architecture as Space: How to Look at Architecture,* New York, Horizon, 1957.

Art in Everyday Life

Faulkner, Ray, Ziegfeld, E., and Hill, G.: *Art Today,* 3d ed., New York, Holt, 1956.

Goldwater, R. (in collaboration with René d'Harnoncourt): *Modern Art in Your Life,* New York, Museum of Modern Art, 1953.

Drawings

Watrous, James: *The Craft of Old Master Drawings,* Madison, U. of Wisconsin Press, 1957.

History of Art

Gardner, Helen: *Art through the Ages,* 3d ed., New York, Harcourt, 1948.

Gombrich, E. H.: *The Story of Art,* New York, Phaidon, 1950.

Hauser, Arnold: *The Social History of Art,* New York, Knopf, 1951.

Myers, Bernard S.: *Art and Civilization,* New York, McGraw, 1957.

Sewall, John I.: *A History of Western Art,* New York, Holt, 1953.

Industrial Design

Giedion, Siegfried: *Mechanization Takes Command,* New York, Oxford, 1948.

Idea 55, Gerd Hatje, ed., bibliography by Bernard Karpel, New York, Wittenborn, 1955.

455

Kouwenhoven, John A.: *Made in America. The Arts in Modern Civilization,* New York, Doubleday, 1949.

Read, Herbert: *Art and Industry,* New York, Harcourt, 1944.

Wallance, Don: *Shaping America's Products,* New York, Reinhold, 1956.

Modern Art

Barr, Alfred H., Jr.: *Picasso: Fifty Years of His Art,* rev. ed., New York, Museum of Modern Art, 1946.

——: *What Is Modern Painting?* New York, Museum of Modern Art, 1953.

Elgar, Frank, and Maillard, Robert: *Picasso,* New York, Praeger, 1956.

Masters of Modern Art, Alfred H. Barr, Jr., ed., New York, Museum of Modern Art, 1954.

Myers, Bernard S.: *Modern Art in the Making,* New York, McGraw, 1950.

See also: Ritchie, Giedion-Welcker, etc., under *Sculpture;* Hayter under *Prints and Silk Screen;* Fitch, Hitchcock, etc., under *Architecture.*

Painting

Constable, W. G.: *The Painter's Workshop,* New York, Oxford, 1954.

Hale, Gardner: *Fresco Painting,* New York, Rudge, 1933.

Mayer, Ralph: *The Artist's Handbook of Materials and Techniques,* New York, Viking, 1957.

Prints and Silk Screen

Guide to the Processes and Schools of Engraving (British Museum Handbook), London, 1923.

Hayter, S. W.: *New Ways of Gravure,* New York, Pantheon, 1949.

Heller, Jules: *Print Making Today,* New York, Holt, 1958.

Hind, A. M.: *History of Engraving and Etching,* Boston, Houghton, 1923.

Ivins, William M., Jr.: *Prints and Visual Communication,* Cambridge, Mass., Harvard U. Press, 1953.

Sternberg, Harry: *Silk Screen Color Printing,* New York, McGraw, 1942.

Weitenkampf, Frank: *How to Appreciate Prints,* New York, Scribner, 1929.

Zigrosser, Carl: *Six Centuries of Fine Prints,* New York, Covici-Friede, 1937.

Sculpture

Giedion-Welcker, Carola: *Contemporary Sculpture,* New York, Wittenborn, 1953.

Lynch, John: *Metal Sculpture. New Forms and New Techniques,* New York, Studio, 1957.

Rich, Jack: *The Materials and Methods of Sculpture,* New York, Oxford, 1947.

Ritchie, Andrew C.: *Sculpture of the 20th Century,* New York, Museum of Modern Art, 1952.

Struppeck, Jules: *The Creation of Sculpture,* New York, Holt, 1952.

Index

Massachusetts Institute of Technology, auditorium of, 88
Masson (André), 417
Matisse, Henri, 13, 137, 139, 221, 257, 418, 431; Vence Chapel paintings, 35; *Young Sailor, The,* 162–163, Fig. 225 (p. 407), 257, 408
Matta (Roberto), 417
Maya, 90
Ma Yüan, *A Sage under a Pine Tree,* 60–61, 63, Fig. 37 (p. 60), 184, 252, 261
Medals, 225–226
Medici, Giuliano de', 54–56, 59
Medici, Marie de', 347
Medieval art, 6, 79, 83, 97, 112–113, 116, 142, 145–146, 150, 157, 162, 168, 179, 182, 216–219, 222, 225, 228, 233, 244, 303, 329 ff., 372, 414
Mediterranean, 40, 42, 78, 142, 150, 319, 324
Meissonier, J. L. E., 2, 269; *Sergeant's Portrait, The,* Fig. 220 (p. 401), 401–402
Méndez, Leopoldo, *Deportation to Death,* 196, Fig. 116 (p. 197)
Merchant George Gisze, The. See Holbein
Mercury, 58–59
Merovingian art, 39, 41, 179
Mesopotamian art, 39, Fig. 27 (p. 40), 28, 145, 317, 319
Metal relief prints, 196
Metal sculpture, 142–146
Metalwork, 223–226
Metropolitan Museum of Art, New York, 175
Mexico, Mexican art, 10, 157, 167, 192, 306, 363, 410, 418, 420, 424–425
Mexico City, 215
Mezzotint, 190, 201, 203–205
Michelangelo, 53, 74, 80, 126, 148, 150, 153, 155, 159–160, 173, 183, 344–345, 353, 355, 375–385, 387, 389, 413, 419, 424, 426–427, 429, 449–450; *Bound Slave,* 379–381, Fig. 212 (p. 379); *Creation of Adam,* 56–58, Fig. 35 (p. 57), 82, 150–151, 159, 165–166, 252, 273, 323, 381, 384; *David,* 377–380, Fig. 211 (p. 377); *Drunkenness of Noah,* 384; *Deluge,* 384–385; *Expulsion from Eden,* 376; *God Dividing Light from Darkness,* 384; *Holy Family (Doni Madonna),* 449; *Jeremiah,* 37–38, Fig. 25 (p. 38), 158–159, 251; *Last Judgment,* Sistine Chapel, 384, 426; *Libyan Sibyl,* 72–73, Fig. 43a (p. 72), Fig. 43 (p. 71), 183; *Moses,* 6, Fig. 1 (p. 7), 129–130, Fig. 87 (p. 133), 132–135, 158, 372, 379, 381; *Pietà,* 378, Fig. 211a (p. 377); *Pietà,* Cathedral of Florence, 382, Fig. 213 (p. 383), 385, 387; *Rebellious Slave,* 380; *Sacrifice of Noah,* 385; Sistine Chapel murals, 56–58,
376, 380, 384–385; Studies for *Libyan Sibyl,* Fig. 43 (p. 71), 72–73, 77, 79, 81–82; Tomb of Julius II, 6, Fig. 1 (p. 7), 379–381; Tomb of Lorenzo de' Medici, 54–56, Fig. 34 (p. 54), 148, 304, 380–382, 384–385
Middle Ages. *See* Medieval art
Middle Stone Age, 317
Middle East, 220
Miës van der Rohe, Ludwig, Lake Shore Apartments, 258; Seagram Building, Fig. 78a (p. 120), 95, 121–122; Tugendhat House, 14, Fig. 64 (p. 101), 88, 100, Fig. 64a (p. 102), 102, 119–120, 267, 301–302, 421
Millefiori glass, 215; Roman glass bowl, 215, Fig. 129 (p. 216)
Milton, John, 58
Minotaur, 366
Miró (Joan), 261, 417, 434
Mohammedan art, 89
Moissac, *Christ Enthroned among the Four-and-twenty Elders,* 360–362, Fig. 205 (p. 361)
Mondrian, Piet, 414, 420–421, 445–446; *Composition,* 14, Fig. 33 (p. 50) 51–53, 66, 151, 158, 245, 264, 266–267, 407, 413, 417–418
Monet, Claude, 13, 24, 74, 183, 259, 429; *Isle on the Seine near Giverny,* 402–403, Fig. 221 (p. 403), 405
Moore, Henry, 74, 139, 260, 429, 435
Moorish art, Moors, 150, 398, 417
Morland, George, 204
Morris, William, 238–239; and Company, 239
Mosaic, 219
Moses. See under Michelangelo
Moslem art, 219
Mount Olympus. *See* Theseus
Mural painting, 163–164
Murano, 215–216
Museum of Modern Art, The, New York, 90, 91, 423, 435, 438
Mycenae, 42
Myron, *Discobolus,* 8, 129–130, 132, Fig. 86 (p. 132), Fig. 86a (p. 132), 134–136, 143, 262, 281, 380

Nanteuil, Robert, 21
Napoleon, Napoleonic, 89, 291–293, 305, 424
National Gallery, London, 235
Nativity and Annunciation to the Shepherds. See Pisano, Giovanni
Naturalism, 399–402
Nazi Germany, Nazis, 65, 241, 411, 437, 439–440

Near East, 97, 116, 227, 292, 314, 316, 329, 398

Neo-Classicism, 227, 393–396, 398–399, 410

Neo-Plasticism, 414

Netherlands, 304

New England, 94, 302–303

New Stone Age, 78, 317

New World, 389

New York Telephone Building, 91

Nicholson, Ben, 139

Night, Medici Tombs, 381

Nonobjective art, 417–419

Norse art, 113

North African art, 306, 329

North America, 396, 420

Northern Europe, 337 ff.

Northern painting, 368

Notre Dame Cathedral, Paris, 254; *Virgin Portal*, 294–296, Fig. 167 (p. 295); view of exterior, 334–336, Fig. 191 (p. 335)

Notre Dame de Bonne Délivrance, 191

Oath of the Horatii. See David, J. L.

Oaxaca (Mexico), 221

Occidental. *See* Western art tradition

Oceanic art, 89–90

Official and commemorative buildings, 90–91

Oil painting, 170–179

Old Masters, 13, 269, 443

Old Stone Age, 41–42, 77–78, 317; *A Wild Horse*, 77–78, Fig. 28 (p. 42)

Old Testament, 37, 145, 332

Olivetti typewriter (Lettera 22), Fig. 143 (p. 231), 258

Olympia, Temple of Zeus, 323

Opéra, Paris, 90, 121

Oriental art, 6, 38, 60, 76, 84, 86, 106, 161, 183, 185, 191, 220, 225, 266, 313, 330, 357, 393, Fig. 23 (p. 36), Fig. 37 (p. 60)

Orozco, J. C., 73, 83, 306, 418, 425; *Christ Destroying His Cross*, Fig. 207 (p. 263), 263–264; *Legs*, 73, Fig. 44 (p. 73), 77; *Miguel Hidalgo y Costilla*, 167, Fig. 100 (p. 167)

Ottonian art, 79, 330

Ovid, *Metamorphoses*, 399

Pacific islands, 121

Packaging, 229

Padua, 166

Paganini. See Ingres, J. A. D.

Painting: color, uses of, 161–163; forms in, 160–161; movement and depth in, 157–159; social functions of, 163–164; spatial devices in, 159–160; techniques of, 164 ff.: (fresco, 164–168; tempera, 168–170; oil, 170–179; water color, 179–181; gouache,

181–183; Oriental water color, 183–185; pastel, 185–187); texture in, 161

Palette of Narmer, 358–359, Fig. 204 (p. 359), 364, 374

Palazzo Farnese, Rome, 25, Fig. 155 (p. 275), 104, 123, 262, 275–277, 281, 283, 286–287, 303

Paleolithic, 438; *see also* Old Stone Age

Panathenaic amphora, 78, 213, Fig. 49 (p. 79), 260–261

Panathenaic Procession, Parthenon, 136–137, Fig. 89 (p. 136), 151, 253, 255

Panel of Hesire, 317, Fig. 179 (p. 318)

Panel painting, 164

Pankration, 78

Panthéon, Paris, 88–89

Pantheon, Rome, 108, Figs. 67, 69 (pp. 109, 111), 328–329

Paradise Gates (Ghiberti), 136–137, Figs. 90, 90a (pp. 138, 139), 142, 153–154

Parthenon, Athens, 23, 25, 89, Figs. 62, 62a (pp. 96, 97), 96–97, 105–106, 151, 225, 251, 253, 255, 260, 266, 281–282, 324, 328–329, 360, 443; *see also* Panathenaic Procession

Pastel, 185–187

Pater (J. B.), 451

Pazzi Chapel, Florence, 25, Figs. 30, 30a (p. 45), 44–47, 49, 52, 101–102, 121, 263

Pazzi conspiracy, 59

Peddler Robbed by Monkeys, 194, Fig. 113 (p. 193)

Pencil drawing, 82–83; *see* Fig. 53 (p. 81)

Peninsular War, 305–306

Pergamum, 397

Persia, 183, 317

Personalities, revealed in art, 291–293

Perspective and space, 364–372

Perugia, 450

Pevsner, Antoine, 126–127, 129, 139, 146, 264–265, 418, 421, Fig. 84 (p. 129)

Phidias, 321

Philadelphia highboy, Fig. 139 (p. 226)

Philadelphia Museum of Art, 142

Philadelphia Savings Fund Society Building, 100, 104–105, Fig. 73 (p. 114), 114, 117, 121, 253, 260

Philip C. Johnson House, New Canaan, Conn., 101

Phoenicia, 317

Phyfe, Duncan, 233

Physical beauty, standards of, 13

Picasso, Pablo, 14, 193, 201, 203, 221, 264, 314, 399, 413–416, 418, 424, 426–439, 443–444, 449–450; *Absinthe Drinker*, 429–431, Fig. 227 (p. 430); Blue Period, 429–430; *Charnel House*, 440; Classicism, 433; Convulsive Cubism, 434; Cubism, 432; Curvilinear Cubism, 434; *Gertrude Stein*,

431; *Girl Before a Mirror,* 435; *Grande Danseuse* (1907), 431, Fig. 228 (p. 431) ; *Guernica,* 74, Fig. 234 (p. 438), 414, 436, 440; *Le grand coq,* 435, Fig. 233 (p. 437) ; *Man with a Lamb,* 437, Fig. 235 (p. 439) *Mardi Gras (The Three Musicians)* 432, Fig. 229 (p. 433), 434; *Metamorphoses,* Ovid, 433; *Owl,* 140, Fig. 236 (p. 439), 141–142, 438; *Peace and War,* 440; *Race, The,* 433, Fig. 230 (p. 434) ; *Red Table Cloth,* 434; Rose Period, 430–431; Stained Glass Cubism, 435; *Three Dancers,* 434, Fig. 232 (p. 436) ; *Violin,* 406, Fig. 224 (p. 406), 432; *Woman in White,* 399, 418, 433, Fig. 231 (p. 435)

Pilasters, 44–45

Pisa, Cathedral and Leaning Tower, 116, 283–285, Figs. 160 and 161 (p. 284)

Pisanello, 225–226

Pisano, Giovanni, Preaching Pulpit, Pistoia, Sant'Andrea, 350–353, Fig. 202 (p. 352)

Pisano, Niccolò, Preaching Pulpit, Pisa, Baptistery of the Cathedral, 350–353, Fig. 201 (p. 351), 376

Pissarro, Camille, 24, 74, 170, 183, 424; *Peasants Resting,* 20, 24, Fig. 11 (p. 24), 161, 258, 373

Planned obsolescence, 232

Planographic. *See* Lithograph

Plato, 278, 322

Pointing machine, 147

Political meanings in art, 304–307

Polyclitus, 286, 321–322, 362; *see also Doryphorus*

Pompeii, 394

Pope Julius II, Tomb of, 379

Portland vase, 215

Portrait of a Young Englishman. See Titian

Portrait of Manet. See Degas, Edgar

Posada, José Guadalupe, 196

Poseidon, 360

Post or column, 105–107

Post-Impressionist, 13, 371–372, 374, 404–405, 411, 418, 424

Post-Renaissance, 97, 161, 266, 344, 367, 387, 408, 414

Pottery. *See* Ceramics

Poussin, Nicolas, 173, 266, 414; *St. John on Patmos,* 177–178, 251, Fig. 106 (p. 176), 263, 266–267, 279

Praxiteles, *Aphrodite,* 18, 22, 27, Fig. 6 (p. 20) ; *Hermes,* 124, Fig. 186 (p. 325), 285, 325–326

Prehistoric art, 41, Fig. 28 (p. 42)

Pre-Machine Age, 233

Principles of design, 249, 268–287

Proportion, 249, 284–287; hierarchic, 359; varieties of, 358–364

Protestants, 304, 387, 390

Protestantism, 63

Pueblo Indians, 116

Puritan, 303

Puvis de Chavannes (Pierre), 431

Pyramids, the, 88, 118, Fig. 76 (p. 118)

Pyrenees, 398

Primitive architecture, 116

Prints: intaglio, 188, 193, 198–206; lithographic, 188, 193; relief, 188, 193–198

Quentin de la Tour, Maurice, 187

Raffaelli, J. F., 187

Raft of the Medusa. See Géricault, Théodore

Ralph Johnson House. *See* Harwell H. Harris

Raphael, 8, 153, 362, 356, 419, 442–443, 449; *Alba Madonna,* 27–29, 53, Fig. 16 (p. 28), 160, 162–163, 261–262, 273, 293–294, 361, 373, 449, 451; *Entombment,* Fig. 239 (p. 450), 449–450; *School of Athens,* 278–279, 449–451, Fig. 151c (p. 269)

Ravenna, San Vitale, mosaics of, 219, Fig. 131 (p. 219), 264, 366

R.C.A. Building, New York, 25, 91, 98, 100, 443, Fig. 58 (p. 92), 104–105, 117, 121–123, 260, 274

Read, Sir Herbert, 230

Realism, Realists, 399–402, 411, 414, 429

Red-figured vase, 78

Reformation, the, 234, 296, 304, 344, 387–388

Regency period, 297

Religion in art, 35–39

Religious buildings, 89–90

Religious outlook, revealed in art, 293–296

Rembrandt, 12, 16, 53, 83–85, 173, 190, 203, 269, 343, 348–349, 353–356, 373, 391, 410, 426, 444, 451–453; *Anatomy Lesson of Dr. Tulp,* 354, Fig. 203 (p. 354), 390; *Man Seated on a Step,* 77, Fig. 47 (p. 78) ; *Man in a Steel Gorget,* 175; *Man with a Beard,* 175; *Man with the Golden Helmet,* 161, Fig. 104 (p. 174), 174–175, 254, 267, 348–349, 354–355; *"Night Watch" (Sortie of Captain Banning Cocq's Company of the Civic Guard),* 270, Fig. 152 (p. 271), 346–348; *Portrait of a Man,* 175; *Portrait of a Young Man,* 175; *Portrait of a Young Woman,* 175

Remington, F., *The Bronco Buster,* 143, Fig. 93 (p. 144)

Renaissance, 9–10, 39, 47, 49, 61, 79–81, 84, 87, 90, 97, 101, 105, 134, 142, 148, 153–154, 157, 161–162, 166–167, 173, 183, 191, 202, 205, 227, 233–234, 245, 255, 265–266, 273, 275, 294, 308